Travellers' Nature Guides

France

Travellers' Nature Guides

Series editor: Martin Walters

This series is designed for anyone with an interest in the natural history of the places they visit. Essentially practical, each book first introduces the ecology, geology, and wildlife of the country or countries it covers, then goes on to describe where to see the natural history at its best. The entries are the personal choice of the individual authors and are based on intensive travel and research in their areas. Sites range in size from a few to thousands of hectares, be they National Parks, nature reserves, or simply common land, but all are open to the public and accessible to the ordinary visitor. The books are designed to complement each other and to build into a nature library, together giving an introduction to the natural history of Europe.

Britain: *Travellers' Nature Guide*
France: *Travellers' Nature Guide*
Greece: *Travellers' Nature Guide*
Spain: *Travellers' Nature Guide*
Portugal: *Travellers' Nature Guide*

Travellers' Nature Guides
France

Bob Gibbons

Photographs
Natural Image

Maps, animal drawings, and panoramas
Michael Wood

Plant drawings
Stella Tranah

OXFORD
UNIVERSITY PRESS

OXFORD

UNIVERSITY PRESS

Great Clarendon Street, Oxford OX2 6DP

Oxford University Press is a department of the University of Oxford.
It furthers the University's objective of excellence in research, scholarship,
and education by publishing worldwide in

Oxford New York

Auckland Bangkok Buenos Aires Cape Town Chennai
Dar es Salaam Delhi Hong Kong Istanbul Karachi Kolkata
Kuala Lumpur Madrid Melbourne Mexico City Mumbai Nairobi
São Paulo Shanghai Singapore Taipei Tokyo Toronto
and an associated company in Berlin

Oxford is a registered trade mark of Oxford University Press
in the UK and in certain other countries

Published in the United States
by Oxford University Press Inc., New York

A catalogue record for this book is available from the British Library

Library of Congress Cataloging in Publication Data

Data available

ISBN 0-19-850431-4

10 9 8 7 6 5 4 3 2 1

Typeset by Pantek Arts Ltd, Maidstone, Kent
Printed in xxxxx
on acid-free paper by xxxxx

Foreword

The primary aim of this series is to act as a guide and a stimulus to holidaymakers, be they specialist naturalist or interested amateur, and to teach them something of the wealth of wildlife that is to be found in the countryside around them, whether at home or abroad.

Despite the continued encroachment of housing and intensive farmland, and the disappearance of so much natural and semi-natural habitat over many decades, the wildlife of Europe is still remarkably varied and rewarding.

One of the major developments of recent years has been the rise of so-called 'ecotourism', which has combined the interests of the naturalist and the holidaymaker. Such tourism ranges from specialist guided tours for small groups of keen birdwatchers or botanists (often both) to more leisurely holidays that involve perhaps a sprinkling of nature study along with the more traditional goals of the tourist, such as visits to famous buildings or architectural sites. At the same time, the general traveller on a private holiday to a hotel, villa, *gîte*, or campsite is frequently keen to learn more about the landscape and countryside of the region he or she is visiting, and such knowledge can considerably enrich and increase the enjoyment of a holiday.

Throughout the books there is a strong emphasis on conservation and the need to ensure that a representative range of habitats remains long into the future for coming generations of naturalists and nature-sensitive tourists to enjoy.

Each book begins with an overview. This is in essence a background sketch of the country – mainly in terms of its ecology and wildlife – with a look at the major habitat types and their importance. The overview also contains some details about the state of nature conservation, and considers the various types of reserve, conservation laws, and related matters.

The overview is followed by a systematic gazetteer of selected sites, grouped by regions, of particular natural history importance. Of course, with so many fascinating areas – not all of them protected – in addition to the large numbers of reserves, our coverage cannot be comprehensive. Nevertheless, we have chosen sites that are generally not too difficult to access and which together give a full picture of the richness of each country. The choice aims to give a representative range of visitable sites, encompassing all the important habitats. The sites vary widely in status and size, but all have something special to offer the visitor, and repay a visit.

The books in this series are highly visual, and are enlivened by the use of colour photographs of landscapes, habitats, species, and locations, many showing the actual sites described. The photographs were provided by the Natural Image photograph agency. The photographer was Bob Gibbons except where otherwise indicated in the caption. In addition, selected animals and plants are also illustrated by black and white line drawings, accompanying the relevant text. Maps of the country, regions, and selected sites enable each site to be quickly located and placed in the context of the country as a whole.

A special feature of these *Travellers' Nature Guides* is the composite painting, painted by wildlife artist Michael Wood, depicting a range of classic habitats for each country, and illustrating a number of characteristic species. This will help to give a flavour of the richness of the wildlife awaiting the informed naturalist traveller.

Martin Walters
Series Editor
Cambridge, 2002

Contents

An index to scientific and English species names used in all the
books in this series can be found at
www.oup.com/uk/travellersnatureguides

Overview

Introduction

France is the largest country lying wholly within Europe, and undoubtedly one of the most interesting and exciting for the naturalist. It is remarkably varied, with an enormous coastline shared ~~between~~ *among* three seas, and vast areas of semi-natural habitats stretching upwards to the highest mountains in Europe. In an ecological sense, it is at the crossroads of Europe, and shares species from virtually all the climatic regions in the continent, as well as having a number of its own. It is also at

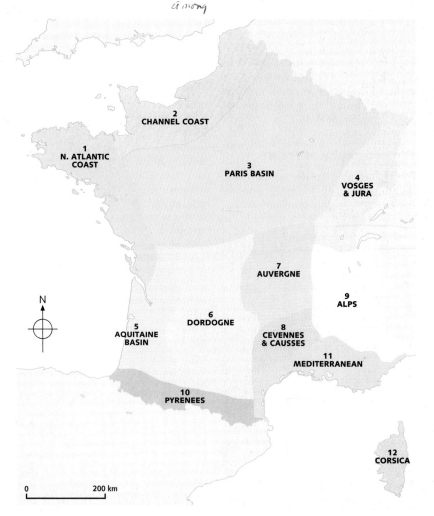

2
CHANNEL COAST

1
N. ATLANTIC
COAST

3
PARIS BASIN

4
VOSGES
& JURA

7
AUVERGNE

9
ALPS

N

6
DORDOGNE

5
AQUITAINE
BASIN

8
CEVENNES
& CAUSSES

11
MEDITERRANEAN

10
PYRENEES

12
CORSICA

0   200 km

Opposite page: **Meadow/Mt. Aiguilles**

the hub of the European migration wheel, and huge numbers of birds that do not actually breed in France (such as common cranes and many waders) pass through on the way to their breeding or wintering grounds.

Thanks to a relatively low population density (half that of Britain), much more habitat has remained unploughed, and is often managed in a traditional way due to the isolation of many communities. Thus even areas of agricultural land may have more species than in Britain, partly because the farmed areas lie in a matrix of woodland and other wilder habitats.

France is also a very relaxed and civilized country, where it is a simple matter to find places to stay and eat well, usually within easy reach of where you want to be. The climate is generally benign, and the southern parts of France are noted for their good weather, almost throughout the year. The possibilities for continuing exploration and discovery are almost endless.

The geography of France

France, including Corsica (but excluding the non-European territories), covers an area of 543 965 square kilometres (or 210 026 square miles), which makes it the largest country in Europe, if you exclude the Ukraine and the European part of Russia. It is over twice (actually 2.23 times) the size of the UK, yet the population of each country is almost exactly the same, which has a considerable effect on the amount of remaining habitats, and space per individual, as discussed later.

The coast of France is one of its great glories, a mainstay of the tourist industry, but also crucial for its natural history heritage. There are roughly 5000 km of coast in France, split between the North Sea/English Channel, Atlantic Ocean, and the Mediterranean, including Corsica. The Atlantic and the North Sea coasts are not so very different in character, though there is a progressive increase in the amount of exposure towards the west, and of course the southernmost parts of the Atlantic coast are much warmer than the Channel and North Sea coasts. All of these western and northern coasts share the characteristics of having extensive unspoilt coastal and intertidal habitats with a very wide tidal amplitude (i.e. the difference in height between high and low tides is considerable), which means that vast expanses of species-rich mudflats, sand, or saltmarsh are exposed every day. This provides very large, normally unfrozen, feeding and roosting areas for truly huge numbers of waders, wildfowl, and associated species, particularly at passage periods and through the winter. There are top-quality bird sites scattered all the way down this coast, from the Belgian border to the Spanish border, particularly where there is a degree of shelter, such as in an estuary or enclosed bay.

The Mediterranean coastlines are quite different. The sea is much warmer and calmer, and has a different range of marine species (although of course there is a fair degree of overlap). It also has a very much smaller variation between low and high tides. This obviously greatly reduces the amount of intertidal habitat exposed each day for feeding, so there are relatively few coastal (in the sense of intertidal) sites of high importance to birds on the French Mediterranean coast. There is also a difference in the way that rivers reach the sea – the absence of strong waves and wide tidal amplitude allows the formation of deltas rather than estuaries. As it happens, relatively few major rivers emerge on the French Mediterranean coast, but those that do, and especially the Rhône, form deltas; these are areas of low-lying land, often triangular (and named after the Greek letter Δ), built upon the quantities of silt deposited by the river as it reaches the sea. In an unspoilt delta, there is likely to be a fascinating and shifting matrix of open channels, mudflats, lagoons, sand dunes, saltmarshes, and dry land, wonderful for wildlife, though sadly no such unimproved deltas remain. The best remaining example of a delta in France is the Camargue, a shadow of its former self but a species-rich area, nonetheless. As a general rule, the Mediterranean coasts of France have also suffered more from tourism-related developments, thanks to the reliably warm, sunny weather, though this is not true in every case. Corsica is still surprisingly undeveloped (though it is changing) and probably has a higher proportion of wild coast than anywhere else in France.

In a list of the most mountainous countries in Europe, judged by proportion of land over a certain height, France would not figure very highly. In fact, it has some very extensive mountain regions, more than most countries, including some of the highest mountains in Europe, but because it is such a large country, it also has very large areas of lowland.

The northern third of France, lying roughly north of a line between Mulhouse and Nantes, is mainly low-lying, with the notable exceptions of the Ardennes and Vosges in the north-east. Apart from much of Brittany, the underlying rocks of this region are largely of sedimentary origin, frequently giving rise to soils that are easily cultivated. There is a huge ring of chalk around Paris, occupying much of north-central France, bounded by a ring of Jurassic and Upper Cretaceous rocks that often produce a hillier landscape than the chalk, with less intensive agriculture. Within the ring of chalk, the rocks are mainly more recent sandstones and clays, giving rise to acidic and often poorly drained soils, which accounts for the preponderance of fine forests and heaths, despite the greater population pressure, because the land is less suitable for agriculture. Wherever there is good soil in a gentle landscape in northern France, the pressure of agriculture has been intense, and this part of France holds some of the most intensively farmed landscapes in Europe.

The western part of north France, roughly equating to Brittany, is underlain by older, harder rocks such as granites and Cambrian and Pre-Cambrian strata, which produce a different landscape, more like Cornwall or south-west Wales in character. The conditions are less favourable to agriculture, which has allowed a rather wilder landscape to survive, with wide views encompassing moors and forests, though there are few high hills of any note. However, this is an area that has changed greatly in the past two decades, partly as a result of greatly intensified agriculture, and partly as a result of the pressure and money generated by tourism. It becomes noticeably less wild with each visit.

The whole of the eastern margin of France is dominated by high hills or mountains, stretching in a virtually unbroken line from the Vosges, in the far north-east, southwards to the Maritime Alps, taking in the Jura and the Alps along the way. Within this line of mountains, there are great differences in geology and climate, which translate into differences in landform, land use, and natural history. The Vosges are underlain by ancient rocks, predominantly acidic, giving rise to a lower and more rounded mountain chain, with a cool northern climate. The Jura are made up of more recent Jurassic (the geological period that takes its name from the Jura) limestones, and reach to a higher altitude, with a more spectacular landscape. From here southwards, there is a continuous variety of high mountains down to the coast, through various named mountain ranges, overlying a variety of different rocks, more heavily folded and convoluted than the northern ranges. They include the highest mountain in Europe – Mont Blanc, at 4810 m – and many peaks over 3500 m, making up a superb selection of varied mountain scenery covering a vast region. The southernmost mountains, especially the Maritime Alps and the Queyras, have a climate quite different from that of the mountains further north, with relatively dry, hot summers and lower rainfall overall. Although a few species are shared between the Vosges and the Maritime

Alps, there are steady changes throughout the range, with more different than shared species at the extremes. Altogether, it is a wonderful area for the naturalist, with a huge variety of species to be seen, and three National Parks and seven natural parks in which to see them.

Central France is dominated by the Massif Central, a large region of hills and low mountains made up of the volcanic mountains of the Auvergne, the granites and schists of the Cévennes, the limestone *causses* (limestone plateaux – see p. 184), and many lesser-known hills. These are not mountains – the highest point is the Puy de Sancy in the Auvergne, at 1886 m – but they are high enough and extensive enough to have their own climate and to be relatively unspoilt. Many of France's great rivers rise in this area, including the Loire, the Lot, and the Dordogne. Many naturalists travelling southwards feel that they have only really arrived somewhere special when they reach this landscape, and it is undoubt-edly true that the natural life suddenly becomes much more varied and interesting as you enter the Massif Central. The hilly countryside and harsh winter climate has helped to ensure the survival of large tracts of semi-natural habitat, and the agriculture itself is relatively unintensive, leaving many more hedges, trees, unimproved pastures, meadows, and marshes to the benefit of wildlife. Around the Massif Central, there are many lower areas of great beauty and interest, such as the limestone hills around Dijon and Beaune, or the intimate wooded–bushy country of the Dordogne Valley and neighbouring areas. Altogether, this is a superb area for the naturalist, with something new at every turn.

Southernmost France is, of course, the warmest part of the mainland, and a Mecca for tourists, fruit-growers, developers, and even industry. Surprisingly, perhaps, there is still plenty of interest for the naturalist, too, and there are many unspoilt areas. The landscape of Provence

Massif des Maures, heath

is familiar to most people, whether they have been there or not, through the paintings of artists such as Van Gogh, and many published photographs – it is an area that has long attracted artists. The mountains of the Massif Central sink down towards the sea, where there are large areas of fertile plains and undulating countryside, dominated by fruit farms, vineyards, and arable agriculture. However, thanks to the constant presence of limestone hills between the valleys, and the hot, dry summers, you are never far from an interesting area of unspoilt rocky hillside, woodland, or cliffs in Provence. Some of the hills – such as the Massif des Maures, the Massif de Sainte-Baumes, Mont Ste. Victoire, or Mont Ventoux – are major features in their own right, and all worthy of exploration.

South-western France is dominated by the great wall of the Pyrenees, stretching right across the neck of the Iberian Peninsula; they separate France from Spain, but also northern and central Europe from Iberia. It is a major barrier in almost every respect, with many differences in the wildlife of either side. The peaks rise to 3404 m at Aneto, and there are many at around 3000 m, with very few low passes in the central area. For the naturalist, it is a marvellous place, especially if you include the Spanish side, with its complex of lower mountains extending away southwards.

Finally, Corsica, which is often described as a mountain rising from the sea, is one of the great undiscovered treasures of the Mediterranean, less developed than any other large island in the area. It has a splendidly pristine coastline, seriously high mountains, vast woodlands, lots of mountain lakes and some coastal lagoons, and a very special flora and fauna. Corsica lies 160 km from the Provence coast, so in many respects it is like another country, sharing more with Italy and Sardinia than with France. There are also other islands off the coast of France, especially the Iles d'Hyères in the Mediterranean, and a number of small islands off the Brittany coast, though their total area is very small.

The climate

As in so many other things, France lies at something of a crossroads in its climatic patterns, being influenced by three major climatic zones – Atlantic, Mediterranean, and central European – together with the locally influenced climates of the higher mountain systems. There is no straightforward and simple division into zones, for the climate is a dynamic and constantly changing force. Each climatic area merges with its adjoining areas over a zone which can vary seasonally and annually.

The western coastal areas, at least as far north-east as Cherbourg, are wholly under Atlantic influences, which produce mild winters, moderately warm summers, and a highish rainfall well spread throughout the year. For example, the whole of the west coast and the Cherbourg Peninsula has an average January temperature 6°C or more warmer than the whole of the rest of France, except for parts of the Mediterranean coast and Corsica. The rainfall is usually in the range of 80–100 cm, spread through the seasons, and snow is rare. This influence pushes eastwards into the country, depending on the strength of the westerly depressions and the forces resisting them, and merges with the central European climate. Central and eastern parts of France tend to have a more Continental climate, dominated mainly by high pressure systems, with clearer and colder winters, and generally warm summers. The further east you go, the more marked this becomes, apart from the complicating influence of the eastern high mountain ranges.

South of the Massif Central and east of the Pyrenees, France has a Mediterranean climate, characterized by hot, dry summers and wet, mild winters with few frosts. Surprisingly, the Mediterranean areas are not necessarily the driest parts of the country, but most people believe they are, because they visit between April and September, when the rainfall is at its lowest. In fact Marseilles, for example, has a higher rainfall than Paris (and many parts of Britain), and is little different from parts of Brittany, but its distribution through the year is quite different. This weather pattern strongly influences the vegetation of the region, and there is a distinctive Mediterranean flora and fauna that occurs throughout much of the Mediterranean Sea area. Most plants, for example, flower in spring or early summer, with a minor peak of activity in autumn as the temperatures cool and the first rains arrive. In the hottest and driest parts, there are very few flowers after June, and much of the vegetation becomes dry and brown. Similarly, birds tend to nest earlier than in the rest of France, and insect numbers peak in May and June rather than later. In especially warm areas, a few butterflies and other insects may be present all year as adults. Drought-sensitive invertebrates, such as snails, tend to aestivate (enter a prolonged state of torpor) to avoid the damaging effects of the long, dry summers; masses of snails cluster on low-growing plants, with their entrances tightly sealed against water loss, avoiding the intense heat at ground level.

The south of France is strongly influenced by the *mistral*, and other locally named winds, from the north, which bring cold air from central Europe, especially down the Rhône Valley. To oversimplify it, the warm air over the south rises, while the cold air over central Europe and the Alps falls and becomes sucked in to fill the vacuum, thus there is a persistent strong wind from the north when the temperature difference is at its greatest in spring. The *mistral* blows, on average, for about 100 days per year.

Overlying these large-scale weather patterns, the local effects of mountains on the climate can be considerable. Average temperature drops rapidly with altitude increase, and precipitation increases up to all but the highest altitudes. Thus almost all the mountain areas are colder and wetter than equivalent lowland regions. For example, the Massif Central and the northern Alps have annual precipitation rates of at least 160 cm per year, in contrast to roughly 70 cm in the adjacent lowlands; and Mont Ventoux in Provence may be experiencing blizzard conditions whilst the Cote d'Azur basks in warm autumn sunshine. There are local exceptions, though; for example, the town of Briançon in the southern Alps (the highest sizeable town in Europe) has a lower rainfall than Marseilles or Nice, because it lies in the rain shadow of several mountain ranges. The influences of these local mountain climates can extend more widely, too, such as through the effects of the *mistral*, or the rain-shadow effect of the Pyrenees on the area around Perpignan, which as a result is the driest part of France.

Vegetation and habitats

As the land warmed after the last ice age, the present-day land area of France became almost wholly forested, with the exception of the highest mountains, open waters, and some coastal areas. Since about Neolithic times (the later part of the Stone Age), people have gradually cleared the forest, initially for grazing animals, then for cultivation, and latterly for a whole range of activities. It is hard to believe, now, that the extensive *garrigue* of Provence, or the vast high pastures of the Auvergne were once forested not so long ago, but all the available evidence indicates that they were, and it is human influence that has caused this change. However, where clearance or grazing has produced a vegetation that is still rich in species, and which still relates closely to the underlying rock and drainage – such as heaths or mountain pastures – it is reasonable to refer to them as semi-natural habitats, which are often at least as interesting to the naturalist as the ancient forest areas which have persisted since post-glacial times.

The natural vegetation cover of France was heavily influenced by climate (includ-

The Tapoul Valley in the Cevennes

ing the effects of altitude), geology and soil, and aspect, and many different woodland types developed. Nowadays, it is much harder to make the straightforward connection between natural conditions and vegetation since the bulk of the country's vegetation has been affected, to a greater or lesser degree, by people, and only a small fraction of the original post-glacial forest exists. The precise percentage is not known; it is not the same as the percentage of forest cover remaining, since this includes planted woodlands, woods that have regenerated on formerly cleared land, and heavily modified woodland. Apart from the obvious effects of climate, it is still worth noting whether the underlying rock is of limestone or some other rock such as schists or serpentine, as this continues to affect the present-day vegetation and landscape. For example, limestone is porous, so water soaks into it immediately. This has many effects, including an absence of surface streams and lakes, very limited soil formation, and a particular topography. Gorges, caves, and dry plateaux with an abundance of bare rock are key features of hard limestone country. In addition, the presence of high amounts of calcium in the soil can be particularly important for some plants; for example, orchids tend to do best on limestone, and most orchid-hunters will seek out limestone areas if they have no other information. Other rocks, which are almost invariably more acid than limestones, are largely impervious, so they support streams and lakes, greater soil formation, and a generally different topography with fewer gorges and more V-shaped valleys, and they often support far more extensive and dense forests, at least in hill areas. The main significant vegetation types in France today are the forests, scrub of various sorts including *garrigue* and *maquis*, alpine areas, wetlands, coastal habitats and agricultural land of various types, and minor habitats such as gorges, cliffs, and screes.

Woodlands

Woodlands are probably the single most important habitat in France. They occupy almost 25% of its land, according to the latest surveys – in other words, a total area about half the size of Britain! The diversity within the general term 'woodlands' is extraordinary: the cathedral-like beech woods of lowland France such as at Compiègne and around Lyons-la-Forêt, or the high-altitude lichen-covered beech woods of the Pyrenees or Auvergne; the oak woods of Fontainebleau, the Bourbonnais or Tronçais; the vast pine woods of the Landes area – the largest planted forest in Europe; the natural larch, spruce, and fir woods of the Alps and other mountains; the evergreen holm oak and strawberry-tree woods of Mediterranean areas, and many other minor types of woodland, such as those dominated by ash, alder, willows, and poplar.

Most woodlands in France are managed, to a greater or lesser extent, and there are strong rural traditions relating to tree and woodland management. The state directly manages or influences about a third of the country's woodlands, mainly those marked as 'Forêt domaniale' (state-owned) or 'Forêt communale'. Many such forests are superb areas for wildlife, with a rich flora throughout, a high density of breeding birds, and an abundance of insects, especially in glades or along rides. Forest such as Grésigne, Fanges, Issaux, or the high coniferous forests of the Auvergne or Queyras are all superb for wildlife, with most of the characteristics of genuine ancient woodland. They tend to lack very old trees, which limits their value for certain birds and insects, and a few epiphytes, but this is not a big problem. The rotational selection system, and the very high proportion of naturally occurring local species in these woods, ensures that there is considerable natural diversity. Unfortunately, this more traditional form of management is tending to decline in favour of more straight-line conifer planting, and

Larch forest in autumn, Queyras Regional Natural Park

larger areas of clear-felling, though this is by no means entirely the case yet. Such changes will inevitably be detrimental for wildlife in general, though a few species – such as siskins, red squirrels, and sparrowhawks – might benefit.

In many areas of France, such as the Dordogne and parts of Normandy, the traditional practice of coppicing is still widely practised. This involves cutting back selected hardwood trees, such as hazel, sweet chestnut, ash, and field maple, to ground level every few years (the length of the cycle varies according to the species, the fertility of the site, the use of the products, and availability of labour). The resulting poles are used for thatching, fencing, firewood, building, and many other things. Where coppicing has a long history, it has provided the habitats for a wide range of species, which do particularly well in the recently cleared areas, then gradually become dormant, or move out, as the canopy closes in. It is always worth looking at a recently coppiced *coupe*, especially in spring and early summer, to see what flowers, butterflies, and other insects are there. Pollarding (i.e. the practice of cutting trees above browsing animal height) is still a common practice, especially on isolated hedgerow trees (and street trees, but that's another story), and these may often provide the ancient trees that are sometimes lacking in the woodlands. They are frequently good nesting sites for redstarts, wrynecks, and other hole-nesters, roosts for bats, and substrates for an abundance of lichens and a wealth of invertebrates.

There are also many tracts of less intensively managed woods in France, such as in steep inaccessible areas and some floodplains. Such woods tend to be more mixed than managed woods, because no single tree type is favoured; typical co-dominants include ash, wild cherry, elms, maples, limes, and hornbeam.

The woodlands are a vital strand in France's ecology and wildlife matrix. Not only do they cover such a large expanse, but their influence also extends much more widely. For example, the short-toed eagle or red kite hunting over the *garrigue* or valley grasslands is almost certain to be nesting in the woods, and many of the insects visiting flowers in limestone grassland will have passed their larval stages in a wooded area. The importance of a large area of semi-natural woodland cannot be overestimated.

Grasslands

The vegetation that develops in fairly damp, temperate climates where regular grazing or mowing takes place tends to be grassland of some sort or another, at least on all but the thinnest or most acid soils. It is estimated that grasslands cover 28–30% of the land area of France, though from the natural history point of view, it is the type and quality of grassland that is more important than its presence or absence. Grasslands cut for hay, which are nearly always enclosed to protect them from grazing animals, are known as meadows, whereas grazed grasslands, often unenclosed, are pastures. Grasslands that have not had regular doses of fertilizers often support masses of flowers (and their attendant insects), and they are one of the most attractive of all habitats in spring and summer. Unfortunately they are also one of the most threatened, and applications of fertilizers or herbicides, or ploughing can quickly destroy this natural variety. Over large sections of the country, enclosed meadows and pastures have steadily lost their wonderful variety of flowers in recent decades, and such places are now a rarity in north and west France. Rather more remain in mountain areas, where agriculture is often less intensive, but they are declining here, too.

Once, not so long ago, large parts of southern France were subject to the grazing pressure of large flocks of sheep and goats. Such flocks were an integral part of the rural economy, and were moved around as necessary to obtain grazing throughout the year, up into high pastures during the summer and down to

Massif des Maures: ❶ Roller *Coracias garrulus* ❷ Cork oak *Quercus suber* ❸ Woodchat shrike *Lanius senator* ❹ Sardinian warbler *Sylvia melanocephala* ❺ Narrow-leaved rock-rose *Cistus monspeliensis* ❻ French lavender *Lavandula stoechas* ❼ Scarce swallowtail *Iphiclides podalirius*

High mountain pasture (Alps): ❶ Alpine chough *Pyrrhocorax graculus* ❷ Martagon lily *Lilium martagon* ❸ Alpine marmot *Marmota marmota* ❹ Lady's slipper *Cypripedium calceolus* ❺ Apollo *Parnassius apollo*

Dordogne: ❶ Cirl bunting *Emberiza cirlus* ❷ Hoopoe *Upupa epops* ❸ Lizard orchid *Himantoglossum hircinum* ❹ Black-veined white *Aporia crataegi* ❺ Pearl-bordered fritillary *Clossiana euphrosyne* ❻ Round-headed rampion *Phyteuma orbiculare*

Camargue: ❶ Bee-eater *Merops apiaster* ❷ Greater flamingo *Phoenicopterus ruber* ❸ Lesser emperor *Anax parthenope* ❹ Stripeless tree frog *Hyla meridionalis* ❺ Giant orchid *Barlia robertiana*

milder localities for the winter. This is known as transhumance, and it had an enormous effect on the wildlife of the region by producing vast open areas of grazed but unimproved grassland, rich in flowers. Although the grazing pressure was often intense, it is quite different from enclosing stock in a field and leaving them until everything has been eaten. Thus, there were always areas of scrub, long grass and woodland, giving rise to a marvellous matrix of habitats, rich in all forms of wildlife, and home to many special species. Transhumance has steadily declined, and many such grasslands have become rank, reverted to scrub or woodland, or been ploughed or enclosed. In more marginal areas, such as around Dijon, or in the Dordogne, there are few signs that it ever existed except to the trained eye, though elsewhere, such as on the limestone *causses* of the southern Massif Central, such patterns persist and there are still superb extensive areas of fine unimproved grasslands.

In mountain areas, such as the Auvergne, Alps, and Pyrenees, the areas around the upper limits of the forest often support grassland. This is frequently at a lower level than the true natural tree-line, thanks to early clearance of the more stunted and open forest areas, followed by continuous grazing. Thus, there is often a wide band of grassland that extends from well below the tree-line, through the natural scrub area, up into a natural alpine grassland (where the altitude permits). Such grasslands may often still be grazed, especially in the Pyrenees, and they will, anyway, tend to persist longer here in the absence of grazing than in the lowlands because the cool climate and long snow cover slows down tree invasion. Such places are often extremely rich in flowers, with an abundance of insects, and they provide feeding or nesting areas for upland birds such as water pipit, red-billed and alpine chough, and snowfinches.

There are also important areas of damp grassland, cut or grazed, such as along river valleys and around lakes, or on exten-sive, low-lying coastal marshes. These areas are especially important for a small group of breeding birds including corncrake and redshank, and may also be rich in flowers. They have declined dramatically in extent in recent years as drainage methods have improved and land values have gone up. Even in semi-protected areas such as Regional Natural Parks they are disappearing, and such habitats, like those in the Marais Poitevin Regional Natural Park (see p. 40), require careful protection. Unfortunately, the populations of all the birds and other life that depends on these areas has decreased in at least equal measure.

Heathlands

Heathlands are roughly the acid-soil equivalent of unimproved pasture grasslands. Although often wild and natural in appearance, they are actually the product of early clearance of woodland, dating back to the Bronze Age or even the Neolithic. Where woodland on acid, free-draining soil is cleared and then kept open by grazing, the soil gradually tends to develop a particular characteristic profile, known as a podzol, which usually supports heathland as its main vegetation. Heathlands tend to develop in areas of medium to high rainfall, and in France they are most likely to be found from the Cherbourg Peninsula southwards through Brittany and down the west coast, almost as far as the Spanish border. They also occur in the lower parts of the western Pyrenees, and in a few acid soil areas in the centre of the country, such as the Sologne and parts of Fontainebleau Forest. Moorlands are broadly similar in their vegetation, but are developed over peat, and they tend to occur in more upland and high rainfall areas, such as the Vosges.

Heathlands are not especially species rich, and are frequently dominated by just a handful of plants such as heather, bell heather, and Dorset heath. However, they do provide habitat for a number of specialized species such as heath lobelia, mossy stonecrop, smooth snake, nightjar,

Dartford warbler, stonechat, and many insects such as tiger beetles, minotaur beetles, and sand wasps. They are a warm habitat, and are often the means by which essentially southern species can survive further north. They frequently occur in conjunction with bogs (see 'wetlands' below) because bogs need the unpolluted and nutrient-poor water that they are only likely to receive from a heathland catchment.

Coastal habitats

As we have seen, France has a coastline of about 5000 km, including Corsica, so it follows that its coastal habitats are of considerable importance. Whilst almost any habitat can occur on the coast, we are concerned here with those that are peculiarly coastal. The main ones are sand dunes, shingle, saltmarshes, mudflats, coastal cliffs, and various rocky intertidal habitats. Cliff-top grasslands often have special species, too. In addition to the fact that many of these habitats are directly formed by the sea, the coast also differs from most of the rest of the land surface in being relatively mild and frost free, and subject to higher levels of salinity. Many species do well in these conditions, for one reason or another, and are rare or absent away from the coast.

The whole northern and western coast of France, from the Belgian border in the north-east to the Spanish border in the south-west, is especially good for sand dunes, which are thrown up by the strong westerly winds and currents. Many of them occur as a result of the material

Sea holly *Eryngium maritimum*

produced in the last ice age, when sea levels were much lower, which was subsequently re-distributed and deposited as the sea levels rose. Good species-rich dunes can be found almost anywhere along this coast, though they are also often in areas of high tourist and visitor activity. The west coast, southwards from the mouth of the Gironde, is especially good for dunes, with an almost continuous line which includes one of the highest dunes in Europe: the Dune du Pilat. Such places have a rich, specialized flora, with flowers such as sea bindweed, sea holly, yellow horned-poppy, sea bedstraw, sea medick, and many more which occur hardly anywhere else. There are many specialized insects, too, including tiger beetles and ant-lions.

Large dune systems may also develop damper dune slacks (marshy hollows) or lakes and pools, where the water table reaches above the surface. Such areas are often especially good for flowers, including marsh helleborine, early marsh-orchid, water germander, and round-leaved wintergreens, and provide key breeding sites for amphibians such as natterjacks.

The south coast of France has fewer good dune systems, thanks to different patterns of erosion and deposition, though some remain at the outer edge of the Camargue, and scattered around the coasts of Corsica. Here they may be home to special flowers such as the widespread sea daffodil, or some of the Corsican specialities such as sand-crocuses and sea-lavenders.

Saltmarshes develop in calm tidal waters where silt accumulates, such as estuaries and sheltered bays, or in the lower reaches of deltas where there is occasional inundation by the sea. The deposited silt is gradually colonized by salt-tolerant plants, including sea asters, glassworts, cord-grasses, sea-lavenders, sea purslane and others, particularly members of the goosefoot family. If undisturbed, the upper reaches may gradually rise above the level of regular flooding and develop into a coastal grassland.

Saltmarshes are important feeding, nesting, and roosting areas for a number of birds including black-winged stilt, redshank, fan-tailed warbler, shelduck, and many visiting waders and waterfowl. They are frequent targets for 'reclamation' by construction of an outer sea wall, and subsequent conversion to grazing marshes or sometimes arable land.

There are good saltmarshes along the north coast in places like the Somme Estuary and Baie du Mont-St.-Michel, and here and there along the west coast, wherever there is shelter. Particularly good areas include the Golfe du Morbihan, the Bassin d'Arcachon, and Aiguillon Bay. In the Mediterranean, there are large areas of saltmarsh in the Camargue, and smaller patches in and around the many coastal lagoons.

Mudflats occur in similar places, but are not vegetated by higher plants because they are covered by the tide for too long, though they may often have good populations of algae. Many estuaries and basins empty at low tide to reveal huge areas of glistening mudflats. In winter and at migration periods, these mudflats are hugely important feeding resources for hundreds of thousands of waders and waterfowl escaping from the harsh northern winters. Because of the salt content and the coastal mildness, such areas are unlikely to freeze, especially towards the south of the country, so they become particularly important in cold periods when inland and more northern feeding sites may become unavailable to the birds.

Shelduck *Tadorna tadorna* (Mike Lane)

Lagoons are large coastal lakes, often brackish or saline. They have many of the characteristics of a very sheltered coastal site, and are often fringed with saltmarsh and filled with many of the invertebrates of mudflats. They can be very important areas for birds and some species – notably greater flamingos and avocets – are virtually confined to these lagoons in France. They are a feature of flat coasts along the Mediterranean, and they dominate the French coast from Marseille westwards to the Spanish border.

Rocky coasts, especially on uninhabited islands, can be very important for breeding seabirds. There are some fine seabird colonies on cliffs around the Brittany coast, and on many of the offshore islands here, and a number of Corsica's islands have seabird colonies, albeit with rather different breeding species. They can be important sites for plants, too, both for widespread species such as rock samphire and for very local ones such as the Bonifacio sea-lavender, confined to granite cliffs north of Bonifacio, on Corsica. Rocky coasts also tend to be better places for studying seashore life, because the water is clearer, there are more solid substrates for organisms to attach to, and rock pools are more abundant. The rocky coasts of Brittany, for example, are exceptionally good places for observing seashore life.

Wetlands and open waters

Wetlands are of considerable importance to wildlife. There are many species of birds, amphibians, invertebrates, mammals, and flowers that are totally dependent on the presence of open water for their survival, in addition of course to wholly aquatic species such as fish.

Despite great losses through drainage in recent years, there are still large areas of wetlands in France, nearly all of them of special interest to naturalists. For example, on the west coast there are several major wetland sites such as Grand-Brière marsh, Lac de Grand-lieu, and parts of the Marais Poitevin, which would be celebrated natu-

White-faced darter *Leucorrhinia dubia*

for birds. Such locations include La Brenne and Sologne in the centre of the country, the wetter areas of the Champagne country, and the Dombes, north of Lyon, all described in more detail as sites. There are also some interesting wetlands developing around reservoirs, especially those to the east of Troyes. The richest wetland areas tend to be those where there is a combination of unpolluted open water with extensive marginal habitats such as reedbeds, fen, and wet woodland, which collectively provide niches for a wide variety of species, especially those that rely on a mixture of habitats.

Other wetland habitats, usually on a smaller scale, include fens with calcareous ground water, such as those near Berck on the North Sea coast, which are often very rich in flowering plants, and grade into wet grassland if grazed or cut regularly. Bogs are widespread in France, though rarely large. They occur wherever there is acid water, low in nutrients, present for long enough to allow bog-mosses to establish and build up acid peat as they die and partially decompose. Bogs tend to occur in higher rainfall areas on more acid soils, sometimes in conjunction with heathlands and often in mountain areas. It is not uncommon for bog gradually to encroach on small acidic upland lakes, forming a surface layer dominated by bog-mosses; there are

ral sites in most other countries but are barely known outside France. These are all essentially natural wetlands, though greatly affected by humans. Elsewhere in the country, there are many artificial wetlands, especially those areas where there are concentrations of ponds, built mainly for fishing and shooting, in such large numbers that the whole area has become of enormous natural interest, particularly

Cranberry *Vaccinium oxycoccos*

good examples at Lac Luitel in the Alps, and Sagnes de la Godivelle in the Auvergne, amongst others. Bogs are not usually rich in species, but there are many specialized or uncommon species such as insectivorous sundews, butterworts and bladderworts, bog-rosemary, and cranberry, and many uncommon dragonflies, such as the white-faced darter.

Garrigue, maquis, and other scrub vegetation

Garrigue and *maquis* are two French words used to cover the whole spectrum of dry, scrubby vegetation that is so characteristic of the warmer parts of France, and else-where around the Mediterranean region. *Garrigue* is a low, rather bare community, with small shrubs and large areas of open ground where there may be abundant flow-ers in spring. The vegetation rarely reaches above about 1 m, and is easily walked through. *Maquis* is taller and more dense, usually at least as tall as a man, and some-times up to 4 m high. Dominant plants include kermes oak, strawberry-tree, myrtle, and Christ's thorn. Although *gar-rigue* and *maquis* are usually clearly distinct, they do intergrade, and other lan-guages make do with one word for both types. Neither is a wholly natural vegetation type – they are a replacement for natural forest, and represent different degrees of grazing and browsing, and responses to varying soil fertility and depth.

Garrigue is usually a good place to see flowers (especially orchids), reptiles, and butterflies, and some birds such as sub-alpine and Sardinian warblers, black-eared wheatear, and stonechats. Insects are abun-dant, especially praying mantises, bush-crickets, grasshoppers, solitary wasps, and many others. *Maquis* holds good popula-tions of birds, though they are much harder to see, and it is a less appealing habitat than *garrigue*. Where *maquis* is left undisturbed by fire or grazing, it will even-tually begin to succeed to woodland, which can soon become quite rich in flow-ers and other species.

Glacier Blanc, Ecrins National Park

Most *maquis* and *garrigue* areas occur around the Mediterranean coasts, and are very extensive in Corsica. However, they also extend inland in Provence, Corbières, and other regions where the conditions are right. Other forms of scrub are relatively rare in France, though in low-intensity agricultural areas such as parts of Brittany there may be large areas of blackthorn or hawthorn scrub, good for birds and occasionally with special lichens near the coast. There may also be natural areas of scrub around the upper edges of mountain forests, particularly in the Alps, dominated by dwarf pine, juniper, hawthorn and other shrubs, or dwarf forms of trees.

High mountain areas

France has a large area of high mountains, and many of these rise above the natural tree-line. Here, there is a wild and often unspoilt region of scrub, open grassland, screes, rocks, cliffs, moraines, and wet flushed areas, reaching eventually up to glaciers or semi-permanent snowfields in the highest places. Most such areas are to be found in the Pyrenees, Alps, and Maritime Alps, with smaller areas in the Auvergne and Cévennes.

Productivity is low here, but the diversity can be astonishingly high. There may be huge numbers of flowers, but also remarkable numbers of butterflies, grasshoppers, and other insects, and a good range of birds and mammals. Mountains are often the last refuge for predominantly lowland birds and mam-

Wildcat *Felis silvestris*

mals that have retreated here as their habitats elsewhere have gone – such as lynx, brown bear, wildcat, and golden eagle – and these mix with mountain specialists like marmots and alpine choughs to provide a wonderful natural experience. Many of the best natural sites in France are in the high mountains.

The natural history of France

France is the largest European country, and has an enormous range of habitats spread over the widest possible altitude range, so it is hardly surprising that it boasts a rich and varied natural life. It also lies at a pivotal point in Europe, so that many migrating birds, which may not breed here, have to pass through.

The flora of France – the higher plants – consists of 4670 species, well over twice the number of Britain's flora, though noticeably fewer than those of Greece, Spain, and Italy. These last three countries all extend much further south than France, into an area where there are more survivors from pre-glacial times, and a generally higher diversity. Nevertheless, 4670 species provides plenty to be going on with. Because France is in such a central position in Europe, it draws its influences from all around, which contributes to its richness. Conversely, this means that it has relatively few endemics (i.e. species confined solely to France or one part of France). High mountain areas are often sources of endemics, as species evolve in isolation here, but France's many Pyrenean and Alpine endemics are nearly all shared with adjacent countries. There are a few mainland endemics, though by far the highest number is on Corsica, where there are about 300 endemic plants, of which 131 are confined to Corsica alone (the others are shared with Sardinia or similar nearby areas), and several endemic races or varieties of birds, butterflies, and amphibians, amongst others.

There are about 350 species of bird that regularly occur in France (plus a long list of occasional visitors), of which about 270 regularly breed. This means that about two-thirds of European bird species occur here, confirming France's ornithological importance. Some 162 birds 'of European concern' breed regularly, of which 6 are of global concern. These latter are black vulture (re-introduced and very rare in France), lesser kestrel, corncrake, little bustard, Audouin's gull, and Corsican nuthatch. Only the last is at all common, and here France has sole responsibility for it occurs nowhere else, not even on Sardinia.

The herpetofauna (reptiles and amphibians) of France is rich and varied, with 68 species recorded in total. As with other groups, the different influences are obvious – Iberian species such as the western spadefoot and Spanish psammodromus (a lizard) reach into south-west France, south-eastern species such as Hermann's tortoise reach into south-east France, and mainly eastern species such as green toad and moor frog reach into eastern France. There are no mainland French endemics, though the Corsican salamander and the Corsican brook salamander are endemic to Corsica, and several other species such as the Tyrrhenian painted frog and European leaf-toed gecko have a very limited distribution. Probably the rarest of the mainland species is Orsini's viper, which just occurs in a few mountain grassland areas in the Haute Provence and Maritime Alps, though it does also occur sparsely in countries further east.

The list of mammals recorded from France stands at 135, of which about 20 marine species are occasional visitors. Some of the most interesting species include the brown bear, which is extremely rare and almost extinct in the Pyrenees, but occurs nowhere else in the country; the European mink, which has a number of populations in west France, well west of their main populations in eastern Europe; and the fascinating Pyrenean desman, an aquatic species closely related to the mole, and confined to the Pyrenees and some other north Iberian mountains. There are also 30 species of bat, with many, such as Brandt's bat, pond bat, northern bat, and parti-coloured bat, towards the edge of their range in France. There are also 65 species of freshwater fish in France, and a further 15 recorded in brackish water, plus the hundreds of vertebrates and invertebrates recorded around the coasts. All this is put in perspective, however, by the number of insects (leaving aside other invertebrates) recorded in France; so far, almost 40 000 species have been recorded (out of a total European insect fauna of about 100 000), which includes a number apparently confined to France.

If you consider that France is also very rich in fungi, lichens, bryophytes, algae, and most invertebrate groups such as spiders, you realize what a treasure house it is.

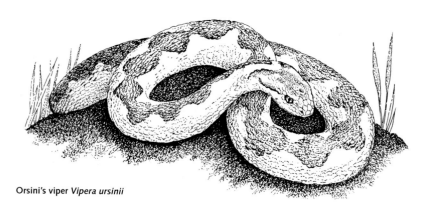

Orsini's viper *Vipera ursinii*

Nature conservation in France

Nature conservation in France is a complex and rather ambiguous business, involving many organizations and individuals. In one sense it is very good, for a wealthy industrial nation, in that there is still a great deal of low-intensity traditional agriculture, which involves retaining woods, hedges, coppice, pollards, and other minor habitats. This happens because it is a large country with a relatively low population density, and many hilly areas where intensive agriculture is difficult. In most official senses, though, it is rather poor, with limited numbers of statutory nature reserves, relatively few strong voluntary bodies, no habitat protection legislation except for that imposed by the EU, and an excessively powerful hunting lobby which has recently succeeded in extending the hunting season when everyone else wants to shorten it.

The National Parks have the highest level of conservation; there are six at the moment, mainly in mountain areas, and covering 0.7% of the land surface. The system is normally based on a core zone, with virtually no inhabitants and a relatively high degree of protection, surrounded by a peripheral zone. The latter is intended as a buffer zone, but in practice often seems to receive all the development that is not allowed in the core zone, and is generally poorly protected. The parks are all lovely places, though their boundaries are usually very tightly drawn around the areas that no one has objected to, so they do not really give much additional protection. On the regional maps, the abbreviation NP in the title indicates a National Park site.

There is also an extensive system of Regional Natural Parks (Parc Naturel Régional), set up under legislation dating from 1967. These are also fine places, but the designation gives no real protection, nor is it necessarily an indication that the area is rich in natural history. The aims of such parks are rather loose, but are generally concerned with helping local people to make a living; indeed one of the specifically stated aims of the Camargue Regional Natural Park is to 'allow the inhabitants of the Camargue to lead a life which they themselves have chosen ...'. This inevitably involves a certain amount of intensive agriculture, forestry, and tourism development, which can be damaging to the wildlife, though in other respects they can be quite wildlife-friendly. Some, such as Grand-Brière, Grands Causses, Queyras, and the Camargue itself, are particularly worth visiting, though others are not. There are currently 38 Regional Natural Parks. On the regional maps, the abbreviation RNP in the title indicates a Regional Natural Park site.

There is a series of National Nature Reserves, which vary enormously in size and quality. Some are managed by separate organizations (see below), while others are managed directly. There are currently 138 in metropolitan France (and another dozen or so overseas). There are also many local and voluntary nature reserves run by regional and specialist organizations, such as La Ligue pour la Protection des Oiseaux, the Société pour l'Etude et la Protection de la Nature en Bretagne, and the Conservatoire du Littoral, amongst others, and no-hunting reserves run by the Office Nationale de la Chasse, whose aim is to have sanctuaries where quarry species can build up their populations; not a laudable aim as far as I'm concerned, as they should not be shot at all, but at least such reserves do provide some sanctuary and are usually good for most forms of natural life.

Other means of protection include the 'Arrêtés de Biotope' which may be invoked locally to protect a specific species or small area of land of conservation importance, though they usually make no provision for subsequent management. The 'Sites Naturels Classés' is an old system designed for protecting features of natural beauty such as a mountain, tree, or waterfall, and may include ecological value, if only peripherally. There are also large numbers of species, from all groups, that are officially protected by law. This includes all bats, many birds, reptiles, and amphibians, and over 400 flowering plants.

The problem with all nature conservation in France is that there may be many laws, and there are certainly many committed individuals, but there is very little official enthusiasm for conservation, and very little is enforced. The hunting, agricultural, and development lobbies are all very strong, and conservation usually loses in any serious contest. Any regular visitor to France cannot fail to notice the continuing loss of habitats, especially in wetlands and coastal areas. Recently, European protective legislation has begun to affect France through the designation of sites such as the Natura 2000 network, and the Special Protection Areas (SPA in the UK, ZPS in France) for birds, and a more serious commitment to species protection. It is hoped that this will gradually improve the official attitude to nature conservation, before much more is lost.

North Atlantic coast

North Atlantic coast

Introduction

This is a predominantly western and coastal region, running from Baie du Mont-St-Michel in the north-east corner down to the mouth of the Garonne River in the south. It runs inland for some distance, east of Rennes and Nantes, but the whole area is dominated by the influence of the Atlantic Ocean and its weather systems, which give it mild winters and relatively cool, damp summers. It has a great deal in common with the southern Celtic fringes of Britain, especially Cornwall and Pembrokeshire, though it is warmer and slightly drier. It has a beautiful and varied coastline that attracts a huge number of visitors, particularly during the main summer holidays. While this brings prosperity, it also means that almost all sandy beaches are heavily disturbed and often built up, and few other sections of coast escape the pressure. The coastal habitats are varied (though limestone rocks are very scarce), with high cliffs, rocky shores, sheltered saltmarshes and mudflats, estuaries, long stretches of sand dunes, shingle beaches, and lagoons, and in a few places woodland or heathland reaches down to the sea. There are also many offshore islands, some uninhabited, which contribute greatly to the variety of the region; many are

Narcissus triandrus

reserves, and some support important seabird colonies of birds such as gannets and puffins. The sea is generally clean and clear, producing ideal conditions for a marvellous diversity of intertidal life, though there have been several devastating oil spills in recent years.

There were once vast areas of heathland here, not natural, but the result of a long history of clearance and grazing over acid soils. The area of heaths has steadily declined through conversion to agricultural land and forests or through lack of management, but there are still large expanses, particularly on the coasts or along the Monts d'Arrée, and they are rich in western species such as Cornish and Dorset heaths. The woods in the area have a distinctly Atlantic character, with slightly deformed and twisted trees thanks to the wind, and a particularly rich covering of lichens. This is a good area in general for lichens, as well as mosses and ferns, revelling in the warm humid conditions, with relatively little frost, and many species that are rare, extinct, or absent from Britain do well here.

In the southern part of the region, there are large tracts of low-lying land and many sheltered bays and harbours,

Gannet *Morus bassanus*

Previous page: **Quiberon**

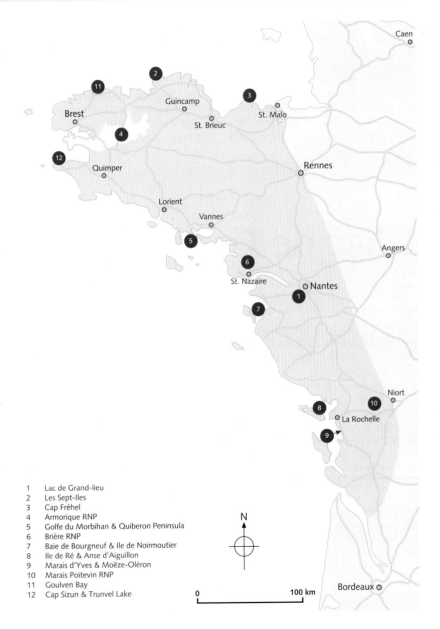

1   Lac de Grand-lieu
2   Les Sept-Iles
3   Cap Fréhel
4   Armorique RNP
5   Golfe du Morbihan & Quiberon Peninsula
6   Brière RNP
7   Baie de Bourgneuf & Ile de Noirmoutier
8   Ile de Ré & Anse d'Aiguillon
9   Marais d'Yves & Moëze-Oléron
10 Marais Poitevin RNP
11 Goulven Bay
12 Cap Sizun & Trunvel Lake

N

0   100 km

which provide some of the very best wet-lands in France. There are vast, yet still little-known wetlands such as the Grand Brière or Lac de Grand-lieu inland, and marvellous bays such as Aiguillon and the Golfe du Morbihan, which remain frost free and productive through the winter, providing superb feeding areas for tens of thousands of birds that have bred in north Europe and Asia.

Altogether, it is a fascinatingly varied part of France. Many southern species reach up the west coast; there are no size-able mountain barriers, so species can extend as far north as their climatic preferences allow. With an overview, it is possible to track the path of mainly southern species – such as sea medick, black-winged stilt, or praying mantis – becoming steadily more rare and confined to warm sites as you move northwards. At the same time, there are many Atlantic and northern species, able to survive because there are no long, hot summers.

It is a region that is changing quickly. Even within the last decade there have been great changes in agricultural intensity, an extensive road-building programme, and a continuing increase in visitor numbers, all putting increasing pressure on the remaining habitats, though with this has come a noticeable increase in the understanding of the fragility and importance of the remaining natural habitats.

SITE 1 Lac de Grand-lieu

A very large and important lake and marsh south-west of Nantes, with a particularly good bird fauna.

The vast Lac de Grand-lieu and its associated marshland lie about 12 km south-west of Nantes. There is a Ramsar Site (an internationally important wetland) covering 6000 ha, and a Special Protection Area taking in virtually the same territory, of which part (mainly to the west) lies in a National Nature Reserve. Although an extremely important and interesting location, it is very frustrating to visit, partly because there is hardly anywhere from where you can see the lake, and partly because – despite its status – it is still heavily shot over in places. Passay, on the eastern side of the lake, is the only realistic access point; the lake can be seen here, and it may be possible to arrange a boat trip with a local fisherman. In winter, the area of open water can cover up to about 3000 ha, shrinking to less than 1000 ha in summer. The lake lies towards the eastern edge of the site, with reedbeds, then extensive grazing marshes, extending away westwards.

Breeding birds here include a strong mixed heronry, probably the single largest in France, with grey and purple herons, little and cattle egrets, night heron, and a few spoonbills – perhaps 2000 birds in all.

Although it is hard to see the heronries, which are mainly in alders and other trees on the lake margin, you can spot their inhabitants along ditches or on marshland all around the area. Other breeding birds include large numbers of marsh harriers, which can always be seen quartering the reedbeds and fields, black terns, gadwall, bearded tit in the reeds, bluethroat along the marshland dykes, masses of marsh and sedge warblers, and honey buzzards and black kites nearby. At passage periods and throughout the winter, there can regularly be 20 000 or more birds, made up particularly of waterfowl such as pintail, shoveler, coot, grebes, and others. About 100 species of birds winter regularly at the site. Corncrake pass through on passage, but do not breed.

Inula britannica

Twelve species of amphibians are found here, of which the marsh and edible frogs are much the most noticeable, with their loud chorus of croaking, especially on early summer nights. There are 26 species of fish recorded, of which eels are probably the most noticeable, forming a key prey item for the herons, and 10 reptiles. It is also an important mammal site, though these are even harder to see than the birds. Over 50 species have been recorded, including otter, European mink, and genet. European mink is a little-known and rather rare species that has declined dramatically in western Europe (though it is more common further east in Europe). It is very similar to the closely related American mink (so widespread in Britain now), but differs in having more white around the face and especially above the mouth, and is usually rather more shy. The genet is an attractive, long, thin, spotted cat, unlike anything else in the wild here; within Europe, it occurs only in the Iberian Peninsula, and western France. Although it is mainly nocturnal and very hard to find, its presence can often be detected by the distinctive droppings, which are very long for a smallish mammal (up to 20 cm or more), horseshoe-shaped, and black when fresh.

As you might expect, Lac de Grand-lieu is an excellent place for dragonflies and damselflies, with almost 40 species recorded, including the Norfolk hawker, hairy hawker, red darter, emperor, vari-

able damselfly, and small blue-tailed damselfly. It is also a fine site botanically, though again not an easy place in which to see species. About 550 species of higher plants have been recorded in the reserve, slightly more in the wider area. The lake itself has large populations of yellow, fringed, and white water-lilies, looking beautiful in early summer, and providing habitat for masses of invertebrates. Water chestnut is present but less common, together with bladderworts, bogbean, pondweeds and other aquatic species. In marshy surrounding areas, there are large populations of royal fern, loose-flowered orchids, pennyroyal, yellow iris, flowering rush, and the rather striking inula *Inula britannica*, with large yellow-orange flower heads, amongst many others.

There is a reserve centre in the village of L'Etier, to the north of the lake, with information and permanent exhibitions.

About 45 km south-east of Nantes there is a much smaller (but considerably more visitor-friendly) wetland reserve called Les Boucheries, lying just west of the village of Les Landes-Genusson. It is sign-posted as 'la cité des oiseaux' from some directions, and has an information centre, hides, and walkways. It is particularly good in winter, but of interest at all times.

Gadwall *Anas strepera* (Peter Wilson)

SITE
2 Les Sept-Iles

The most important seabird colony in France, on a group of islands
just off the north Brittany coast.

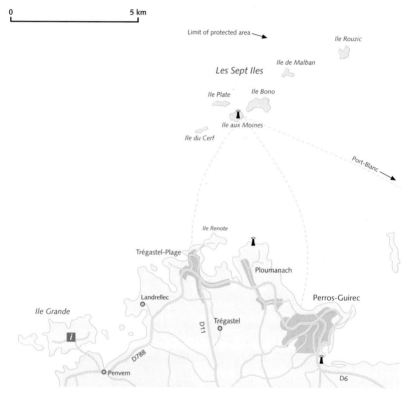

There are relatively few seabird colonies in France, and the best ones are in Brittany. This one, run as a nature reserve by La Ligue pour la Protection des Oiseaux, is easily the best, overall, in most respects. It is a granite archipelago made up of five main islands and some rocks, lying roughly 5 km off the Brittany coast at Perros-Guirec. There are 12 species of seabirds breeding here: puffin, gannet, shag, Manx shearwater, storm petrel, kittiwake, fulmar, guillemot, razorbill, common tern, and gulls, together with oystercatchers, ravens, rock-pipits, shelduck, and wheatears. Grey seals can be seen all around the islands throughout the year. The best island is Rouzic, the most northerly, which has the main gannet colony. Currently about 11 000 pairs of gannets live here, the only significant gannet colony in France, and about 230 pairs of puffins, representing 90% of the French breeding population. The Breton coast lies towards the southern edge of the breeding range of many seabirds, and there are few colonies to be found southwards from here.

In addition to the breeding birds, it is quite a good site for seeing migrants, with 56 species recorded, and birds such as

North Atlantic coast

Shag *Phalacrocorax aristotelis*

curlew, oystercatcher and turnstones pass the winter here. Records list 160 species of flowers, including sea kale (rare in France) and sea spleenwort, a distinctive fern that grows almost exclusively on coastal rocks.

Access is limited. Landing is restricted to Ile aux Moines, where there is a lighthouse, though boat trips can be arranged from Perros-Guirec. There is an information centre on Ile Grande, described as a 'Station ornithologique', run by La Ligue pour la Protection des Oiseaux, which is excellent for information, bookings, books, and leaflets, and live video footage of the seabird colonies. The best time for a visit to the islands is between mid-April and early July.

Ile Grande itself is worth a visit. It has beautiful, unspoilt rocky coastline, with particularly good intertidal and marine life, lovely rock pools, and superb displays of coastal flowers such as thrift and sea heath. Many of the islands' breeding birds can be seen fishing offshore, and the passage and wintering birds are similar.

SITE
3 Cap Fréhel

A very attractive coastal heathland site, with impressive cliffs, home to a wide range of species.

Chaffweed
Anagallis minima

landscape feature with its lighthouse and striking cliffs. The plateau areas are predominantly heathland, with smaller areas of bog and woodland.

Botanically it is very rich, with a mixture of heathland and coastal species, together with a few extras. There are two tiny members of the gentian family: yellow centaury, which reaches 10 cm (in favoured sites!) and has tiny yellow flowers that open only in the sun, and the even smaller annual Guernsey centaury, which grows less than 5 cm high. The much larger marsh gentian occurs in

Cap Fréhel projects northwards from the Côte d'Emeraude, forming a major coastal

The cliffs of Cap Frehel in spring

boggy areas. The distinctive, white-flow-ered, Kerry lily is fairly common towards the cliff edges, the rare small adder's tongue fern occurs in short turf, and other uncommon plants such as smooth cat's ear, Cornish heath, Dorset heath, pale violet, spring and autumn squills, and a variety of other species occur. *Pulmonaria azurea*, a lungwort with unspotted leaves and blue flowers that normally occurs in mountains, can be found on steep slopes and cliffs. In

Guernsey centaury *Exaculum pusillum*

boggy areas, there are two species of sundew, pale butterwort, bog asphodel, and many others. Sea spleenwort grows on the cliffs.

It is a good bird-watching site, with Dartford warblers, stonechats, linnets, nightjars, and various others on the heath, and occasional melodious war-blers (rare this far north in France) in damp scrub areas. The cliffs support breeding colonies of fulmar, shag, kitti-wake, gulls, and a small, declining colony of guillemots and razorbills. There are also breeding ravens, peregrine, genuine-ly wild rock doves, stock doves, jackdaws, and black redstarts.

It is a good area for heath and bog invertebrates such as large marsh grasshopper, bog and grey bush-crickets, a few dragonflies, emperor moths, and the striking wasp spiders.

The site is easily accessible and well signposted via minor roads north of the main Dinan to St. Brieuc road. Part of the heath is run as a reserve by the Société pour l'Etude et la Protection de la Nature en Bretagne, and there are guided walks on offer in summer. It is a popular tourist spot in busy periods.

SITE 4 Armorique Regional Natural Park

A large park which stretches through the central part of Brittany, encompassing a wide range of habitats.

Armorique Regional Natural Park covers 172 000 ha, stretching from the offshore islands of the Ile d'Ouessant group, through the Crozon Peninsula eastwards along the Monts d'Arrée and on to Huelgoat and its famous forest. Like most Regional Natural Parks (see p. 19) it encompasses much that is far from being natural habitat, and its conservation management falls well short of that of a reserve or National Park. Nevertheless, it includes many localities of great natural interest, especially its offshore islands, coastal habitats such as dunes and salt-marshes, heaths, bogs and moorland, a few marshes, unimproved grassland, and some fine old forests.

The offshore islands are both beautiful and of particular importance for their wildlife, though access to the best parts is limited. The archipelago off the coast west of Brest is a superb area, including the little, uninhabited archipelago known as Iroise, the Ile Moléne area, and the larger inhabited island of Ile d'Ouessant. Within the area, there is a vast biosphere reserve, a National Nature Reserve, a Special Protection Area, and various other protective designations, as well as a permanent bird observatory on Ouessant. It has a rather similar character to the Scilly Isles, and the French believe it to be even better for birds (although, of course, it isn't!). It is excellent for birds at any time between March and November (and winter is not bad); passage periods bring large numbers of birds: up to six species of shearwaters, many waders, birds of prey, shrikes, flycatchers, and numerous other passerines, including a few rarities each

Land quillwort
Isoetes hystrix

year. Breeding species include good populations of storm petrel, Manx shearwater, little, common, and Sandwich terns, shag, oystercatcher, kittiwake, fulmar, red-billed chough, and ringed plover on the coasts, and heathland birds such as Dartford warbler, stonechat and wheatear elsewhere. There are superb displays of coastal flowers, notably thrift and sea campion in late spring, and a number of less common plants such as shore dock, small adder's tongue, the curious little quillwort *Isoetes hystrix*, and various others. Both grey and common seals occur in the area, and dolphins are not uncommon offshore.

Access to Ouessant is open, reaching it by boat from Brest or Le Conquet, or by air from Brest. Access to the smaller islands can be arranged locally, but is restricted.

There are extensive heathlands and moorlands within the park, particularly

Oystercatcher *Haematopus ostralegus* (Mike Lane)

Huelgoat Forest

along the Monts d'Arrée, on the Crozon Peninsula, east of Berrien, and in various areas just outside the park boundaries, such as south of Guerlesquin. Such areas have a fine array of heathland species: flowers include Cornish and Dorset heaths, marsh gentian, chamomile, dodder (often in remarkable abundance, parasitizing gorse and heather), sand spurrey, yellow centaury, and others. Breeding birds include Dartford and grasshopper warblers, curlew, hen harriers, stonechats, and other specialized species. The Société pour l'Etude et la Protection de la Nature en Bretagne has an excellent reserve, covering 300 ha, called the Landes du Cragou, close to the village of Le Cloitre–St. Thégonnec, where there are guided walks in summer and an open botanical trail. There are many areas of bogs, particularly associated with heaths, or more extensive areas such as La Tourbière de Venec and other areas around the St. Michel Reservoir. These are the places to see sundews, at least 12 species of bog-moss

Sphagnum, marsh clubmoss, pale butterwort, lesser bladderwort, bog asphodel, lousewort, and cotton-grasses. They are good places to see dragonflies, such as several species of emerald damselfly *Lestes*, small red damselfly, golden-ringed dragonfly, keeled skimmer, and various others. There is a museum and information centre at nearby Brennilis, where there is also information about, and examples of, the reintroduced beavers from the Rhône Valley.

There are some old forests in the area, most noticeably at Huelgoat, which is a remnant of the original ancient Argoat forest, albeit a rather managed one. It is now made up mainly of oak and beech, with birch, rowan, and other trees, made more varied by the presence of large granite boulders and stony valleys, which make the trees more stunted and the whole area more complex. There are clean rivers, sunny clearings, and patches of heathland providing a mosaic of habitats for an extensive range of species. It is a good area

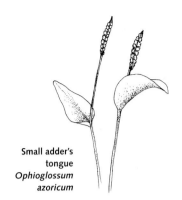

Small adder's
tongue
*Ophioglossum
azoricum*

for lichens, bryophytes (mosses and liver-worts), and ferns; some of the more humid rocks, for instance, are covered with moss-es and filmy ferns, particularly Tunbridge filmy-fern, and royal fern grows along the valleys. Flowers of interest include Cornish moneywort (quite common), the pretty little ivy-leaved bellflower, slender St. John's-wort, angular Solomon's seal, Dorset heath, sheep's-bit, early purple and heath spotted orchids, and many others. Golden-ringed dragonflies are abundant

along the streams, and birds such as red-starts and wood warblers breed here. Huelgoat has a small botanic garden, which at present specializes mostly in exotic species, though there are plans to feature the local species more.

Throughout the park, and in adjacent regions, there are patches of unimproved pastures and wet meadows, sometimes red with green-winged orchids or blue with heath lobelia. The whole coastline is of interest, and – away from the main built-up areas – there are many good examples of coastal habitats such as dunes and salt-marshes, and the Conservatoire du Littoral protects a number of sites such as Pointe de Keric and L'aber, south of Telgruc-sur-mer, and Cap de La Chèvre and Pointe des Espagnols on the Crozon Peninsula.

The park HQ has an information centre, wooded reserve, and animal park, near Hanvec, at the western end of the Monts d'Arrée, north-east of the Crozon Peninsula, which is open every day in summer, or Wednesdays and Sundays in winter, except for January, when it is closed.

SITE 5 Golfe du Morbihan and Quiberon Peninsula

A superb, varied coastal area, particularly important for birds and with a fascinating range of flowers, insects, and reptiles.

Golfe du Morbihan is a large, tidal, and almost completely enclosed bay immedi-ately south of Vannes. It is dotted with about 40 islands of various sizes, some of which are accessible at low tide. It covers about 23 000 ha – a huge area – and is large enough to have very varied salinity and tidal currents within it. At low tide, about 4000 ha of mudflats become exposed, providing a huge feeding resource for birds, though much is dis-turbed by shellfish farming.

Common tern *Sterna hirundo* (Peter Wilson)

The gulf is exceptionally important for birds, with all possible international designations. In winter, up to 100 000 birds use the site, including large numbers of brent geese, shelduck, wigeon, shoveler, pintail, goldeneye, red-breasted merganser, and waders such as grey plover, avocet, redshank, dunlin, and curlew. Some species winter in significant numbers, for example up to 1500 black-necked grebe, 2000 red-breasted merganser, 30 000 dunlin, and almost 1000 avocets. It is not particularly important for birds of prey, though there are marsh harriers about most of the time, and other species pass through. At passage periods, there are additional species such as spoonbill, spotted redshank, terns, whimbrel, and many more. The density of breeding birds here is not high, but it includes marsh harrier, little egret, fan-tailed warblers, black-winged stilts (over 50 pairs), avocet, common redshank, and a few bluethroat. Good areas to visit include the no-hunting reserve on the south side, north of Sarzeau, and the Falguérec reserve (or Marais de Séné) at Séné, just south-east of Vannes, though roads encircle the site and lead on to some of the islands, giving many opportunities for viewing, especially at high tide.

The area to the south of the gulf has many other places of interest. The Anse de Sucinio, on the coast south-east of Sarzeau, has a mixture of coastal habitats including lagoons, saltmarshes, mudflats, dunes, and coastal grassland. There are breeding fan-tailed warblers, water pipit, little and common terns, little egrets and ringed plovers, amongst others. On the dunes and sandbars, interesting flowers include sand bedstraw, sea medick, sea-holly, Ray's knot-grass, yellow horned-poppy, marsh mallow, hairy rupture-wort, sea radish, and the saltwort *Salsola soda*. Sand lizards are quite common, and there are blue-flashing grasshoppers. The Pointe du Grande-mont, a few kilometres west of here, has goldilocks aster and praying mantis, towards the northern edge of its range. At Penerf, especially in the Penerf Estuary, there are large areas of good saltmarsh and mudflats with abundant birds, and further east at Kervoyal, sand dunes harbour species of interest such as green lizards and wintergreens. The whole Vilaine Estuary, south-east of Muzillac, is an important area for wintering birds such as avocets (with over 2000 regularly appearing), brent geese (almost 4000), curlew, scaup (over 5000), pintail, and other wildfowl and waders.

To the west of Morbihan, the Quiberon Peninsula curves southwards in a protective arc. It is a very busy holiday area but still retains some fine habitat, particularly the rocky, exposed 'Côte Sauvage', parts of which are protected by the Conservatoire du Littoral, and the sand dunes northwards towards the mainland from Panthièvre. The dunes are largely protected as a reserve, and mainly covered with semi-stable grassland that is particularly flowery. Notable species include yellow rattles, burnet rose, the little joint-pine *Ephedra distachya*, masses of a lovely everlasting *Helichrysum stoechas*, sand toadflax, several stork's-bills, sea-holly, stocks, sea medick, sand bedstraw, hare's tail grass, broomrapes, and many others. The sheltered Quiberon Bay can hold large numbers of birds in winter, especially dunlin, turnstones and brent geese. On the island of Belle-Ile (easily reached from Quiberon), there are some seabird colonies; for example, the Société pour l'Etude et la Protection de la Nature en Bretagne reserve at Pointe du Vieux

North Atlantic coast

Château (known generally by its Breton name Koh Kastell) on the north-west coast has shags, kittiwakes, ravens, and red-billed choughs, amongst others.

Whilst in the area, it is likely that you will visit the famous standing stones, or *alignements*, around Carnac. These lie in an area containing significant amounts of heathland, with flowers such as Dorset heath and heath lobelia, and plentiful Dartford warblers. Ponds in the area often contain the rare floating water-plantain, and are good for dragonflies such as keeled skimmers and scarce chasers.

^{SITE}6 Brière Regional Natural Park

Extraordinary wetlands with a primitive and unspoilt atmosphere, lying just north of the Loire Estuary.

The Brière is the second largest region of wetlands in France, after the Camargue. The park covers about 40 000 ha, with the core section of wetland habitats occupying about 19 000 ha. It is a quite remarkable area, which has the feeling of being little changed over the centuries, and which is still both little known and relatively inaccessible. The key to the site is its varying water levels, which rise to flood vast areas in wet periods, then retreat at drier times, making intensive agriculture and extensive habitation impossible. The result is a vast matrix of open water, grazing marshes, fen, reedbeds, carr wood-

Whorled caraway
Carum verticillatum

land, and a few other habitats which are hard to penetrate deeply, except by boat in a few places. Unfortunately, artificial changes in the adjacent Loire Estuary, with which the Brière is intricately associated ecologically and hydrologically, are causing water levels to drop, and flooding to become less frequent. This is shifting the ecological balance, and the area is in danger of becoming steadily less valuable as an ecological resource.

It is a superb location for wetland birds, at most times of year. Breeding birds include a large population of bitterns (with up to 20 or so pairs breeding), spotted crake in small numbers, the largest breeding colony of black tern in France (with up to 100 pairs in some years), whiskered terns, and dozens of marsh harriers, which can be seen at almost any stop in the area.

Water rail *Rallus aquaticus* (Mike Lane)

North Atlantic coast

Marshland and open water in Brière

There are also relatively large numbers of bluethroats (with an estimated population of about 200 birds), a few hen harriers, black kite, abundant water rail, and the usual assemblage of more common wetland species such as grey and purple heron, little egret, sedge, reed, and Cetti's warblers, reed buntings, and many more. It is also a good stopover for passage migrants such as corncrake, spoonbill, and masses of passerines, ducks, and a few waders. In winter, if conditions are right, there can be large numbers of ducks such as shoveler and wigeon, coot, grebes, and other birds, attracting birds of prey such as spotted eagle, whitetailed sea eagle, and merlin in addition to the residents.

It is a rich area botanically, too, especially if you are interested in wetland plants. Flowering-rushes (which are not rushes at all, and have large pink flowers), yellow iris, ragged-robin, and marsh-marigold, amongst others occur around the edges of water;

Viper's-grass
Scorzonera humilis

in the water, there are yellow and white water-lilies, insectivorous yellow-flowered bladderworts, half a dozen or more water-crowfoots, masses of species of pondweeds, and a few colonies of the curious water chestnut, towards the northern edge of its range here. Wet fields are good for marsh, loose-flowered and green-winged orchids, meadow thistle, whorled caraway, lousewort and viper's grass, and the drier fields can be blue with heath lobelia in late summer.

Not surprisingly, amphibians are abundant (though of relatively few species), mainly common and edible frogs, common toads and natterjacks, and tree frogs. Dragonflies are plentiful, notably hairy hawker, Norfolk hawker, orange emerald, emperor, scarce chaser, and many more common species. It is rich in other insect life (including a number that bite), such as the striking musk beetle wherever there are old willows or poplars. It is also an interesting locale for mammals, though most of them are hard to see. There is a good population of muskrat (which is rather like a large water vole, up to 40 cm long excluding the tail), water voles, otters, brown hare, and the usual wild boar, red foxes, and other more widespread species.

Roads encircle the area, though few penetrate far. It is probably best to aim for Ile de Fédrun on the east side, which has a park information centre offering boats and horses for hire, and various guided walks. A few kilometres to the south-east of here are an animal park and nature trail.

The coast to the west of Brière is also worth visiting, especially south-west of Guérande, where there are saltmarshes, saltpans, mudflats, dunes, and other good habitats. The Société pour l'Etude et la Protection de la Nature en Bretagne has

Black tern *Chlidonias niger*

a reserve near Le Croisic, and an education centre at Bois-Joubert.

SITE
7 Baie de Bourgneuf and Ile de Noirmoutier

A vast area of intertidal and coastal habitats, particularly good for birds.

The Ile de Noirmoutier stretches northwards from the coast west of Challons, protecting and partially enclosing an area known as the Baie de Bourgneuf. There are vast expanses of mudflats, saltmarshes, saltpans, dunes and other coastal habitats, and a certain amount of freshwater marshland, such as the Marais de Machecoul, stretching away eastwards inland. Almost 50 000 ha of the bay and peninsula are considered to be particularly important for birds.

The site is excellent for birds in winter and at passage periods, though a number of species also breed here. Some examples from the long list of birds to be seen in winter include: brent geese (up to almost 10 000), shelduck (4000–5000), avocet (up to 2000), grey plover (up to 6000), dunlin (up to 15 000), curlew (3500) and smaller numbers of redshank, knot, oystercatchers, godwits, grebes, eider duck, and many other waders and waterfowl. Similar species occur on pas-

sage, with additional numbers of terns, harriers, osprey, white-tailed sea eagle, and spotted redshank. Breeding birds include little egrets, common and little terns, redshank, avocet, black-winged stilts, Kentish plover, bluethroat (quite common here), and remarkably large numbers of both marsh and Montagu's harriers. It is not an easy area to watch, especially as shooting

Dunlin *Calidris alpina* (Mike Lane)

can disturb the birds. Towards high tide is generally best as the area of feeding grounds is reduced, and good places include the roads south of Les Moutiers, the coast just west of Beauvoir-sur-mer, and the remarkable little causeway road (known as the Passage du Gois, and only safe to use around low tide) that crosses the bay to the island from west of Beauvoir.

The Ile de Noirmoutier (now a peninsula thanks to the main road connecting it to the mainland) has a good range of coastal habitats, and many of the same birds as the bay. Additional breeding species here include melodious warbler, cirl bunting, and fan-tailed warbler. There is a small National Nature Reserve at the Marais de Müllembourg, run by La Ligue pour la Protection des Oiseaux, and covering just 48 ha, yet home to many of the birds recorded in the area. It lies just south-east of Noirmoutier town, on the north bank of the channel, and consists of old saltpans, saltmarsh, dunes, and other sandy areas. There are strong breeding colonies of shelduck, avocets, black-winged stilts, Kentish plover, bluethroat, and many others, and Montagu's and marsh harriers feed over the reserve.

The coastal habitats of the island are good places for an abundance of coastal plants such as sea medick, sea-holly, joint-pine, *Helichrysum stoechas*, sea stock, cotton-weed, Jersey pink, sage-leaved cistus (at its northern limit), and various clovers on the dunes and other sandy areas; sea-lavenders, saltwort including *Salsola soda*, annual and shrubby sea-blites, various glassworts, sea purslane, sea club-rush and many more in saltmarsh or similar areas; and interesting species in the ditches and other fresh or brackish water sites, such as the water-crowfoots *Ranunculus trichophyllus*, *R. baudotii*, and *R. droueti*. About 160 species of flower have been recorded for the 48 ha of Müllembourg alone.

The vast grazing marshes to the east and south of Baie de Bourgneuf, though largely drained, are still of great interest to the naturalist, with good dragonflies such as hairy and Norfolk hawkers, breeding birds such as bluethroat along some of the ditches and, in places, interesting flowers such as loose-flowered orchids, greater spearwort, and flowering-rush.

South of the bay, just south of the small town of Fromentine, lies the Pays de Monts forest, mainly on old dunes. There are interesting birds here such as hoopoe, woodlark, and serins, and remnants of a dune flora with extra species such as *Daphne gnidium*.

Ile de Ré and Anse d'Aiguillon

A vast area of sheltered coastal habitats, particularly rich in birds.

The Ile de Ré, now connected to the mainland by a main road, stretches westwards from the coast at La Rochelle, sheltering the bay to its north. Within this area, there is a further, more sheltered bay known as the Anse d'Aiguillon. Although part of this area lies within the Marais Poitevin Regional Natural Park (see p. 40), we have treated it separately as a coastal area, quite different from most of the park. Much of

Greylag geese *Anser anser*

the Anse d'Aiguillon is now a National Nature Reserve, in two separate parts, though the level of management and protection is still being sorted out. In winter, the bay is particularly good for birds, and is noted as one of the best sites in France, though it is not an easy area to watch. Each year 20 000 or more birds winter here.

Species of interest to be seen in the bay in winter include brent geese (up to 4000), avocets (8000), knot (10 000), grey plover (2000), with smaller numbers of many others such as dunlin, curlew, godwits, oystercatchers, and shelduck. Passage periods can bring large numbers of greylag geese, with spoonbills, spotted redshank, wood, green, and curlew sandpipers, whimbrel, little gulls (in surprisingly large numbers), terns, and numerous others. Tawny pipits and short-toed larks appear in small numbers, and at times hen harriers can be abundant. There are also some interesting breeding birds around the area, including Montagu's and marsh harriers, bluethroat, black-winged stilts, avocets, little bittern, purple heron, black kite, redshank, and fan-tailed warbler.

Good access points to the bay include the Pointe de l'Aiguillon, and north from here to where the D60 runs south from St. Michel; or at Port du Pave or Pointe St. Clément on the east side.

The Ile de Ré has a good mixture of coastal habitats and a mild winter climate, but is more built up than it appears on the map. There are grassy sandy areas in the interior of the island, sometimes dominated

Mass of biting stonecrop *Sedum acre* and other dune flowers

by wall-pepper, sometimes by other flowers. Towards the western end of the island, just south of the Portes de Ré, there is a National Nature Reserve, run by La Ligue pour la Protection des Oiseaux, called Lilleau des Niges. It encompasses a mixture of coastal habitats, especially saltmarsh, saltpans, foreshore, grassy areas including sea wall, and open water. It is particularly important for birds, with vast numbers passing the winter here or on adjacent intertidal land. In all, over 300 species of birds have been recorded on the reserve, of which 43 breed, 214 occur on passage, and 135 pass all or part of the winter here. Breeding birds include bluethroat, shelduck, avocet, black-winged stilt, and Cetti's warbler. Natterjacks breed in the warm shallow pools, calling loudly at night; there are green lizards and wall lizards, and an abundance of coastal flowers. Flowers of interest here or nearby include two uncommon water-crowfoots *Ranunculus trilobus* and *R. ololeucos*, dwarf eelgrass (as well as the more common species), and various saltmarsh and sand species, including masses of clovers. Elsewhere on the island, the endemic borage relative *Omphalodes littoralis* occurs quite commonly; it is a smallish plant, up to 15 cm high, with white or bluish flowers, confined to this part of coastal France.

The reserve is signposted (not very well) from the D101 near Portes en Ré, and there is limited access around the site. There is a summer-only information centre – the Maison des Marais – at St. Clément des Baleines.

On the mainland north of here, there is a no-hunting reserve on the dunes and other habitats south of L'Aiguillon-sur-mer on the Pointe d'Arcay, with a reasonable range of birds, including red-backed shrike and hoopoe, and some interesting flowers. As well as the usual dune species such as wild asparagus and joint-pine, there are also wintergreens, lizard orchids, and narrow-leaved helleborine in the woods. Red squirrels are frequent in the pine woods.

SITE
9

Marais d'Yves and Moëze-Oléron

Two interesting and varied coastal nature reserves, with a marvellous variety of birds and flowers.

Around Rochefort (where, as it happens, the main French bird protection organization, La Ligue pour la Protection des Oiseaux, is based), there is a fine variety of coastal habitats, including two state nature reserves. The Ile de Ré to the north (see p. 36) and the Ile d'Oléron curving up from the south protect a large area of sea which has developed extensive mudflats and saltmarshes. The

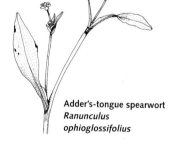

Adder's-tongue spearwort
Ranunculus ophioglossifolius

area as a whole supports 40 000 or more birds in winter, and is one of the most important sites in France.

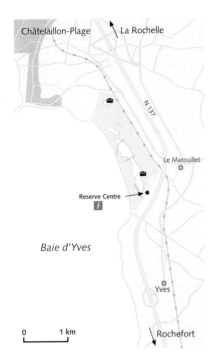

The Marais d'Yves lies on the mainland coast midway between Rochefort and La Rochelle, 2–3 km north of the small town of Yves. The reserve covers 185 ha, though it also draws its interest from the relatively unspoilt area around it, and includes saltmarsh, dunes, freshwater marshes, reedbeds, grassland, and other habitats. It is primarily known for its bird life and some 250 species have been recorded, of which 66 nest, 230 pass through on migration, and about 120 overwinter. Breeding birds include spoonbill, black-winged stilt, redshank, little bittern, marsh harrier, bluethroat, fan-tailed and Cetti's warblers. Passage and wintering birds, as they are less specific to an area, are considered below for the wider region. The reserve is also important for most other forms of wildlife. Eight reptiles have been recorded, including western whip snake, and green, wall, and sand lizards, and nine amphibians including natterjack, western spadefoot, tree frog, agile frog, and marbled newt. (The spadefoots are a little-known group of amphibians, rather intermediate between frogs and toads, differing from toads in having a vertical pupil and the eponymous spade-like structure on the hind feet. Western spadefoot is primarily Iberian, reaching northwards up the French coast.) There are also 18 mammals recorded, and 4 fish including eels. There is a good range of dragonflies recorded for such a small site, with 23 species in all, including the rare damselfly *Lestes macrostigma*. This is one of the emerald damselflies, distinguishable by the very large pterostigmas (a patch of colour on the front edge of the wings); it lives mainly in southern and eastern Europe, but has an outpost here. Other species include hairy hawker, emperor and lesser emperor, and a variety of darters. There are also 32 species of butterflies, mainly common ones such as grayling, wall brown, and silver-studded blue, but including large copper, well away from its more normal central European locations.

The reserve is also rich botanically, with over 450 species recorded, including a number of rarities amongst the more typical coastal species. Nationally rare species include the little endemic borage

Bluethroat *Luscinia svecica* (Peter Wilson)

Western spadefoot *Pelobates cultripes*

relative *Omphalodes littoralis* (see p. 38), the rare buttercup *Ranunculus ophioglossifolius*, dune willow (a subspecies of creeping willow), and the fragrant form of bug orchid, now defined separately as *Orchis fragrans*. Regionally rare species include the form of loose-flowered orchid now known as *Orchis palustris*, a form of butterfly iris *Iris spuria* subspecies *maritima*, a subspecies of yellow-wort, and the rush *Juncus striatus*. Altogether it is an excellent site. The main access is from a parking area on the N137 (the Aire du Marouillet), where there is an information centre which is normally open at weekends and during holidays.

The Moëze-Oléron reserve comprises a broad strip across the bay between Moëze on the mainland and Oléron, covering 6500 ha of largely intertidal land. It differs relatively little from the rest of the bay (except in reduced hunting pressure), so it is easiest to describe the area as a whole. The bay is especially important for wintering and passage birds, with about 250 species recorded and peak numbers of around 40 000 birds. Particularly significant species include brent geese (up to 7000 birds), avocets (up to 2000), grey plover (up to about 2000), knot (up to 13 000), dunlin (up to 36 000), and smaller numbers of curlew, redshank, oystercatcher, wigeon, and many other waders and wildfowl. Birds of prey include marsh and Montagu's harriers, black kite, short-eared owls, and others.

Access is not especially easy, though a road south from St. Froult reaches the reserve, and there is an information centre here. On the island, there are good roads along the side of the bay.

A vast expanse of marshland and low-lying country, seamed with ditches and canals and rich in wildlife of all types.

Marais Poitevin Regional Natural Park (strictly speaking, it is an inter-Regional Natural Park, as it spans several regions) covers 142 000 ha of low-lying marshy ground between Niort and the Atlantic. It is by no means all made up of good semi-natural habitat, and some parts are quite intensively farmed, but large areas of interest remain and the ditches, canals, and rivers that cross the park act as corridors and oases for wildlife. It has many similarities with the Somerset Levels in Britain, in formation, structure, and wildlife. The coastal sections have been covered on pp. 36–38, and this account deals largely with the inland areas, especially the main marshland.

The best habitats in the area are those which are wettest, especially any unimproved damp marshy areas, wet woodland, and the canals and ditches themselves.

An old ditch lined with pollards in the Marais Poitevin

Anywhere drier tends to be subject to more intensive agriculture. The waterways remain relatively unpolluted and free from eutrophication (excessively nutrient-rich water, often caused by run-off from land), since there are few large boats and no large areas of intensive arable agriculture. Thus they are rich in aquatic life and all that goes with it. Dragonflies, for example, are abundant, with about 40 species recorded, including Norfolk, hairy, and southern hawkers, orange-spotted emerald, brilliant emerald, banded demoiselles by the thousand, and the pretty orange damselfly *Platycnemis acutipennis*. Other insects, such as musk beetles, longhorn beetles, water beetles, soldier flies, and a reasonable range of butterflies are abundant. Amphibians are common in and around the waterways, and these include pond terrapins, edible and common

Cut-grass
Leersia oryzoides

frogs, common toads, and several species of newt, and grass snakes can often be seen swimming out in the water. There are several mammals particularly associated with the waterways, including muskrat, water voles, otters, and several species of bats which particularly feed over the water.

The same areas also tend to be best for birds. Breeding birds include bluethroat, purple and grey herons, little egrets, kingfishers, a few white storks, black kite, marsh harrier, extremely few pairs of corncrake, yellow wagtails, whinchat, and many more common species. Waterside and marsh plants are both beautiful and abundant – purple and yellow loosestrifes, yellow iris, white and yellow water-lilies, fleabane, mints, water-crowfoots, and many others. Nowadays, one of the most frequent and conspicuous species is the introduced *Ludwigia uruguayensis*, an American species with large golden yellow flowers which has spread vigorously throughout the waterways. Though attractive, its long-term effect on the native flora and fauna is unlikely to be positive.

Rarer species include butterfly iris, adder's-tongue spearwort, loose-flowered, marsh, and green-winged orchids, yellow-vetch, hairy vetchling, strawberry clover, reversed clover, and many others. There is a nature reserve just east of St. Denis du Payré, covering 205 ha, which conserves and manages a fragment of old marshland. It is a fascinating place, well worth a visit, though it points up the difference between the good and bad habitats in the park. The reserve is made up of open water and marshland, with water levels varying according to the season. Botanically, it is rich, with about 270 species recorded, including many of those already mentioned for the area, plus the rare and striking starfruit (a nationally protected plant) and an annual loosestrife *Lythrum tribracteatum* confined to seasonally wet places in the

Butterfly iris *Iris spuria*

south. It is said to be the best site for butterfly iris in France. The 11 amphibian species include pool frog, and marbled and crested newts. More than 200 bird species have been recorded, of which 44 breed, including a small colony of black terns, together with black-winged stilts, marsh harriers, and redshank, in addition to most of those already mentioned. On the main D25, which passes the site, there is a reserve centre open daily in the summer, and on the first Sunday of each month for the rest of the year. There is limited public access to the reserve, and guided walks at times.

The remainder of the marais can be appreciated from the maze of roads or footpaths, or boats can be taken from various places such as St. Hilaire le Palud, Magné, La Garette, and Arcais. Outlying, detached parts of the park include some fine extensive forests such as the Forêt de Chizé south of Niort. There is an interesting no-hunting reserve on grazing meadow common land at Velluire, about 8 km south-west of Fontenay-le-Comte, with abundant birds at most times, including little bustard which gather in autumn before migrating.

SITE 11 Goulven Bay

An attractive stretch of coast, with two important bird areas and some species-rich protected dunes.

Goulven Bay is a large, north-facing bay on the west Breton coast, with two distinct 'arms' – the western Gréve de Goulven, and the eastern Baie de Kernic – with some notable protected dunes on the coast between them at Keremma. It lies about 30 km north-east of Brest, with good road access around the site between Plouescat and Brignogan.

About 2000 ha of the bay are considered important for birds, and most of this is protected as a no-hunting area. It is particularly valuable at passage periods and through the winter. The site regularly supports 20 000 or more birds at a time in spring and autumn, with more variable numbers in winter. Typical migration-period figures include up to 2000 each of sanderling, turnstone, bar-tailed godwit, redshank, dunlin, lapwing, and ringed plover, often with large numbers of waterfowl and a wide variety of passerines. The northernmost point of the western arm, Beg-ar-scaf head, is particularly good for terrestrial migrants, if conditions are right. This is also a good point for sea-watching, especially in autumn, when there are likely to be gannets, shearwaters, terns, gulls, and skuas passing by.

In winter, regular visitors include many waders such as turnstone, oystercatcher, purple sandpiper, snipe and jack snipe, ringed and Kentish plovers, golden and grey plovers, goldeneye, wigeon, shelduck, and many more.

The Keremma Reserve, run by the Conservatoire du Littoral, is a site of almost 200 ha consisting mainly of sand dunes. There is a good flora, which includes sea-holly, sea bindweed, the prostrate form of lady's bedstraw (which progressively replaces sand bedstraw northwards through Brittany), common restharrow, wild asparagus, sea stock, several stork's-bills and centauries, and a variety of others. Other species of interest here include green lizard, blue-headed wagtail, and wheatear.

About 20 km to the west, there is another important stretch of protected dunes at the Dunes de Sainte Marguerite, north-west of Lannilis. Two sites totalling 70 ha are managed as reserves here, at Tevenn Santez Vac'harid and Pointe du Vill near Landéda.

SITE 12 Cap Sizun and Trunvel Lake

An important seabird colony on cliffs, and an unspoilt expanse of coastal lakes, sand, and marshes.

Cap Sizun is a rocky headland with heathland, bounded by cliffs with off-shore stacks. It is one of the best-known bird-watching sites in Brittany, and part of it has been a reserve since 1959, run by the Société pour l'Etude et la Protection de la Nature en Bretagne. The cliffs are home to breeding colonies of shag, fulmar, kittiwake, guillemot, and great black-backed gulls, with smaller numbers of ravens and red-billed choughs. The choughs have been the subject of research and experiments to find which type of sheep-grazing best suits their feeding requirements. Shelduck breed here and there in suitable holes. The heathland is broadly similar to other

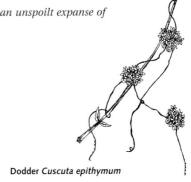

Dodder *Cuscuta epithymum*

Breton coastal heathlands, with several species of heather, western gorse, dodder, and other plants, and breeding Dartford warblers and stonechats. About 600 ha are considered to be an important area for birds. Guided tours take place throughout the spring and summer. Tel: 02 98701353.

Southwards, in the centre of the Audierne Bay, there is an unspoilt group of habitats around the lakes of Trunvel and Kergalan. The site consists of three small valleys whose exits to the sea have become blocked by a sandbar, producing a complex of three lakes, extensive sand dunes and beach, and associated wetland and coastal habitats. It is considered to be internationally important for its birds: breeding birds include bittern and little bittern, marsh harriers, sedge, reed, and Cetti's warblers, bearded tits, purple heron and reed buntings, amongst others. At pas-sage times, large numbers of waders, wild-fowl and passerines pass through, and in winter there are large numbers of water-fowl, waders, and a few birds of prey.

The Société pour l'Etude et la Protection de la Nature en Bretagne has a small reserve here, and the Conservatoire du Littoral has a series of sites totalling about 550 ha. The sand dunes are good for flowers, and relatively undisturbed, because access into the heart of the site is rather difficult.

The best access into the area is via the minor roads to the coast from Tréogat and Plavan, or on the D156 from Tréguennec to the coastal car park.

Channel coast

Channel coast

Introduction

This region covers the northern coast of France, stretching from Baie du Mont-St.-Michel in the west to the Belgian border in the east, including the Cherbourg Peninsula, and extending inland beyond Amiens, Rouen, and Caen. It includes most of Normandy and Nord Pas de Calais, with the more coastal parts of Picardie. Whilst this is perhaps not the most dramatic part of France, with no high hills or spectacular landscapes, it is generally pleasantly unspoilt, with many areas of low-intensity agriculture where small farms have old orchards and unimproved pastures. There are large forests in the region, usually run by the state, and many smaller woods, and large expanses of marshland along the coast where regular flooding has prevented intensive agricultural improvements. As a generalization, with exceptions, the rocks tend to be more acid in the west, grading towards chalk and limestone in the eastern part, and there is a gradual trend of decreasing rainfall eastwards. These two factors, and other reasons (such as the proximity of large cities) have influenced the intensity of agriculture, and there is noticeably more in the way of large arable fields without hedges in the east of region; some parts, such as Picardie, are extremely poor for wildlife and best passed through as quickly as possible!

The Cherbourg Peninsula is a surprising and interesting region, full of secret locations and interesting places. The western coast is distinctly Atlantic in character, exposed to the west winds, and has some fine dune areas and rocky coasts, with a rich variety of seashore life. Not surprisingly, it shares many species with the Channel Islands, which are just off-shore, and also has many in common with south-west England. It is a good area in which to see species that are very rare or absent from the UK, too, such as summer lady's-tresses, scarce emerald damselfly, tree frog, marbled newt, and woodlarks. The east coast has a very different character, with more sheltered sandy and muddy bays sheltering large saltmarshes, and there are some excellent sites here for wintering and migrating birds. Inland in the peninsula, there are large tracts of grazing marshes which flood virtually every winter and remain largely unspoilt and unchanged. The Marais du Cotentin et du Bessin Regional Natural Park (which is not covered in detail here) includes most of the best marshes, and is worth exploring especially on foot or by bicycle, though there are few key sites within it except the ones described.

Southwards from the peninsula, towards Fler and Argentan, is true Normandy countryside, almost always interesting but with few specific sites to visit. Much of the underlying rock is hard limestone, which supports a countryside that is pleasantly species-rich yet not too exploited. Any of the woodlands will have something of interest, and there are often small-scale habitats such as ponds, roadsides, and damp fields which collectively support an abundance of species.

Eastwards from here, the landscape and agriculture is dominated by the great chalk massif which encircles the Paris basin. Where there are valleys, such as along the course of the Seine and its tributaries, one often sees steep slopes which have retained some of their semi-natural vegetation such as chalk downlands or woodland, but elsewhere, and in particular further east and on the lower-lying sections, arable agriculture now domi-

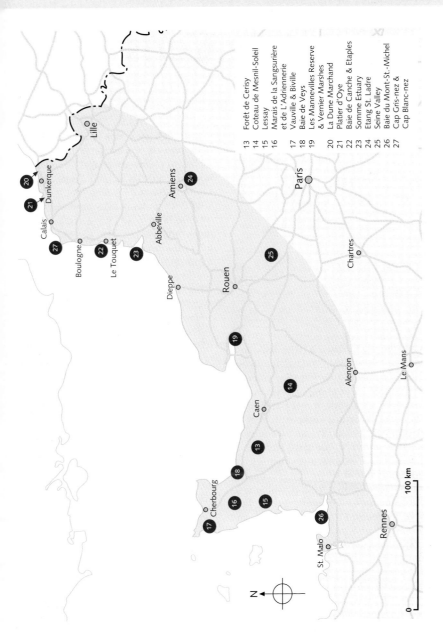

13 Forêt de Cerisy
14 Coteau de Mesnil-Soleil
15 Lessay
16 Marais de la Sangsurière et de L'Adriennerie
17 Vauville & Biville
18 Baie de Veys
19 Les Mannevilles Reserve & Vernier Marshes
20 La Dune Marchand
21 Platier d'Oye
22 Baie de Canche & Etaples
23 Somme Estuary
24 Etang St. Ladre
25 Seine Valley
26 Baie du Mont-St.-Michel
27 Cap Gris-nez & Cap Blanc-nez

100 km

nates. Some of the best habitats tend to be along the coast, where there are base-rich fens, high chalk cliffs, dunes and saltmarshes in more sheltered areas. The estuaries, especially those of the Somme and the Canche, provide superb areas of habitat for wintering and passage birds; they lie on a main migration route and usually remain frost free throughout the winter. Inland, there is relatively less to see, but we have selected some of the best remaining areas where protection or chance have allowed good locations to survive.

13 Forêt de Cerisy

SITE

An extensive forest, run partly as a nature reserve and noted for its insect life.

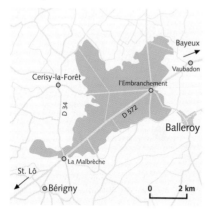

The Forêt de Cerisy is a large deciduous forest covering over 2000 ha, dominated mainly by beech, with smaller amounts of oak, and alder along the valleys. It is managed as a state forest but has the status of a nature reserve. It was so designated primarily on account of *Chrysocarabus auronitens* subspecies *cupreonitens*, an endemic subspecies of ground beetle with strikingly reflective wing-cases, known from nowhere else. Other beetles of interest here include stag beetles and lesser stag beetles, and longhorns such as *Rhagium bifasciatum* and *Strangalia maculata*. It is also notable for woodland butterflies, including lesser purple emperor, wood white, orange tip, brimstone, white-letter and purple hairstreaks, large tortoiseshell, and Camberwell beauty. Moths of interest include the impressive Clifden nonpareil, the largest of the underwings, with a striking blue and black underwing, and lobster moth with its amazing caterpillars, looking rather like tiny terrestrial lobsters.

It is not a great area botanically, but it does possess a reasonable flora which includes yellow archangel, moschatel, lungwort, angular Solomon's seal, orpine, sanicle, bastard balm, and violets. Woodland birds breeding or resident here include tawny and long-eared owls and black woodpecker, plus the more common woodpeckers, buzzard, redstart, and many more. Also living here are red and roe deer, a few red squirrels, badgers, and other mammals, the impressive fire salamander skulking in the humid leaf litter, and agile frog in the ponds.

The main D572 Bayeux to St. Lô road passes through the wood, and the smaller D13 and D10 give access deeper into it. There are numerous paths and tracks within the wood, with open access on foot. Wider rides and clearings are generally the best places.

The botanic garden (Jardin des Plantes) in nearby Caen is worth a visit, with a good range of well-labelled flowers, including some special local species. It is located at 5 Place Blot, Caen, and is open every day, without charge.

Clifden nonpareil *Catocala fraxini*

SITE 14 Coteau de Mesnil-Soleil

Limestone grassland and woodland with a rich flora and abundant butterflies.

Although this reserve only covers 25 ha, it provides an oasis of nature – flowers and butterflies in particular – in an otherwise unexceptional area. It consists mainly of warm, south-facing limestone grassland and scrub, with mixed deciduous woodland (common oak, beech, and birch) mainly on the plateau, where there are areas of more acidic clay soil. The flora and fauna is a fine mixture of the anticipated north European species together with a few more typical southern ones, reflecting the particular warmth of this corner of Calvados.

Chiltern gentian
Gentianella germanica

Botanically it is very rich, with about 350 species, including grassland plants such as autumn and Chiltern gentian, dwarf sedge, horseshoe vetch and the very similar *Coronilla minima* (see p. 149), which both act as important butterfly and moth food-plants, mountain germander with its ring of yellow flowers, and the spurge *Euphorbia seguierana*, which is more characteristic of southern grasslands. Both common and large-flowered

selfheal occur, and in early spring there are masses of cowslips and pasqueflowers. It is also a fine spot for orchids, including lady, bee, fly, greater butterfly, early spider, pyramidal, and dark-red helleborine in more open areas, and white and narrow-leaved helleborine, bird's-nest orchid, and even creeping ladies tresses in the wooded parts. Not surprisingly, it is also good for butterflies, with grassland species such as Adonis and chalk-hill blues, Duke of Burgundy, common and scarce swallowtails, silver-spotted skipper, marbled white, dark green fritillaries, and many others. As well as the more common burnet moths, the distinctive *Zygaena fausta* is also found here, feeding on *Coronilla* and close to the northern edge of its range. It has more red on the forewings than five-spot or six-spot, and a fine edging of white around the spots. There are also stag beetles around the woods, and a general abundance of insect life, thanks to the combination of flowery grassland, scrub, and old woodland.

A good range of birds breed on the reserve including nightingales and melodious warbler, close to the northern edge of its range.

Access is from the D511 Falaise to St. Pierre-sur-Dives road, with parking on the minor road to Falaise airport, following the GR path southwards from there.

Mountain germander *Teucrium montanum*

15 Lessay

Heathland, woodland, and bogs, with many specialized species and rarities.

Around the little abbey town of Lessay, and especially south-east of it, there is a large expanse of heathland, pine woodland, and bogs. Although the heathland once extended over a large area, it is almost entirely unprotected and has gradually been cultivated, drained, developed, or left to proceed to woodland, so that the interesting sections are now quite discontinuous. There are still some remaining good locations, and even the roadsides and fragments of heath hold much of interest. There is one small reserve, the Tourbière de Mathon, covering 16 ha of bog and associated habitats, but the remainder is unprotected and unmanaged.

It is very rich botanically, with a good mixture of heath and bog species, particularly all three sundews – great, round-leaved, and oblong-leaved – heath lobelia (sometimes in abundance), summer lady's-tresses (which is surprisingly common here, despite its extinction in Britain and rarity elsewhere), the little marsh clubmoss, the attractive yellow viper's grass, slender centaury, bog pimpernel, marsh gentian, bog asphodel, bogbean, coral-necklace, pale butterwort, blunt-flowered rush, saw sedge, marsh cinquefoil, and others. Altogether about 40 lichens – with a particularly good range of the ground-living *Cladonia* species – and 80 bryophytes have been recorded, mainly on the reserve, though there must be many more in the whole area.

Nightjars, tree pipits, stonechats, Dartford warblers, and another 30 or so species breed here, and there are adders, common lizards, common frogs, and natterjacks. It is also an interesting area for invertebrates: at least 100 species of spider occur, including the striking wasp spider, together with sand-wasps, rove

Golden-ringed dragonfly *Cordulegaster boltonii*

Heath with pines, south of Lessay

beetles, tiger beetles, velvet ants, bee-killer, and many more. Dragonflies have declined as the area has dried out, but there are still keeled skimmers, scarce emerald damselfly and golden-ringed dragonfly, amongst others.

The Tourbière de Mathon lies about 3 km east of Lessay, just north of the railway, though access is restricted to paths.

The remaining area lies east of the main D2 south of Lessay, and is easily seen, for example, from the minor road to Heugueville.

Just west of Lessay, towards the coast, there are some good marshy fields with loose-flowered orchids, and the Ay Estuary provides shelter for many birds in winter.

SITE 16 Marais de la Sangsurière et de L'Adriennerie

Low-lying grazing marshes, bog, heath, and woodland, with a rich flora and fauna.

Marais de la Sangsurière et de L'Adriennerie National Nature Reserve covers about 400 ha of low-lying drained marshland with ditches, grazed by cattle and often flooded in autumn and winter, together with extensive areas of wet heath and woodland on peat. It has a fascinating mixture of wetland species, including some rarities. Botanically, it has a rather

Tawny sedge
Carex hostiana

Ditch on Sangsunère grazing marshes

have been agriculturally improved and are rather dull, most of the ditches remain of interest; there are flowers such as frogbit, arrowheads, flowering-rush, and a number of pondweeds, and a rich invertebrate fauna that includes many molluscs and water beetles. Medicinal leeches still occur, and are the origin of the name Sangsurière (*sangsue* is French for leech). Interesting dragonflies can also be found, including southern damselfly and hairy hawker, and the list of butter-flies includes marsh fritillary, which is generally rare in France. There are abun-dant frogs in the ditches, and grass snakes can often be seen swimming in search of tadpoles in summer.

similar mixture to that of Lessay (see p. 50) in the wet heath and bog areas, including all three sundew species, summer lady's-tresses, bog asphodel, pale butterwort, lesser bladderwort, devil's-bit scabious, white-beaked sedge, and many others. In the rougher grazing marshes, there are other flowers such as purple loosestrife, water dropworts, marsh fern, brown galingale, and numer-ous sedges including *Carex hostiana* and *C. lasiocarpa*. Although some of the fields

About 55 species of bird breed here, mainly common ones, but including a few marsh harriers, some curlews, lap-wings, yellow wagtails, and nightjars, amongst others.

Access is restricted to footpaths or with organized groups. The main D900 passes through the reserve (with signs on the roadside indicating this), and there is parking and access just west of it, on the south side of the reserve at La Pitoterie.

(see p. 50)

17 Vauville and Biville

SITE

Extensive mixed coastal habitats with species-rich dunes, marshes, and lagoons.

On the north-west coast of the Cherbourg (Cotentin) Peninsula, there is an exten-sive area of unspoilt coastal habitats lying roughly between the villages of Biville and Vauville. Part of the site is a National Nature Reserve, the Mare de Vauville, which comprises 45 ha of lakes, dunes, dune slacks, reedbeds, and scrub, but the coast around the reserve is also of general interest southwards into the lightly used military firing range.

It is particularly rich botanically, with most of the dune species that one might expect in this region. These include mass-es of burnet rose, Jersey thrift, spiked speedwell (which can colour parts of the dunes blue at times), lady's bedstraw (including subspecies *littorale*), moon-wort, hare's tail grass, wild chamomile, the prostrate form of wild asparagus, Portland and sea spurges, sea bindweed, sea kale, sea-holly (covered in burnet moths and other insects), several stork's-bills, and many more. In wetter areas, such as the dune slacks and on the margins of the lakes, there are masses of the pink spikes of water germander, greater spearwort, dune willow (a variant of creeping willow, sometimes described as *Salix repens* variety *argentea*), a dozen species of sedges, mudwort, large clumps of sharp rush (and the leaves *are* extremely sharp), knotted pearlwort, bladderwort, galingale, purple loosestrife, and many others. In the lakes, there are several species of pondweeds *Potamogeton* and tassel-weeds *Ruppia*, with water-crowfoots and the hornwort *Ceratophyllum submersum.* There is also a long list of fungi recorded from the reserve, including *Lepiota littoralis, Tricholoma singularis*, and the distinctive bolete *Suillus bellini*, with its white stalk dotted with brown granules.

However, it is by no means only good botanically. Tree frogs are quite common here, 'chacking' loudly from the reeds, and natterjacks breed in the shallower lagoons or temporary pools. Midwife toads breed here in suitable places –you occasionally come across them under a

Cteniopus sulphureus

log or similar structure – and marbled newts occur at the very northern limit of their European range. These are impressive creatures, unlikely to be confused with any other amphibian in the area thanks to their relatively large size (up to 15 cm long, including the tail), and bright green colour marbled with black; unlike the bright orange great-crested newt, they are dull underneath. Although they breed in the lakes, marbled newts may be found well away from them for the rest of the year. Great-crested and palmate newts also occur here. In fact, all the amphibian species recorded for Basses Normandie are known from the reserve. There are also adders, grass snakes, and common lizards to be seen.

It is also a good site for insect life, including some specialized coastal species. Almost 250 species of beetle have been recorded, including uncommon ones such as the coastal tiger beetles *Cicindela maritima* and *C. germanica*, bloody-nosed beetles which feed on lady's and hedge bedstraws, and the straw-coloured *Cteniopus sulphureus*, which can be seen in thousands on the dunes, on flowers in summer. There are masses of grasshoppers and crickets, including great green bush-cricket, grey and Roesel's bush-crickets, long-winged and short-winged cone-heads, mottled grasshopper, and the blue-flashing grasshopper *Oedipoda caerulescens*. Butterflies such as grayling, wall, and gatekeeper are common, and there are hundreds of burnet and cinnabar moths, amongst others.

Although this is not a major bird site, there are 36 breeding species, including reed, sedge, and Cetti's warblers, nightingales, reed-bunting, and Kentish plover. There is a no-hunting area around the reserve so it acts as a safe haven through the shooting season in otherwise shot-over countryside.

Access is easy. The D237 from Beaumont through Vauville to Biville passes around the edge of the site, and tracks lead down into it. There is an information board at a parking area near the beach, just south of Vauville.

There are good heaths nearby on the slopes and plateau to the east, with Dartford warblers and other heathland species.

SITE 18 Baie de Veys

A vast expanse of mudflats and other coastal habitats, grading into saltmarsh and grazing marshes, with a very rich bird fauna.

Baie des Veys lies at the south-east corner of the Cherbourg Peninsula, where the land turns sharply eastwards to run along the Normandy coast, known here as the Côte de Nacre. Part of the bay is protected within the Domaine de Beauguillot National Nature Reserve, which covers 650 ha of coastal habitats and mudflats on the western shoulder of the bay, around the Banc du Grand Vey. The whole area lies within the Marais du Cotentin et du Bessin (i.e. Cotentin and Bessin Marshes) Regional Natural Park, which covers a large area of inland grazing marshes and intervening countryside across the southern part of the peninsula.

This is primarily a bird site, designated as both a Ramsar Site (an internationally important wetland) and a Special Protection Area for its bird life (see p. 20), with something to see at all times of year. Breeding birds include shelduck, Montagu's harrier (in small numbers), marsh harriers, Kentish plover, terns, corncrakes in reasonable numbers, a few white storks, lapwings, snipe, curlew, black-tailed godwit, teal, garganey, yellow wagtails, marsh warblers, and many more in the area as a whole. At passage periods there can be very large numbers of birds, especially waders, wildfowl, terns and gulls, including thousands of common, black, and Sandwich terns, ringed plover, shoveler, pintail, brent geese, and spoonbill, and smaller numbers of hundreds of other species. In winter, the site regularly holds more than 20 000 waterbirds such as brent geese, great-crested grebes, cormorants, pintail, velvet scoter, oystercatcher, and dunlin in huge numbers, well over 10 000 curlew, golden plover, and many more.

However, the site is also worth a visit for other reasons. For example, the Beauguillot reserve has records for over 300 species of flowers, almost 400 beetles, 22 species of dragonfly and damselflies, 9 amphibians, and 32 mammals! Some specialities include marsh-orchid, loose-flowered orchid, and marsh helleborines in wet areas, with yellow bartsia, adder's tongue fern, purple broomrape, sea-holly, lesser water-plantain, and other interesting flowers. There are good numbers of bats including Daubenton's, grey long-eared, and Nathusius' pipistrelle. Common seals can often be seen out on the mudflats.

The whole area is of interest, especially the low-lying grazing marshes and other wet habitats to the west of Carentan, which regularly flood in winter. The HQ for the Regional Natural Park is at Rond-Point de la Liberté, 50008 St. Lô. The Beauguillot reserve centre is at Fondation de Beauguillot, 50480 Ste. Mairie-du-Mont. Access to the reserve is along the D329, off which there is parking and a hide.

SITE
19 Les Mannevilles Reserve and Vernier Marshes

Lovely, low-lying coastal marshes near the mouth of the Seine with a rich and varied flora and fauna.

Les Mannevilles Reserve covers about 100 ha of grazing marshes, wet woodland, bog, and reedbed, part of a much larger area known as the Marais Vernier (Vernier Marsh). Both of these areas lie within the 42 000 ha Brotonne Regional Natural Park, which extends roughly from here up the Seine as far east as Duclair. There are extensive stretches of low-lying grazing marshes along the lower reaches of the Seine on both sides, though most have been at least partly drained and agriculturally improved.

Les Mannevilles Reserve provides an excellent introduction to the area, and most of the local species occur here. In boggy places, there are sundews, pale butterwort, lesser bladderwort (all of these are insectivorous plants), white-beaked sedge, lesser water-plantain, marsh arrow-grass, and a variety of sedges and *Sphagnum* species, amongst others. In damp woodland or grassland one may see royal ferns, marsh fern, marsh spurge, loose-flowered orchids, and southern marsh-orchids, as well as more common species which lend colour and variety, such as purple and yellow loosestrifes, and yellow iris. In ditches and pools, there is an abundance of frog-bit, with arrowheads, water plantain, and the rare submerged aquatic *Najas marina*, amongst others. In total, there are about 260 species of higher plants within the reserve.

It is a superb area for dragonflies and other insects. For example, there are downy emeralds, hairy hawker, Norfolk hawker, and variable damselflies; bush-crickets such as bog, great green, and Roesel's, and the impressive moth *Mamestra splendens*. The strikingly large green musk beetle occurs here, passing its larval stages in poplars or willows. Not surprisingly, amphibians are abundant, with agile and common frogs, tree frogs, common toads, natterjacks, and great-crested newts, amongst others.

Holly-leaved naiad *Najas marina*

Great green bush-cricket *Tettigonia viridissima*

It is not an important bird site, but there is a good range of marshland and wetland species, including breeding short-eared owl, corncrake, curlew, snipe, redshank, shelduck, a selection of marsh-land warblers, and even the occasional white stork.

Access to the reserve is restricted. There is a footpath in from the D103 just to the west, or more detailed visits can be arranged through CEDENA, Centre de la Découverte de la Nature, Place de l'Eglise, 27680 Sainte-Opportune-la-Mare. The Regional Natural Park HQ is at Maison du Parc, 2 Rond-Point Marbec, 76580 Le Trait.

SITE 20 La Dune Marchand

A species-rich area of mobile and stable dunes with dune slacks.

La Dune Marchand Nature Reserve protects an area of about 100 ha of fine sand dunes and associated habitats in an area where they were once widespread but are now largely lost to industrial, residential, and holiday developments. It provides an essential oasis of natural countryside here, close to the Belgian border. The history of the dunes is well known here, and their progress can be traced back for over a thousand years.

Botanically, the site is particularly important, with about 350 species of higher plant, many of them rare, pro-tected, or both. The dominant plants on the reserve are, typically, marram grass,

Seaside centaury *Centaurium littorale*

lyme grass, sea buckthorn and privet. On the drier parts of the dunes, the flora includes Curtis's wild pansy, common rock-rose, masses of burnet rose, sea bindweed, sea spurge, biting stonecrop, the little early forget-me-not *Myosotis ramosissima* (considered to be a glacial relict species here), yellow-wort, several centauries including *Centaurium littorale*, common spotted orchid, Jersey cudweed, sheep's bit, umbellate chickweed, the uncommon eyebright *Euphrasia tetraquetra* and purple broomrape, to name a few. In the extensive dune slacks and other wet areas, there are other flowers of interest, such as round-leaved wintergreen, knotted pearlwort, grass-of-Parnassus, early marsh-orchid, marsh helleborine, creeping willow, and sedges such as *Carex trinervis* and *C. serotina*. Altogether, it is an exceptionally rich site, containing most of the possible dune species for this area in a relatively small location.

Round-leaved wintergreen *Pyrola rotundifolia*

Other features of interest include a good colony of sand-lizards, natterjacks which breed in the sun-warmed, temporary pools among the dunes, and great-crested newts. In addition to the common and expected birds such as common whitethroats and skylarks, there are also breeding icterine warblers (a distinctly yellowish warbler, which is right at the western edge of its breeding range here), crested lark, and stonechats.

There is access and parking at both ends of the site, such as off the D947 road to Bray-Dunes, with open access on foot on the made-up paths.

Platier d'Oye

Coastal wetlands, open water, and dunes that provide an important migration stopover for birds.

Platier d'Oye Nature Reserve lies on the north coast of France, roughly midway between Calais and Dunkerque. It covers almost 400 ha, of which over half is publicly owned foreshore, and the remainder is made up of dunes, scrub, and a series of pools that vary from freshwater to brackish. This was once – not so long ago – a coast of wide open wild spaces, but developments are steadily encroaching and reserves such as this are assuming an increasingly important role.

Platier d'Oye is best known as a bird site. The pools and scrub are magnets for migrating and wintering birds, and altogether well over 300 species have been

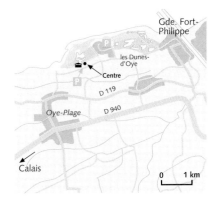

Gde. Fort-
Philippe

les Dunes-
d'Oye

Centre

D 119

P

Oye-Plage   D 940

Calais

0   1 km

Kentish plover, black-winged stilts, oystercatcher, black-necked grebe, short-eared owls, shoveler, snipe, and many smaller birds in the scrub, notably whitethroats and Cetti's warblers.

It is also an interesting site for other reasons. Natterjacks and great-crested newts breeding in the pools, with another four or five species of amphibians, and sand-lizards in drier areas. The dunes themselves, rising to over 13 m and quite impressive, are made up of sand that contains large amounts of calcareous material derived from marine and terrestrial molluscs. This has allowed a good flora to develop, and also suits present-day molluscs such as white-lipped snails, *Helix barbara*, and the distinctive, mainly southern species *Theba pisana*, which tends to gather in large quantities on plant stems in dry periods. There are well over 200 species of flowering plants on the dunes, including Curtis's wild pansy, sea-holly, sea bindweed, lady's bedstraw, pyramidal and spotted orchids, lyme grass, purple broomrape, sea rocket, sea spurge, cowslips, and many more in the drier parts, and seaside centaury, knotted pearlwort, round-leaved wintergreen, creeping willow, common scurvy grass, and others where it is a little damper. Although not as rich as La Dune

recorded here. Typical passage birds include common, Arctic, Sandwich, and little terns, ruff, greenshank, redshank, spotted redshank, sandpipers such as common and wood, Temminck's stint, spoonbills, ringed plover, dunlin, brent geese, wigeon, teal, and a host of passerines such as swallows, martins, wagtails, and warblers. In winter, there can be large numbers of ducks, geese, cormorants, some waders, and smaller birds such as snow bunting, shore lark, and a few Lapland buntings. There are also about 65 species breeding here, which gives the site year-round interest for the bird-watcher. Breeding birds include avocets,

Little grebe *Tachybaptus ruficollis* (Mike Lane)

Marchand Reserve, it is certainly worth a look. There are a fair number of insects, though it is not strikingly rich, and has not been fully studied. Butterflies including grayling, hedge brown, ringlet, and common blue are there in abundance if not great variety, and there are five-spot and six-spot burnet moths, often flying with cinnabars. A little, gall-forming fly *Chlorops pumilionis* attacks the sand couch grass here and causes distorted growth.

Access to the site is by minor roads, northwards to the coast from Oye-Plage, then eastwards towards Gde. Fort-Phillipe, from where there are parking areas and paths.

Travel 30 km south and you will come to another reserve of special interest for birds at the Etang de Romelaere, about 4 km north-east of St. Omer. It is a rather picturesque area of lakes – which are old peat diggings – with marshes, reedbeds, wet meadows, and woods, mixed with agricultural land. It is a good location for breeding marshland birds, including marsh harri-

ers, reed, great reed, grasshopper, Savi's, and Cetti's warblers, bluethroats, grey herons, great-crested and little grebes, and others. It is also good in winter for ducks and visiting birds of prey such as hen harriers, and masses of waders, passerines, and other birds at passage periods.

The reserve is signposted from the centre of Clairmarais. There is a seasonal information centre, walks, and hides.

Cetti's warbler *Cettia cetti*

22 Baie de Canche and Etaples

A superb collection of coastal habitats around Etaples, including dunes, fens, saltmarshes, and mudflats, with a rich flora and fauna.

Etaples lies at the mouth of the river Canche. On the north side of the estuary there is a large and varied nature reserve, the Baie de Canche, which covers over 500 ha of varied coastal habitats such as dunes, marshes, fen, woodland, open water, saltmarsh, and foreshore, and southwards from here there is a fine series of habitats, largely unprotected.

The site has a rich flora, with about 500 species of flowering plants (including 13 species of orchids and 16 species of sedges), and a good range of fungi,

Fen orchid *Liparis loeselii*

Channel coast

Moonwort *Botrychium lunaria*

such as common and red darters, emperor dragonfly, black-tailed skimmer, and broad-bodied chaser, though there are also hairy hawkers and the inconspicuous overwintering damselfly *Sympecma fusca*. The wolf spider *Pardosa monticola* is common in sandier areas.

The whole Canche Estuary, of which the reserve is just a small part, is notable for birds. There is a no-hunting reserve and a Special Protection Area covering over 4000 ha, which gives migrating and wintering birds a good chance. The site regularly holds over 20 000 birds in winter, and up to 50 000 at times, including very large numbers of herring, lesser black-backed and great black-backed gulls, shelduck, brent geese, curlew, and others, and a number of birds of prey such as merlin, hen harrier, rough-legged buzzard, and the occasional white-tailed sea eagle. At passage periods, there can be large numbers of gulls, terns, waders, ducks, and geese, amongst others. At least 76 species of birds breed in the reserve and surrounding area; there are masses of whitethroats and lesser whitethroats, up

bryophytes, and lichens. Some plants of special interest in the damper areas, such as the dune slacks, include the rare (and not very conspicuous) fen orchid, round-leaved wintergreen, greater spearwort, flowering-rush, the beautiful grass-of-Parnassus, water germander, knotted pearlwort, bog pimpernel, southern marsh-orchid, blunt-flowered rush and others – a typical assemblage of rich fen plants. In drier areas, there are Curtis's wild pansy, seaside centaury, lyme grass, Jersey cudweed, the little moonwort (a curious relative of ferns), sea-holly, and burnet rose, amongst others. It is an attractive and interesting mixture.

Besides the plants, there is much else to see. As with other coastal sites in the area, there are breeding natterjacks, with midwife toads in damp, sandy places, great-crested newts, and tree frogs in the reedbeds and other dense vegetation. Common lizards are frequent on the more stable dune areas. Over 20 species of dragonflies and damselflies have been recorded, mainly more common species

Wheatear (Northern) *Oenanthe oenanthe*
(Peter Wilson)

to 1000 pairs of nightingales, reasonable numbers of nightjars, woodlarks, redpoll, Kentish plovers, wheatears, linnets, and many others.

There is an information centre at Boulevard Bigot-Descelers, BP 102, 62630 Etaples, open every day in summer, weekdays in winter. Access to the reserve is directly off the D940 from Etaples towards Camiers, which passes through the reserve. There are footpaths around it.

To the north of the estuary, there are good dunes between Dannes and Hardelot-Plage, and the forest of Hardelot is worth a visit for flowers, birds, and butterflies. Mont St. Frieux dunes and woods are now a reserve, with forest birds such as black woodpecker, goshawk, and

crossbills in addition to the dune species. Southwards from the Canche Estuary, one can find some fine habitats; just east of Cucq, there is a rich fen with fen orchids and other species, with larger areas of similar habitat in the Marais de Balançon just east of Merlimont, where three species of bladderwort grow in close proximity. The dunes and associated habitats southwards from Merlimont-Plage towards Berck are very good in places, and have similar species to those described for Baie de Canche Reserve, and others. It should be emphasized, though, that these sites – despite their quality – are not well protected and development or drainage could take place at any time, unfortunately.

SITE
23 Somme Estuary

One of the most important sites in France for birds in winter and at migration times.

The estuary of the Somme, on the coast north-west of Abbeville, forms a narrow enclosed bay about 3 km across, stretching about 10 km inland. It is a major ornithological site, of international importance, recognized by its designation as a Ramsar Site and Special Protection Area for birds, covering about 17 000 ha. Within this broader area, there is a large National Nature Reserve – Baie de Somme – covering 3000 ha, plus an ornithological park and several no-hunting areas. It is twinned with Rye Bay in England (comprising Rye Harbour and Dungeness Reserves) and ideas are shared under what is called the Two Bays Initiative. The bay as a whole easily meets the 'important bird area' criterion of regularly supporting more than 20 000 birds both in winter and at passage periods. Huge numbers of birds may appear in winter, including shelduck, pintail, velvet scoter, oystercatcher, grey plover, knot, dunlin (over 20 000 of these alone), bar-tailed godwit, curlew, red- and black-throated divers, red-necked grebes, great white egret, bean geese, red-breasted merganser and goosander, short-eared owls, great grey shrike, and passerines such as snow and Lapland buntings. At passage periods, all manner of birds can pass through, with regular numbers of spoonbill, white stork, brent geese, waders such as spotted redshank and Temminck's stint, pintails, black terns and other more common terns, amongst others.

Although not a major breeding bird site, there is plenty of interest with at least a hundred species. There is a mixed heronry of grey herons and cattle and little egrets, shelduck, avocets, occasional black-winged stilts (this is at the northern edge of their breeding range), Kentish and ringed plovers, bluethroat, a few short-eared owls, nightjars, crested larks, and sand martins, amongst others.

The Parc Ornithologique du Marquenterre forms part of the nature reserve. There is a mosaic of semi-natural habitats here, with many wild birds and good numbers of captive birds, together with walkways, hides, a shop, and an information area. This section of the reserve requires payment for entry; it is open daily between March and November, and only at weekends in winter. There is also a bird museum on the south side of the bay, which has some open water and a hide, and birds of prey in captivity, just west of St. Valéry-sur-Somme, open between mid-February and mid-November.

The reserve and park are signposted from the main D940. Apart from the park, limited access into the rest of the reserve is provided by a coastal footpath from La Maye northwards. There is also good access to the bay on the south side at Le Hourdel.

The reserve has much of interest in addition to the birdlife. There are breeding natterjack and common toads, tree frogs and wall lizards, and 30+ species of mammals. There is a small colony of resident common seals (which are very rare in France), bats such as grey long-eared and Geoffroy's, and many more common species. It is also quite important botanically. There are areas of shingle (a rare habitat in France) with sea kale, yellow horned-poppy, viper's-bugloss, sea pea, and red hemp nettle; in saltmarshes, there is an abundance of common species such as sea aster, but also rarer species such as *Atriplex pedunculata*. On the dunes and dry, sandy places and their associated dune slacks, one can find some particularly showy flowers such as lizard and pyramidal orchids, grass-of-Parnassus, narrow-leaved helleborine, early marsh-orchid, water germander, adder's tongue fern, several broomrapes, and spiked speedwell, amongst others.

On the coast south of the Somme Bay, there is a sizeable no-hunting reserve at Hable d'Ault, just south of Cayeux-sur-Mer. It includes an old lagoon, now separated from the sea, with reedbeds, marshy fields, and dunes, with much of the flora and fauna already described.

The dunes and woodlands on the coast north of the estuary are worth visiting, from Quend-Plage-les-Pins southwards, and there are fragments of rich fen, with good flowers, between Quend and Villers-sur-Authie. The flood plain of the Somme up towards Abbeville has many ditches and wet areas which still hold an interesting flora and fauna despite agricultural improvement.

24 Etang St. Ladre
SITE

A small, but interesting and well-managed wetland reserve, just south-east of Amiens.

In the flood plain of the river Avre, about 5 km south-east of Amiens, is situated a nature reserve covering 13.5 ha of mixed wetlands. It lies on old peat diggings that were started in the eighteenth century and finally abandoned in 1925. Although small, it is a rich site, with a wide variety of flowers, birds, and other wildlife. Botanically, it is quite rich with over 300 species, including a number of protected plants. Not surprisingly, there is a good range of aquatic plants, including pondweeds such as *Potamogeton coloratus*, two water-milfoils *Myriophyllum spicatum* and *M. verticillatum*, frogbit, the insectivorous bladderwort *Utricularia vulgaris*, which flowers well here, and least bur-reed. There are also several stoneworts or charophytes – algae that resemble flowering plants in their form – including *Chara hispida* and *C. major*. In boggy areas, there is marsh gentian, sedges such as tufted sedge, various willows, marsh fern, the rare crested buckler-fern, bog pimpernel, and about a dozen bog-moss *Sphagnum* species.

The site has a good range of dragon-flies, including emperor and black-tailed skimmer, together with tree frogs, agile frogs, palmate newts, grass snakes, and common lizard. There is a surprising variety of breeding birds, including king-fisher, water rail, great-crested and little grebes, reed, sedge, and marsh warblers, and the cricket-like reeling of the grasshopper warbler can often be heard. Nightingales are abundant, and the songs of the occasional bluethroat vie with them (the bluethroat song is more scratchy and less powerful, but it has

something of the same character, and is also often sung at night). There is an intermittent small population of little bit-terns, which can be seen occasionally as they break cover from the reeds, and they also breed elsewhere in the area. Both hen harriers and marsh harriers breed nearby and feed over the reserve at times. The site provides good feeding areas and safe roosts for another 50 or so species of birds at passage periods and during the winter, including large numbers of field-fares, redwings, and other thrushes.

A minor road running south from the D935 towards Boves skirts the eastern edge of the site, and there is limited access and views from here.

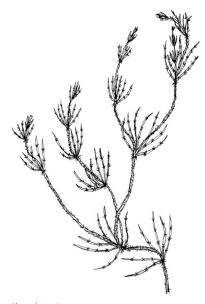

Chara hispida

SITE
25 Seine Valley

A series of small, chalk downland sites, with a rich flora and associated fauna, along the lower Seine Valley.

North-west of Paris, between roughly Mantes-La-Jolie and Rouen, the Seine wriggles its way through an extensive chalk massif. Most of the more level parts of the chalk are under cultivation or well wooded, especially where there are patches of more acidic clay overlying the chalk. However, in the Seine Valley, and in adjacent tributaries such as the Epte, or dry valleys, there are many slopes which are too steep to cultivate. Scattered around the area are a number of chalk downlands of interest, though virtually none is managed for conservation, so they tend to be undergrazed, used for motor-cycling, and hunted over in season, and are often progressing towards scrub or secondary woodland.

Collectively, they are very rich botanically. For example, there are numerous orchids including military, monkey, and lady (and some difficult hybrids between these three), bee, man, early purple, pyramidal, fragrant, and early spider; in more shady places there are narrow-leaved helleborines, bird's-nest orchid and broad-leaved helleborines, amongst others. Other flowers of interest include the Rouen pansy *Viola hispida*, which is endemic to this small area – it is a perennial, with large violet or yellowish-violet flowers, found mainly on chalk cliffs or other open chalky areas. There are also both yellow and white rock-roses, bastard balm, large speedwell with distinctive twin spikes of dark blue flowers, knap-

Flowery chalk downland in the Seine Valley

weed broomrape and other broomrapes, and many other fine downland flowers. In places, one or more of manna (flowering) ash, laburnum, and false acacia have invaded the downs – all attractive trees, but damaging to the downland ecosystem here. The associated butterfly fauna is rich, and includes common and scarce swallowtails, Duke of Burgundy, dark green fritillary, brown argus, chalk-hill and Adonis blues, and others. Those that like ungrazed conditions, such as marbled whites and meadow browns, have done well, usually at the expense of the more demanding short-turf species such as silver-spotted skipper and Adonis blue. Other insects include field crickets, woodland grasshoppers, and wood crickets.

The sites are usually quite easily found by travelling along the valley roads and scanning the side slopes. There are good sites at Roches d'Orival, near Bennecourt, above Amfreville, north and south of Les Andelys, and above La Roche Guyon, amongst others.

There is a bird reserve in the Seine Valley just east of Val de Reuil, a few kilometres south-east of Rouen.

26 Baie du Mont-St.-Michel

A vast expanse of mudflats, saltmarshes, and other coastal habitats, particularly rich in birds.

Baie du Mont-St.-Michel covers a huge area at the south-west corner of the Cherbourg Peninsula. Apart from its fame as the site of Mont-St.-Michel itself (a World Heritage Site), it is also an internationally important site for birds: 62 000 ha are designated as a Ramsar Site, and within this 18 000 ha are designated as a Special Protection Area for birds. Parts of it are a no-hunting reserve. Although it straddles two of our regions, we have included the whole site in this region for simplicity.

Grazed saltmarsh in the Baie du Mont-St.-Michel

The main habitats within the bay are the vast mudflats, with areas of raised saltmarshes, often grazed, and other coastal habitats.

Its primary importance is for birds. In winter there are enormous numbers of birds of a wide range of species: brent geese, wigeon (up to 25 000), common scoter (up to 15 000), oystercatchers (up to 20 000), grey plover, knot, dunlin (up to 35 000 birds), bar-tailed godwits, curlew and black-headed gulls, with smaller numbers of golden plover, hen and marsh harriers, short-eared owls, peregrine, merlin, white-fronted geese, and both Lapland and snow buntings, to name but a few. At passage periods, there are large numbers of common scoter, ringed plover, grey plover, black-tailed godwit, whimbrel, spotted redshank, redshank, greenshank, swifts, and hirundines, and smaller numbers of many other birds such as hobby, various warblers, and finches, including bramblings. It is also quite an important breeding site, taking the bay as a whole. There are Kentish and little ringed plovers, quail, skylarks in plenty, yellow wagtails, shelduck, reed buntings, Cetti's warbler, raven, and many more. Schools of common dolphin often come into the bay in summer, and common seals are seen occasionally.

The road across to Mont-St.-Michel gives good views (though it is too busy at peak periods). There are footpaths following the sea-wall on the west side (e.g. Sentier des Douaniers) and good access on the east side at Genets. A fragment of old, windswept forest survives on the cliffs just west of Champeaux. There is also an information centre, the Maison de la Baie du Mont-St.-Michel at 50530, Genets, in addition to the normal tourist offices.

Snow bunting *Plectrophenax nivalis*

27 Cap Gris-nez and Cap Blanc-nez

SITE 27

A marvellous coastal site, consisting of the headlands at either end of Wissant Bay, well known for their bird life.

South-west of Calais, from Cap Blanc-nez south-westwards to Cap Gris-nez, there is a particularly attractive stretch of coastline, comprising high chalk cliffs around Blanc-nez, sand dunes, coastal marshes with pools, and mixed wildlife-friendly countryside, culminating in the Jurassic cliffs of Cap Gris-nez. This is the part of France closest to England (only 28 km), and is also one of the best sites for watching bird migration anywhere in France.

Cap Gris-nez is particularly good for birds, and 8600 ha is a Special Protection Area for birds, under European legislation. It is estimated that hundreds of thousands of birds of all types pass by or over the headland at migration periods each year, and they are relatively easy to see. Overall, the autumn migration is easier to watch than the spring one due to the layout of the site. At sea, there can be very large numbers of gulls, terns, shearwaters, skuas, divers, ducks such as scoters and eiders (which are usually also present around the area all year), grebes, cormorants, auks, and herons. On or close to the land, there are often vast numbers of passerines, depending on the

Great Cormorant *Phalacrocorax carbo* (Mike Lane)

conditions, such as flycatchers, warblers, thrushes, pipits, wagtails, finches, and even dotterel. Rarities such as Richard's pipit, red-breasted flycatcher, and yellow-browed warbler, often turn up here.

Eastwards, there are good areas of marshland and freshwater lakes blocked off from the sea by a line of dunes. The flora and fauna here is broadly similar to that of, for example, Platier d'Oye (see p. 58). The marshland around Tardinghen is an excellent locale for birds, natterjacks, and other features of interest. Cap Blanc-nez is part of a line of high chalk cliffs, and has a reasonable chalk flora on its unimproved parts. There is a limited seabird colony on the cliffs, with fulmars and gulls. Some stretches of the coast between the two headlands have limited access for conservation reasons, and this coast is remarkably unspoilt.

The whole region is part of the Nord-Pas-de-Calais Regional Natural Park, which covers 1670 square kilometres of this part of France. There are three parts, with three HQs, and the relevant one is at Manoir de Huisbois, Le Wast, 62142 Colembert.

Paris basin and north-east France

Paris basin

Paris basin and north-east France

Introduction

This is easily the largest of the regions into which we have divided France. It essentially covers that part of central northern France bounded by the Vosges and Jura to the east, the Massif Central in the form of the Auvergne to the south, the Belgian border to the north-east, and the coastal fringes to the west and north-west. It is an extremely varied region, though lacking in any coast or significant mountains, and has many fine areas of habitat, though it also includes many of the most intensively farmed parts of France. The reason it is the largest of our regions is simple enough – sites are fewer and further between here than anywhere else. Conversely, it is probably the most useful area in which to have some guidance as to where to visit: huge sections are almost entirely lacking in interest for the naturalist, with vast hedgeless fields sprayed with enormous quantities of pesticides, and the sprawl of Paris occupying a substantial area. However, we should not give the impression that it is all like this, because here and there little gems exist that one could easily overlook; there are some extremely fine areas where one can walk or ride all day in good quality

habitats and see an enormous variety of interesting features.

In the north, along the Belgian border north of Charlevilles-Mézières, the Ardennes (not described as a site) is a splendid region of hilly woodland cut through by the Meuse River. It is a good place for woodland birds, and superb walking country. From Reims eastwards, there are increasing amounts of wilder countryside, in the *champagne humide* and hilly areas to the east; the Argonne Forest and its accompanying area of lakes is wonderfully unspoilt and full of birds, and the Montagnes de Reims (just south of Reims) is a surprising area – though hardly a mountain range – designated as a Regional Natural Park and with some fine woodland areas. The Lorraine Regional Natural Park covers a vast area of woodland and lakes in two blocks either side of Nancy and Metz, with more than enough of interest for a week or two's holiday.

Southwards, from Auxerre to Dijon and beyond, there is an enormous territory of hard limestone, cut into valleys by the Yonne, Cure, Armançon, and many minor rivers. It is well wooded, with remnants of flowery grassland surviving from the time when it was all grazed by vast, wandering flocks of sheep. We have picked out a number of sites of interest, such as Le Bois du Parc and Plateau de Langres, but it is one of those regions – more common in the south of France – where almost anywhere is likely to be worth a visit. South of Orléans and Tours, there are two large areas with a wealth of interest: the Sologne is a huge, heathy area with lakes and forests lying south of Orléans; collectively, it has an enormous range of species, but the interest is dif-

Four-spotted chaser *Libellula quadrimaculata*

Previous page: **Limestone gorge, Combe de Lavaux**

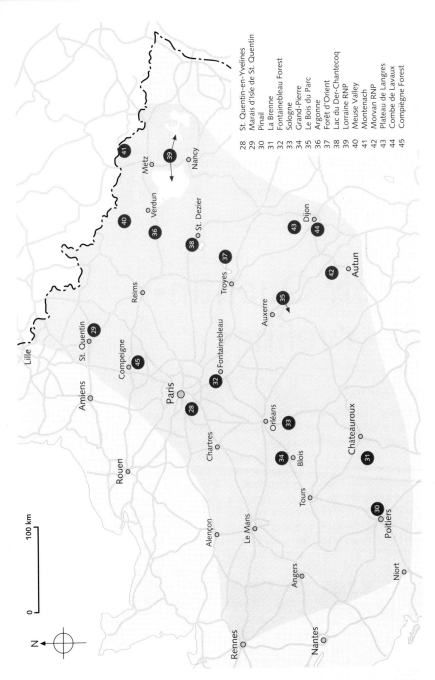

28 St. Quentin-en-Yvelines
29 Marais d'Isle de St. Quentin
30 Pinail
31 La Brenne
32 Fontainebleau Forest
33 Sologne
34 Grand-Pierre
35 Le Bois du Parc
36 Argonne
37 Forêt d'Orient
38 Lac du Der-Chantecoq
39 Lorraine RNP
40 Meuse Valley
41 Montenach
42 Morvan RNP
43 Plateau de Langres
44 Combe de Lavaux
45 Compiègne Forest

fuse, and it suffers from being the hunting capital of northern France. La Brenne, between Chateauroux and Chatellerault, is an area of lakes and marshes, a little more accessible than the Sologne and with a superb range of species. Both of these areas, though internationally important, are almost entirely lacking in reserves or any statutory protection, which makes visiting more difficult and frustrating. However, they do bear out the old adage that the interesting wildlife areas in France only begin south of the Loire; not quite true, but not far wrong if you are heading due south-wards from the channel ports.

This is a region of great state forests. There are some huge ones within easy reach of Paris, managed for their timber but in such a way as to keep a good variety of native wildlife, and with excellent public access. Most are dominated by native trees, often naturally regenerated, so most of the flora and fauna has survived, though admittedly they tend to be lacking in very old trees and the wildlife that depends on them. Some of the best examples are Fontainebleau, Compiègne, Rambouillet, Retz, and Chantilly, in a ring around Paris, though there are many others, too.

Altogether, although it does not have the spectacular scenery or the cachet of the south, there is plenty to see here, within easy reach of the channel ports or Paris.

SITE 28 St. Quentin-en-Yvelines

A sizeable wetland reserve with a remarkably rich flora and fauna, right on the edge of Paris.

Covering about 90 ha, St. Quentin-en-Yvelines National Nature Reserve consists of open water (the western part of the Etang de St. Quentin), reedbeds, grassland, carr woodland, and other wetland habitats. It lies only 30 km from the centre of Paris.

Botanically, the reserve is quite rich, with about 300 species of higher plants recorded. The fringing vegetation consists of bulrush and lesser bulrush, reeds, the grass *Glyceria maxima* and reed canary-grass, yellow and purple loosestrifes, and various willows. In other wet areas, there are bur-marigolds, including the rarest of them, *Bidens radiata*, the inconspicuous but uncommon six-stamened waterwort, and *Elatine alsinas-trum*, the cinquefoil *Potentilla supina*, southern marsh-orchid, marsh stitchwort, mudwort, pennyroyal, and many others. The aquatic vegetation includes pondweeds such as *Potamogeton trichoides*, and two rare aquatic bryophytes: *Riccia fluitans* and *Ricciocarpus natans*. It is also a good locality for insects, including over 200 beetle species, a good selection of wetland butterflies with common swallowtails and the fascinating map butterfly, 15 species of dragonflies, and many more – not exceptional, but a good selection for an almost urban site.

It is particularly notable for birds, with over 230 species recorded, of which about 70 breed, and the reserve was originally acquired for ornithological reasons. Breeding birds include Cetti's, grasshopper,

Potentilla supina

reed, sedge, and other warblers, masses of nightingales, marsh harriers, and ducks such as pochard and shoveler. At passage periods, there can be huge numbers of birds, depending on the water levels and the amount of mud exposed. Waders such as redshank, greenshank, spotted redshank, spoonbill, ringed plover, with little egrets, herons, terns, shelduck, and others, turn up in variable numbers, and there can be large quantities of waterfowl in winter.

There is an information centre nearby at: Base des Loisirs, RD 912, 78190, Trappes, open all year. Access is normally limited, or guided walks can be arranged here. The site is signposted off the N10 at Trappes, just south-west of Versailles.

29 Marais d'Isle de St. Quentin

SITE

A surprising, semi-urban nature reserve made up of wetland habitats along 2 km of the upper Somme.

This National Nature Reserve covers about 50 ha of open water, wet woodland, reedbeds and sedge beds, gravelly banks, and other flood-plain habitats along the Somme Valley on the eastern edge of the town of St. Quentin, between the old and new Somme channels. The reserve is surprisingly rich in species. There is a good range of more widespread wetland and aquatic species such as purple and yellow loosestrifes, yellow iris, bur-reeds, angelica,

comfreys, pondweeds, sedges, ragged-robin, and white and yellow water-lilies, together with some rarer species such as cowbane, tufted loosestrife (a predominantly northern plant), greater spearwort, and *Potamogeton coloratus*. There are edible and common frogs, common toads, wall-lizards, and grass snakes, including large numbers of melanic individuals within the population.

Not surprisingly, as in most unspoilt wetland environments, there are many insects here, including masses of hoverflies, soldier flies, rove beetles, and other groups. Some species of particular interest include scarlet tiger moths in abundance (their larvae feed mainly on comfrey), and the fascinating water spider, which lives much of its life underwater with the aid of a bubble of air that it carries down with it. The list of dragonflies includes an abundance of white-legged and variable damselflies, emperor dragonfly, and scarce chaser.

It is also a good site for birds. About 65 species breed here regularly, including marsh harriers, bluethroats, grasshopper,

Kingfisher (Common) *Alcedo atthis* (Peter Wilson)

Tufted loosestrife *Lysimachia thyrsiflora*

Cetti's, sedge, and reed warblers, kingfishers (which can be seen regularly, streaking along the canals or river channels), little bittern, nightingales and many other wetland and woodland species. The open waters are well used by wildfowl in winter, and birds such as waders on passage. It is designated as a Special Protection Area for birds.

Access is controlled to maintain the interest in a potentially much-disturbed environment, with limited paths and nature trails.

The marshes along the Somme downstream of St. Quentin are fragmented, but still hold much worth seeing.

SITE 30 Pinail

An extraordinary site where heathland, bog, and pools have developed on old stone workings.

Green heather *Erica scoparia*

The Pinail Nature Reserve covers 135 ha, made up almost entirely of a site which was excavated over a period of at least 200 years for a high-quality stone used mainly for millstones. The excavations ceased at the end of the eighteenth century, leaving a vast flat landscape studded with around 3000 hollows, looking like a lunar landscape or an area that has suffered intensive bombing. Since then, it has gradually developed into an extremely rich area of heathland and bog, studded with ponds of varying character. It is surrounded by the 3000-ha Forêt des Moulières, so the reserve's ecological value is enhanced by its position.

Botanically it is very rich, with about 450 species of higher plants recorded to date. There is a wide range of heath and wet heath species, such as Cornish heath, cross-leaved heath, and the less common *Erica scoparia*, sometimes known as green heather on account of its tiny greenish flowers, which is common here; marsh gentians are also common, producing their intense blue flowers in autumn, with marsh clubmoss, saw-wort, heath spotted orchid,

A pool at Pinail, full of water lilies

the rare and protected summer lady's-tresses orchid, the little white-flowered gratiole, wild chamomile in abundance, dwarf gorse, and many other heathland species. In the wettest areas, there are various insectivorous plants including sundews, pale butterwort, two species of bladderwort, including the inconspicuous pale yellow lesser bladderwort, with pillwort (a grass-

Bog bush-cricket *Metrioptera brachyptera*

like fern with little balls of spores at the bases of the fronds), bogbean, white water-lilies, lesser water-plantain, an umbellifer *Peucedanum cervaria*, and many more. It is one of the best places in northern France to see a range of heath, bog, and acid water plants all together.

It is also a remarkably fine place for watching birds. There is a good range of typical heath and forest-edge birds, including abundant Dartford warblers, stonechats, nightjars, linnets, and grasshopper warblers. The site has a strong population of hobbies, and this is a perfect place to watch them hawking over the ponds for dragonflies, particularly on warm summer evenings but possible at any time during the summer. Both Montagu's and hen harriers breed in the area, with particularly good numbers of the latter, and short-toed eagles drift over from time to time. Around the edges of the site, where there are more trees, one may see tree pipits, woodlark, short-toed treecreepers, and middle spotted woodpeckers, amongst others.

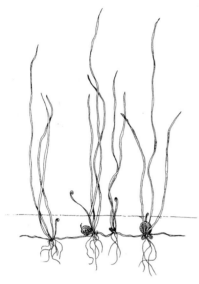

Pillwort *Pilularia globulifera*

Dragonflies are both diverse and abundant. Almost 50 species have been recorded, thanks to the abundance of clean acid-to-neutral water with a wide range of depths, aspects and flow-rates. Species of particular interest include the white-faced dragonfly and its close relative *Leucorrhinia caudalis*, which is an essentially Siberian species right

at the western edge of its range here, downy emerald and four-spotted chaser (both abundant enough to be the favoured food of hobbies here), hairy hawker, southern hawker, darters, small red damselfly, white-legged damselfly, the rare emerald damselfly *Lestes barbarus* with its distinctive bi-coloured pterostigmas (prominent spots near the wing-tips), and the overwintering *Sympecma fusca*. There is also a good range of grasshoppers and bush-crickets here, including large marsh grasshopper and bog bush-cricket. Amphibians are common, including western spadefoot toads, tree frogs, agile frog, great-crested and marbled newts, and natterjacks – 13 species in all. There are also red deer, wild boar, and another dozen or so mammals.

The reserve lies about 15 km northeast of Poitiers, close to the village of Vouneuil-sur-Vienne, from where it is well signposted. It has ample parking, information boards, and a network of paths.

The rest of the forest around the site, the Forêt des Moulières, is well worth visiting, with a wide range of forest birds including honey buzzards, five species of woodpecker, Bonelli's warbler, and many more, as well as good flowers.

31 La Brenne

A large area of outstanding interest for the naturalist, particularly for its birds and dragonflies.

La Brenne is a vast area of low-lying land lying between the Indre and the Creuse Rivers, roughly between Chateauroux and Chatellerault. The whole site lies within La Brenne Regional Natural Park, which covers 1660 square kilometres stretching in a rough square southwards from Buzançais. The park covers all the best habitats, though – as explained on p. 19 –

Caldesia parnassifolia

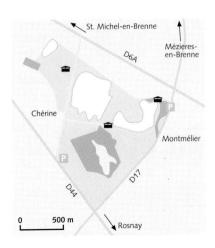

Western whip snake *Coluber viridiflavus*

Regional Natural Park designation does not signify any degree of protection or conservation management. In fact the lack of protection for La Brenne at a national level is impressively poor: 140 000 ha are designated as a Ramsar Site (internationally important wetland), and large sections are considered to be particularly important to birds, yet there is only one small reserve in the area (145 ha – see below), some limited no-hunting

Red deer *Cervus elaphus*

areas, and nothing else. At the moment, it works, more or less, and the area remains of great interest to the naturalist, but it could easily change, and there are signs of steady deterioration in the overall habitat as old meadows are turned into fish ponds, fish farming is becoming more intensive, and there is too much shooting.

Essentially, it is a huge expanse of poor or poorly-drained soil on which over 1000 lakes of various sizes have been created (they are virtually all artificial or artificially enlarged); the lakes lie in a mosaic of woodlands, reedbeds, wet meadows and pastures, fens, and other habitats, with relatively little intensive agricultural land. Because the lakes are essentially fish ponds, they are managed for this purpose and may be arbitrarily drained, cleared, flooded, or enlarged, which makes it difficult to predict where the best spots will be. However, there is enough for there always to be something of interest.

Almost 300 species of bird have been recorded here in total. It is particularly good during the breeding season, but it also meets international criteria for importance during passage periods and in the winter. Overall, it is of enormous significance for breeding populations of bittern, little bittern, grey and purple herons, night heron, little egret, marsh harriers, wetland warblers such as Savi's, great reed, grasshopper, sedge, melodious, and Cetti's, bearded tits, whiskered

Lake at Gabrière

tern (in large numbers) and black tern (in very small numbers), black-necked grebe, stone curlew, black-winged stilts, red-backed shrike, and kingfishers, as a start. In wooded areas, there are Bonelli's warblers, several woodpeckers including black and middle spotted, crested tits, short-toed treecreeper, and nightjars.

In addition to all the bird interest, La Brenne is a superb area for most other

Little bittern *Ixobrychus minutus*

forms of natural life. There are 26 species of reptiles and amphibians, including fire salamanders in the wooded areas, several species of newts including marbled, midwife, natterjack, and common toads, parsley frogs, tree frogs, agile and pool frogs, pond terrapins, grass snake, western whip snake, and smooth snake, amongst others. It is well known as a marvellous site for dragonflies and damselflies, not only in number of species but also abundance. Almost 60 species have been recorded – just about everything you might expect in this area – though you would have to work hard to find them all. Some highlights include orange-spotted emerald, the mainly southern powder-blue skimmer *Orthetrum brunneum*, emperor and lesser emperor, Norfolk, hairy, and southern hawkers, the gomphids *Onychogomphus forcipatus* and *O. uncatus*, downy and brilliant emeralds, variable damselfly, and many others. Likewise, about 60 butterfly species are known here, including map and lesser purple emperor. It is also superb for many other insects groups,

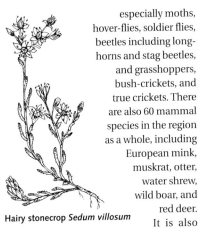

Hairy stonecrop *Sedum villosum*

especially moths, hover-flies, soldier flies, beetles including long-horns and stag beetles, and grasshoppers, bush-crickets, and true crickets. There are also 60 mammal species in the region as a whole, including European mink, muskrat, otter, water shrew, wild boar, and red deer. It is also very rich botanically, though without any clear-cut locations for seeing a wide range of species. About 1000 species are recorded within the Regional Natural Park, and apart from the vast range of widespread waterside and aquatic species, such as purple and yellow loosestrifes, yellow and white water-lilies, pondweeds, water-milfoils, water-plantains, and arrowheads, there are also many less widespread species. There are 30 species of orchids: southern plants close to their northern limits, such as water chestnut, green heather, or parnassus-leaved water-plantain, and attractive species such as heath lobelia and viper's grass. Other plants of interest include the semi-aquatic fern pillwort, the rare small fleabane (as well as common fleabane), hairy stonecrop, pennyroyal, and loose-flowered orchid. Spring and early summer are good times to visit.

The Chérine Nature Reserve is the best-protected section of La Brenne, see map p. 77, and probably has the highest concentration of species. It covers 145 ha of open water, reedbeds, fen, woodland, and other wetland habitats. The flora and fauna are roughly typical of that described above for the area; highlights include 40 species of dragonfly, including the rarity *Leucorrhinia pectoralis*, 8 species of amphibians, 80 species of breeding birds (and almost 200 in total), and 39 species of mammals including wild cat, red deer, and beech martens. There are well over 500 species of flowers, including many unusual ones. Access is limited to certain trails, with hides and observation platforms. A new information centre at the reserve should be open by the time of publication.

Virtually all the area is good, and much can be seen by simply driving around and stopping at promising spots; the site is also ideal for cycling, which makes access down quiet tracks easier. Some good localities to visit include the lakes around Gabrière and Gabriau, Beauregard Lake, the lakes around Migné, and the Lancosme Forest near Vendoeuvres. The Maison du Parc for the Regional Natural Park is at: Le Bouchet, 36300 Rosnay. Tel: 02 54281213.

SITE 32 Fontainebleau Forest

A huge forest lying just south of Paris, remarkably rich in all forms of wildlife.

Fontainebleau Forest is enormous, covering about 170 square kilometres around the town of Fontainebleau, not far south of Paris. It is very popular as a recreation area for Parisians, so it becomes extremely busy at weekends and holidays, though this does have the advantage that shooting and hunting are reduced and there is

Redstart (Common) *Phoenicurus phoenicurus*
(Robert Dickson)

some conservation management. The forest is underlain mainly by rather acidic sandstones capped by hard blocks on the ridges, which have weathered into a jumble of rocks impossible to farm. This supports extensive deciduous woodlands, with heathy and boggy areas in clearings. In a few places, the Brie limestone outcrops to give another dimension to the habitats, and on the east side, towards Milly-la-Forêt, the sand is rather more calcareous. Here and there, patches of planted or natural coniferous woodland occur.

The plant life is a marvellous mixture of woodland, bog, heath, chalk downland, and steppe species, with an enormous diversity. In the woods, there are angular Solomon's seals in abundance, bastard balm, lady orchids, narrow-leaved helleborines, yellow bird's-nest and bird's-nest orchid, orpine, and many more; along roadsides and in grassy clearings, one can find cypress spurge, blue bugle, pasque-flowers, swallow-wort, and others, while monkey and military orchids, red helleborine, spiked speedwell, and many more common species grow on downland. In the dry, open steppe-like areas, there is a flora not dissimilar to that of the East Anglian Breckland in England, with spring speedwell, grape-hyacinth, perennial knawel, and similar species. In boggy areas, there are sundews, bog asphodel, white-beaked sedge, marsh gentian, and other typical bog or wet heath species.

Butterflies are common in clearings and along rides, and most of the woodland and grassland species for the region

occur here, such as Camberwell beauty, large tortoiseshell, purple and lesser purple emperors, map, various fritillaries, hairstreaks, coppers, blues such as Adonis, and many more. Other insect life is rich and varied.

It is also an excellent place for the bird-watcher, with an abundance of forest species: woodpeckers are of special interest here, with black, great spotted, middle spotted, lesser spotted, green, and grey-headed (a good place to check some of the differences!); there are breeding pied flycatchers (which are rare generally in this area), common redstarts, wood and Bonelli's warblers, short-toed treecreeper, tawny owls, crested tits, firecrests, wryneck, and hawfinches. Birds of prey include honey and common buzzards, common kestrels, sparrowhawk, and hobbies. Golden orioles call loudly from poplars and other trees – my first experience of them was here, many years ago, when I was woken up by several singing at a campsite near La Musardière. Wild boar are common, and signs of their digging can be seen everywhere, and there are good numbers of deer. Amongst other

Lady orchid *Orchis purpurea*

Lesser purple emperor *Apatura ilia*

reptiles, there are lots of the impressive green lizard.

Access is generally open, with just a few exceptions. It is worth buying the IGN 1:25 000 map of the area, which covers the forest fully and shows many routes and sites of interest. Some places worth visiting include: Rocher Cuvier Chatillon, north of the N7, with good plants; the Gorge et Platières de Apremont for impressive stony areas and abundant wild boar; the reserves at La Tillaie and Le Gros-Fouteau, north-west of Fontainebleau for good forest birds; the route of the east–west aqueduct south of Fontainebleau crosses some limestone and is good for flowers, butterflies, etc; the Gorge de Franchard; the area east of the Croix du Grand Veneor on the N7 for flowers; the Plaine de Chanfroy, just east of the A6, for its breckland flora and insects; and the Marais de Couluvreux, just east of the A6, for bog and wet heath species. If you are travelling by car, watch out for car thieves in the area.

33 Sologne

Fascinating lakes, woodland, and heathland, particularly rich in birds and insects.

Sologne is a vast area of heathy woodlands, studded with hundreds of lakes. Collectively, it is one of the most important wetlands in France, though it is a hard area to get to grips with, partly because it is so spread out, and partly because virtually all the lakes and woods are private and often jealously guarded. There are no reserves of any significance, no national or international protection to speak of, and the area is heavily shot over, sadly. However, its importance can hardly be ignored.

For birds, it is extremely good. Breeding birds in the area as a whole include bittern, little bittern, night heron and purple heron, honey buzzard, short-toed eagle, marsh and hen harriers, whiskered and black terns, kingfishers, nightjars, grey-headed and black woodpeckers, woodlarks, grasshopper and Savi's warblers, great-crested, black-necked, and little grebes, and many more widespread species. Ospreys have started to breed nearby, at the first mainland France site in recent years, and can sometimes be seen in the area. There are large numbers of waterfowl on the lakes in winter, depending on the weather, and cranes and greylag geese pass through. Dragonflies and damselflies are abundant, with at least 40 species, though it is not quite as good as La Brenne. Typical species of interest here include downy and brilliant emerald, scarce, broad-bodied, and four-spotted

Bembix rostrata

chasers, golden-ringed, variable damselfly, and small red damselfly. Amongst the other insects, there are strong populations of orthoptera such as blue-winged and mottled grasshoppers, wood-crickets, and bog bush-crickets, and praying mantises are common. On sandy, heathy areas, one can see abundant specialized hymenopterans such as bee-wolves, sand-wasps, digger wasps, mining bees, and the striking *Bembix rostrata*, amongst others.

There is an abundance of amphibians in and around the lakes, including edible and agile frogs, tree frogs, spadefoot toad, pars-ley frog, midwife toad, various newts, and reptiles such as pond terrapins, green lizards, western whip snakes, and smooth snakes. It is not exceptional botanically, though there is a good range of wetland species tolerant of slightly acid conditions, and heathland species such as cudweeds, mossy stonecrop, and heath lobelia.

The best lakes are at St.Viâtre, Marcilly-en-Gault, L'Arche, Marguilliers, and in the Bruadan Forest. It is an excellent area for cycling, with many small roads and tracks, and few hills. Neung-sur-Beuvron makes a good centre.

Grand-Pierre

St. Lucie's cherry
Prunus mahaleb

A fine area of limestone grassland, woodland, and marshland with a rich flora and fauna.

Grand-Pierre Nature Reserve covers 300 ha of countryside just north of Blois, in an area that is otherwise rather intensively cultivated. It is underlain mainly by hard limestone, and there are flowery grasslands, cliffs, scrub, woodland, and some wetland areas along the valley floor. The reserve is botanically rich, though a good deal has been lost or suppressed during the long post-war period without grazing, and some species are only just beginning to return now. Plants of the dry

grassland and scrub include pasque-flower, white and yellow rock-roses, mountain germander, the blue composite *Carduncellus mitissimus*, species of pink *Dianthus*, several orchids, horse-shoe vetch and *Coronilla minima*, St. Lucie's cherry, box, downy oak, and the yellow-flowered, semi-parasitic bartsia *Odontites jaubertiana*, which is endemic to France. Among the lower plants, over 250 lichens and 113 bryophytes have been recorded on the reserve, including a handful new to France.

The mixture of habitats is good for butterflies, with at least 40 species, including Adonis blue, chalk-hill blue, brown argus, the rare and endangered false ringlet, silver-spotted skipper, and many others. Praying mantises are common in the warmer, south-facing long grass and scrub areas, and ascalaphids *Libelloides longicornis* (see p. 200) fly actively in the sunshine.

This is also a good site for birds, with at least 60 breeding species and many more passing through. Interesting breeding species include wryneck, spotted flycatcher, Bonelli's warbler, and Savi's warbler, together with more widespread species such as skylarks, woodlarks, and tree pipits. There are also roe deer, beech marten, wild boar, and other common mammals.

The D162 passes through the reserve, and there is footpath access from Marolles just to the south. There is a Maison de la Nature at: Rue de la Mairie, 41330, Marolles.

The surrounding area, known as the Petit Beauce, has some important breeding birds which require open country, particularly hen and Montagu's harriers, and stone curlew.

35 Le Bois du Parc

A woodland nature reserve on the banks of the river Yonne, with a lovely combination of northern and southern species.

South of Auxerre, the river Yonne cuts through hills of coralline limestone, producing cliffs and steep slopes along the valley. Le Bois du Parc (park wood) lies on the slopes of the valley and up onto the adjacent plateau, covering 45 ha of deciduous woodland and open dry limestone slopes. It is situated in an area of extensive woodland, with flowery grasslands, so the reserve draws on its surroundings for part of its variety.

It is of particular interest botanically, with many uncommon species in addition to more typical and widespread plants of calcareous woodland and grassland. Some species of particular interest include the snowdrop windflower (similar to, but larger and more solid than wood anemones, and much less common); delicate white spires of St. Bernard's lily, pink crown vetch, least scorpion grass, both yellow and white rock-roses, the pink-flowered perennial bindweed *Convolvulus cantabrica*, crested cow-wheat, two rare grasses: *Koeleria*

Snowdrop windflower
Anemone sylvestris

vallesiana and the feather-grass *Stipa pennata*, spring cinquefoil, alpine squill, and various orchids including lizard orchid. In open stony areas, there are several unusual cresses such as *Thlaspi montanum*, *Cardaminopsis arenosa*, and *Cardamine impatiens*. Shrubs and trees of special note include snowy mespil, hornbeam, downy oak, and box – more typical of the southern *causses* (see p. 184) than here. Recent management work has improved the quality of the open habitats, and to the benefit of the flowers.

It is a good site for butterflies and other insects: woodland grasshoppers, wood-crickets, various bush-crickets, praying mantises, ascalaphids, and the uncommon small cicada *Cicadetta montana*, which is particularly inconspicuous as its call is much quieter than those of its larger southern cousins. There are both asp vipers and aesculapian snakes here, as well as wall lizards and green lizards – all potential food for the short-toed eagles that can be seen hunting over the area at times.

Parking is available alongside the D130, which runs along the Yonne between Mailly-le-Chateau and Merry-sur-Yonne. There is open access on the paths, with a marked nature trail.

The whole site has superb limestone woodland; the D950 from Mailly to Voutenay-sur-Cure, a little to the east, passes through fine woods containing plants such as pasqueflowers and mezereon in abundance.

36 Argonne

Extensive wooded hills with areas of marshland and lake, collectively very rich in birds.

Argonne is a long, thin, and rather amorphous stretch of land running southwards from south of Salon on past Ste. Menehould towards Bar-le-Duc. In the north it is largely forested on an acidic ridge with beech and oak forest, whereas towards the southern end there are extensive marshes, lakes, and bogs, especially south of Ste. Menehould. The whole area is of interest and provides a welcome respite from the flat, intensively cultivated champagne country to the west of it. The wetlands are particularly important, and 1350 square kilometres have been designated as a Ramsar Site (internationally important wetland), though there is little active protection or conservation on the ground.

In the wetland area, birds are abundant, and many species are of special interest. The site supports good breeding populations of bittern, little bittern, honey buzzard, both black and red kites, marsh and hen harriers, and a few booted eagles. There are purple and grey herons, kingfishers, warblers such as great reed, grasshopper and Cetti's, hoopoes, three

species of shrikes (red-backed, great grey, and occasional woodchat), melodious warblers, woodlarks, and cirl buntings. In the more extensively wooded areas, there are collared flycatchers, and woodpeckers of interest including grey-headed, middle spotted, and black.

A good area for seeing a range of wetland birds lies in the triangle between Belval, Vaubécourt, and Beaulieu-en-Argonne, where there are fine lakes, marshes, and woodland. There are no reserves, but generally access is not difficult, and some good viewpoints can be found along the roads.

The woodlands on the higher ground are pleasant and extensive, with a good range of birds. On the more flowery rides butterflies are abundant, and there are flowers such as common spotted orchids, columbine, tower-cress, bird's-nest orchid, may-lily, lily-of-the-valley, and wintergreens. Ste. Menehould makes a fine base, with interesting areas to the north and south. Forêt de Lisle to the south, near Triaucourt-en-Argonne is a good oak woodland.

SITE 37 Forêt d'Orient Regional Natural Park

A large, Regional Natural Park dominated by forests and lakes, particularly good for birds.

Forêt d'Orient Regional Natural Park covers an area of about 715 square kilometres to the east of Troyes, comprising mainly extensive old woodlands with three large lakes and many smaller ones. The largest lakes, the Reservoir d'Aube (or Lac du Temple) and the Lac d'Orient are both over 2000 ha in extent, and all the significant lakes here are artificial in origin. Lac d'Orient is the oldest, and has a well-established vegetation and fauna, while the two other main lakes were completed in 1990 and are still developing. The bird life is particularly rich, and the Lac d'Orient is a Special Protection Area for birds, while the whole region is part of an internationally recognized wetland.

It is marvellous for birds at all times, but particularly at passage periods and in winter. The lakes, and especially Lac d'Orient, hold large numbers of common cranes on migration – a fabulous sight – together with large numbers of wildfowl such as great-crested grebes, bean geese, teal, mallard, pochard, ferruginous duck, red-breasted geese, white-headed duck, black stork, little gulls, and various waders, amongst others. In winter, there are many of the same species, together with great white egrets, Bewick's and whooper swans, white-fronted geese, goldeneye, smew, goosander, and birds of prey such as white-tailed eagle, peregrine, and hen harrier. The numbers of birds on show can be very large, depending on the weather both here and elsewhere. In the breeding season the site is less exciting, and more like others in the region, but there are honey buzzards, black and red kites, goshawk, marsh harrier, little bittern, grey-headed and black woodpeckers, hawfinches, and a few of the secretive black storks.

The forests around the lake, and especially to the east, are vast and mostly ancient, and dominated by oak on heavy soils. The flora includes interesting trees such as wild service-tree and two species of lime (with huge quantities of mistletoe), spotted and marsh-orchids along the rides, and a wide range of ancient woodland flowers. The area is also famed for its fungi (especially edible ones, but there are many others, too). Butterflies are good without being exceptional, and include map, purple emperor, white admiral, poplar admiral, purple and brown hair-

Edible frog *Rana esculenta*

Foret d'Orient – lake

streaks, pearl-bordered fritillaries, and many others, plus a wealth of other interesting insects such as longhorn beetles, grasshoppers and crickets, wood-crickets and hornets.

The lakes have become steadily better for amphibians, and now there are huge populations of some species in favoured areas, particularly common frogs, common toads, agile frog, and edible frogs (the noise can be deafening on warm evenings in spring!), with smaller numbers of spadefoot toads, several species of newts, and fire salamanders in the woods. Similarly, the dragonflies have continued to increase in both numbers and diversity, though they do not yet match those of La

Whooper swan *Cygnus cygnus*

Brenne as there is not the variety of habitat. Frequent species here include downy and brilliant emeralds, emperor, black-tailed and broad-bodied skimmers, several darters including ruddy, common, vagrant, and occasionally others, together with white-legged, southern, and other damselflies. There are red and roe deer, wild boar, red squirrels, and brown hares, amongst other mammals.

The site is relatively easy to study, especially if you have a car, though it is also an easy area for cycling and walking. There are good bird-watching spots all up the east side of Lac d'Orient along the Lusigny–Géraudot road. The D79 on the north side runs past the bird reserve, which is always of interest, though close views may be difficult to achieve. The D50 to Brevonnes from just east of Géraudot gives good views of Lac du Temple, and the dam area, on the D11, and is often good for cranes. There is a Regional Natural Park HQ at 10220 Piney (on the D960), and a good information centre nearer the lake on the D79 east of Géraudot.

The Etang de la Horre, about 15 km north-east of Brienne, is a large lake, particularly good for birds in autumn and winter.

SITE 38 Lac du Der-Chantecoq

Paris basin

A vast artificial lake that is rapidly gaining a reputation as a major ornithological site.

Lac du Der-Chantecoq covers almost 5000 ha in the low-lying wooded country to the south-west of St. Dizier. It was created in 1974–75, and has steadily gained in importance as an ornithological site since then. It lies on a major migration route, and is surrounded by damp, well-wooded countryside (part of the *champagne humide* area) that was already rich in many forms of wildlife.

Its special value is as an ornithological site of international importance; it is part of a much larger Ramsar Site, and the whole of the lake and immediate surroundings (5000 ha) is a Special protection Area for birds under EU legislation. It is of particular interest in winter, with vast numbers of birds feeding and roosting, the main attraction being the common cranes; at least 6000 birds regularly winter here, and more than 20 000 stopover on migration. They can be watched relatively easily, and at the *ferme de Grues* ('crane farm') they are fed and can be viewed from a hide. In winter, too, there are thousands of waterfowl, such as Bewick's and whooper swans, greylag, bean, and white-fronted

A well-vegetated bay on the Lac du Der-Chantecoq

Paris basin

Crane (common) *Grus grus*

geese, common and velvet scoter, golden-eye, smew, scaup, shoveler, and pochard, and birds of prey such as white-tailed eagle (with up to half a dozen individuals), peregrine, hen harrier, and merlin amongst others. At passage periods, there are many of the same birds (and many more cranes, especially in November and March), with more waders, cormorants, a

few ospreys, terns such as black tern, and gulls including little gull.

It is also quite an important site for breeding birds in spring and summer, with its combination of woodland, wet grassland, marsh, reedbed, and open water. There are black and red kites, honey buzzards, marsh harriers, red-backed and great grey shrikes, bittern and little bittern, purple heron, gadwall, a few booted eagles, kingfishers, and a good range of woodpeckers in the woods, including black, middle spotted, and grey-headed. The rest of the wildlife is of interest, too, broadly similar to that of the nearby Forêt d'Orient Regional Natural Park (see p. 85).

Roads encircle the lake, with several side roads leading to harbours and peninsulas. There are good areas around Larzicourt beach and peninsula, Port de Chantecoq, Giffaumont-Champaubert, and St. Rémy-en-Bouzemont to the north-west, where the 'crane farm' is open throughout the main crane period.

SITE 39 Lorraine Regional Natural Park

A vast expanse of rolling, well-wooded countryside studded with lakes of various sizes, particularly rich in birds.

Lorraine Regional Natural Park covers over 2000 square kilometres of countryside, in two separate blocks. The larger block lies to the west of the Moselle between Nancy and Metz, with the smaller about 30 km further east, between Château Salins and Sarrebourg. The park boundaries are marked on most maps and atlases. It is made up of a mixture of quiet habitats – huge areas of woodland, an abundance of lakes of all sizes, limestone

Noctule *Nyctalus noctula*

Old beechwoods in autumn, in the western part of the park

grassland, marshes, reedbeds, and the valleys of the Meuse and Moselle in part.

It is a particularly well-known area for birds, thanks mainly to the extensive lakes and wetland habitats. Some of the main sites, such as Lachausée and Madine Lakes, are designated as Special Protection Areas, bird sites of European significance. The lakes are part of a system in which fishing is of major importance, and regular drainage plays a central part in management. Although this has disadvantages, it does provide large areas of mudflats which are good feeding areas for waders on passage. The park comes into its own in the breeding season, in particular, and the diversity and range of breeding birds is impressive. The list includes waterside and wetland species such as bittern and little bittern, purple and grey herons, marsh and Montagu's harriers,

spotted crakes, white (reintroduced) and black storks, kingfishers, a variety of warblers, notably sedge, reed, great reed, melodious, and grasshopper, and a few penduline tits. In more wooded areas, there are black and red kites, honey buzzard and common buzzard, hobby, grey-headed, black, and middle spotted woodpeckers (amongst others), icterine and wood warblers, collared flycatchers, and hawfinches, and in more open areas there are red-backed and great grey shrikes, hoopoes, whinchats, corn buntings, and woodlarks. At passage periods, there can be great white egrets, Bewick's swans, common cranes, greylag geese, terns such as common and black, gulls, waders, and birds of prey including osprey, white-tailed and booted eagle, and others. In winter, there can be large numbers of geese and ducks with some birds of prey and variable numbers of cranes.

The park offers other features of interest, too. There are 17 species of bats recorded (over half of the European species), including Daubenton's, whiskered, Natterer's, Geoffroy's, Bechstein's, greater mouse-eared, noctule, serotine, and barbastelle. There are also a few otters, water-voles, wild boar, red and roe deer, and small numbers of wildcats at the western edge of the isolated Vosges–Black Forest population. Botanically, entomologically, and herpetologically (reptiles and amphibians), it is broadly similar to Forêt d'Orient (p. 85). There are inland saltmarshes along the valley of the Seille, and in particular around Marsal – there was an important salt-mining industry here, reflected in the numerous place names with 'sel' or 'sal', and saltwater reaches the surface in a number of places. The flora in these areas includes many salt-tolerant species such as sea-spurreys, sea aster, and oraches *Atriplex* species. In the north-west corner of the western zone of the park, around Genincourt-sur-Meuse (in the Meuse Valley), there is an area of limestone with patches of fine limestone grassland, rich in flowers, including abundant orchids.

Good locations to visit in the western section include Etang de Lachaussée and Madine, the two large lakes west of Thiaucourt-Regnieville, both very rich in bird life, and the scattered smaller lakes further south between Raulecourt and Sanzey, and in particular the wooded area with lakes known as the Forêt de la Reine. The Meuse Valley, especially the limestone area around Génicourt, is both beautiful and interesting. In the eastern section, the Etang de Lindre is a dominant feature with particularly good birds and other wetland species; also worth visiting are the Etang de Parroy and nearby Forest of Parroy, and the valley of the Seille around Marsal.

The main park HQ is at: Domaine de Charmilly, BP 35, Chemin des Clos, 54702, Pont-à-Mousson (midway between Metz and Nancy), and there are other information centres at Beaumont, Bruley, Vigneulles, Hattonville, and St. Maurice. The park has a good range of useful leaflets.

The botanic gardens in Nancy (the Jardins Botanique du Montet, 100 Rue du Jardin Botanique, 54600 Nancy) is one of the best in France, with many local plants of interest.

SITE 40 Meuse Valley

River flood plain with marshes, particularly good for breeding birds.

Around the small town of Stenay, the Meuse passes through a broad flat flood plain which still has relatively unimproved hay meadows in parts. The best known are just west of Mouzay, to the south of Stenay, between the river and the canal, though there are similar meadows just north of Stenay. Their particular interest lies in the presence of breeding corncrake, curlew, and other birds. The corncrakes can be best picked up by their distinctive double 'crek-crek' call, uttered mainly at night, and are rarely seen. Other breeding birds here and nearby include both black and red kites, kingfishers, blue-headed wagtails (a race of yellow wagtail), whinchat, grasshopper warblers, golden orioles, Montagu's harriers, and other birds of damp, open country. Unfortunately, the site is not protected either at the national or international level, and the best meadows are steadily being drained and/or fertilized and ploughed, with a continuing loss of

Whinchat *Saxicola rubetra* (Mike Lane)

ing cranes. This was known and protected long before the Lac du Der-Chantecoq became important and famous. There is a protected section with hides just west of the village, and the whole area is of interest with its intimate mosaic of ponds, woods, and grassland. Other birds here include breeding common and little bitterns, purple heron, marsh and Montagu's harriers, hobby, great reed, grasshopper, and melodious warblers, red-backed shrikes, and black and red kites. At passage periods, there are more cranes, birds of prey such as ospreys, and a host of passerines. In winter, besides the cranes, there are merlins, hen harriers, and various wildfowl.

the breeding birds and other wildlife. The Woevre Forest, just to the east, is a good all-round deciduous woodland.

About 30 km south-east of Mouzay, near the village of Billy-sous-Mangiennes in the Loison Valley, there is an area of special interest for migrating and winter-

The protected section lies immediately west of Billy-sous-Mangiennes, but the whole area is of interest, especially southwards beyond the A4 Reims–Metz motorway.

41 Montenach

A group of limestone grasslands and woods, with a very rich flora and butterfly fauna.

Around the village of Montenach, in the far north-eastern corner of France, lies an outstanding area of limestone grassland. A section of just over 100 ha, split into five separate sites, is protected and managed as a National Nature Reserve run by the Conservatoire des sites Lorrains. It consists mainly of steep, grassy downland slopes with scrub, and woodland in places dominated by downy oak. There is also a series of calcareous springs along the line of the junction between the limestone and the impermeable rock below it, and these have formed a line of tufa-rich marshes with different species.

It is best as a botanical site, with over 400 higher plants recorded. On the warm,

Stinking hellebore
Helleborus foetidus

open grasslands and patchy scrub areas, there is a rich mixture of flowers including cut-leaved selfheal (as well as common selfheal and occasional hybrids), common rock-rose and the closely related but rarer *Fumana procumbens*, which is a more southern species, the pretty European Michaelmas daisy, the hawksbeard *Crepis praemorsa*, sedges such as *Carex dioica*, and a pretty blue flax *Linum leonii* that is endemic to this area of France and adjacent Germany. It resembles the more

Late spider orchid *Ophrys fuciflora*

widespread blue perennial flax, but differs mainly in being homostylous – that is, it has anthers and stigmas of about the same height. There are also some 30 species of orchids and 6 hybrids in the reserve, mainly on the grassland areas. These include man, lizard, fragrant, fly, bee, late spider, pyramidal, greater butterfly, and the rare hybrid between late spider and fly orchid, sometimes known as *Ophrys × devenensis*. In more wooded areas, there are white and narrow-leaved helleborines, bird's-nest orchid, stinking hellebore, and many others characteristic of warm, shady, calcareous sites. In the spring-line fens, there are early marsh-orchids, black bog-rush, marsh arrow-grass, and grey club-rush, together with a selection of mosses and liverworts.

Entomologically, it is also very rich, with, for example, over 60 species of butterflies recorded – an exceptional tally for a small site in the north of the country – often in abundance. The list includes common swallowtail, black-veined and wood whites, pale clouded yellow, brimstone, purple and ilex hairstreaks, large copper (rather surprisingly, as it is not a typical site), a selection of blues including Adonis, small, short-tailed, holly, mazarine, and chalk-hill, Duke of Burgundy, dark green fritillary, and Camberwell beauty. There are also over 400 moths recorded, including a nice selection of day-flying species such as the

burnets, burnet companion, and latticed heath. Other insects of interest include glow-worms, and two species of tiger beetle *Cicindela hybrida* and *C. campestris*. There are sand lizards and wall lizards, slow-worms, smooth snakes, and fire salamanders in the shadier parts of the woods.

Black-veined whites *Aporia crataegi*

It is also a surprisingly good location for birds, with over 100 species known to occur. Breeding birds of special interest include red-backed shrikes, who use the hawthorn trees as their 'larders' by impaling insects on the thorns, red kites in the woodland, skylarks, woodlarks, tree-pipits, and a dozen or so more.

The reserve is generally open on the marked paths, which include nature trails, and other parts can be visited by arrangement. There is no reserve centre, but information and permits can be obtained from: Conservatoire des sites Lorrains, 7, Place Albert Schweitzer, 57930 Fénétrange, which lies well to the south-east near Sarrebourg. Montenach lies just south of Sierck-les-Bains, close to the Luxembourg–German border, and the sections of the reserve are all around the village.

SITE 42 Morvan Regional Natural Park

A vast, hilly Regional Natural Park with large areas of forest and lakes, rich in birds, mammals and other wildlife.

Morvan Regional Natural Park covers almost 2000 square kilometres to the west of Dijon and Autun. It consists largely of a range of mid-altitude granite mountains, providing a contrast to the generally calcareous terrains in the vicinity. The mountains rise to 900 m at the highest point (Haut-Folin) and are heavily wooded, with a number of large lakes and any number of streams and rivers draining the relatively high rainfall from the hills. It is a pleasant and little-known area, not exceptional, but with plenty of interest, particularly in spring and summer. Despite the modest height of the peaks, this is quite a cold area and snow lingers late.

There are 90 000 ha of woodland within the park – almost half of its area – dominated by beech, oak, hornbeam, and pines, partly planted but with some old forest. The flora is typical of acidic situations: wild daffodils, pheasant's-eye narcissus, whorled caraway, wild tulips, harebells, foxgloves, St. John's-worts such as the uncommon *Hypericum linariifolium*, and orchids which are tolerant of less calcareous soils, such as early purple, green-winged, broad-leaved marsh, and heath spotted.

There is a good range of birds, without anything exceptional. The forests have breeding black and middle spotted woodpeckers amongst others, short-toed treecreepers, honey buzzard, goshawk and sparrowhawk, red kite, firecrest and goldcrest, crested tits, Bonelli's warblers, crossbills, serins, and many more. Wild boar, red deer, roe deer, beech martens, and red squirrels are all common. There are several parks or reserves where animals are kept semi-wild and are easy to see: these include the Anost Reserve east of Château-Chinon, in the Forêt de Breuil-Chenue and at La Vernuie in the Forêt au Duc near Quarré-les-Tombes. There is a botanical garden specializing in local flowers at the park HQ, which also has information on flowers and other wildlife available. The HQ is at: Maison du Parc, St. Brisson, 58230 Montsauche (west of Saulieu), and there is also a deer park and prehistoric burial chamber here.

SITE
43 Plateau de Langres

A dissected limestone plateau, heavily wooded, with a rich flora and fauna.

Pasqueflower *Pulsatilla vulgaris*

To the north and north-west of Dijon lies an extensive, little-known area of hilly limestone country, reminiscent of the Dordogne (see p. 143) but more heavily wooded and much less visited. Beautiful old stone villages nestle in a hilly landscape with huge forests, expanses of limestone grasslands, wet flushed areas with fen vegetation, streams and ponds, occasional cliffs and rocky areas, and a scattering of agricultural land.

It is botanically very rich. In the forests, there are often large quantities of columbine, lily-of-the valley, bastard balm, bugle and blue bugle, snowdrop windflower, tower cress and tower mustard, mezereon, alpine squill, snowdrops, wild liquorice, asarabacca, winged broom, orpine, spiked star-of-Bethlehem, with the distinctive yellow coronets of *Coronilla coronata* and the deep blue flowers of perennial cornflower in clearings or along shady roadsides. The orchids are good,

Reserve of Marais de Chalmessin

Bedstraw broomrape *Orobanche caryophyllacea*

too, with white, narrow-leaved, broad-leaved, and red helleborines, bird's-nest, lady, violet limodores, twayblade, and others. In a few places, such as in the Forêt du Mont de l'Echelle, north-west of Marcilly-sur-Tille, there are colonies of the rare and exotic lady's-slipper orchid. In open grassland, scrub, or rocky areas, including along the better roadsides, one finds a different range of plants: military and monkey orchid, early spider, greater and lesser butterfly, fragrant, pyramidal, bee, woodcock, fly, man, lizard, and other orchids; cowslips, bedstraws parasitized by bedstraw broomrape, with its pleasantly clove-scented flowers, dragon's teeth, greater hay rattle, pasqueflowers, St. Bernard's lily, white and common rockroses, viper's-bugloss, St. Lucie's cherry, and the great yellow gentian in places. In wet fen areas, there are other plants such as black bog-rush, marsh helleborine, early marsh-orchid, blunt-flowered rush, broad-leaved cotton-grass, and many more. Butterflies are abundant, especially where flowery grassland, woodland, and scrub all meet in a sunny but sheltered valley. At least 70 species occur in the area.

The Reserve of Marais de Chalmessin combines and protects many of the best features of the region, in an area of 124 ha.

It is a mixture of limestone grassland, scrub, and woodland with calcareous marsh and tufa springs, at the source of the Tille River. It has many of the species described for the whole plateau plus a few of its own.

Botanically, the reserve is rich, with European Michaelmas daisy, sedges such as *Carex davalliana* and *C. ornithopoda*, Chiltern gentian, the rare Teesdale violet (so-called because within Britain it is confined to the sugar limestone of Upper Teesdale; on the Continent, it is widespread but rare), larkspur *Aconitum napellus*, the buttercup *Ranunculus polyanthemoides*, and various others. There are also truffles *Tuber aestivum* in the woods.

The 70 or so butterfly species include the large heath, from the fen area, and the little-known and rather uncommon woodland brown, amongst the usual limestone grassland and woodland species. There are interesting odonata (dragonflies and damseslflies) in the fen and along the stream, including southern damselfly, the rarer relative of golden-ringed *Cordulegaster bidentatum*, and the emerald *Somatochlora flavomaculata*. Other features of interest within the reserve include midwife toad, pool frog, palmate newt, breeding black woodpeckers, and a pair of hen harriers, and several species of bats including Daubenton's and whiskered.

Access to the reserve is restricted to marked paths or by guided walks. The site is managed by: Conservatoire du Patrimonie Naturel de Champagne-Ardenne, 08240 Boult-aux Bois. It lies 2 km north-east of

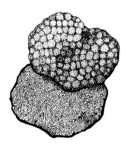

Summer truffle *Tuber aestivum*

Chalmessin village, or 2 km west of Musseau on the D112. Other sites worth visiting in the area include the attractive causse-like (*causses* are hard limestone plateaux – see p. 184) grassland and cliffs just north of Baulme-la-Roche (west of Dijon), protected by the community, the woods and other habitats just north of Moloy on the D996, and the Forêt d'Auberive around Auberive. There is a good botanic garden in Dijon, the Jardin de L'Arquebuse, at: 1, Avenue Albert 1er, 21033, Dijon. It has mainly exotic species, but with some French and local collections.

SITE
44 Combe de Lavaux

A rocky limestone valley with good birds, flowers, and butterflies.

Southwards from Dijon towards Beaune, there is an extensive area of limestone hills, cut through by valleys which are often dry. Once, it was extensively grazed by sheep and other stock, but in recent years it has steadily reverted to scrub and woodland, or been ploughed or planted. Some of the steeper valleys have retained much of their interest, and the Combe de Lavaux is probably the best example; it is a steep-sided valley with cliffs in places, sloping down to the east, with scrub, woodland, open grassland, and warm rocky areas. Most of the site is common land.

Although not of exceptional importance for birds, there is plenty to see, mainly in spring and summer. Breeding birds in the woods include black, great spotted, and lesser spotted woodpeckers, turtle doves, wood and Bonelli's warblers

Pale clouded yellow *Colias hyale*

(a good opportunity to compare the short rattle of Bonelli's with the longer, descending shivering song of wood warbler), and firecrests. In scrub and more open areas, there are nightjars, cirl buntings, yellowhammers, and occasional red-backed shrikes, while peregrines and hobbies pass overhead from time to time.

It is a splendid place for flowers, with rather similar species to the Plateau de Langres (p. 94) in general. Some specific plants here include pale St. John's-wort, yellow woundwort, bloody crane's-bill, *Tanacetum corymbosum*, perfoliate pennycress, St. Lucie's cherry, narrow-leaved red valerian, downy and alpine woundworts, wolfsbane, field eryngo, spiked star-of-Bethlehem, cut-leaved selfheal, mountain clover, St. Bernard's lily, *Coronilla minima*, horseshoe vetch, Cheddar pink, dyer's greenweed, swallow-wort, and wild roses such as *Rosa squarrosa*. Not surprisingly, it is also rich in butterflies and other insects, with Adonis blues, skippers, pale clouded yellows, Duke of Burgundy, fritillaries and the occasional Camberwell beauty. Woodcrickets purr mellifluously from the woodland edges, and glow-worms produce their eerie green light on warm, early summer evenings.

Access is easy. The D31 westwards from Gevrey Chambertin passes through the valley, which has parking places and paths along its length. Entry is unrestricted. The whole area to the west of here is of interest, though fragmented by agricultural activities, for many similar species, plus a few short-toed eagles and hen harriers, woodlark, and a small population of Orphean warbler, with Tengmalm's owls and grey-headed woodpeckers in the woods.

45 Compiègne Forest

SITE

One of the largest single forests in France, with a marvellous diversity of birds and other wildlife.

Compiègne Forest, just east of the town of the same name, and only some 70 km from Paris, covers 14 500 ha – a huge area – and lies adjacent to another large forest, the Forêt de Laigue, just across the river Aisne to the north-east. So, although it is well visited and used, it absorbs the pressures quite easily and quiet places are not difficult to find. It is essentially an oak and beech forest, with some hornbeam, and patches of pine and other conifers. It is intensively managed but allows for ample wildlife, though as usual in managed forests there is an absence of very old trees.

It is a well-known bird-watching site, with several species that are rare in this area as well as a good range of the more common woodland birds. Honey buzzards are positively common (though usually hard to spot) with perhaps 15–20 pairs breeding in the woods, as well as common buzzards and sparrowhawks. Woodpeckers abound, with perhaps 50 pairs each of black and middle spotted as well as the more common species, and a few grey-headed. Wrynecks, generally rare in the region, breed here, with common redstarts, pied flycatcher, Bonelli's warblers (close to the northern edge of their range), crossbills, both common and short-toed treecreepers, firecrests and goldcrests, crested tits, and hawfinches. Woodcock nest deep in the woods, and there are nightjars and stonechats in clearings, with grasshopper and melodious warblers and kingfishers in the wetter parts. In autumn and winter, it provides good feeding for flocks of red-

wings, fieldfares, bramblings and siskins, though they are not always easy to find. Botanically it is not exceptional, though there is a reasonable range of woodland flowers including wood anemones, lily-of-the-valley, wood spurge, spurge laurel, wood sanicle, bastard balm, and others, and butterflies such as purple emperor, white admiral, purple hairstreak, large tortoiseshell, and most northern woodland species.

The forest, which comes right to the edge of Compiègne, has numerous roads and tracks throughout, with free access. The Forêt de Laigue stretches north-eastwards from Choisy-au-Bac.

Just south-east of here, south of Villers-Cotterêts, lies the Forêt de Retz, another important and interesting site, with good forest birds.

Pied flycatcher *Ficedula hypoleuca* **(Peter Wilson)**

Vosges and Jura

Introduction

The Vosges and the Jura form the northern part of the great barrier of mountains that runs down the whole of the eastern side of France from the German border to the Mediterranean Sea. Although the two ranges are roughly similar in height, with the Jura being rather higher on average, they are very different in character. The Vosges mountains are made up of ancient crystalline and volcanic rocks, which are hard and acid and have generally weathered to a rounded range of hills, reaching 1424 m at the highest point. The rock is largely impervious, so there are many surface streams, lakes, and boggy areas. The soil is poor, so there has been relatively little clearance of forest for pastures or arable land, and hence the Vosges have remained heavily wooded, with open moorland and grassland only at the upper altitudinal limits. Thus their main interest is for species of forest and bog, and it is a particularly good region for forest birds such as capercaillie, hazel grouse, Tengmalm's owls, and woodpeckers. Botanically it is rather poor, thanks to the acid soils, and there is not a huge diversity of species, though there are a few endemics and a few acid-loving mountain species. Biogeographically, however, the Vosges are of particular interest in that their height, northern position, and cool climate make them the southern or south-western outpost for many northern or north-eastern species, such as the northern bat, bog arum, least water-lily, and the white-faced darter and *Aeshna subarctica* dragonflies. Around the lower fringes of the Vosges, there is an outcrop of limestone that provides a complete contrast, with very different soils, topography, and even climate, so it has a quite dissimilar range of species. The adjacent Rhine Valley corridor is different again, making the Vosges a superb place for an extended stay.

The Jura mountains begin almost immediately to the south of the Vosges, then stretch away south-westwards to well beyond Geneva, eventually merging into the complex of pre-alpine mountains such as the Chartreuse, and the Alps themselves. The Jura extend into Switzerland, where they are very similar in character, while the underlying rocks continue into Germany to form part of the Black Forest and Schwabian Alps regions. The Jura are composed almost exclusively of a medium-hard limestone named after the area – Jurassic limestone – which gives rise to a rather different scenery and vegetation from that of the Vosges, and they also extend much further south, which gives them an altogether warmer feeling. Like the Vosges, they are well forested, but lack the bogs, lakes, and streams, except in a few broad valleys such as the Drugeon, where silt has collected and peat has built up over it. At the highest levels, the *chaumes* moorlands of the Vosges are replaced by flowery, limestone grasslands and scrub, with cliffs and frost-shattered outcrops in places. The Jura reach higher than the Vosges, to 1718 m at their highest point, so there are greater expanses of high-altitude habitats, and the proximity to the Alps means that quite a number of alpine species occur here. On the higher sites there is an extraordinary variety of species, ranging from warmth-demanding southern species on the sunny lower slopes, through a selection of central and north European species, to genuine alpine species.

Opposite page: **Drugeon Valley – Lake**

Vosges and Jura

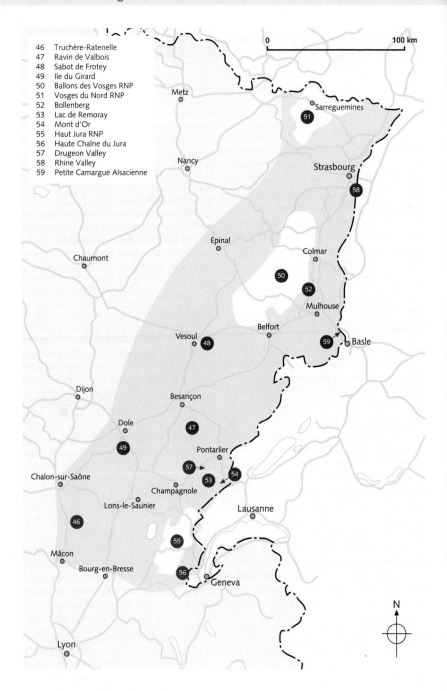

46 Truchère-Ratenelle
47 Ravin de Valbois
48 Sabot de Frotey
49 Ile du Girard
50 Ballons des Vosges RNP
51 Vosges du Nord RNP
52 Bollenberg
53 Lac de Remoray
54 Mont d'Or
55 Haut Jura RNP
56 Haute Chaîne du Jura
57 Drugeon Valley
58 Rhine Valley
59 Petite Camargue Alsacienne

0   100 km

Metz

Sarreguemines
51

Nancy

Strasbourg
58

Epinal

Colmar

Chaumont

50

52

Mulhouse

Vesoul
48

Belfort

59   Basle

Dijon

Besançon

Dole
47

49

Pontarlier

Chalon-sur-Saône

57
53   54

Champagnole

Lons-le-Saunier

Lausanne

46

55

Mâcon

Bourg-en-Bresse

56   Geneva

N

Lyon

The Vosges and the Jura are worth a visit at any time between spring and autumn. The flowers and butterflies continue throughout the summer, thanks to the slightly cooler and wetter climate compared to the low-lands, and in autumn the colours of the trees and shrubs are superb, with plenty of fungi in the woods. It is a friendly and welcoming region, with numerous paths and small roads allowing easy exploration.

SITE 46 Truchère-Ratenelle

Fascinating inland sand dunes, with heaths, woodlands, and lakes in an unspoilt area.

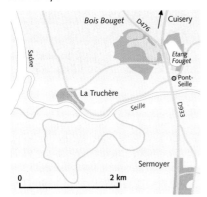

Truchère-Ratenelle Reserve covers about 100 ha of inland sand dunes, heathland, bog, woodland, marsh, and lake. The dunes are a post-glacial relict, at least 10 000 years old, whose instability and infertility has prevented them from being wholly colonized by woodland. The result is an unusual habitat, with many species that you might not expect in the area. There are 300 species of flowers recorded, including the little gratiole *Gratiola officinalis*, water-violet, early sand-grass, least cudweed, shepherd's cress, the plantain *Plantago arenaria*, sheep's-bit, fingered speedwell, and two species of sundew. There are extensive areas of lichen-dominated heath, with abundant *Cladonia* and *Cetraria* species together with

mosses such as *Rhacomitrium canescens* and hair mosses *Polytrichum* species. Near the boggy areas, there is a particu-larly rare moss *Brucha vosegiaca*, in addition to more widespread species such as marsh clubmoss and the sedge *Carex elata*.

It is a good habitat for insects, with the intimate mosaic of different habitats. The scarce emerald damselfly breeds, together with downy emerald dragonfly, four-spotted chaser and other characteristic bog species. The site has about 50 species of butterfly, mainly common or wide-spread species, but including colonies of marsh fritillary and large copper. It also boasts 250 species of moth, with probably many more to be discovered. There are also at least 150 beetle species, from all groups, including several species of tiger

Large copper *Lycaena dispar* (Peter Wilson)

Lichen heath in the Truchère-Ratenelle reserve

beetles, together with wood-crickets, mole crickets, and other crickets and grasshoppers. In the open sandy areas, there are colonies of ant-lions, far from their more usual coastal habitats. The reserve is an entomologist's delight, especially as there are large areas of deciduous woodland around the reserve.

It is not exceptional for birds, though one may see breeding water rail, purple heron, marsh harrier, sedge, grasshopper and other warblers, reed buntings, nightjars, stonechats, and hobby, amongst others. There are also tree frogs, green and sand lizards, and brown hares.

The reserve lies east of the Saône river, about 8 km south-east of Tournus. The D933 and D476 pass through the site, and there is easy direct access on foot via a network of paths.

47 Ravin de Valbois

SITE

A limestone valley cutting back into the Jura plateau, with a rich flora and fauna.

Ravin de Valbois National Nature Reserve is a deep valley on the western side of the Jura, cutting back into the hills, with limestone cliffs all around. The reserve covers 335 ha of mainly deciduous woodland, with dry calcareous grassland, cliffs and scree, and damper more humid habitats along the stream at the base of the ravine.

Honey buzzard (European) *Pernis apivorus*

It is botanically rich, with a nice mixture of mountain and southern species, including several which find their northern limit in France here. The typical species of limestone grassland and woodland occur, such as burnet rose, bloody crane's-bill, lily-of-the valley, rock-roses, great bellflower, and angular Solomon's seal. In addition, though, there are a number of less common species such as hoary rock-rose, mountain kidney vetch, the umbellifer *Athamantha cretensis*, and the rock-rose relative *Fumana procumbens*, which are all at their northern limit in France here; dwarf sedge, the rare moon carrot, alpine daphne, Haller's

pasqueflower, the candytuft *Iberis intermedia* (similar to common candytuft but with narrower, undivided upper leaves), mountain germander, and others. It is also a fascinating place for insects, with a similar blend of southern and upland species: for example, the Apollo butterfly – a steadfast mountain species – occurs, but so do praying mantises, ascalaphids and Faust's burnet moth – all warmth-demanding species. There are hundreds of species of moths, masses of beetles, hymenopterans, and other insects, including one particularly rare ruby-tailed wasp *Chrysis brevitarsis*.

Over 60 bird species breed in the ravine. Peregrines nest here intermittently, with honey buzzards, red kite, ravens, and wood and Bonelli's warblers; wallcreepers often pass the winters here searching the cliffs for invertebrates. There are green and sand lizards, smooth snakes, and the impressive western whip snake, with the delightful little yellow-bellied toad along the stream. The mammals are nothing special, though lynxes are said to pass through occasionally, and bats are abundant.

Access is generally open, and there is a botanical trail. There are entry points from Chassagne St. Denis or up the valley from Castel St. Denis. There is a Maison de Reculées at 25330 Cléron, just west of the reserve.

The nearby Loue Valley is an excellent place to see bats hunting over the water at dusk, masses of calcareous stream invertebrates such as stoneflies and mayflies emerging, or kingfishers and dippers.

48 Sabot de Frotey

Fine limestone grassland with a particularly rich orchid flora.

Just east of the town of Vesoul lies an area of dry limestone grassland and woodland, famous for the presence of a

curious, boot-shaped limestone rock at the western end – the 'sabot' of the reserve's name. This may be the devil's boot left behind while he was fleeing on the return of a jealous husband, or it may be a piece of eroded Jurassic limestone. This National Nature Reserve, covering almost 100 ha, is made up of pine wood (largely planted), scrub, and a sheltered section of dry, short, limestone turf, which is the real gem of the site.

It is especially rich botanically, and well known for its orchid populations, with 20 or more species, often in abundance. There are masses of late spider, fly, woodcock, and bee orchids (including a form of the last-named sometimes known as the Jura bee orchid, though more commonly treated just as a variant of bee orchid), with pyramidal, fragrant, narrow-leaved, white and broad-leaved helleborines, and the rarer narrow-lipped helleborine. Other flowers of interest include white rock-roses, restharrow, carline thistle, horseshoe vetch, and bladder senna. The insects of the site are indicative of its warmth and

sheltered nature: ascalaphids, praying mantises, and cicadas (albeit only the little *Cicadetta montana*), all more characteristic of warm southern grassland and scrub than here, butterflies that include Adonis, little, and chalk-hill blues, plus a wealth of other species. It is also surprisingly good for birds, with over 40 breeding species. Red-backed shrikes, cirl buntings, yellowhammers, nightjars, and woodlarks all occur in open areas with bushes or trees, and in the wooded areas there are marsh tits, crested tits, a few wryneck, hawfinches, nightingales, and possibly grey-headed woodpeckers. Montagu's harriers breed in the area, sometimes within the reserve, and can be seen quartering the open grassland at times.

There is open access on foot along paths leading in from the N19 Vesoul–Belfort road to the south, or from the N57 which runs along the north-west edge of the reserve.

SITE 49 Ile du Girard

A flood-plain reserve where two rivers meet, with a fascinating assemblage of animal life.

Where the Doubs and Loue meet, just south of Dôle, there is a complex of flood-plain habitats consisting of old river channels and banks, woodland, willow scrub, and incipient woodland, ponds, and grassland. The National Nature Reserve covers almost 100 ha of the best of the habitats.

It is particularly good for birds. Over 150 species have been recorded, of which about 70 breed here. Bluethroats nest in scrub and trees along the river channels, kingfishers are common,

Mole cricket *Gryllotalpa gryllotalpa* (Peter Wilson)

Little ringed plover *Charadrius dubius*

Cetti's warblers sing explosively (but usually invisibly!) from the bushes, and hobbies fly overhead in pursuit of martins or dragonflies. Other breeding birds here include red-backed shrikes, little ringed plover, black kite, grey-headed woodpeckers, water rail, great-crested grebe, nightingales, and hawfinches – a diverse but interesting mixture. The reserve also lies on an important migration route, especially in autumn for birds moving southwards, and all sorts of things can turn up: ospreys, occasional rough-legged buzzards, white storks, purple herons, little bittern, cormorants, and black-necked grebes, amongst others. Winter can also bring good numbers of birds, depending on the season, with interesting species such as great white egrets, pintail, wigeon, and shoveler, and masses of feeding thrushes.

The site is also good for mammals, with a reasonable chance of seeing some of them, thanks to the observation hides. Otters are quite frequent, wildcats occur occasionally, and there are roe deer, wild boar, foxes, and beech martens, plus abundant bats revelling in the insects emerging from the river: Daubenton's, Bechstein's, serotines, noctule, and pipistrelle, amongst others. Midwife toads call softly from damp, sandy banks, natterjacks and tree frogs are rather noisier, and there are resident great-crested newts and sand lizards. To round off the vertebrates, there are also 21 species of fish recorded in the reserve.

Invertebrates have been relatively well recorded, and it turns out to be something of an entomological crossroads between southern, northern, and mountain species. Around 70 hymenopterans are known here, a good number of butterflies including map butterfly and at least 15 species of dragonflies or damselflies, with two specialities – the bright blue hawker *Aeshna affinis*, close to the northern edge of its regular range here, and the green and brown hawker *Boyeria irene*, which is at the extreme northern edge of its range.

There is free access to the reserve along the marked paths, with the use of two hides. Entry is via Gevry from the north, where there is an information board, or from Rahon, to the south, to a tower hide looking across the river.

Not far east of the reserve, just east of Dôle, lies the state forest of Chaux, which is well worth a visit. It is an extensive, low-lying and generally level forest on neutral to slightly acid clay, with small streams and a few ponds, dominated by oak and beech, with some hornbeam, ash, hazel, and conifers. It is well managed, with open access, some nature trails, information boards, and an animal park. There are good woodland butterflies such as large tortoiseshell, Camberwell beauties, map, black-veined and wood whites, silver-washed fritillaries, brimstone, white admiral, purple hairstreak, and many more. Mole crickets and a variety of bush-crickets such as Roesel's are abundant. Dragonflies from nearby rivers or lakes – such as southern hawker, broad-bodied chaser, or the yellow and black *Onychogomphus forcipatus* – often hunt along the rides. There is also a good variety of woodland flowers, including herb-Paris, lily-of-the-valley, Solomon's seal, orpine, sanicle, violets, cowslips, and many others.

Entry to the wood is easy. Minor roads encircle it, and there are forest roads into it, with ample parking and numerous paths and tracks.

50 Ballons des Vosges Regional Natural Park

A beautiful, forested mountain range, with a marvellous range of birds, flowers, and other wildlife.

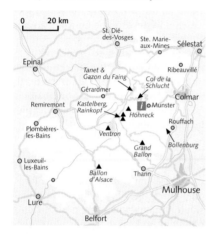

The Vosges mountains rise like a wall from the plains of eastern France, dropping sharply again on the east side to the Rhine Valley. There are two Regional Natural Parks within the Vosges covering the wilder and higher areas: the Vosges du Nord (see p. 110), which lies well to the north, and the Ballons des Vosges, which covers 3000 square kilometres of high land based around a chain of old volcanoes (the 'ballons'). The mountains here rise to 1424 m at the highest point at Grand Ballon – not high compared to the Alps, but higher than any mountain in Britain, and quite high enough to create a cool and wet climate. It is a heavily forested region – the largest natural forest in France – with over 50% of the land covered with woodlands dominated by beech, silver fir, and Norway spruce. Higher up, there are extensive grassy and heathy moorlands – the *chaumes* – often partly tree-covered, as they are not above

the true tree-line. There are fine undisturbed bogs near the summits with some natural lakes on the west side, and spectacular cliffs in a few places, such as at Frankenthal-Missheimle. This last named is one of four important nature reserves along the chain of peaks that collectively cover and protect some of the best habitats in the region. They are described later in this section.

The Vosges are a superb terrain for certain birds, very different in character to the surrounding lowlands. Because they are relatively cool and wet, and the soil is generally acidic, the mountains are not particularly productive, but the vast extents of forest and other wild habitats, and the relatively undisturbed quality of the Vosges, are perfect for certain species. At the highest levels, there are citril finches, alpine accentors, water pipits, rock buntings, and wheatear, with ring ouzels and ravens amongst the craggier parts, and very occasional rock thrushes. Peregrines breed on the cliffs, but other large birds of prey are scarce or absent, due partly to the limited

Wild boar *Sus scrofa*

range of cliffs and the absence of extensive open areas for them to hunt over. In the forests, there are breeding hazel grouse, capercaillie (see below), buzzard and honey buzzard, Tengmalm's and long-eared owls, nutcrackers, common cross-bills, black, grey-headed, and other wood-peckers, firecrests, crested tits, and other more common birds. Capercaillies used to be moderately common and widespread in the wilder forests, but numbers dropped dramatically a few years ago due probably

Tree lungwort *Lobaria pulmonaria*

Lesser twayblade *Listera cordata*

tree lungwort. May-lilies are quite frequent, with other species such as purple lettuce, several large ragwort species, yellow bird's-nest, coral-root and bird's-nest orchids, wintergreens, white butterbur, bitter-cresses, yellow star-of-Bethlehem, spring snowflake, and a full range of clubmosses such as stag's horn and interrupted; the Vosges are one of the easiest places to see clubmosses, as they do especially well here, even along roadsides. In the high pastures or among cliffs, there are a few special flowers – though the Vosges do not have the richness of the southern alpine areas – such as arnica, globe-flowered orchid, lesser twayblade orchid, alpine and other clubmosses, common moonwort (but also the rarer *Botrychium matricariifolium*, which differs in having twice-pinnate fronds; it is near the south-western edge of its European range here), alpine lady fern, a rare hawkweed *Hieracium jachenii*, and *Streptopus amplexifolius*, the attractive relative of the Solomon's seals. In general, the Vosges are also good for fungi, bryophytes, and lichens.

The Vosges are also superb for insects – the vast tracts of forest, the interfaces between woodland, grassland, and wetland, and the bogs all contribute to a wealth of species. Butterflies are not particularly conspicuous, as so many do better on the warm calcareous soils, but there are plenty, including Apollo, the mainly northern cranberry fritillary as well as other fritillaries, moorland clouded yellow, ringlets, and other mainly northern or upland species. The dragonflies are of special interest, with

to increased disturbance and changes in forest management. Some key sections of forest, such as in the Gazon du Faing Reserve, have been designated as sanctuaries and closed to the public, and numbers are beginning to rise again, though obviously this makes it more difficult to get to see the birds. Pygmy owls used to breed in the Vosges but probably no longer do so.

Botanically, the high Vosges areas are interesting rather than outstanding, with the acid soil and the damp, cool climate limiting the range of species, but what does occur is usually here in abundance. These include a good range of bog plants, such as lesser bladderwort, sundews, bog-rosemary, bog bilberry, cranberry, crowberry, Rannoch-rush (so-called because in Britain it is virtually confined to Rannoch Moor), heath spotted and early marsh-orchids, marsh clubmoss, grass-of-Parnassus, marsh gentian, and diverse sedges, with a wealth of bog-moss *Sphagnum* species and abundant lichens, especially *Cladonia* species. In the woods, there are impressive amounts of corticolous (bark-dwelling) lichens including huge colonies of *Parmelia*, *Pseudevernia*, *Evernia*, and *Lobaria* species such as the

Hazel grouse *Bonasa bonasia*

upland or northern species such as downy emerald, alpine emerald, Arctic emerald, white-faced darter and other *Leucorrhinia* species, and the rare hawker *Aeshna subarctica*, right at the extreme south-west of its predominantly Arctic range here. Most other groups of insects are well represented, and there is always something to see – huge musk beetles visiting flowers, stag and longhorn beetles, hoverflies, soldier-flies, day-flying moths, giant lacewings, and caddis-flies, often in abundance. This suits the bats, and there are a dozen or so species here including the northern bat, also at the extreme south-western edge of its range in the Vosges. Other mammals of interest include red and roe deer, pine and beech martens, wild boar, red squirrels, and a small population of reintroduced lynx.

Working north to south, the four reserve areas are as follows. The Tanet-Gazon du Faing Reserve covers 500 ha of high-altitude moorland and grassland, bogs, lakes, and forest and has many of the species already mentioned, plus common butterwort, 24 species of pteridophytes, hairy greenweed, alpine newt, wildcat, and a huge range of invertebrates. There is a special no-access reserve set aside mainly for capercaillie and other shy species. The Frankenthal-Missheimle Reserve covers about 750 ha of spectacular high country between the Col de la Schlucht and the Hohneck (1362 m), with extensive forests and some fine glacial cliffs, visible from the main road over the col. There are also extensive mid-altitude bogs here. It is one of the most species-rich and scenic parts of the Vosges, and the area of interest extends southwards to well south of the Hohneck, outside the reserve. The Tourbière de Machais lies south-west of the high points of Rainkopf (1304 m) and Kastelberg, and comprises about 150 ha of superb bog forming in the basin of an old glacial lake, with forests all around. The site has both mature bog and floating bog ('*Schwingmoor*'), with a central area of open water. It is the best example of an intact bog in the Vosges, and has a fine range of forest, lake, and bog species,

Stag's-horn clubmoss *Lycopodium clavatum*

including least water lily, narrow-leaved marsh-orchid, the sedge *Carex limosa*, and most of the species described above. Immediately south of here, from the Col de Bramont southwards, lies the Massif du Ventron Reserve, covering 1600 ha of lovely wooded land up to 1200 m, with scattered areas of moorland and grassland, drained by clear mountain streams. It is unspectacular, but quiet and full of interest.

Other places of interest within the area include the fine botanic garden on the Col de la Schlucht, open daily in summer. Apart from the collection of mountain plants from around the world, there is also a good collection of local species, and it borders a bog in the Frankenthal-Missheimle Reserve, with boardwalk access to it. There are interesting forests and bogs on the west side of the range, mostly unprotected but rich in species; they are marked on the 1:25 000 IGN maps of the area. On the east side of the range, on the edge of the Rhine Valley, there is a fringe of limestone, mainly cultivated for vines but with a few unspoilt areas including Bollenberg (see p. 111). The HQ for the Regional Natural Park is at: Maison du Parc, 1 Cour de l'Abbaye, 68140 Munster. Tel: 03 89779020. There are also information centres in most of the larger nearby villages.

SITE 51 Vosges du Nord Regional Natural Park

Low, wooded mountains, particularly rich in birds.

Bog arum *Calla palustris*

Vosges du Nord Regional Natural Park covers 1200 square kilometres of the northern Vosges stretching up to the German border (where it adjoins the Pfälzer Wald Natural Park) and southwards to Saverne. It is different from the high Vosges in the

Ballons; no peak is higher than 581 m, and the rock is mainly acid but not volcanic. It is a heavily forested area (mainly beech, oak, pine, fir, and spruce), with lakes, moorland, bogs, and grassland, and a few areas of limestone. It shares many species with the high Vosges, though it lacks the high-altitude species such as alpine accentor, citril finch, and Apollo butterfly.

The park is ornithologically rich, however, with about 85 breeding species, including a few capercaillie, hazel grouse, honey buzzard, peregrine, and Tengmalm's owl, and the usual common crossbills, crested tits, and firecrests. Where there are lakes, such as at the Etang de Hanau north of Bannstein, one can also find great-crested grebes, reed and sedge warblers, icterine warblers, and ducks.

Marsh cinquefoil *Potentilla palustris*

Botanically, it is broadly similar to the high Vosges, lacking some high-altitude and endemic species, but with a few of its own. All the bog species are here – sundews, butterworts, bladderworts, cranberry, bog-rosemary, crowberry, marsh cinquefoil, and others, with the rare and mainly eastern bog arum in places, and narrow-leaved marsh-orchid. There are particularly good bogs in the Schwarzbach Valley north of Niederbronn-les-Bains. Otherwise, Vosges du Nord broadly resembles the lower parts of the Ballon des Vosges, with red and roe deer, red squirrels, good butterflies and other insects, and similar amphibians.

Near Saverne there is a botanic garden that specializes in orchids and local species of interest. There are about 20 native species of orchids, including drifts of some species such as fragrant orchids, and a good range of lady's-slipper orchids *Cypripedium* species from around the world. The garden is on the Col de Saverne on the N4 west of Saverne, open most days between May and mid-September.

SITE
52 **Bollenberg**

Hilly limestone grassland rich in flowers, especially orchids.

Along the eastern edge of the high Vosges mountains, there lies a band of limestone on the edge of the warm and sunny Rhine Valley. Although much of the original vegetation has been replaced by vineyards, farmland, and a golf course, there are still areas of interest, the best of which is the hill called Bollenberg, just south-west of the village of Rouffach. It lies just on the edge of the Ballons des Vosges Regional Natural Park (p. 106), partly outside the boundary, and is so different in character from most of the Vosges that it is treated separately.

The grassland area is particularly rich in orchids, with about 20 species recorded. These include greater and lesser butterfly, military, green-winged, man, burnt (dwarf), lizard, bee, and fly; however, the most impressive feature is the quantity of late spider orchids, in a wide variety of colour forms. Late spider orchid is by no means common in France, and it is rare to find it in this quantity. It is a good place to watch for the pollination process in the *Ophrys* orchids (i.e. spider, bee, fly, etc.), in which the males of certain hymenoptera, such as the little wasp *Argogorytes mystaceus*, are attracted to attempt to mate with the flowers because they look – and even smell – like the females of the species, a process known as

Green-winged orchid *Orchis morio*

pseudocopulation. Male wasps emerge before the females, and the pollination process only takes place before the females emerge. Real females prove more attractive than the flowers, so it is a finely balanced system that can easily fail, but fascinating to observe if you get the chance. There are other limestone flowers here, such as masses of pretty pink crown vetch, horseshoe vetch, pasqueflowers, broomrapes, and others. Butterflies are abundant, and include Adonis, chalk-hill, little and silver-studded blues, Duke of Burgundy, Glanville and dark green fritillaries, and common swallowtails.

Access is via the D18b off the N83 south of Rouffach, then left to climb up the Bollenberg on a minor road.

The Forêt de la Harth, to the north and south of Mulhouse, is a large area of woodland on the flood plain of the Rhine, worth a visit if nearby.

SITE
53 Lac de Remoray

An old glacial lake now partly surrounded by bog and reedbeds, with a rich flora and fauna.

Lac de Remoray National Nature Reserve covers 427 ha of lake, fringing bog and reedbeds, grassland, and woodland, lying at an altitude of about 900 m in the Jura mountains. The remnants of a much larger glacial lake that has gradually filled in, it is now fed by two streams, and has one small outflow. It has matured into a

Fringing bog and woodland by the Lac de Remoray

fine mixture of mid-altitude habitats, surrounded by limestone hills.

Lac de Remoray is a good place for birds, with well over 200 species, of which over half breed here. Water birds include water rail, spotted crake, snipe, and tufted duck, and the highest-altitude heronry in France. In the woodland or other areas away from the lake, there are breeding hazelhen, both black and red kites, Tengmalm's owl, red-backed shrikes, black woodpecker (which are quite common here, and can often be heard in the woods), corncrakes, redpoll, and fieldfare (this was its first known breeding site in France when discovered in 1954).

The flora is a rich mixture of bog, fen, grassland, and woodland species, totalling about 550 in all. Bog plants include sundews, bog-rosemary, cranberry, common butterwort, cotton-grasses, grass-of-Parnassus, sedges such as flea sedge, *Carex hostiana*, and *C. caespitosa*, amongst others, and several bog-mosses including *Sphagnum magellanicum*, while in more lime-rich areas you can find narrow-leaved marsh-orchid,

Jacob's ladder, round-leaved wintergreens, bird's-eye primrose, marsh arrow-grass, snake's-head fritillaries (a rare plant in France), the ragwort *Senecio helenitis*, greater spearwort, and the only population in France of the rare creeping spearwort.

The site has been relatively well studied entomologically, and proved to be very rich – a fact which is immediately obvious if you visit the reserve on a warm day in summer. There are 24 species of dragonflies and damselflies, 15 mayflies including *Baetis nubecularis*, known nowhere else in France, 73 species of hymenopterans, and 55 species of dipterans – just numbers, but they indicate the richness and unpolluted nature of the site. There are dozens of butterflies, including large heath, moorland clouded yellow, and the pretty little violet copper, which feeds mainly on bistort. There are also 78 gastropods.

Access is restricted to footpaths and guided groups. There is a Maison Réserve at 28, Rue de la Gare, 25160, Labergement-Sainte-Marie for information and guided walks.

54 Mont d'Or

One of the highest peaks in the Jura, surrounded by forests with a fine range of birds and flowers.

Mont d'Or is one of the highest peaks in the Jura, reaching to 1463 m. It lies on the Swiss border, and fine forested mountains extend away in all directions. To the west, the slopes are mainly clothed with forests of beech and silver fir, with alpine pastures and scrub at higher levels; eastwards, there is an impressive line of cliffs and scree, with forests below. Its flora and fauna are a blend of alpine, subalpine, and lowland.

It is a particularly good site for birds, and there is a 500 ha no-hunting reserve which gives protection to a number of species. Breeding birds here include both hazelhen and capercaillie (with numbers recently estimated at about 250 and 50 birds, respectively), goshawk, peregrine, sparrowhawk, Tengmalm's and long-eared owls, black woodpecker, woodcock, water pipit, crag martins (at the northern edge of their range), both Bonelli's and wood warblers, crossbills, siskins, citril finches, nutcrackers, ravens, ring ouzels and fieldfares – to mention just a few! There are also small numbers of the distinctive little pygmy owl (see p. 226), though numbers are probably declining.

Martagon lily *Lilium martagon*

It is a very rich area botanically, too. The woodlands contain Martagon lilies,

alpine sow-thistle, bastard balm, bird's-nest and coral-root orchids, narrow-leaved, narrow-lipped, and red and white helleborines, asarabacca, bitter-cresses such as *Cardamine heptaphylla*, herb-Paris, rampions, whorled Solomon's seal, baneberry, and many more. In more open areas, there are monkshood, yellow gentians, globeflowers, alpine pasqueflowers, and perennial cornflower – a lovely mixture, best in June, depending on the snow. It is also a good area for butterflies, including apollos, various ringlets, clouded yellows, and fritillaries.

Access is unrestricted, and the mountain can be reached via the N57 (E23) south from Pontarlier, then the D45 to Longevilles, then south-eastwards to the summit; or from the col on the N57 on the Swiss border.

The Fôret du Risol and Mt. Risoux, south-west from here along the Swiss border, contain many similar species and are quieter. The Dent du Vaulion, just over the border in Switzerland, is also worth a visit.

SITE 55 Haut Jura Regional Natural Park

Marvellous limestone mountains clothed in forest, with an enormously rich flora and fauna.

This Regional Natural Park, covering about 760 square kilometres, encompasses some of the highest parts of the French Jura, along the Swiss border southwards from near Morez as far as Giron. It lies almost exclusively on Jurassic limestone (named after the area), and has a superb landscape of plateaux, valleys, and peaks rising to almost 1700 m, seamed with gorges, and

clothed with forests. The whole area is of special interest, marvellous walking country with the additional benefits of waterfalls, caves, pretty villages, and a good network of paths. Most parts are worth investigating, although perhaps the most unusual sections are the high forested areas on the east of the park, close to the Swiss border. From the Fôret du Risoux and the southern part of Mont

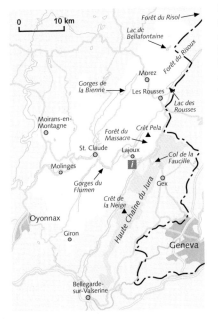

there is superb high-altitude forest with occasional lakes and bogs. It is excellent country for birds, including capercaillie in small numbers, hazel grouse, honey buzzard, Tengmalm's, pygmy, and long-eared owls, black woodpeckers, the rarer three-toed woodpecker at the western edge of its range (easily identified, not so much by its three toes as by the yellow crown and bold white stripe down its back), firecrests, crossbills, and many others. Ring ouzels, usually rather uncommon, are here in considerable abundance. Red and roe deer are reasonably common, with red squirrels, pine marten, polecats and the occasional lynx. Flowers are abundant, with red and narrow-leaved helleborines, martagon lilies, lily-of-the-valley, whorled Solomon's seal, bird's-nest orchids, bastard balm, wintergreens, yellow bird's-nest and many more in the woods; in higher pastures, such as around Crêt Pela, there are aconites, alpine pasqueflowers, spring and yellow gentians, crocuses, mainly *Crocus albiflorus*, snowbells, and the yel-

Risoux (which runs northwards into the Forêt du Risol – see p. 114) southwards to the Forêt du Massacre and the Crêt Pela,

A superb Jura hay meadow, dominated by yellow rattle

Vosges and Jura

Meadow saffron *Colchicum autumnale*

low anemone *Anemone ranunculoides*, amongst others. In limestone scree, there may be masses of dark-red helleborines, with perennial honesty, cresses such as *Cardaminopsis arenosa*, and other interesting flowers.

The grasslands and forest rides are great places for butterflies and other insects, such as Apollo, silver-washed and high brown fritillaries, black-veined moths, the pretty little day-flying moth *Psodos quadrifaria*, which is brown with a large orange patch on all four wings, burnets, longhorn beetles, including the rare and protected *Rosalia alpina* – one of the most striking of beetles, usually associated with higher beech woods – and many more. The upper edges of the forests and the high grasslands are marvellous places from May through to September or later, retaining their interest throughout the summer.

Elsewhere in the park, there are rich hay meadows, with greater yellow rattle, scabiouses and rampions in June, and

meadow saffron in August–September; lovely, clear limestone rivers full of invertebrates and fish, with dippers, grey wagtails, and kingfishers along them; caves; and lakes, such as Lac des Rousses north of Les Rousses, or Lac de Bellafontaine north of Morez, often with fringing reeds and surrounding fen or bog rich in flowers. There are also some fine gorges with their own special plants and animals, such as the Gorges de la Bienne, south-west of Morez, and the Gorges du Flumen, south-east of St. Claude, which contains masses of wild cyclamen in late summer.

The park HQ is at 39310 Lajoux. Tel: 03 84341230.

The Cirque des Baume-les-Messieurs is an impressive site situated outside the north-west park boundary. A beautiful wooded valley leads up to a large double cirque of high cliffs, with tufa springs, limestone grassland rich in orchids and other flowers, masses of butterflies, and flower-rich woods dominated by such southern species as box and downy oak. The cirque is home to breeding peregrine, short-toed eagle, ravens, crag martins, alpine swifts, ortolan and rock buntings, and many other birds. The limestone stream issuing from the valley is wonderfully clean and full of life, with vast numbers of giant stoneflies. Clove pinks and other good flowers grow on the cliffs.

Ring ouzel *Turdus torquatus* (Robert Dickson)

SITE 56 Haute Chaîne du Jura

A superb chain of limestone peaks reaching to over 1700 m, with marvellous flowers, butterflies, and birds.

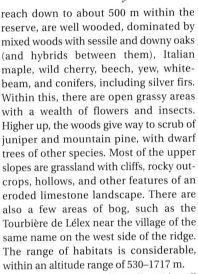

Bog-rosemary
Andromeda polifolia

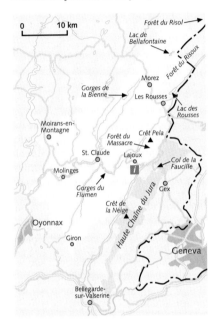

This is a major National Nature Reserve which covers almost 11 000 ha of the highest parts of the Jura. The reserve runs southwards from just north of the Col de la Faucille to Bellegarde-sur-Valserine – a distance of almost 40 km – and includes peaks reaching to over 1700 m at Crêt de la Neige (snow crest). The greater altitude of this ridge takes it into a different category from the rest of the Jura – there is more snow, more erosion, a more shattered landscape, and a greater area of scrub and grassland above the tree-line, which in turn gives a more alpine feel to the flora and fauna. It can be extremely cold up here for all but a few months of the year. The warmer lower slopes, which

reach down to about 500 m within the reserve, are well wooded, dominated by mixed woods with sessile and downy oaks (and hybrids between them), Italian maple, wild cherry, beech, yew, whitebeam, and conifers, including silver firs. Within this, there are open grassy areas with a wealth of flowers and insects. Higher up, the woods give way to scrub of juniper and mountain pine, with dwarf trees of other species. Most of the upper slopes are grassland with cliffs, rocky outcrops, hollows, and other features of an eroded limestone landscape. There are also a few areas of bog, such as the Tourbière de Lélex near the village of the same name on the west side of the ridge. The range of habitats is considerable, within an altitude range of 530–1717 m.

It is a superb site botanically, with well over 600 species of flowering plants, including many rare and protected species. In the lower, wooded areas, the flowers are typical of the southern Jura, with orchids such as red, narrow-leaved, white and broad-leaved helleborines, bird's-nest and coral-root orchids, violet limodore, lily-of-the-valley, Solomon's seals, bastard balm, alpine sow-thistle, purple lettuce, and many others. One may also spot the rare and unpredictable ghost orchid, flowering when it feels like it, always in deep shade. The flora of the higher areas is more unusual, with a more alpine character to it. Around the upper edges of the woods, there are lady's-slipper orchids (as well as lower down,

European Michaelmas daisy *Aster amellus*

here and there), European Michaelmas daisy, Queen of the Alps (an attractive flower, but this is not a very appropriate name for it), yellow stars-of-Bethlehem *Gagea* species, mountain bladder-fern, alpine garlic, pinks such as Cheddar pink and *Dianthus superbus*, fragrant orchids, spring gentian and trumpet gentians, snowbells, mountain alison, mountain valerian, rare grasses such as *Festuca pulchella*, and a wealth of others. There is also the smallest of the moonwort ferns *Botrychium simplex*, rarely more than 10 cm high, with simple or slightly divided fronds – a mainly Arctic species towards the southern edge of its range.

In boggy places, there is the usual range of species such as sundews, bog-rosemary, and cotton-grasses, but also the beautiful, large-flowered butterwort with its large violet flowers.

Butterflies, moths, and other insects are abundant here. There are apollos, of course, but also mountain small white, wood white, orange tip, pale and common clouded yellows, brimstone, hairstreaks, purple-shot and other coppers, long-tailed and green-underside blues, fritillaries such as niobe, dark green, and Weaver's, Piedmont and other ringlets, and many more. Day-flying moths are common, and the flowers are visited by a constant procession of other insects. Sheltered, sunny areas around the edges of the woodland or scrub are particularly good, drawing insects from both habitats. It is also a marvellous place for birds – over 100 species of birds are recorded as breeding within the reserve. These are broadly similar to those

described elsewhere for the higher parts of the Jura, with highlights such as capercaillie, hazel grouse, and black grouse in small numbers, Tengmalm's owl and possibly still pygmy owl, the rare three-toed woodpecker, citril finch, rock thrush, rock bunting, peregrine, and many more in the higher areas. Lower down, there are crossbills, firecrests, crested tits, Bonelli's and wood warblers, small numbers of nutcrackers in the coniferous areas and most of the birds you would expect in this region in woodland. Small herds of chamois graze the high grasslands, moving down into the woods as the weather worsens, and there are both red and roe deer in and around the woods. Wildcats are spotted occasionally, and apparently lynx can be seen now and again, though the chances of meeting one are low!

Access to the reserve on foot is open. There is road access from the Col de la Faucille north-west of Gex, or *telecabines* from several villages around the massif. The reserve HQ is at GERNAJURA, Les Orchidées, Rue Briand-Stresemann, 01710 Thoiry, which is just east of the reserve.

Just south of the reserve, where the Rhône leaves Switzerland and passes through the Défilé de l'Ecluse, there is another site of high ecological interest, though largely unprotected, known as Etournel Marsh. It is particularly well known as an ornithological site: there are breeding wetland birds such as reed, sedge, marsh, grasshopper, and aquatic warblers, reed-bunting, and various ducks. At migration periods, it acts as something of a funnel, especially in autumn, and the gorge itself makes an excellent viewpoint. Storks, cranes, birds of prey such as eagles and harriers, and a multitude of smaller birds pass through between August and October, with smaller numbers in spring. Wallcreepers pass all or part of the winter on the cliffs here. The marsh is also rich botanically, with a number of fen and marsh plants, such as narrow-leaved marsh-orchid. The N208 crosses the river, and there is access along the south side; the gorge can be reached from the D908a on the south side or the N206 on the north side.

Drugeon Valley

SITE
57

A lovely damp valley surrounded by woods, with an enormously varied flora and fauna.

The Drugeon River rises in the Jura, then flows for 36 km westwards and northwards to join the larger Doubs at Pontarlier. Although its whole length is of interest, there is a particularly good stretch in the area between Frasne, Bonnevaux, and Bouverans, where the river begins to slow down on the flatter alluvial plain. This area has been the subject of an especially interesting project; not so long ago, all the wetland habitats were being exploited by activities such as gravel extraction, drainage, canalization of the river, ploughing, and over-hunting, and were steadily declining in size and value. In about 1990, spurred by the threat of further large-scale gravel extraction, the inhabitants of the local communes grouped together in a determined effort to reverse the decline and improve the ecology of the area. With EU and local funding, there have been dramatic changes, including the establishment of a large locally run nature reserve. It would be wrong to say that everything is now perfect, but it is an excellent example of how a major site can be saved and protected with local agreement. The main habitats of note, extending over several thousand hectares, are peat bogs, open water, hay meadows, grazing marshes, fens and old woodland – a marvellous combination, in which each habitat draws part of its value from the others.

It is very rich, botanically. In the bogs, especially those north of Bonnevaux, there are sundews, cranberry, Rannochrush, bog bilberry, crowberry, cowberry, lesser bladderwort, and introduced pitcher plants, amongst others. In fens and damp grassland areas there is a wealth of thistles such as meadow, alpine, brook, and *Carduus personata*, with the large, white-flowered buttercup *Ranunculus*

Marsh saxifrage
Saxifraga hirculus

aconitifolius, bay willow, orchids such as early marsh, narrow-leaved marsh, and frog, butterwort, bird's-eye primrose, marsh valerian, Jacob's ladder, and the rare marsh saxifrage, which flowers very well here. There are nice patches of dry calcareous grazed grassland with scattered juniper bushes, and trumpet gentians, fragrant, small white, and butterfly orchids, and many other flowers. The woods around and within the site also have an abundance of flowers such as bird's-nest orchids, narrow-leaved helleborines, several species of wintergreens, may-lilies, lily-of-the-valley, whorled Solomon's seal, herb-Paris, coral-root bittercress, and many more. In the open water areas, there are white and yellow water-lilies, sedges, yellow iris, and other aquatic plants.

It is also an excellent place to see a variety of birds: about 220 species have been recorded so far. In the woods, there are hazel grouse, honey buzzards, black kites, black and other woodpeckers, firecrests, crossbills, crested tits, and other species of mid-altitude mixed woodlands. Corncrakes can still be found in the hay meadows (though extremely rare), and spotted crakes in wetter places. The Etang de Frasne – Frasne Lake – on the west side of the area is particularly good for birds. Breeding species include great-crested grebes, mute swans, teal, garganey, shoveler, and marsh warblers on or close to the lake, with lapwings, snipe and woodcock in nearby pastures, and fieldfares not far away. At spring passage periods, there are large numbers of waders (depending on water levels), ducks such as pochard and red-crested pochard, raptors such as osprey, harriers, hobby, black and red kites and even red-footed falcons, and smaller birds such as wagtails, swallows and martins. It provides a useful feeding and roosting station on their journey northwards. In autumn, there are similar species, though black storks are an additional possibility.

Other features of interest in the area include 40 or so species of dragonflies and damselflies, abundant butterflies, includ-

ing large heath and moorland clouded yellow, and nine species of amphibians. It is a splendidly varied and unspoilt landscape.

The D471 south-west from Pontarlier skirts the site; from Frasne, the D46 passes the lake and goes through some good habitat on the way to Bonnevaux; or one can take a minor road that goes south from Frasne to Bonnevaux, passing through fen areas and by the entrance to the bog along a boardwalk. East and south of Bonnevaux, there are some fine woodlands.

58 Rhine Valley

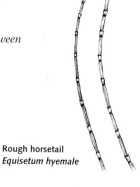

A series of flood-plain reserves along the Rhine Valley between Lauterburg and Rhinau, with Strasbourg at the centre.

The broad Rhine Valley, with its multitude of old channels, canals, and subsidiary rivers, is a long wetland complex of considerable importance. Many sections

Rough horsetail
Equisetum hyemale

have been drained, altered, and built on, but much remains and there is a series of five reserves between Lauterburg – almost on the German border – and Rhinau to the south of Strasbourg, totalling about 1000 ha. The main habitats are riverine forests, reedbeds, drier forests, open water, grasslands, and sandbanks. Typical trees include elms, white and grey poplar, willows, ash, and oak. It is a superb terrain for birds, both as a migration corridor and for nesting species. At least 70 species breed here, including kingfishers, icterine warbler, black and middle spotted woodpeckers, black kite, goshawk, honey buzzard, hawfinch, water rail, and little ringed plover. The range of plants is surprising, with many widespread woodland and

Sand lizard *Lacerta agilis*

waterside species, and less common plants such as fen violet, the uncommon rough horsetail *Equisetum hyemale*, half a dozen species of pondweed *Potamogeton*, whorled water-milfoil, river water-dropwort, flowering rush, bladderworts, and the willow *Salix daphnoides*, amongst others. There is also a fine range of fungi, mosses and liverworts, and lichens.

Other features of interest include 30 or so dragonflies and damselflies, such as golden-ringed, scarce chaser, and red-eyed and white-legged damselflies; the site also boasts a good range of amphibians, including yellow-bellied toad, tree frog, agile frog, and great crested newt, with sand lizards and grass snakes. Amongst the 30 or so mammals the bats are of special interest, and include Daubenton's, noctule, and grey and brown long-eared bats; the valley is also home to polecats, martens, wild boar, roe deer, and common dormice.

The sites are the Sauer Delta near Seltz, Offendorf Forest, a reserve in Strasbourg, Erstein Forest just east of Erstein, and Ile de Rhinau, just south of Rhinau. Access is generally limited to marked paths and by guided groups. Management is carried out by the Conservatoire des sites Alsaciens, Ecomusée de Haute-Alsace, 68190, Ungersheim.

SITE 59 Petite Camargue Alsacienne

Flood-plain wetlands teeming with birds, amphibians, and other wildlife.

The name 'Petite Camargue' gives the impression, perhaps, of a superb piece of wetland, comparable to the Camargue itself, but smaller. This is not the case: the Petite Camargue covers just 120 ha, and it is about as far from the coast as anywhere in France can be. That said, it is nevertheless a surprising site, with a remarkable diversity of species. It comprises a mixture of Rhine Valley flood-plain habitats, including old courses of the river, alluvial forests, and damp grasslands, similar to the Rhine Valley reserves but treated separately as it is much further south, managed by a different organization, and more accessible.

Common frog *Rana temporaria* (Peter Wilson)

This is a superb ornithological location. This stretch of the Rhine Valley is classed as important for birds on the basis of its large wintering populations of waterbirds (including tufted duck, pochard, mallard, coot, black-headed gulls, and a few ferruginous ducks), and the reserve plays a part in this. It is probably more interesting, though, in the breeding season, with a wide range of species to be seen. There are nesting black kite and sparrowhawks, six species of woodpeckers, including black, grey-headed, and middle spotted, as well as a few wrynecks. Kingfishers are common; there are penduline tits nesting in the old willows and poplars, and nightingales in marvellous abundance; and several warblers are found here, including reed, Savi's, and grasshopper. The last two of these have similar songs but can be distinguished (with practice) – the grasshopper warbler does sound like a cricket, but it goes on for hours, while Savi's song is lower in tone and faster, almost like a buzzing sound. Little bitterns and water rails also breed around the ponds, and there are red-backed shrikes here and there. White storks – the symbol of the Alsace area – and even occasional black storks, can be seen on or around the reserve, though neither breed here at present.

This is also a surprisingly good place for mammals, given its small size and fragmented nature. Thirty different mammals

Nightingale *Luscinia megarhynchos*

have been recorded, including wild boar, badger, and roe deer – all widespread species in France – but also polecats, common dormice, and the tiny harvest mouse, nesting in reed canary-grass and old meadows. Bats are frequent, including Daubenton's, noctule, and common pipistrelle. There are also 16 species of

Petite Camargue Alsacienne

amphibian here – just about all the species that occur in the region! There are tree frogs in the reedbeds (we often think of tree frogs as mainly coastal and southern, though actually they occur throughout France and as far north as southern Scandinavia), yellow-bellied and common toads, natterjacks, crested, alpine and smooth newts, common, agile, and pool frogs (see below), together with five species of reptile. This part of France is surprisingly warm in summer, and conditions suit a wide range of insects. About 40 species of dragonflies and damselflies occur here – as many as are resident in the whole of the UK! – including red-eyed, variable and emerald damselflies, demoiselles, common, brown, and southern hawkers, emperor, hairy hawker, scarce chaser, and several darters. Remarkably, 35 species of orthopterans (grasshoppers and crickets) have also been recorded, including large speckled bush-cricket, large sword-tailed bush-cricket, three coneheads, great green and Roesel's bush-crickets, wood cricket, mole cricket, ground-hoppers, and an abundance of grasshoppers. There are also 12 species of fish recorded from the reserve.

There is plenty for the botanist, and a botanical footpath has been set up to show some of the more interesting species. Amongst the hundreds of species recorded, some plants of special interest include the beautiful blue Siberian iris (more commonly seen in upland marshes), common and large meadow-rue, grass-of-Parnassus, marsh helleborine, parsley water dropwort, and the rare marsh gladiolus in grasslands and fens, with white water-lilies and bladderworts in the water. There are a few stretches of old, slightly calcareous, sandy river deposits, now dry grassland, which

support a rich flora, including orchids such as military, pyramidal, bee, late and early spider, and European Michaelmas daisy. It is a rich and varied area.

There is access on foot from parking at St. Louis, or along the canal south from Rosenau to another parking area. There is a Maison de la Réserve at CINA, Rue de la Pisciculture, 68300, St. Louis, open weekends and holidays.

Although they are just over the border in Switzerland, the two botanic gardens in Basle – which is just a few kilometres away – are both worth a visit and have collections of species of local interest. They are: the Botanic Garden at Brülingen, and the Basle University Botanic Garden at Schönbeinstrasse 6.

Frogs

Common frog and agile frog are very closely related species of brown frogs that can occur in similar habitats, and which need to be looked at closely to identify them. Common frogs are more familiar to most people, and are usually larger, more robust, and relatively shorter-legged than agile frogs. Agile frogs tend to have a more pointed snout (though you need to be able to compare adults, not immatures), and their colouring is more delicate, without bold markings. If you catch them, it is possible to see that the two longitudinal folds that run the length of the underside come closer together at one point in the common frog, but remain parallel in agile frog.

Aquitaine basin

Introduction

This relatively small region of south-west France is dominated by the area known as Les Landes – a huge, flat triangle with sides of about 200 km, where sand has blown inland over the millennia since the last ice age (and before). Once it was a huge region of shifting dunes, marshes, and lakes, spreading inland from the Atlantic shore, with hardly any settlements, and endemic malaria and other fevers. From the late eighteenth century onwards, plans were made – and ultimately realized in the nineteenth century – to drain Aquitaine and plant massive tracts of pine, now classed as the largest artificial forest in Europe. The loss of biological diversity was probably huge, though elements of the old landscape and wildlife remain in a landscape that is now almost entirely artificial. In the north, our area includes the rolling Cognac region and the edge of Dordogne country, and southwards it extends to the foothills of the Basque Pyrenees. Virtually all the key sites are within the coastal belt, where there is a line of natural lakes and associated habitats cut off from the sea by quite recent strings of dunes. The combination of unspoilt dunes, forest, natural lakes, and associated wetland habitats is superb for a range of natural history features, with a mixture of southern and northern species, plus a few local endemics. The climate here is warm and generally frost free, but strongly influenced by the Atlantic Ocean; so it allows a wide range of species to flourish, including those that need warm winters as well as those that require the summers not to be too hot and dry. Mediterranean species such as sea medick, *Daphne gnidium*, the cam-

pion *Silene laeta*, cistuses, Perez's frog, stripeless tree frog, ocellated lizard, and Kuhl's pipistrelle all occur here, alongside northern species such as eider duck at the southernmost part of its range. There are special species confined to this region, too, such as the milk vetch *Astragalus bayonensis*, the angelica *Angelica heterocarpa*, and the toadflax *Linaria thymifolia*. As with many warm, mild areas, there are large numbers of naturalized species; some are inconspicuous, but others threaten to engulf the native flora and fauna, such as the large, shrubby composite *Baccharis halimifolia* on saltmarshes and the edges of coastal creeks, and the yellow *Ludwigia uruguayensis* and related species that are taking over wetlands and canals. South American coypus and muskrats have become abundant in some of the wetlands.

The marine and intertidal life is very rich here, thanks to the cool clean Atlantic waters. Although there are virtually no rocky coasts, the abundance of life in and around the mudflats and sandy beaches is remarkable, and sheltered areas such as the Garonne Estuary and the superb Arcachon Bay provide feeding areas for huge numbers of ducks and waders on passage and through the winter. The offshore waters at Arcachon are noted for their abundance of seahorses – a relatively uncommon feature.

This is a part of France which has probably changed more than any other rural area over the last 100 years. Not so long ago it was largely empty, but the planting of the forests and then the huge boom in tourist demand for sandy beaches has changed the region totally. The coast is dominated by one vast sandy beach, and it is also good for surfing, and these two

Aquitaine basin

factors have contributed to a steady and continuing development of the seaboard. Its saving grace is its vastness and the rel-ative absence of older settlements from which expansion can take place, but even the more remote areas are changing fast.

60   Etang Noir
61   Etang de Cousseau
62   Marais de Bruges
63   Banc d'Arguin
64   Courant d'Huchet
65   Marais d'Orx
66   Bassin d'Arcachon
67   Landes de Gascogne RNP

0   100 km

N

La Rochelle
Rochefort
Ruffec
Saintes
Royan
Angoulême
Périgueux
61
Lacanau-Océan
62
Bordeaux
Bergerac
66
63 Arcachon
Langon
Marmande
67
Agen
64 Castets
Mont-de-Marsan
60 Dax
Auch
Biarritz 65
Pau
Tarbes

SITE 60 **Etang Noir**

An attractive natural lake surrounded by forest and bog, with a particularly rich flora.

Etang Noir – or Black Lake – lies in the far south-west part of the sandy Les Landes region. The reserve covers about 60 ha, of which roughly half is made up of a large shallow lake, surrounded by wet carr woodland, bog, wet heath, and reeds, with some open grassland. It is a noted botanical site, with over 400 species of higher plants recorded, and a good range of lower plants. Apart from widespread wetland plants such as greater skullcap, purple and yellow loosestrife, white and yellow water-lilies, bell heather, cross-leaved heath and yellow iris, which make superb displays at times, there are also some less common species: water-chestnut, with white flowers and curious spiky fruits, grows in the lake, and the undistinguished but uncommon Hampshire-purslane (so-called because in Britain it is virtually confined to the New Forest in Hampshire) is found around the lake margins. In wet grassland, there are loose-flowered orchids, saw sedge and several true sedges, with sundews, bog asphodel, cotton-grass, bog-myrtle, and white-beaked sedge in the boggy areas. Royal fern, marsh fern, tussock sedge, and other species are abundant in the wet woodland, and there is a fine range of mosses, liverworts, and lichens. The information centre (see below) displays

Great-crested grebe *Podiceps cristatus* (Peter Wilson)

labelled examples of interesting plants from the reserve at times.

The birds are rather disappointing, partly because both hunting and fishing are still allowed, with too much disturbance (the site is best avoided in winter – it is too depressing to see a nature reserve treated like this!). There are breeding great-crested grebes, water rail, night herons, teal, shoveler, and warblers, but no significant winter gatherings of birds. Marbled newts breed in the lake, and there are edible frogs (including some unusual varieties probably caused by viral infections) and pond terrapins. Dragonflies are not exceptional, but include species such as the downy emerald, emperor, and four-spotted chaser. The fish population is largely introduced, and there are really too many for the aquatic ecosystem to function satisfactorily.

The reserve HQ and information centre are on the edge of Seignosse, at Pavillon de la Réserve, Route du Penon, Bourg 40510. From here there is access on foot, with boardwalks and marked paths, and guided tours can be arranged. It is open from spring until autumn.

Not far away to the south-west, on the coast, Hossegor Lake is an interesting natural lake held back by the dunes but

Hampshire-purslane *Ludwigia palustris*

Fen carr around the Ètang Noir

connected to the sea, so it varies from saline, through brackish, to freshwater. Large portions of saltmarsh and mudflats are exposed daily at low tide, providing extensive feeding areas for waders and other birds. At migration periods, there is a good range of species, particularly waders such as curlew, both godwits, avocets, black-winged stilt, stints, grey and golden plovers, common and wood sandpipers, spoonbills, and others, with terns and gulls. In winter, there can be large numbers of gulls including common,

little, Mediterranean, great and lesser black-backed, and even a few ring-billed gulls (a mainly North American species). Offshore, there may be gannets, shearwaters, petrels, kittiwakes, eiders, great northern and red-throated divers, razorbills, and other birds.

The outflow channel of the lake runs southwards towards Cap Breton, then westwards to the sea. There are good views from the bridge across it at the southern end, and from the sea wall running seawards on its north side.

SITE 61 Etang de Cousseau

A reserve that is a microcosm of the best of the Landes area, with a rich flora and fauna.

The 600 ha Etang de Cousseau Reserve comprises a medium-sized shallow lake, wooded sand dunes, open sandy areas,

marshes, and dune slacks. Part of the forest consists of managed maritime pine stands, but there are also tracts of more

Genet *Genetta genetta*

natural forest with holm oak, common oak, and cork oak and an understorey that includes strawberry-trees, tree heather, broom, and gorse. East of the lake, in the quietest part of the reserve, lies the huge Talaris Marsh, which reaches westwards as far as the channel joining two larger lakes north and south of here. It is one of the very best areas to sample the habitat mix of Les Landes (see p. 125) which elsewhere is often disturbed or over-managed, and it has a pleasantly natural atmosphere.

It is a superb area for birds, and the whole reserve has been designated as a Special Protection Area in recognition of this. There are about 70 breeding species here, including birds of prey such as black kite, honey buzzard, short-toed eagle, marsh harrier, and sparrowhawks; other breeding birds include water rail, Dartford warbler, tree-pipit, nightjar, stonechat, woodlark, and reed warbler. Tawny pipits breed in the general area in small numbers. At migration times, large numbers of common cranes pass through, and some may winter here. Other passage visitors include ospreys, greylag goose, and small numbers of waders, and in winter there can be hundreds, sometimes thousands, of teal, mallard, and other ducks, and small flocks of thrushes such as redwings.

One may see tree frogs and stripeless tree frogs (see p. 160), along with agile frogs, natterjacks, European terrapins, green and sand lizards, and several species of snakes. Otters live here in small numbers, there are both red and roe deer in the woods and marshland edges, and a few genets (see p. 25), red squirrels and polecats, amongst other mammals.

It is less important botanically, though there is plenty of interest. Wetland plants include several species of the insectivorous bladderworts, white and yellow water-lilies (which colour large parts of the lake in early summer), round-leaved and oblong-leaved sundews, the little, grass-like fern pillwort, and Hampshire-purslane. There is also an uncommon and little-known aquatic insectivorous plant here – *Aldrovanda vesiculosa* – which has a floating, rootless rosette of leaves, each hinged to allow them to close over any unwary insect. In seasonally flooded parts that become drier in summer, there are some interesting plants such as the little white umbellifer *Thorella verticillatinundata* (which is little known, rare, and confined to this part of France and a small

Aldrovanda vesiculosa

Pine woods in the Etang de Cousseau reserve

area of Portugal), and coral-necklace. Growing in drier places are pretty white-flowered bushes of the cistus relative *Halimium umbellatum*, several species of cudweed, and relict dune flowers such as *Helichrysum* species.

North of the reserve is Lac d'Hourtin-Carcans, and to the south, Lac de Lacanau. Both are too disturbed to be great sites but they are worth a look, and

their presence contributes to the value of Cousseau. To the east of the reserve, the marshland, then forest, continues for some distance, while to the west there are extensive and partly unspoilt flowery dunes along the coast to the north and south of Lacanau-Océan.

Pointe de Grave, at the northern tip of the Médoc Peninsula on the outer edge of the Gironde Estuary, is worth a visit. It has saltmarshes, mudflats, and other coastal or estuarine habitats, and is a well-known spot for watching migration northwards in spring; unfortunately it is also well known to hunters. There are regular mass movements of white storks, honey buzzards, black kites, turtle doves, and many passerines here.

SITE 62 Marais de Bruges

Marsh and open water on the edge of Bordeaux, particularly rich in birds.

Marais de Bruges Reserve covers 262 ha of open water, reedbeds, woodland, and marshland with varying degrees of inundation. Although lying only 6 km from the centre of Bordeaux, and hemmed in by roads and railways, it is large enough to survive and flourish, supporting a marvellous array of wildlife. The reserve is a Special Protection Area for birds, under EU legislation, a designation that is well deserved: almost 200 species have been recorded, of which about 60 breed. There are a few white storks, a heronry (grey herons), and a few purple herons, marsh harriers, black kites, surprisingly large numbers of red-backed shrikes and a few woodchat shrikes, and kingfishers, amongst others. Penduline tits breed in small numbers, wrynecks can be heard calling, and there are a few red-necked grebes. Masses of birds pass through and stop for a while on migration, including waders of all sorts, common cranes, ospreys, black stork, little bittern, peregrine, and masses of passerines. In winter there can be considerable numbers of ducks, snipe, cormorants, little egrets, marsh harriers, and much else of interest.

In addition to the birds, there are 18 species of fish including eels, six species of amphibians including marbled newts, Perez's frog (= Iberian waterfrog) and tree frogs, and reptiles such as western whip snake and European pond terrapin. It is also quite an interesting location for its flowers, with around 300 species of higher plants including flowering rush, frogbit, water-violet, the local endemic angelica *Angelica heterocarpa*, which grows mainly on muddy river banks, narrow-leaved bird's-foot trefoil, and many others. There are European mink, genets, polecats, and introduced coypus.

The reserve lies just north of the motorway ring-road; take junction 6, then travel north on the D210 to the reserve entrance. There is a reserve centre at Le Baron, 33520, Bruges, and entry to the reserve is free on the marked paths. The reserve itself is a fragment of the much larger 'Marais de Bordeaux' along the Garonne, and there are many areas that still retain some wetland interest.

Black Kite *Milus migrans*

^{SITE}
63 Banc d'Arguin

A cluster of offshore sandbanks and adjacent dunes, with large colonies of breeding birds.

Banc d'Arguin Nature Reserve is made up of five offshore sandbanks, just south of the Bassin d'Arcachon, which are about 500 m offshore at the closest point. They are home to a large breeding colony of Sandwich terns (usually 4000–5000 pairs), with nesting Kentish plovers, oystercatchers, herring gulls, crested larks, and the southernmost breeding eiders in France (or Europe), albeit rather erratically and only in small numbers. It also acts as an important safe haven and feeding ground for waders and other birds on passage, and large numbers of wintering birds including, for example, tens of thousands of dunlin, and large numbers of curlew, oystercatcher, and sanderling. The banks

are a Special Protection Area for birds, thanks mainly to the terns. Bottle-nosed dolphin are regularly seen in the vicinity, and at times become almost resident here. Many notable birds such as gannets and shearwaters pass by offshore at migration periods, or spend the winter fishing around the banks. There is a reasonable dune flora here, but access limitations make it easier to study it on the nearby shore dunes (see below). Access to the reserve is now limited, because of the enormous damage done to the birds by uncontrolled visiting until a few years ago. Boats can be taken from Arcachon or Cap Ferret, and there is limited access outside designated zones where the birds breed.

Mixed saltmarsh in the Prés-Salés and Lège reserve (see p. 138)

The adjacent coast has some of the highest dunes in Europe, including the famous Dune du Pilat, which reaches 103 m. There is a good varied dune flora here which includes sea bindweed, sea-holly, sea stock, sand bedstraw, the toadflax *Linaria thymifolia*, spotted rock-rose, wild asparagus, restharrow, a variety of clovers such as sea clover and rough clover, and many more. Parts of the dunes are well-wooded with similar flowers, and also crested tits and red squirrels. There is easy access off the minor road running south from Pyla-sur-Mer. It is a very busy area in high summer.

64 Courant d'Huchet

A fine combination of natural lake, forest, dunes, and sea with a range of wildlife.

As the ice retreated after the last ice age and the sea level rose, a new line of sand dunes was formed down this sandy south-west coast of France, cutting off former coastal lagoons and altering the courses of rivers. A glance at a map of the region shows that the same has happened all down the coast from Médoc to Biarritz, with almost all the lakes lying a few kilometres inland. Here, the Etang de Léon lies inland, and as its exit river is blocked by the dunes, it turns southwards and runs between two dune areas before issuing into the Atlantic. The reserve covers over 600 ha of mixed coastal habitats – part of the lake and associated marsh, bog, and reedbeds, pine woodland on the dunes, river valley woodland dominated by alders, a fine range of dune habitats from bare to quite stable, and the river itself. It has a rich flora and fauna, and is designated as a Special Protection Area for birds.

Botanically it is very rich, with a broad spectrum of typical *landaise* plants, and a few special ones. On the dunes, one can find sea bindweed, sea stock, sea-holly, sand bedstraw, immortelle, clumps of *Daphne gnidium*, the little endemic toadflax *Linaria thymifolia*, the semi-parasitic *Osyris alba*, the blue-flowered Bayonne milkvetch, dune hawkweed *Hieracium eriophorum* (unusually distinctive in this genus by being covered with long, white woolly hairs), and many more dune flowers. In shady, damp areas, there are clumps of royal fern, with other commoner ferns in abundance, and marsh-marigolds. The marshy and boggy areas, and adjacent open water, on the western edge of the lake and in places along the long outflow channel, have bog plants such as round-leaved and oblong-leaved sundews, aquatics such as least bur-reed and water plantain, and marsh plants including mints, yellow iris, and purple loosestrife.

It is an important area for breeding, wintering, and migrating birds. Over 200 species have been recorded here, of which 72 breed. There are about 10 pairs of little bitterns, kingfishers in plenty, honey buzzards and black kites in the woods, abundant nightjars, a few red-backed shrikes in scrub and open woodland, and Dartford warblers on the more open, heathy areas. Usually grey herons, night herons, and a few purple herons are to be seen at the site, though not necessarily breeding here. At passage periods, all sorts of things can turn up depending on the weather and the water levels, though regular visitors include ospreys, black and white storks, common cranes in small numbers, various waders including godwits, stints, redshanks, and sandpipers, and birds of prey including the occasional white-tailed sea eagle. There can be masses of passerines such as swallows and martins, wagtails, and

Astragalus bayonensis

warblers, including the uncommon aquatic warbler. Winter often brings good numbers of little egrets, marsh and hen harriers, ospreys for short periods, lots of kingfishers, and a variety of ducks. Tree frogs, palmate newts, agile frogs, pond terrapins, and grass snakes live in the wetter spots, and on the drier sandy or heathy areas there are green and ocellated lizards, and snakes such as the southern smooth snake. Bats are reasonably abundant, though there are relatively few roosting or breeding sites within the reserve. Other mammals include otters and European mink (which is moderately frequent in the lakes and marshes along this stretch of coast – see p. 25 for differences from the North American mink), polecat, the elusive genet (most often seen as a road casualty), and the usual red and roe deer. There are also dragonflies, butterflies, and other invertebrates to be seen, but nothing exceptional.

Access is generally open, with a good network of paths. Entry points include the extreme southern end where the river joins the sea, where the D328 crosses the river, and on the south side of Lac de Léon. Boats can be hired here for trips around parts of the reserve.

Most of the dunes and dune forests in this area, such as those at Vieux-boucau to the south, are of interest.

Helichrysum stoechas

<small>SITE</small>

65 Marais d'Orx

A rich wetland reserve, teeming with life at almost any time of year.

The Marais d'Orx is one of the conservation success stories of this part of France. Originally there were extensive marshes here, where several small rivers met before flowing westwards through the dune barrier to the Atlantic. They were steadily drained and converted to arable fields, latterly particularly maize, until the 1970s, when efforts to keep the drainage pumps going were relaxed. In 1985, a large area was flooded to provide a reservoir, and the future of the marshes looked poor until 1989 when the World Wide Fund for Nature, in co-operation with the Conservatoire du Littoral, and thanks to a large legacy, bought almost 800 ha of the remaining marsh to run it as a reserve. Since then, it has been managed for wildlife, and is steadily getting better.

It is particularly important for birds, and designated as a Special Protection Area for its wintering and passage bird numbers (which regularly exceed 20 000), though the breeding birds are also of interest. About 240 species of birds have been recorded here, including 36 which breed. Regular nesting birds include night herons (about 10 pairs), little egrets (about 10 pairs), both grey and purple herons (which can be easily seen feeding in the marsh along the roadside), kingfishers, a few black-winged stilts, and Cetti's warblers. Spoonbills have bred in small numbers and are usually about, but they are not very successful at the moment. In the surrounding drier areas, including parts outside the reserve, there are breeding hobby, black kites, nightjars, red-backed shrikes, and other more widespread species, often visiting to feed in the marsh. It is common to see whiskered terns over the marshes, and they may now breed; there is also the occasional black tern.

Passage periods are excellent times to visit the reserve, both in spring or autumn, with a slightly different range of birds in each season. Common cranes stop here and may spend part of the winter, and there are masses of waders such as curlew, bar-tailed and black-tailed godwits, golden plover, sandpipers, avocets, terns such as whiskered, black, little, and common, masses of hirundines, warblers, and other passerines including bluethroats. In winter, there are often thousands of ducks, especially shoveler, wigeon, garganey, teal, and pintail, with greylag geese and sometimes smaller numbers of whitefronts, barnacle, bean, and pink-footed in

Coypu *Myocastor coypus*

late winter for a while on their way north-wards. There are usually good numbers of birds of prey in winter, such as marsh harrier, peregrines, merlin, and occasional spotted eagles, and a variety of herons that have stayed on. There is always something to see, and the provision of hides and trails is gradually being improved.

It is also steadily becoming more important for mammals as the habitat has developed and shooting pressure has declined. At least 26 mammal species have been recorded here, including the European mink, otters, genet, and roe deer, but much the most obvious mammal is the coypu, an introduced species from South America. They are a problem in that they undermine banks and compete with native species, though they are quite appealing and can be readily seen on their nests relatively close to the road. There also muskrats, another introduced species, though they are more nocturnal and less likely to be seen. Bats are abundant, with several species that include Daubenton's, both common and Nathusius' pipistrelles, and Kuhl's pipistrelle towards the northern edge of its range (though it is currently spreading northwards), as well as horseshoes and long-eared bats. Amphibians are abundant and noisy, especially the marsh frogs, with agile frogs, natterjacks, and tree frogs joining in at times, and there are pond terrapins, green lizards, and aesculapian and western whip snakes amongst others.

The striking *Ludwigia uruguayensis* invading the Marais d'Orx

The fish fauna numbers at least 10 species, including eels and carp, with fewer tench and pike. It is also an excellent place to see dragonflies, whose numbers seem to be increasing, including southern and blue hawkers (*Aeshna affinis*), emperor, and lesser emperor, with an abundance of skimmers, darters, and damselflies. Mole-crickets and marsh crickets call incessantly in early summer, and bush-crickets are abundant in the marshy areas.

Botanically, it is interesting rather than exceptional, and not very easy to get to see the plants. The most obvious feature at the moment is the vast extent of the South American water plant *Ludwigia uruguayensis*; it is very pretty, with its large yellow flowers, but extremely invasive and is pushing out the native flora as well as reducing the area of open water, though it does provide quite a good feeding area for birds. It is related to the inconspicuous native Hampshire-purslane that also occurs in this area,

but looks nothing like it. Other flowers of interest here include whorled water-milfoil, yellow and white water-lilies, frogbit, bladderworts, flowering-rush, several pondweed *Potamogeton* species, and a good range of willows.

Access is easy on the minor road eastwards from Labenne on the N10, from where it is signposted. The D71 crosses the reserve on the dam, and passes the reserve centre which lies at the western end of the dam at: Maison du Marais, Domaine du Marais d'Orx, 40530, Labenne.

The whole area southwards from here towards the Adour River is generally unspoilt and rather damp. Along the Adour itself, the marshy area known as the Barthes d'Adour is still of great interest, and there is a small reserve called Reserve des Barthes, just south-east of Quartier neuf, with a hide. There are similar birds here to Orx, though in smaller numbers, and France's first black-shouldered kites bred near here. The whole area is very pleasant and full of interest.

66 Bassin d'Arcachon

A superb, enclosed, sheltered bay, with vast areas of intertidal habitat and several reserves, particularly good for birds.

The Bassin d'Arcachon is a significant feature on the west coast of Gascony, lying just to the south-west of Bordeaux, and extending over about 20 000 ha. The coast is rather built-up, but there are a few undeveloped areas and large expanses of mudflats and saltmarshes exposed at low tide. There are several important reserves in the area which are described below as examples, though there are birds and other things to be seen almost throughout the bay. It is also very close to the Banc d'Arguin Reserve (see p. 132). Parts of the

Spoonbill *Platalea leucorodia*

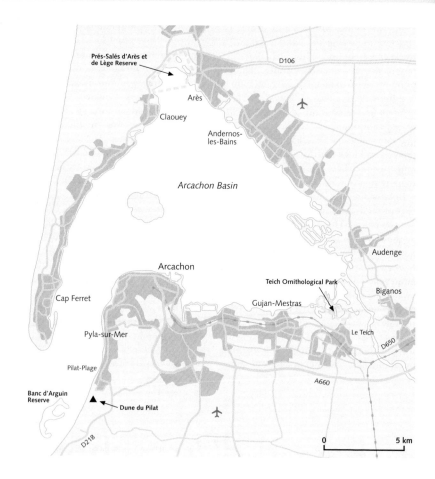

bay, especially at the south-east corner, are designated as Special Protection Areas for birds.

At the northernmost point of the bay, the **Prés-Salés d'Arès et de Lège Reserve** covers 500 ha of foreshore, saltmarsh, fishponds, grassland, forests, and other habitats as a prime example of the littoral habitats of the area in what is probably the warmest and most sheltered part of the bay. Over 140 species of bird have been recorded, of which about half breed regularly. Nesting species of interest here include bluethroats, nightjars, kingfishers, fan-tailed warblers (now also known by their much less pleasant name of zitting cisticolas), little bittern, a few wrynecks, and good numbers of water-side warblers such as reed, Cetti's, and grasshopper. At passage periods, there are masses of waders including knot, dunlin, whimbrel, curlew, sandpipers, godwits, oystercatchers, common and spotted redshanks, a few spoonbills, and many others. Birds of prey include marsh harriers and ospreys, and many waterfowl such as greylag geese and shelduck. The reserve has a wealth of marine and intertidal life; it is a noted oyster fishery, but the basin as a whole is also noted for its abundance of seahorses; other species of interest include pipefishes, mullets, eels, and of course the wealth of ragworms, lugworms, molluscs, and other invertebrates that make it such a rich feeding ground for birds.

About 200 species of higher plants have been recorded for the reserve, mainly widespread coastal species such as goosefoots, oraches, sea-blites, glassworts, and spurreys, though there are a few unusual species. A dominant plant here and elsewhere in the bay is *Baccharis halimifolia*, the large shrubby composite, up to 2 m high, introduced from North America – now all too common down the south-west coast and into Spain. Several mainly southern species reach northwards here, notably the sea-spurrey *Spergularia heldreichii* and the campion *Silene laeta*.

The most exciting place in the bay to visit, certainly for the ornithologist, is **Parc Ornithologique du Teich**, at the south-east corner of the bay. This is a combination of nature reserve and bird park, with better facilities for viewing wild birds than anywhere else in France. It was constructed from the remnants of old fish farms, and now has a series of pools whose levels can be controlled. The park covers a large area within which there are 6 km of walkways and 20 hides, thus ensuring that there is always something to see, often at close quarters. In winter, there can be large numbers of birds of many kinds: wildfowl such as shoveler, pintail, garganey, wigeon, tufted duck, shelduck, brent geese, and mute swan, and birds of prey such as osprey and marsh harrier. White storks (which nest here) are staying longer and longer in the winter, and in December 2000 there were over 100 present. Spoonbills regularly pass through on passage, and are more frequently staying on for the winter. Common cranes are regular migrants which are increasingly wintering here, too. There are also abundant waders in winter, including dunlin, curlew, and ringed plover in large numbers, and a few avocets, and many herons such as grey heron and great white, and little egrets. Offshore, there are great-crested, black-necked, and red-necked grebes, and sea ducks; strong autumn gales may bring three species of skua and Leach's storm petrel into the reserve. At passage periods, there are many of the same birds, with more waders such as whimbrel, spotted redshank, godwits, and sandpipers, and an abundance of passerines. It is also worth a visit during the breeding season: there are strong heronries, with grey and night herons and little egrets in large numbers, active from very early in spring. A few white storks breed, and again they are active from very early in the year, in this case on specially constructed platforms. Bluethroats are common in and around the reserve (with 60 pairs or more estimated for the bay as a whole), shelduck are abundant, and in the wooded areas there are breeding black kite, short-toed eagle, golden oriole, wryneck, lesser spotted woodpeckers, and nightingales. Warblers are abundant in the reedbeds and around the pools, especially Cetti's, Savi's, reed, sedge, and melodious, with fan-tailed in more open areas. Other breeding birds include bearded tits and reed buntings.

The park is well signposted and easily reached via the Teich turning off the A660 spur motorway from the main A63 south of Bordeaux. It is open every day between 10 am and 6 pm (winter) or 8 pm (summer), and at the time of writing costs five euros – money well spent on a good day. The park has an information centre and shop at: Parc Ornithologique du Teich, Rue du Port, 33470, Teich. Tel: 05 56228093. It also has a good website: www.parc-ornithologique-du-teich.com, in French, and information on site is in both French and English.

Just east of the park, there is a reserve run by the Conservatoire du Littoral at the estuary of the Eyre or Leyre in the south-east corner, and the whole of this area is worth looking at. Bassin d'Arcachon actually lies just within the Landes de Gascogne Regional Natural Park, but as it is the only coastal area within the park, and so different from the remainder, we have treated it separately.

SITE 67 Landes de Gascogne Regional Natural Park

Some of the most unspoilt parts of the great Landes pine forest.

This Regional Natural Park covers 2620 square kilometres of Les Landes (see p. 125) south of Bordeaux. In 1857, Napoleon III decreed that Les Landes should be planted with pines and other trees to make it more useful, and it became the largest artificial forest in Europe. It is now mature, and forest covers about 80% of the park. Pines dominate the landscape, though there are oak woods and sweet chestnut in places, and alders and willows along the river valleys. It is a hard site to describe satisfactorily: there *is* plenty of interest – almost anywhere has something of value – but there are no single places where one can see a great range of species. The few remaining lakes and river valleys are often of particular interest (though they tend to be well used for other purposes), and any tracts of heathland are especially good, though these are both scarce and transient, depending on the tree-felling rotations.

Heath and pines

Breeding birds in the park include black kite, hobby, sparrowhawk, marsh harrier, red-backed and woodchat shrikes, nightjars in reasonable abundance (best located by going into suitable habitats at dusk and listening), crested tits, Dartford warblers, and stonechats. There are red squirrels, genet, wild boar, red and roe deer, and a few other mammals, with green, common, wall, and ocellated lizards, and the normal range of amphibians for the area around the lakes. Botanically it is not exceptional, though the total list of species is considerable. Typical plants of interest include immortelle, narrow-leaved helleborine, coral-necklace, sand spurrey, cudweeds, and a good range of fungi.

The valleys of the Petite Leyre and Eyre are worth looking at wherever there is access, and there are lakes around Sore and Hostens. Small areas of heath are often visible from roads and always worth a look, especially for their insects and spiders (including the striking ladybird spider). The park HQ is at: 33 Route de Bayonne, BP 8, 33830, Belin-Beliet, and there is a good museum near Sabres, the Ecomusée de Marquèze.

Dordogne

Introduction

Strictly speaking, this region includes many areas that are not in the Dordogne, and excludes some that are, but it is a useful general term for this part of southern France. Our region stretches from north of Limoges southwards to the edge of the Pyrenees, and eastwards as far as the edge of the Auvergne and the real *causse* country (see p. 184). The Dordogne river itself flows westwards across the centre of the region, and other main rivers include the Garonne and the Lot. It is dominated by limestones in the southern part, giving rise to a warm land of small towns set amidst a matrix of woodland, grassland, scrub, and farmland, with occasional gorges and cliffs. The limestone does not make for very easy cultivation, except in a few places, or where it is replaced by alluvium in the valleys, and the resulting countryside is marvellous for the naturalist. In the best areas, such as those described below, there is always something to see, and there are usually masses of paths, tracks, and small roads with which to explore. Although the climate is by no means Mediterranean, with much more of the rainfall spread through the summer months, many southern species find a congenial home here. Winters can be quite cold, especially as much of the region is well above sea level, so the number of more demanding southern species is limited, except in the extreme southern areas around Carcassonne.

For the naturalist, probably the best areas of limestone are the *causses*, which are marked on most maps by names spreading across large tracts of country, such as 'Causse du Larzac'. These are described in more detail in the Cévennes and *causses* region, where they reach their peak of development, but essentially they are dry, hard limestone plateaux, often dissected by valleys or gorges, hard to plough and with virtually no surface water. Traditionally, *causses* have been used for extensive sheep and goat grazing in a largely unenclosed landscape, which has produced an open steppe-like countryside with a thin covering of flowery grassland. In this area, the *causses* are neither harsh enough nor extensive enough to have remained unimproved, and the practice of extensive grazing has declined considerably. Now the *causses* are much more fragmented, with an increasing number of areas devoted to arable land, fenced, improved pastures, invading scrub, and

Burnt orchid *Orchis ustulata*

Opposite page: **Rocamadour**

Dordogne

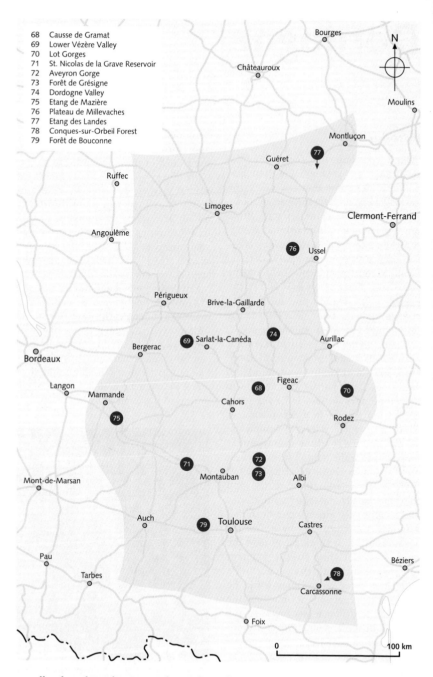

68 Causse de Gramat
69 Lower Vézère Valley
70 Lot Gorges
71 St. Nicolas de la Grave Reservoir
72 Aveyron Gorge
73 Forêt de Grésigne
74 Dordogne Valley
75 Etang de Mazière
76 Plateau de Millevaches
77 Etang des Landes
78 Conques-sur-Orbeil Forest
79 Forêt de Bouconne

woodland, and you have to seek out the remaining areas of interest. Such places can be marvellous for flowers and butterflies, but they are usually too small here for the specialist steppe birds such as little bustard and stone curlew – you need to go further east to see the remaining populations of these.

Traditional wooden boats moored in the Dordogne river, below overhanging branches of willows and the introduced box-elder (Martin Walters)

In the north of the region the rock is more varied, especially in the north-east where the edge of the great complex of volcanic Auvergne rocks is reached. East of Limoges, the Plateau de Millevaches lies on granites at moderately high altitude, giving rise to a wet, hilly, unspoilt landscape of bogs and lakes set amidst forest. Although not far north of the limestone areas, it has a much more northern or central European feel, thanks to the altitude, the higher rainfall, and the impervious colder rock. The range of species to be seen here is almost completely different, apart from some shared woodland birds and mammals, and the two areas provide an interesting contrast.

The Dordogne is generally at its best through May and the first half of June, but thanks to the climate there is something of interest right through the summer, and there is a superb range of fungi in autumn.

68 Causse de Gramat

A marvellous, dissected limestone plateau with a superbly varied flora and fauna.

The Causse de Gramat is the most westerly (together with the Causse de Limogne) of the great *causses* that stretch across south central France. It is roughly a triangle, lying between Gramat-Rocamadour to the north, the river Lot to the south, and the main Souillac–Cahors road on the west side. It is much lower and gentler than the *causses* further east, and less severe; there is more farmland, woodland, and gentle limestone grassland here, with little in the way of

Adonis blue *Lysandra bellargus*

Sometimes there are great masses of rock soapwort, with sticky leaves and pink flowers, tumbling down a small cliff. Although these dry slopes do have orchids, they are not as good as the slightly more fertile fields and roadsides described below.

In general, this is marvellous country for orchids. Almost any patch of flowery grassland or woodland will have some, and it is easy to find 30 or more species in the better places. A typical list for a good patch of grassland, frequently to be found next to the road, would include monkey, military, lady, man, bee, woodcock, green-winged, early purple, fly, wasp, early spider, fragrant, pyramidal, burnt, twayblade, lizard, red helleborine, and greater butterfly, with rarer ones such as late spider here and there. Such places might also have St. Bernard's lily, small Solomon's seal, masses of meadow clary, adder's tongue fern, cypress spurge, tassel hyacinth, pink flax, and many more. In damper meadows, which occur along some of the valleys, you can find loose-flowered and even early marsh-orchids, the stately *Dactylorhiza elata*, meadow saffron, and occasionally pheasant's-eye narcissus.

The flowery limestone grasslands are perfect for butterflies, which can reach very high densities by summer. Typical grassland species here include Adonis blue, Provençal short-tailed blue, pale and common clouded yellows, Glanville, heath, spotted, meadow, and pearl-bordered fritillaries, pearly and small heaths, common and scarce swallowtails, grayling, and many more. Glow-worms are common, bee

extensive limestone steppe country. It is a great area to explore, as almost all parts have something of interest. It is hard to define specific locations within it, as the terrain is an intimate mixture of small-scale habitats and agricultural land throughout, so we will describe what can be found in the various habitats, and make some suggestions as to where to look. It could also be described as a microcosm of the limestone parts of the Dordogne region, and most of the species described here occur elsewhere.

In places, especially towards the north, there are quite large expanses of dry limestone grassland, sometimes with exposed rock. These are superb for flowers in spring and early summer: there is a pretty, dwarf shrubby legume *Argyrolobium zanonii*, with silvery leaves and yellow flowers, the purplish-flowered Montpellier milk-vetch, pink flowers of the perennial bindweed *Convolvulus cantabricus*, blue-flowered globularias, mainly *Globularia punctata*, the little yellow-flowered prostrate toadflax, Cheddar pink, two little yellow legumes – horseshoe vetch and least scorpion grass – rock-roses and the rather similar *Fumana procumbens*, and hairy inula, to name a few. Where the ground is slightly broken, there are grey-leaved pink-flowered shrublets of *Staehelina dubia* and the related *Leuzea conifera*, which has a mass of swollen bracts looking like a little globe artichoke topped with a tuft of purplish flowers. Here and there, you can find plants of a striking dwarf composite, *Carduncellus mitissimus*, with blue knapweed flowers at ground level.

Argyrolobium zanonii

Hay meadow awash with pyramidal orchids

chafers and other insects visit the flowers, and ascalaphids (mainly *Libelloides cocca-jus* – see p. 200) pursue insects. Ascalaphids are distinctive, highly predatory insects related to ant-lions, which look like small dragonflies with long antennae and yellow and black wings. There are also abundant grasshoppers and crickets, of which perhaps the most conspicuous are those with colour-flashing wings, especially the red flashing *Oedipoda germanica* and the blue-flashing *O. coerulescens* and *Sphingonotus caerulans*. The grasslands are not the best places for birds, although

Macromia splendens

quail are quite commonly heard and sky-larks sing overhead.

There are patches of woodland and scrub everywhere, with some larger woods. The main trees include downy and sessile oak, Scots pine, common juniper, ash, whitebeam, limes, and wild service-tree. Often, the boundaries of the wood are not clearly defined, perhaps where scrub and woodland are invading old grassland, which makes for particularly diverse habitats. Such places are especially good for birds. Nightjars often nest in dry scrub areas, Bonelli's warblers call from the oaks, golden orioles are common especially where there are poplars, and hobbies can often be seen dashing across the fields between woods, or feeding on large insects. There are four species of woodpecker here – the three British species plus middle spotted – while other woodland or scrub birds include turtle dove, woodlark, short-toed treecreeper, tree pipit, nightingale, honey buzzard, and many more. Melodious warblers are common in isolated bushes, especially where close to wet areas. Other denizens of the wooded locations include fire salamanders (which are quite abundant, but only likely to be seen at night or in wet weather), additional butterflies such as woodland grayling, ilex hairstreak, and speckled wood, and moths such as the blotched emerald and the goat moth. Stag beetles, lesser stag beetles, woodland grasshoppers, and a vast range of other insects can be found. Red squirrels are quite common, mainly in pine woods.

Botanically, the woods can be very rich, especially in clearings. Many grassland species occur, but there are also violet limodores, helleborines such as white, broad-leaved, narrow-leaved, and small-leaved, bird's-nest orchid, crested cow-wheat, orpine, the delightful bastard balm in pink and white, swallow-wort, fly honey-suckle, winged broom, and lots more.

In more rocky areas, such as around Rocamadour, different birds are found, such as short-toed eagles, alpine swifts, and crag martins, while Scops owls call from most villages or gorges. Incidentally, midwife toads are quite common here, mainly around old stone buildings, and their call is very like that of Scops owl, only much quieter!

It is also worth looking at small, arable fields in less fertile areas, as the cornfield weeds can be particularly abundant, though they are declining even here: poppies galore, corn cockle, cornflower, broad-leaved spurge, corn-salads, blue woodruff, fluellens, and many others can be found.

Good general areas can be found around Beaumat and Vaillac in the west, to the south of Rocamadour and along the valley either side of it, around the Peche-Merle caves in the south, and all along the Célé and Lot rivers.

The Lot and the Célé valleys are also worth exploring for their more specific waterside and aquatic flora and fauna, too. Of these, the Lot is much the larger river (and is a generally busier valley), while the Célé is small, beautiful, and mainly peaceful throughout. In parts, the rivers can be white with a water-crowfoot

Prostrate toadflax *Linaria supina*

Ranunculus penicillatus in early summer, and a wider range of common water plants grow in quiet backwaters. These are good rivers for dragonflies and other aquatic insects, thanks to their unpolluted nature and relatively even flow: scarce chasers, emperors, the green and brown hawker *Boyeria irene*, club-tailed dragonflies (in particular the rare *Gomphus graslini* that is basically found only in this area), and the most impressive of all: *Macromia splendens*. This is a striking insect, with green eyes and a greenish-black body marked with yellow, up to 7 cm long. It is virtually confined to this part of south-west France, though not uncommon where it is found. It flies between mid-June and late July in an average year, and is worth looking out for on either of these rivers within this area. Other notable insects in the valleys include a striking bright blue beetle *Hoplia caerulea* on riverside vegetation, mole crickets which constantly churr like a grasshopper warbler, and damselflies, such as the white-legged and red-eyed, and the large *Cercion lindeni*.

There are also a few particular riverside flowers including the pretty crane's-bill *Geranium nodosum* and occasionally *G. endressii*, both attractive enough to be widely grown in gardens, Mediterranean coriaria, dragon's teeth, Deptford pink, and tutsan, amongst others. Butterflies that tend to be more common here

Dordogne

include southern white admiral, orange tip, and spotted fritillary. The birds are broadly similar to those seen elsewhere, especially the cliff species such as crag martins, but there may also be dippers, grey wagtails, and kingfishers along the river, and melodious warblers and golden orioles nearby.

The Causse de Limogne lies immediately to the south of the Lot, and is broadly similar, though slightly less rich and varied.

SITE
69 Lower Vézère Valley

Beautiful limestone country threaded by gorges, with a rich flora and fauna, and countless prehistoric remains.

This is a large area covering the valley of the Vézère between Terrasson and its confluence with the Dordogne, the surrounding area of hilly limestone countryside, and a rather similar area northwards towards Hautefort. It is mainly Cretaceous limestone, and has something of the character of the *causses*, though generally lower and more rolling.

The Vézère is an impressive river, with good cliffs in places, famous for a series of prehistoric discoveries: Lascaux, the sites around Les Eyzies de Tayac, and the striking cliff settlement in an open cave at La Roque St. Christophe. Crag martins, house martins, alpine swifts, kestrels, jackdaws, and black redstarts nest on the cliffs and are constantly in evidence, while kingfishers and grey wagtails are common along the river. The Vézère is similar in character to the Célé (see p. 148) and has a broadly similar range of species of dragonflies and other insects, though slightly less rich.

The surrounding limestone hills are dry and infertile in places, with poor, thin soils and little surface water. Much of it is open grazing land (though the area is declining year by year as modern techniques and grants have made more cultivation and enclosure possible), and is superb for flowers and butterflies. Orchids are abundant, with early purples, green-winged, military, lady, monkey, early spider, fly, and burnt in the first flush, followed soon after by woodcock, bee, white helleborine, narrow-leaved helleborine, red helleborine, greater butterfly, and eventually by the tall spikes of the strange lizard orchid. There are masses of other flowers, too: horseshoe vetch and the remarkably similar dwarf *Coronilla minima*, which has more rounded, greyer leaflets (both are important butterfly caterpillar food-plants), Montpellier milk vetch, chalk milkwort, pink flax, blue flax, cut-leaved selfheal (and sometimes the hybrid with common selfheal), blue bugle, thyme broomrape and other broomrapes, white and yellow rock-roses, lesser meadow rue, swallow-wort and much else. In cultivated fields, one often finds poor crops of wheat

Trichodes alvearius

Limestone cave and cliffs at Roque St. Christophe

accompanied by abundant cornfield weeds, though there has been a noticeable decrease over the past few years.

The grassland and scrub areas are superb for butterflies throughout the late spring and summer. In early summer, there are large tortoiseshells, brimstones (both overwintered as adults, so they may look rather tatty at this time), common and scarce swallowtails, pale, Berger's, and common clouded yellows, Adonis blues, orange tips, and the earlier fritillaries such as heath, pearl-bordered, and meadow. The peak numbers and diversity are reached from mid-June onwards, with marbled whites, Cleopatras, black-veined whites, various larger fritillaries such as dark green, silver-washed, cardinal, and Queen of Spain, blues such as chalk-hill, long-tailed, and short-tailed, graylings such as great-banded and woodland, and hairstreaks including sloe, ilex, purple, brown, and white-letter (not an easy group to sort out, especially as they begin to lose their colour!). Around more wooded areas, there are purple emperors, lesser purple emperors, southern and common white admirals, Camberwell beauty, and occasional map butterflies. The latter is a fascinating little butterfly, exhibiting more

marked seasonal dimorphism than any other European species – that is, the spring and summer broods look completely different from each other, so much so that they were thought at first to be different species. These flowery grasslands and woodland edges are also good for other insects such as bee chafers, longhorn beetles of all colours, the strikingly

Cut-leaved selfheal *Prunella laciniata*

Cardinal fritillary *Argynnis pandora*

coloured beetle *Trichodes alvearius*, which is striped red and blue and frequently feeds at flowers, though its larvae feed on solitary bee larvae; humming-bird hawk-moth, burnet companion, and burnet

moths, with many others. At night other moths are abundant, and glow-worms shine gently in sheltered spots.

It is not an exceptional area for birds, though there is a good mixture of relatively common species: cirl buntings, woodlarks, and Bonelli's warblers can be heard everywhere, with skylarks overhead; red-backed shrikes are not uncommon, and wrynecks call loudly as they pass through in spring, but only a few stay to breed. Short-toed eagles hunt for snakes and lizards over the more open patches, and hobbies are fairly common.

It is a beautiful and varied area, where almost any walk will turn up something of interest.

SITE 70 Lot Gorges

A varied and interesting area where the river Lot cuts through limestone and acid rocks, producing a fine range of habitats.

Between Espalion and Entraygues, via Estaing, the Lot cuts through a range of rock types including limestone, granite, and schist, producing a diversity of fascinating scenery, well wooded in parts, heathy in others, and more open where there is limestone.

The Lot is clean and clear, as there is little industry or intensive agriculture upstream of here, and it is rich in aquatic life. There is a good selection of dragonflies and damselflies, including golden-ringed, common club-tailed, and its close relative *Onychogomphus forcipatus* (which frequently perches on riverside rocks), scarce chaser, downy emerald, white-legged damselfly, red-eyed damselfly, and many more, and the usual waterside birds such as kingfishers. The river in places is white with water-crowfoot, of several species but mainly *Ranunculus penicillatus*, and these more vegetated stretches are particularly rich in mayflies, caddis flies, stoneflies, and

other aquatic life. In June, there are often huge numbers of giant stoneflies (such as *Dinocras cephalotes*), looking almost like dragonflies.

In the more wooded areas, one can find honey buzzard, sparrowhawks, goshawks, red kite, booted and short-toed eagles, a good range of woodpeckers including middle spotted and black, Bonelli's and melodious warblers, whinchat, and many others.

South of the river, above Estaing, the terrain is mainly of limestone, with typical causse plants as you head towards the Causse de Lanhac. These are broadly similar to those described on page 146, and there are good orchids amongst the oak, pine, or juniper scrub, and in open grassy fields: military, lady, monkey, lizard, green-winged, frog, bee, and woodcock are all tolerably common, with smaller numbers of violet limodore and red helleborine; other flowers include pasqueflower and pheasant's-eye narcissus (usually over by late April), chalk milkwort, winged broom, and many more.

It is also a good area for butterflies (though not as rich as the more typical causse areas) with Adonis blue, pale clouded yellow, large tortoiseshell, woodland grayling, and a wide selection of fritillaries, blues, and coppers.

The nearby Causse de Lanhac and Causse du Comtal, just north of Rodez, are well worth exploring.

River water crowfoot *Ranunculus penicillatus* in the River Lot

SITE
71 St. Nicolas de la Grave Reservoir

An artificial lake in the Garonne Valley, particularly noted for its birds.

Just downstream from the Tarn–Garonne confluence, near the small town of St. Nicolas de la Grave, there is a reservoir covering about 400 ha on the flood plain. Although the northern parts of the lake are heavily used for water sports and recreation, the southern section is quieter and well used by birds. There is a lakeside track and a hide, both giving good views of the birds. It is particularly good in winter, when there can be large numbers of grebes (mainly great-crested), waders such as redshank, ducks including gadwall, shoveler, teal, pochard, tufted duck, and small numbers of red-crested pochard and ferruginous duck at times. There may also be small numbers of red and black-throated divers, cormorants, yellow-legged gulls, black-headed gulls and others. At passage periods, there are good numbers of waders such as wood sandpiper, golden plover, black-tailed godwit, spotted redshank, and greenshank, together with little gulls, black

terns, the occasional osprey, and many more. In the breeding season, there is a small colony of common terns, breeding purple heron, and night herons are not far away, while kingfishers, little egrets, little grebe, coot, mallard, Cetti's warbler, and a few other birds are present all year. Black kites are generally common in this area.

Access is easy, following signs southwards from the N113 west of Moissac to St. Nicolas de la Grave, then signs for 'base de loisirs' and finally 'observatoire ornithologique' (i.e. bird hide).

South of here, in the Garonne Valley west of Grisolle and north of Grenade, there is an area of marshland, reedbed, and carr woodland, assessed as an important area for birds, which has a substantial colony of night herons, with little egrets, purple heron, and spotted crake, and golden orioles nearby. It is not an official reserve, and access is difficult, though the birds may be seen round about.

SITE
72 Aveyron Gorge

A partly wooded gorge on the edge of limestone country, with a marvellous array of birds, flowers, and other wildlife.

The beautiful river Aveyron cuts several gorges on its passage south-westwards to meet the Tarn and Garonne, though the main one, and the best for the naturalist, is in the section between Bruniquel and St. Antonin, to the east of Montauban

(and adjacent to Forêt de Grésigne – see p. 155). It passes through limestone and other rocks, giving a variety of terrain and habitats, with impressive views.

Breeding birds here in the woods and on the cliffs include short-toed eagles,

and a variety of woodpeckers and more common birds. There are rock sparrows in a few of the villages, or around deserted buildings, easily distinguished from house sparrows by their white eye stripe and the absence of brown on the head, though you often pick them up first by the distinctive, wheezy, single-note call. Scops owls are common around the villages, golden orioles call melodiously from the woods, especially in the poplar plantations near the river, and there are dippers, kingfishers, and grey wagtails along the river itself. Partly wooded areas, including orchards and fields around the villages, are good for cirl buntings, hawfinches, red-backed and woodchat shrikes, and short-toed treecreepers (these may be difficult to differentiate from common tree-creepers, but their calls are quite different; the short-toed tree-creeper has a short song reminiscent of a coal tit's in tone, in contrast to the loud, ringing, monotonous call of the common treecreeper.) In winter (roughly

eagle owl, peregrine, crag martins, alpine swift, black kite, kestrel, sparrowhawk,

The Aveyron Gorge near Bruniquel

from November to March), this is a good area for wintering wallcreepers, probably from the north side of the Pyrenees, and they are regularly seen around the villages of Bruniquel and Penne (both, incidentally, lovely old villages).

The limestone surroundings to the north, essentially the southernmost part of the Causse de Limogne, are good for flowers, birds, and butterflies. Breeding birds here include short-toed eagle, hobby, red-backed shrike, cirl buntings, and Bonelli's and subalpine warblers. The flowers and butterflies are broadly similar to those described for the Causse de Gramat (p. 145).

SITE

73 Forêt de Grésigne

One of the finest lowland forests in France, with an exceptional array of wildlife in an attractive setting.

grasslands on some of the thinner soils, with outcrops of rock in places. The combination provides habitat for an exceptional range of species. I first visited the forest over 20 years ago, before getting to know much of the rest of France; it seemed like a naturalist's paradise then, and fortunately it still does.

It is an excellent area for breeding woodland and scrub birds, both in diversity and quantity. Birds of prey are common here, and include honey buzzard, common buzzard, goshawk, short-toed and booted eagles, hen harriers, sparrowhawk, hobby, and both red and black kites. There is usually one or other of these visible on a good day, and

The Forêt de Grésigne is the epitome of a French forest. It lies in a beautiful hilly setting, rising to 500 m, with river valleys on three sides, and ancient villages all around. Although naturally it is predominantly wooded, mainly with oak, beech, and hornbeam, there are also many open areas – rides, clearings, scrub, and flowery

Strangalia maculata

Gresigne Forest

there are several viewpoints which are particularly good for raptor watching: Montoulieu is the highest point (468 m) actually within the forest, just to the north of the village of Puycelci, and there are good views from here; or the parapet of the Lafage Château, in the north-east of the forest, is ideal. There are also owls here, especially Scops and tawny, but eagle owls have been released on the northern edge of the forest and should still occur. They are best found by going out at night in late winter or very early spring, and listening for their highly distinctive deep double call (an eerie sound!), though they will continue to call until May, albeit less frequently.

Other birds in the forest in the breeding season include a good population of hawfinches, wood and Bonelli's warblers, at least five species of woodpeckers including black and middle spotted, marsh tit, red-backed shrike, nightjar, Dartford and subalpine warblers, firecrests, and – of course – abundant nightingales.

However, it is by no means of interest only for its birds. There is a great variety of woodland or woodland edge flowers, such as bastard balm (in a wonderful array of colour forms including deep red), whorled and angular Solomon's seal, spiked star-of-Bethlehem, tassel hyacinth, martagon lily, white, narrow-leaved, red, and broad-leaved helleborines, violet limodore, bird's-nest orchid, lady orchid, blue bugle, orpine, cowslips, several lungworts, pasqueflower – and many more. The dominant trees are sessile oak, but there are also downy oaks, whitebeam, pines, hornbeam, yew, wild service-tree, limes, and lots more. It is a state forest and generally managed as such, though this leaves plenty of scope for wildlife in the managed sections, and there are many peripheral areas, such as on steep slopes or thin soils,

Chanterelle *Cantharellus cibarius*

Goshawk *Accipiter gentilis*

There are also stag beetles and lesser stag beetles in good quantity. Other insects include blue-flashing and woodland grasshoppers, wood crickets in abundance, glow-worms of several species, ascalaphids (see p. 200) in the clearings, masses of hoverflies, shield-bugs, conopid flies, solitary bees, and hornets, and a good selection of butterflies. Most of the woodland and scrub species that you might expect occur: large tortoiseshell, Camberwell beauty, southern white admiral, lesser purple emperor, cardinal, silver-washed fritillary, heath fritillary, tree and woodland graylings, skippers, blues, and hairstreaks, to mention but a few. Day-flying moths include several burnet moths, burnet companion, latticed heath, humming-bird hawkmoths, and a large selection of nocturnal moths.

It is not an easy place to see mammals, partly because they are made secretive by hunting pressure in season, which includes hunting with dogs. There are red and roe deer, wild boar, red squirrel, beech marten, badger, and red fox, plus a selection of bats and small rodents.

There are minor roads all around the area, and a number of forest roads which are open to traffic at times. Access on foot is entirely open, and there are many tracks and footpaths.

which have more of the character of a nature reserve.

Not surprisingly, given the variety of plants and the diversity of habitats, it is a good place for insects of many kinds. There seem to be more longhorn beetles here than almost anywhere else, from the common and widespread *Strangalia maculata* and the bright red cardinal beetle to larger and less common species such as *Cerambyx cerdo* and *Monochamus galloprovincialis*.

SITE 74 Dordogne Valley

Where the upper stretches of one of France's best-known rivers cut through the hills, they provide some first-class habitat for birds and flowers.

The great Dordogne passes through some superb country, providing spectacular settings for some of France's best-known villages. In its western sections (within this area) it cuts through hard limestone, producing beautiful, warm, honey-coloured cliffs along its route, whilst further north

Hairy inula
Inula hirta

and east it passes through the complex acidic rocks that surround the Auvergne, and has a quite different character.

Between Souillac and Beaulieu-sur-Dordogne, roughly, the river passes through some fine limestone country, and a good site with easy access lies at Gluges, near where the Brive–Figeac road crosses the valley. On and around the cliffs, there are nesting crag and house martins, kestrels, peregrines, and

Beynac

alpine swifts, with black redstarts, serins, firecrests, kingfishers, and hobby nearby. The Belvedere de Copèyre usually provides good views of the birds. There is a rich limestone flora here, too, generally similar to that of the Causse de Gramat, with species such as Cheddar pink, ivy broomrape, hoary mullein, and hairy inula, and a reasonable range of orchids. Many other sites along this stretch provide a similar range of species, though this area is particularly attractive and accessible. The North American tree box-elder is naturalized along many of the Dordogne riversides, and its pretty foliage droops towards the water.

North-east of Argentat, as far as Bort-les-Orgues, the Dordogne passes through hard acid rocks, and much of this section is described as the 'Gorges de la Dordogne'. It is now mainly a series of reservoirs, but has retained its importance for birds, thanks to the wildness of the surrounding countryside. It is particularly good for breeding raptors, and acts as a migratory corridor, so there is usually something to see. Breeding species include short-toed and booted eagles, black and red kites, common and honey buzzards, hen harriers, and peregrines, many of them in considerable numbers. At passage periods, there can also be ospreys and a host of small birds. Good viewing points include the Site de St. Nazaire (west of Bort), the Belvedere de Gratte-Bruyère (about 10 km south) and the village of Madic.

The river is good for dragonflies of flowing water throughout (and for many still-water species, which manage to breed in backwaters), though much depends on water levels and the severity of winter and spring floods. The rather delicate viperine snake can often be seen hunting for fish in the shallows.

SITE 75 Etang de Mazière

A former ox-bow lake of the Garonne, now protected as a species-rich area of marshland and open water.

The Etang de Mazière National Nature Reserve covers 65 ha in the flood plain of the Garonne, west of Tonneins, on the west side of the main river. The habitats include open water, reedbeds, freshwater marshes, and poplar plantations.

Over 170 bird species have been recorded, of which 64 are known to breed, such as black kite, water rail, and various warblers including reed, sedge, melodi-

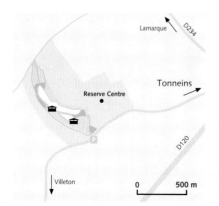

Common tree frog *Hyla arborea*

Stripeless tree frog *Hyla meridionalis*

esting, but not exceptional for flowers – about 100 species have been recorded, including frogbit, fine-leaved water dropwort (which can grow to almost 2 m in favourable conditions), marsh sow-thistle, yellow iris, purple loosestrife, and the duckweed *Lemna polyrrhiza*. Dragonflies have not been fully recorded, though the list includes scarce chasers, black-tailed skimmer, and hairy hawker.

ous, and Cetti's. Hen harriers breed in the area and hunt over the reserve. At passage periods and in winter, there is a wide variety of visiting species.

Thirty species of mammals have been recorded – a good total for such a small reserve. These include the rare native European mink (not to be confused with the north American mink, now widely naturalized – see p. 25), water vole, the pygmy white-toothed shrew (a southern species, at the northern edge of its range here), several bats including grey long-eared, and the European genet, closely related to mongooses (see p. 25). Twelve species of freshwater fish have been recorded, including eels, and nine amphibians. It is one of the few places where you can find both common and stripeless tree frogs together, and there are also natterjack and midwife toads, green frogs, marbled newts, and others. European pond terrapins are common in and around the lake. It is inter-

Tree frogs

There are two species of tree frog in Europe. Common tree frog is widespread, except in northern areas and parts of France and Spain; stripeless tree frog is confined to southern France and southern Spain. Their ranges overlap in this area. Both are beautiful little bright green amphibians, though common tree frog has a dark stripe all along its side, while stripeless tree frog just has a stripe on its head. Common tree frog has a staccato call almost like a duck, with the pulses repeated at about four per second, whilst the call of stripeless is slower and deeper, at about one per second. They are not usually in trees, despite their name, but are most frequently found up in rough vegetation such as reeds.

SITE 76 Plateau de Millevaches

Extensive peat bogs and woodland at about 1000 m altitude.

The Millevaches Plateau is a fascinating and little-known area on the western edge of the hills rising towards the Auvergne. Its name is said to derive not from the French for a thousand cattle, but from an older word meaning a thousand springs. This fits, as it is

Dipper *Cinclus cinclus* (Mike Lane)

Dordogne

a noticeably wet site, not infrequently shrouded in cloud, probably because it is one of the first areas of high land reached by the westerly winds from the Bay of Biscay. On the plateau, which is actually a hilly area at high altitude, there is a mosaic of forests, bogs, and small lakes, dotted with a few villages and cultivated areas. Although some of the forests are replanted and dull, and some of the bogs have been drained, there is still a remarkable amount of semi-natural habitat left, mainly on acid soils overlying granite. The Longéroux Peat Bog is a reserve cover-

ing 255 ha, one of the largest bogs, but by no means the only place of interest here.

In the Longéroux Reserve, there is a mixture of habitats typical of the area: bog, open water, heath, acid grassland, and pines. It is a good place for heathland, moorland, and pine wood birds: birds of prey include both hen and Montagu's harriers, honey buzzards, short-toed eagle, and occasional red kites. Nightjars churr from the heathy scrub areas, and firecrests, tree pipits, whinchat, crested tits, linnets, and even rock buntings can all be seen.

The bogs have a typical range of acid bog flowers – limited, but interesting. These include marsh gentian, bog-rosemary, the beautiful summer lady's tresses orchid (a rare plant of bogs and wet heathland), bog asphodel, round-leaved sundew, marsh cinquefoil, a mass of bog-moss *Sphagnum* species, heathers, cotton-grasses, club-mosses, and a few others. It is also a good area for lichens, thanks to the clean air; there are various *Cladonia* species on the heath, and the trees and even fence posts are festooned with beard lichens:

An extensive bog on the Millevaches plateau

Lichens

dull fawn) and small red, with dragonflies such as golden-ringed and four-spotted.

The beech woods in the wider landscape can often be interesting, with flowers such as may-lily, wintergreens, clubmosses, wood-sorrel, bird's-nest orchid and yellow bird's-nest (not related and quite different, despite their similar names and lifestyles), and a fine range of mosses, liverworts, lichens, and fungi. Birds include great spotted, lesser spotted, and black woodpeckers. These are good areas for old woodland insects such as longhorn and stag beetles, hoverflies, and moths.

The Vézère River, which flows from the site, has dippers and grey wagtails along its upper stretches, and this is where the golden-ringed dragonflies breed.

The reserve is not particularly easy to find, though it is marked on the Michelin 1:200 000 maps. It lies about 10 km north-west of Meymac, just east of the hamlet of Celle, and there is an information board and access point on the D109 Celle to St. Merd-les-Oussines road. However, any drive around the area will reveal other good bogs scattered across the plateau.

The Dauges Peat Bog, although in a rather different setting, has many similarities. It is a National Nature Reserve, officially declared in 1998, covering about 200 ha of bog, heath, and surrounding habitats. Amongst other things, about 300 species of moths and butterflies, and 200 species of beetles have been recorded. It lies about 25 km north-east of Limoges, north of Ambazac, and close to the village of St. Léger la Montagne, from where it is signposted.

Hypogymnia, Parmelia species, and many more, including rare ones. On drier areas, there are heathers and bilberries. Acid grassland has harebells, pepper saxifrage, whorled caraway, and viper's grass, with occasional common tongue orchids. They are good areas for insects, though mainly of less well-known groups – masses of beetles, hover-flies and other flies, and several hundreds of moths including fox moth and emperor moths. Damselflies include the overwintering *Sympecma fusca* (not the most conspicuous of species, being a rather

SITE

77 Etang des Landes

A natural, shallow, freshwater lake, with good birds at all times of year.

Etang des Landes (which has no geographical relationship with the area known as Les Landes closer to the Atlantic coast – see p. 125) is a natural lake in a depression in the

quiet hilly area known as Combraille. It is noted as a good bird site in all seasons.

About 1800 ha are considered to be especially important to birds, made up of the lake and surrounding reedbeds and other fringing aquatic vegetation, wet pastures, mixed woodland, and carr. In the breeding season, there are grey and purple herons, a few bittern, large numbers of little and great-crested grebes, teal, pochard, marsh harrier, spotted crake, and water rail. Warblers are abundant, including reed, sedge, great reed, Savi's, and grasshopper around the lake, with melodious not far away. The spotted crakes are not very likely to be seen, but their monotonous, loud single-note phweet, constantly repeated, can quickly be picked up. Bitterns can also be heard booming here in spring.

Winter is the least rewarding season on the site (depending on the weather) but by March there is a flurry of activity as birds arrive on their way north. About 3000 common cranes regularly pass through,

and up to 10 000 have been recorded – a fantastic sight. Other spring passage birds include greylag geese, wigeon, gadwall, pintail, scaup, goosander, and merganser, and at least four species of terns, including whiskered and black. In autumn, there are many of the same birds plus both white and black storks, osprey, night herons, and cormorant, to name but a few.

Remarkably the site has no formal national or international designation or protection, and no conservation management, though it is identified as being an important area for birds (a non-statutory designation). It is privately owned, so access is limited. It lies about 30 km south-west of Montluçon, just west of Lussat village. There is a road to the lake on the east side, from Lussat, and a car park, from where there are tracks.

78 Conques-sur-Orbeil Forest

Forest and open limestone hills just north-east of Carcassonne.

Around the village of Conques-sur-Orbeil, just north-east of Carcassonne, there is an extensive area of 'forest', which in practice is a lovely mosaic of woodland, scrub, grassland, and *garrigue* (see p. 16) mainly on limestone, on south-facing slopes. It is a rich area botanically, with a range of orchids including lady, military, fly, early spider in different forms, man, and the very pretty *Ophrys catalaunica*; this is a relative of the distinctive *O. bertolonii* with a narrow, slightly slipper-shaped lip with a bright mirror in the centre, and pinkish-red petals and sepals. It is confined to the general Catalonian region and nearby, and is quite frequent here. With the orchids grow masses of the strik-

ing *Aphyllanthes monspeliensis*, looking like a shrubby, leafless, blue-flowered flax, though the six petals help to identify it as a member of the lily family; culinary

Squacco heron *Ardeola ralloides* (Mike Lane)

thyme, sun-roses such as *Cistus albidus*, Montpellier milk-vetch, white, yellow, and annual rock-roses, and various yellow legumes such as winged broom, *Genista pilosa*, *Argyrolobium zanonii*, and the more familiar horseshoe vetch. The main trees are pines, including Scots pine, holm oak, kermes oak, and some round-leaved oak. It is a good area for butterflies, though, surprisingly, not as good as the *causses* (limestone plateaux) further north. Birds to be found here include Bonelli's warbler (following its Massif Central habit of singing from oaks rather than its Pyrenean habit of breeding in conifers), red-backed shrike, woodlark, subalpine warbler, and many more. Access into the area is easy via minor roads running east from the D118 north to Mazamet.

About 40 km to the north-west, at Cambounet-sur-le-Sor, there is a quite different habitat, a bird reserve managed by La Ligue pour la Protection des Oiseaux, consisting of a collection of lakes and associated habitats, mainly in old gravel pits. It is particularly important and interesting for its large mixed heronry, which has substantial numbers of breeding night heron, cattle egret (spreading and increasing here), little egret, and grey heron, with smaller, irregular numbers of purple heron, little bittern, and squacco heron. Other breeding birds here include bee-eaters, kingfisher, grebes, and many common birds. Large numbers of birds pass through on passage, and there can be good numbers of waterfowl in winter, so it is worth a visit at any time, though March–May for the heron activity is favourite.

It lies about 10 km south-west of Castres, signposted from the N126 towards the village of the same name.

79 Forêt de Bouconne

A large managed forest close to Toulouse, rich in flowers and birds.

The Forêt de Bouconne lies less than 20 km from the centre of Toulouse, and, as such, receives a considerable number of local visitors, with much cycling and dog-walking, so it is best avoided at busy periods. However, there is good parking and access, and much of interest.

Botanically, it is best in spring before the leaf canopy becomes too thick, when there is white asphodel, several lungworts, butcher's-broom, orpine, bastard balm, Bithynian vetch, *Lathyrus niger*, angular Solomon's seal, spiked star-of-Bethlehem, sage-leaved cistus, tree heather, sanicle, and a few orchids such as greater butterfly, early purple, narrow-leaved helleborine, and lady. Butterflies including large tortoiseshell, lesser purple emperor, and black-veined white are

Bithynian vetch *Vicia bithynica*

frequent along the rides, though it is not a great site for this group.

It is also well known as a good bird-watching area. Breeding birds within the forest include honey buzzard, common buzzard, hobby, and black kites (which are remarkably common in the area west of Toulouse), while Montagu's harriers regularly hunt over the surrounding fields. There are also firecrests, short-toed treecreepers, Bonelli's warblers, woodpeckers, and a variety of tits. Wherever there are cleared areas on slightly more acid soil, there are often nightjars and Dartford warblers. There are a few streams and lakes in the forest, harbouring dragonflies such as downy emeralds, though there is no great diversity of species.

Access is easy via the Toulouse–Auch road, from where the forest is sign-posted along the D24.

South-westwards towards the Pyrenees, there is another fine state forest, though much quieter and less visited. The Forêt de Cardheilac is an area of hilly forest, part native and part planted, with a similar variety of birds to Bouconne, and an arboretum. In fact this whole region to the north east of Lannemezan is full of interest and variety, and remarkably unspoilt and unvisited.

Auvergne

Introduction

Auvergne is a well-defined hilly or mountainous region, forming the northern part of the Massif Central, stretching from the lower-lying limestone country south of Dijon southwards to the edge of the limestone *causse* country (see p. 184), and eastwards to the Rhône Valley. It is dominated, and virtually defined, by an area of former volcanic activity; most of the mountains in the region are either remnants of old volcanoes or are made up of rocks often associated with volcanic activity, such as granites. The volcanoes vary in age; the older ones are often difficult to recognize as such, but the more recent, in particular the Puy de Dôme range west of Clermont-Ferrand, are very distinctive.

It is a rather cool and damp landscape, thanks to its high average altitude and position. It is the first significant range of mountains which the Atlantic depressions reach as they sweep eastwards, and considerable amounts of rain may be deposited here. The higher parts of the Auvergne receive around 2000 mm (partly as snow) per year, which is quite enough to spoil a visit, but there are many fine days, too, and the air can be marvellously clear at times. Winters are generally cold, with snow down to quite low levels at times.

The flora and fauna are a mixture of southern, northern, Pyrenean, alpine, and Atlantic, with a few Auvergne specialities, too. The central position of the Auvergne, linked through smaller ranges to both the Alps and the Pyrenees, has laid it open to a wide variety of influences. It is very rich in species – for example, about 2000 flowers are known – yet remarkably different from the adjacent *causses* to the south. There are Arctic species living here as relicts of the last ice age, hanging on in a cool climate while all around has changed, such as the tall orange spikes of *Ligularia sibirica*, or the Lapland willow. The little damselfly *Coenagrion lunulatum* has one of its few French sites here, an outpost from its mainly north-eastern distribution. There are alpine species such as alpine pasqueflowers and the grasshopper *Podisma* (*Miramella*) *alpina*, together with species that are mainly Pyrenean, such as the mignonette *Sesamoides pygmaea*. There are also a few endemics such as the sheep's bit *Jasione crispa* subspecies *arvernensis*, though these tend to be only slightly different from species occurring in nearby areas.

One of the great strengths of the Auvergne, for the visiting naturalist, is its relatively unspoilt character. There are huge expanses of semi-natural habitat such as moorlands, and deciduous and coniferous forests, but also most of the agricultural land is managed at low intensity, so there are hedges, ancient flowery pastures, and old hay meadows, with abundant trees. This provides homes for a huge range of species from almost all groups, including many that were once widespread but are now rare elsewhere thanks to agricultural intensification. It is changing, of course, but the damp climate and hilly terrain, coupled with a resistance to change, has slowed the process. Although it lacks the spectacular displays of flowers and butterflies of the Pyrenees or Alps, it does have the advantage of providing something of interest at every turn, whether it be a field full of wild daffodils, an ancient pollard ash, or a mass of copper butterflies in a marshy hollow.

Opposite page: **A lake in the Sagnes de la Godivelle reserve**

For most reasons, it is best visited from May onwards, and there are flowers, butterflies, and other insects to be seen right through the summer and into the autumn. It lies on a migration corridor for birds, which means that there is something noteworthy to be seen at any time between late spring and late autumn.

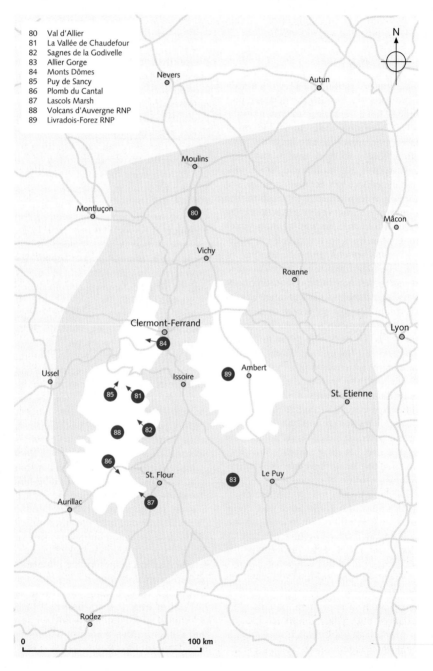

80　Val d'Allier
81　La Vallée de Chaudefour
82　Sagnes de la Godivelle
83　Allier Gorge
84　Monts Dômes
85　Puy de Sancy
86　Plomb du Cantal
87　Lascols Marsh
88　Volcans d'Auvergne RNP
89　Livradois-Forez RNP

N

Nevers

Autun

Moulins

Montluçon

Mâcon

80

Vichy

Roanne

Clermont-Ferrand

Lyon

84

Ussel

Ambert

Issoire

89

85　81

St. Etienne

88　82

86

St. Flour

Le Puy

83

Aurillac

87

Rodez

0　　　　　　　　　　　100 km

SITE 80 Val d'Allier

A 20-km stretch of unspoilt river with associated habitats, rich in birds and other wildlife.

The Allier is a braided river with multiple channels separated by shifting gravel banks. A 20-km stretch, covering about 1500 ha of land, is protected as a reserve, southwards from Moulins towards Vichy. It has long been known for its ornithological importance and is designated as a Special Protection Area under European legislation, which covers most of the reserve, but it is also of interest for its flowers, dragonflies, and other features.

Well over 100 species of bird breed within the reserve or nearby and use the river valley at some time. It is also a migration corridor, and a great variety of birds have been recorded at passage periods. There are several heronries with both grey and purple herons, little egrets, and night herons, and other breeding birds include stone curlews, common and little terns, and little ringed plovers on the gravel banks. Kingfishers and sand martins nest in the river banks, and there are black kites, honey buzzards, and hobbies in the nearby woods. Other species of interest which breed here include tawny pipit, corncrake, red-backed shrike, and Cetti's warbler. The valley is an important migration route, and black and white storks, ospreys, common cranes, corn-crakes, little bustard, sandpipers, black and whiskered terns, and many others pass through in spring or autumn, or both. There is an interesting variety of other vertebrates, including great-crested newt, yellow-bellied toads, pond terrapins, and 37 species of fish such as Atlantic salmon, pike, and brown trout. Beavers breed in the reserve, and there are polecats, wild boar, roe deer, and a range of bats including pipistrelle and Daubenton's.

The reserve was created originally in 1994 for its ornithological interest and the value of the habitat, and it is only gradually revealing its botanical secrets. Within the woodlands there are ashes (including the uncommon and mainly southern narrow-leaved ash), alders, poplars, and willows, and the rather rarer European white elm, distinguishable from other native elms by the longer leaf stalks, the white-hairy undersides to the leaves, and the hairy fruits. Small fleabane (a rare plant generally, and protected in France) is quite common, and the little-known *Lindernia procumbens*, a waterside plant with pale pinkish solitary flowers, in the figwort family, is not infrequent. There are several species of bur-marigold, flowering-rush, and strapwort growing on the bare gravelly banks, the white crucifer *Berteroa incana*, and masses of willows, goosefoots, and other plants of damp or open areas. Other special plants here include narrow-leaved lupin, a rare hawkweed *Hieracium peleterianum* subspecies *ligericum*, a sedge *Cyperus michelianus*, and arrowheads.

This is an excellent site for dragonflies and damselflies, with at least 36 species recorded. Like many larger French rivers, the Allier is large enough to provide a

Beaver *Castor fiber*

Purple lettuce *Prenanthes purpurea*

range of breeding habitats, from virtually stagnant to fast-flowing and gravelly, with additional riverside flushes and other small-scale habitats. Thus the list includes river species such as golden-ringed, club-tailed, scarce chaser, and the gomphid *Ophiogomphus cecilia* (a mainly eastern species confined to just a few places in France), species of still waters such as the darters and chasers, and species of damp flushes such as the southern damselfly.

The N7 and N9 southwards from Moulins run either side of the reserve, and the N145 and the road to La Ferté Hauterive pass through it, giving direct access. The reserve is run by a combination of the Office National des Forêts (the forestry authority) and La Ligue de la Protection des Oiseaux. The local office of the latter is at: 9, Route de Montilly, 03000 Moulins.

The Val d'Allier is of interest at a number of points. Another location upstream from here, south of Vichy at St.Yorre, is a good migration corridor and has breeding night herons, amongst other species.

81 La Vallée de Chaudefour

SITE

A high valley on the slopes of Monts-Dore with a notably rich and varied flora.

La Vallée de Chaudefour is a high, glacial valley cutting back into the volcanic slopes of the Puy de Sancy (1885 m), part of the Mont-Dore section of the Auvergne mountains. The reserve covers 820 ha of the valley, reaching up to an altitude of about 1850 m on Puy Ferrand, and consists of woodland – mainly beech – with scrub, grassland, and moorland, punctuated by some fine cliffs, remnants of glacial cirques (half-open, steep-sided hollows at the head of a valley or on a mountainside, formed by glacial erosion).

The flora is particularly rich, a fascinating combination of southern, northern, and upland species, partly as a result of the region's history of glaciation, but also reflecting its position in the centre of the country. Typical Arctic plants to be seen here include the pretty mountain avens, dwarf willows such as *Salix herbacea* and the rare *S. lapponum* and *S. bicolor*. There are more alpine species such as *Androsace carnea*, snowbell, alpine erigeron, and alpine pasqueflower in its form *Pulsatilla alpina* subspecies *apiifolia*, with pale yellow flowers rather than the typical

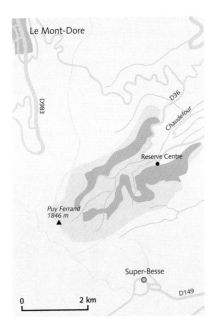

For example, about 200 species of birds have been recorded, of which 70 are known to breed. Typical upland breeding birds include peregrine, crag martin, ring ouzel, rock thrush, raven, northern wheatear, and water pipit. Eagle owls breed around the interface between woodland and cliffs, helped by artificial nestboxes, and there are more characteristically woodland birds such as honey buzzard, black woodpecker, crested tits and goldcrests, with nightjars in more open areas. Alpine accentors are often present but do not normally breed, perhaps due to disturbance by climbers. In autumn, the valley acts as something of a migration funnel, especially for birds of prey, and is a good place to watch honey buzzards, common buzzards, red and black kites, marsh and hen harriers, white storks, and even cranes between August and early November. Masses of passerines such as swallows and martins, thrushes, pigeons, flycatchers, and golden orioles also pass through.

There are small herds of chamois here, and a few mouflon, originally introduced for hunting, in addition to more wide-

white. There are saxifrages such as musk saxifrage and the endemic *Saxifraga bryoides* variety *auvernica*, the pretty little *Sesamoides pygmaea*, related to mignonettes, as well as martagon lily, alpine clubmoss, orange hawkweed, and alpine garlic. There are bog plants such as sundews, cotton-grass, and marsh gentian, and plants that reflect the fact that there is high rainfall coming in from the Atlantic – such as Welsh poppy, and Irish spurge with its distinctive warty fruits. There is also a pretty, cushion-forming variant of one of the sheep's bits, which is confined to this area: *Jasione crispa* subspecies *arvernensis*. There are more widespread woodland plants such as wintergreens and bird's-nest orchid, and typical upland grassland species such as common juniper, purging broom, wild daffodil, poet's-eye narcissus, and Carthusian pink. Altogether it is a very rich mixture, although it does not have quite the luxuriant abundance of the best sites in the Pyrenees or southern French Alps.

Although primarily a botanical site, everything else is of interest here, and the scenery is spectacular (in good weather).

Sesamoides pygmaea

spread, upland woodland mammals such as polecat and red squirrels. Butterflies are not exceptional, but it is high enough for Apollos and a good range of blues, whites, and fritillaries, and the delightful alpine grasshopper *Podisma* (*Miramella*) *alpina* is common, amongst many other orthopterans. Spiders are abundant and diverse, including the local speciality *Diplacephalus arvernus*, and there is a rare glacial relict pseudoscorpion.

The site is open to those on foot, with good paths up from the D36 where it runs along the edge of the reserve. There is a small café here in which to wait for the rain to stop!

The whole area around is of interest, with many good woods and upland pastures worth exploring.

Vallée de Chaudefour

SITE 82 Sagnes de la Godivelle

Interesting high-level marsh and lakes with many unusual species.

The Sagnes de la Godivelle Reserve is only 24 ha, but it is part of a larger area of interest around two lakes in a remote part of the southern Auvergne. Sagnes is an old dialect word for marsh, and La Godivelle is the name of the nearest

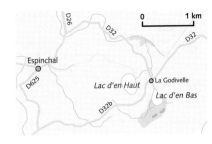

hamlet to the site. The reserve itself comprises an area of bog, marsh, and boggy woodland at the head of a small lake, plus a separate patch of bog about a kilometre to the north, and access to these areas is restricted. However, there are two natural lakes and other areas of interesting grassland and marshland around, so it is worth describing the reserve as a prime example of the habitat here. It lies at an altitude of about 1200 m, so the climate is distinctly montane, cold and snowy in winter and liable to be wet in summer.

The easternmost lake, the Lac d'en Bas, is being slowly invaded by floating bog, producing an interesting habitat that will eventually become a *Schwingmoor* (a floating bog with a thick raft of peat and a central pool). The bog areas are botanically rich, with bog-rosemary, sundews, bog asphodel, hare's tail cotton-grass, numerous bog-moss *Sphagnum* species, several sedges such as *Carex limosa* and *C. lasiocarpa*, and others. The open water has bur-reeds and the uncommon reddish pondweed *Potamogeton alpinus*. In marshy patches, there are other plants of interest including the striking orange-yellow spikes of the composite *Ligularia sibirica*, a relict of ice-age times here and attractive enough to be grown in gardens, cowbane, grass-of-Parnassus, heath spotted orchids, and a good selection of willows such as bay willow, *Salix bicolor*, and *S. lapponum*. In unimproved grasslands around the area, there are wild daffodils, orchids such as elder-flowered, the little moonwort fern, pignut, mountain pansies, and other attractive flowers. Overall, there are about 100 species of flowering plants in the reserve, and many more in the surrounding area.

It is also a particularly interesting area entomologically, more for the quality of the species rather than their diversity, which is hardly surprising in a cool, damp, upland area. There are about 20 species of dragonflies and damselflies, mainly widespread species but including the rare Irish damselfly (so-called because within the British Isles it is known only from Ireland), which is an essentially north-eastern species, absent from most of France. There is an interesting collection of bush-crickets, including the mainly lowland Roesel's bush-cricket, the more northern bog bush-cricket, and the mainly alpine *Metrioptera saussuriana*. The reserve is the type locality for two small moths, first described here, and there are half a dozen species of more obscure groups currently known from nowhere else in the world. Butterflies are not outstanding, though the occurrence of the little violet copper is a notable feature – the males are suffused with violet on the upper surface of both wings, making them easy to identify.

Both natterjack and midwife toads breed in the reserve, and common lizards are frequent in the drier areas. It is not a great bird site, though there are breeding red kites, little grebes, wheatears, and meadow pipits amongst others, and Montagu's harriers roost in the lakeside vegetation at times. Mammals are not present in any great abundance, though common, pygmy, and water shrews occur, enjoying the wealth of insect life.

La Godivelle lies well away from the busy centres of the Auvergne, about 15 km due south of Besse-en-Chandesse, on the D32 east of Espinchal.

SITE 83 Allier Gorge

A steep river valley bordered by woodland and basalt cliffs, with a marvellous selection of birds.

Between Prades and Monistrol d'Allier, to the west of Le Puy-en-Velay, the river Allier passes through an attractive landscape featuring heavily wooded surrounding hills with patches of moorland, and sections of impressive basalt cliffs that include some spectacular named features such as the Rocher de Prades. A large section of the upper Allier valley, including this stretch, is considered to be particularly important for birds, though there are no reserves and no national or international protective designations.

The breeding birds here are of particular interest. On and around the basalt cliffs, there are breeding crag and house martins, alpine swifts, ravens, rock buntings, and just a few booted eagles. In the surrounding woodlands and other habitats, there are many birds of prey, including both red and black kites, short-toed eagles, common buzzard, honey buzzard, goshawks and sparrowhawks,

and eagle owls; other birds of interest include red-backed shrikes, woodlark, black woodpecker, common sandpiper, and dippers along the river, with kingfishers here and there, and nightjars in open, heathy places. Both Montagu's and hen harriers breed in the area and hunt along the valley.

In winter, there are ravens, dippers, and grey wagtails (resident all year), with great grey shrikes and a few alpine accentors. Wallcreepers come here to feed on the cliffs, and can be seen at any time between November and April.

There is road access to the valley at Prades and at Monistrol, and it is possible to walk the whole length between the two.

The whole area is quiet and unspoilt with many areas of interest; for example, there is the Monts du Devés just to the east, the crater-lake Lac du Boucher at the southern end, and the forested areas to the west of the valley.

SITE 84 Monts Dôme

Fascinating old volcanic mountains, clad with forest and with an abundance of wildlife.

The Monts Dôme lie just to the west of the large city of Clermont-Ferrand, yet they are a world apart. They represent the youngest volcanoes in the Auvergne, not

long extinct, and retain the characteristic form of active volcanoes. Puy de Dôme is the highest point at 1465 m, forming a familiar and distinctive landmark. There

Clouded apollo *Parnassius mnemosyne*

are extensive woods of beech and silver fir, separately or mixed, and areas of scrub or moorland at higher levels. The natural tree-line here lies at 1500 m or more, though it has been lowered in many areas by felling and grazing over a long period. There is a pleasantly unspoilt feel to the landscape – despite the number of visitors – and many of the meadows and pastures are still rich in flowers such as wild daffodils and poet's-eye narcissus, orchids such as green-winged, early purple, and elder-flowered, pignut, meadow saxifrage (often in luxuriant abundance), master-wort, and other attractive species. At higher levels in the mountain pastures, there are alpine pasqueflowers, globe-flowers, yellow gentian, narcissus-flowered anemones, alpine clover, lady's-mantles, mountain cinquefoil, spring sandwort, and many others. The woods have a good montane woodland flora which includes large-flowered calamint, herb-Paris, wintergreens, purple lettuce, whorled Solomon's seal, bitter-cresses, and bird's-nest orchid.

It is a good bird-watching area. There are black woodpeckers, Tengmalm's owls, both treecreepers, firecrests and goldcrests, crossbills, crested and other tits, red kites, goshawks and spar-rowhawks, and short-toed eagles to be seen in and around the woods. In more open areas, there are red-backed shrikes, tree pipits, woodlarks, and a few hen harriers.

The whole range is excellent for but-terflies, including Apollo and the scarce clouded Apollo (looking rather like a

A flowery clearing in the fir woodland

black-veined white that has lost most of its scales, though actually they are not closely related; the black spots, especially on the forewing, of the clouded Apollo help to distinguish them), with swallowtails, fritillaries, coppers, blues, and many others. It is a good area for insects in general, such as bush-crickets, longhorn beetles, and hover-flies.

The main D941b and D941 pass through the area, and there is a network of minor roads and paths. It lies within the Volcans d'Auvergne Natural Park (see p. 178).

(see p. 178).

SITE 85 Puy de Sancy

The highest mountain in the Auvergne, with a rich mountain flora.

The Puy de Sancy reaches 1886 m – not huge, but far higher than anything in the UK, for example, and quite high enough to give it a distinctly alpine character, with long, snow-clad winters. Like most mountains in the Auvergne, it is the remains of an extinct volcano, and lies at the centre of an interesting landscape of high hills and forests.

There is a rich mountain flora, with elements of both the Alps and the Pyrenees at higher levels. Species of interest here include alpine pasqueflower (in both yellow and white subspecies, but mainly white), narcissus-flowered anemones, arnica, alpine clover, alpine aster, pink rock-jasmine, alpine forget-me-not, some alpine speedwells, louseworts including whorled lousewort, a few orchids such as globe-flowered, burnt, and small white, alpine lady's-mantle, globeflowers, cinquefoils including alpine cinquefoil, and a few snowbells, amongst many others. The invasive purging broom is abundant in places, and there are wet flushes and boggy areas where willows, starry saxifrage, lousewort, bog violet, and sedges do particularly well. In the woods, there is a wide range of flowers similar to those described for the Monts Dôme, and there are daffodils and poet's-eye narcissus in the grasslands. On the lower slopes, such as the area just south of Super-

Alpine aster *Aster alpinum*

Besse, there are some extensive peat bogs with sundews, masses of marsh gentian, early marsh-orchids, meadow thistle, viper's grass, and a wealth of sedges and other plants.

This is also a good place for birds, with a very similar range of species to that described for La Vallée de Chaudefour (p. 170), with rock thrush, alpine accentor, and crag martins as highlights. Mouflon still occur as remnants of an introduction, and there are chamois in the area. Skiing has become increasingly popular here, with a noticeable amount of damage and disturbance.

Access to the higher areas is on foot from the Mont-Dore side or from Superbesse, and there are many well-marked paths in the area. There are also ski-lifts.

SITE 86 Plomb du Cantal

The second highest mountain in the Auvergne, rich in flowers, butterflies, and birds.

The Plomb du Cantal, rising to 1858 m, is the highest point in a range of mountains called the Monts du Cantal, with other peaks such as the Puy Mary reaching almost as high. They are the remains of a huge ancient volcano, and this is the southernmost significant mountain area in the Auvergne, reaching almost to the edge of the limestone *causses* region of the south. There is a marvellous range of unspoilt habitats here, including high-altitude flowery pastures, scrub, deciduous and coniferous woodland, peat bogs, and rocky outcrops, providing homes for a great variety of species.

It is an excellent area for birds, and particularly noted as a migration viewpoint. About 6500 ha is designated as an 'important area for birds', while the best 1500 ha of the 'Monts et Plombs du Cantal' is designated as a Special Protection Area for birds. Breeding species include a fine variety of upland birds such as ring ouzel, rock thrush, water pipit, northern wheatear, and alpine accentor, and lower down there are crossbills, crested tits, red kites,

crag martins, nightjars, woodlarks, and other more widespread species. But the site really comes into its own at migration time, particularly post-breeding, between early August and late October. Raptors are especially good, with red and black kites, honey buzzards, Montagu's harriers, ospreys, short-toed eagles, peregrines, sparrowhawks, and merlins passing through at some time or other. Some recent counts show that 2000 or more red kites and honey buzzards pass through, and almost as many black kites. Other birds of interest coming through include both black and white storks, hirundines, wood-pigeons, ring-ouzels, warblers, finches, and many more.

The Prat de Bouc pass is particularly good, and there is information about the migrant birds here. There are numerous forest walks, mountain walks, and ski-lifts here giving good access to all parts, though it is very busy in the ski season and in high summer. There is also a fine variety of flowers here in late spring and summer, and a good mixture of butterflies.

SITE 87 Lascols Marsh

Important high-altitude marsh, open water, and reedbed, with good birds.

To the west of the little village of Lascols, just north of Cussac, there is an extensive area of open water, reedbeds, and marshland, covering 100 ha or so at an altitude of about 1000 m on the volcanic plateau

west of St. Flour. There is very little habitat of this type left in the Auvergne or adjacent regions. It is an important site for breeding marshland birds, some of them at their altitudinal limit for France.

Red-backed shrike *Lanius collurio*

Spotted crakes are probably the rarest birds here, breeding only in very small numbers, but their piercing and rather monotonous single-note call can be readily picked up at dawn or dusk in spring and early summer. Other breeding birds include lapwings, curlew, snipe, water rail, black-headed gull, grey heron, whinchat, teal, and garganey, amongst others. Red-backed shrike are common in the general area, with dozens of pairs, and red kites and buzzards are regularly seen overhead. The marsh is also of interest in spring and autumn, at passage periods, when there are terns such as whiskered and black, all three common harriers, wagtails, warblers, white storks, and even a few common cranes, mixing with the resident birds.

Cussac lies on the D57 about 20 km south-west of St. Flour. Lascols is signposted from near Cussac, and the site is obvious when you reach the village.

A few miles to the south, the Truyère Gorges are also worth a visit. The stretch north of Chaudes-Aigues, for about 10 km either side of the D921 crossing at Pont de Lanau, is of special interest. It is noted for its breeding birds of prey such as honey buzzard, black and red kites, short-toed eagles, a few booted eagles, hen harriers, and peregrines, and any of these may be seen on a visit. The extensive woods on both banks are good for forest birds such as black, grey-headed, and middle spotted woodpeckers. There are minor roads throughout the area; any of the sign-posted *belvédères* (viewpoints) are worth visiting for good views of both scenery and birds.

SITE 88 Volcans d'Auvergne Regional Natural Park

The largest Regional Natural Park in France, covering a vast expanse of rich and varied mountain country.

The Volcans d'Auvergne Regional Natural Park covers almost 4000 square kilometres of beautiful volcanic mountain scenery, stretching southwards from north of Volvic and Riom, through the Monts Dôme and the Puy de Sancy areas, almost to Aurillac. It includes several of the sites described separately (such as Plomb du Cantal, Chaudefour, and Puy de Sancy), but it is so vast and loosely protected that it is easier to separate out the key sites for individual descriptions. There is, of course, much else of interest in an area such as this. It is an almost exclusively volcanic landscape, dominated by the remains of volcanoes of varying ages, including the quite recently extinct. The Chaîne des Puys just west of

Clermont-Ferrand, for example, contains 80 individual volcanoes in a line of peaks stretching for just 35 km. Most of the area lies at an altitude of over 500 m, with peaks up to 1800 m, and it has a distinctly cooler and damper climate than the surrounding lowlands. Although there is little protection or organized conservation management, there is a vast expanse of interesting habitats such as deciduous and coniferous woodlands, montane grasslands, peat bogs, marshes, and scrub. Many of the enclosed pastures and meadows have retained a rich flora and fauna, thanks to traditional management and the difficult terrain and climate.

Over 2000 species of flowers are known from the park, and they are often present in great abundance. It is a good place to see plants of traditional pastoral countryside that have become rare elsewhere, such as wild daffodils, green-winged orchids, meadow saxifrage, adder's tongue fern, whorled caraway, and viper's grass, as well as the more specialized

plants of the high areas, such as those described for La Vallée de Chaudefour. The older native woodlands are also good for flowers, though the soil is generally neutral to acid, so the spectrum of calcicolous woodland flowers (i.e. those that grow best in calcareous soil), such as lily-of-the-valley or some orchids tends to be rare or absent. At Riom-ès-Montagnes, south-east of Bort-les-Orgues, there is a small botanic garden specializing in local and medicinal flowers.

The bird life is rich and varied, both in terms of breeding species and what can be seen at migration periods. Many of the more terrestrial breeding birds of northern Europe pass through, especially on their way south, and there are some notable bottlenecks where observation is relatively easy. Prat de Bouc (p. 177) is described separately, but another good area is the Montagnes de Serre, just south of Clermont-Ferrand, and north-west of St. Amant. This is a low range of wooded hills – an old lava flow – with numerous paths, and about 1.5 km west of Chadrat village there is a good migration observation post where records have been kept for many years. Typical species here include large numbers of honey buzzards, kites, eagles, and cranes, and passerines of all sorts. The hilly area southwards from here, through Champeix and on towards Ardes, is known as Les Couzes, and is par-

Montagu's harrier *Circus pygargus*

ticularly good for breeding short-toed eagles, Montagu's harriers, corncrakes, Ortolan bunting, red-backed shrike, and surprisingly large numbers of eagle owls in a matrix of woodland and old-fashioned farmland.

In general, the countryside of the Auvergne is friendly to butterflies and other insects, and they can be marvellously abundant in places. Typical butterflies include swallowtails and scarce swallowtails, Apollos and a few clouded Apollos on higher ground, black-veined whites, Bath white and wood white, orange tips, brimstones, purple and brown hairstreaks, and a few blue-spot hairstreaks, coppers such as sooty, purple-shot, and purple-edged, green-underside, alcon and large blues,

purple emperor and lesser purple emperor, large tortoiseshell, and fritillaries such as high brown, niobe, pearl-bordered, knapweed, spotted, heath, and meadow, amongst many others.

There are a number of natural volcanic lakes in the park; while sometimes well-used for sailing, fishing, and other activities, they are usually worth visiting for their waterside flowers, dragonflies, damselflies, and other aquatic life, and birds. Some good examples include the Lac d'Aydat, Lac Chambon, and Lac Pavin.

The park HQ is at Montlosier, 63970, Aydat. Tel: 04 73656400. There are information centres in most of the towns and larger villages.

Lac Chambon

SITE
89 Livradois-Forez Regional Natural Park

A huge area of wooded hills and moorland, with a rich bird fauna.

Livradois-Forez Regional Natural Park covers over 3000 square kilometres, running southwards from north of Thiers to Allegre. It is effectively the eastern part of the Auvergne, largely volcanic or granitic, consisting of two parallel ranges – the Monts du Livradois and the Monts du Forez – and the valley between. It is a heavily wooded area, with about 50% of the land surface covered by forests of beech, silver fir, and other trees. On the higher mountains, there are extensive moorlands, and conditions on the very highest points (of which the highest is Pierre-sur-Haute, 1634 m) are harsh, usually with snow throughout the winter and early spring.

Breeding birds here include buzzard and honey buzzard, short-toed eagle, goshawk, Montagu's harrier, red kite, ring ouzel, woodcock, black woodpecker, wryneck, tree pipit, rock thrush, and others. The park mascot is the hazelhen, though they are far from common here. The park also lies on a major migration route, and in autumn there are common cranes, the same range of raptors as in the Volcans d' Auvergne, a few black and white storks, citril finches and other finches, thrushes including ring ouzels, and waders such as dotterel. The Col du Béal at 1390 m, roughly between Olliergues and St. Georges-en-Couzan, gives good access to high ground, including the highest point of the park a few kilometres to the south.

The park is not as rich botanically as the Auvergne, but it is a flowery place and there are many unspoilt habitats. The high moorlands, or *chaumes*, are good for some of the more montane species such as arnica, alpine roses, Pyrenean angelica, asphodels, elder-flowered orchids, and louseworts. The lower pastures tend to be agriculturally unimproved and have wild daffodils, poet's-eye narcissus, early purple orchids, and others, with a good range of typical acid–neutral woodland flowers such as wintergreens, wood-sorrel, may-lily, and many more. Fire salamanders are common in the woods, especially the beech woods, and the most frequent mammals are wild boar, red squirrel, polecat, pine marten, and red and roe deer. There is a zoological park at Le Bony, south-west of Ambert, which includes local species in semi-wild conditions.

The park HQ, at St. Gervais-sous-Meymont BP 17, 63880, Olliergues, is open all year, with a good range of leaflets and other information, and guided walks are offered in summer. There are tourist offices in most of the towns and villages.

To the east of the Regional Natural Park, on plains in the Loire Valley, there is an area of special interest for birds,

Fire salamander *Salamandra salamandra* (Peter Wilson)

Arnica *Arnica montana*

known as Forez Plain. It is dotted with lakes and ponds, mostly artificial, used for hunting and fishing, with limited access. However, there are strong populations of a number of less common birds here, which can often be seen from roads and tracks. Black-necked grebes are remarkably abundant, along with great-crested and little grebes. A few bittern breed, as well as numerous herons such as grey, purple, night, and little egrets, and ducks such as gadwall. There are strong populations of whiskered terns, with a few black terns, plus marsh and Montagu's harriers. Small numbers of short-toed eagles hunt over the area, and both red and black kites are common. It is also a good area for nightjars, stone curlews, red-backed shrikes, kingfishers, waterside warblers, and sand martins. In winter, there can be large numbers of ducks (regularly exceeding 20 000 birds over the whole area), and waders and birds of prey including osprey and white-tailed eagle pass through at migration times. The area of interest is roughly defined by Montbrison and Montrond-les-Bains in the south, the Loire to the east, the D8 to the west, and the A72 motorway to the north as it begins to curve westwards. There is another area of interesting lakes east of the Loire around Feurs.

The Pilat Regional Natural Park is covered in the Alps region (p. 219).

Cévennes and
causses

Cévennes and causses

Introduction

Although small, this is one of the most distinctive and interesting areas of France from the natural history viewpoint. There is probably a higher proportion of wild countryside and semi-natural habitat here than anywhere else except in high mountain areas, and the region has more sites of interest than in the whole of central France. It is one of those rare places where it is really hardly necessary to pick out any sites at all because everywhere is of interest, though it is true that some locations are rather better than others.

Like much of southern France, the area is dominated by limestone, with Jurassic limestone to the west and Cretaceous to the east, separated by the hard granites and schists of the high Cévennes around Mont Aigoual and Mont Lozère. The western Jurassic limestones are the highpoint for the development of the *causses*, a southern French dialect word. The *causses* are extensive limestone plateaux, flat in places, though frequently dissected by minor valleys and often deeply cut by gorges into separate, named areas. In this region, they tend to be at quite a high altitude, often as much as 1000 m on average, so they have cool or cold winters, while the summers are often hot. Since the soil is highly porous, there is usually no natu-

ral surface water, and this combination has limited the introduction of intensive arable agriculture. For centuries, the *causses* have been part of a pastoral way of life in which vast flocks of sheep and goats have grazed them extensively, producing an open landscape dominated by short, flowery turf. Although the *causses* in this area *are* still grazed, the pattern is changing, with fewer large flocks, more enclosure for the use of individual farms, and an overall reduction in the intensity of grazing pressure. Extensive grazing, especially if not too heavy, tends to produce a lovely countryside without boundaries, ideal for species that require open conditions (such as little bustard and stone curlews) or which like the dynamic boundaries between habitats (such as many butterflies, green lizards, and numerous other species). At present there is still plenty of this, and the existing amount of invading scrub and woodland produces a perfect habitat, but it is likely eventually to become less species-rich if woods invade much more. It is noticeable that older fields on the *causses* tend to follow closely the areas of higher fertility, such as in a natural sinkhole depression, and these are usually full of cornfield weeds. Newer fields, ploughed using heavy machinery, cut across natural contours and are much larger and more intensively managed, so they are often completely lacking in cornfield weeds.

The centre of the region is dominated by the Cévennes, including the National Park. This includes areas of limestone, but is dominated by harder, more acid granites and schists which have weathered to higher, rounded mountains reaching almost to 1700 m. This is a damper, more wooded landscape, with a

Bee-eater *Merops apiaster* (Peter Wilson)

Previous page: **Gorges du Tarn**

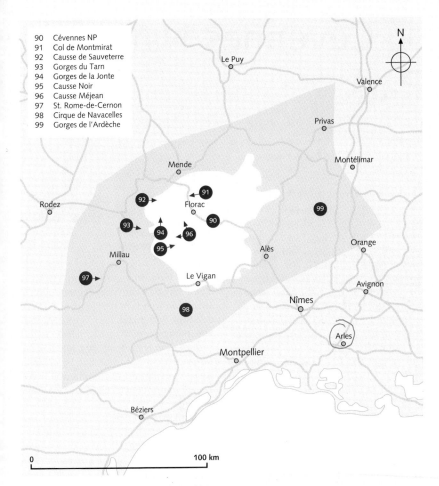

90	Cévennes NP
91	Col de Montmirat
92	Causse de Sauveterre
93	Gorges du Tarn
94	Gorges de la Jonte
95	Causse Noir
96	Causse Méjean
97	St. Rome-de-Cernon
98	Cirque de Navacelles
99	Gorges de l'Ardèche

0   100 km

quite different range of species. This area extends northwards and merges with the crystalline and volcanic rocks of the eastern part of the Auvergne.

Tulipa australis

Eastwards from the Cévennes, the limestone returns, mainly as Cretaceous limestone, at slightly lower altitude. This has more the character of Mediterranean coastal hills, with extensive, open flowery *garrigue*, and less in the way of definite plateaux. The Ardèche River cuts through these limestone hills on its way to join the Rhône, producing some spectacular gorges with high cliffs.

Collectively, the region is enormously diverse, with well over 2000 species of flowers, and all other groups in abundance. Altogether it is a wonderful area to visit, good at almost any time between April and November, but especially in May and June.

SITE 90 Cévennes National Park

A splendidly varied mountain area with an exceptionally rich flora and fauna, including many endemics.

Provence orchid
Orchis provincialis

The Cévennes National Park lies in central southern France, and its core protected area covers 913 square kilometres, with a further outer buffer zone of 2300 square kilometres. Only the core zone is considered here, partly because it is very large and varied, but also because the interest of the peripheral zone is diffuse and widespread, and better discussed under a number of separate sites. It is a mountainous area, not as spectacular as the Alps or the Vercors, but rugged and varied, and high enough to have a decidedly mountainous climate in places. The highest point is Mont Lozère in the north (1699 m), with Mt. Aigoual (1600 m) reaching almost as high in the south. It is a varied and convoluted area, difficult to characterize simply, and difficult to explore quickly, thanks partly to its varied geology. To the west lie the vast limestone *causses* – high plateaux (see, for example, p. 197–201) – which form the western part of the park along the edges of the Causse Noir and Causse Méjean. These are dry places, often open or with scrub and light woodland of downy oaks and pines. The high central zones, including the two

highest mountains, are granite with a characteristic heathy vegetation in open areas, and woods of beech, fir, and sweet chestnut, with much more surface water. The remainder of the park, mainly on the eastern side, is made up of acidic schists, with sweet chestnut woodland and some similar vegetation to the granite areas. There is almost 60 000 ha of forests within the park.

Thanks to its position close to the Mediterranean, and its considerable altitude range, there is a great diversity of vegetation types, and a corresponding diversity of flora and fauna, ranging from Mediterranean on the lowest south-facing slopes to subalpine on the higher northern slopes. The park core is considered to be nationally and internationally important by almost any measure: it has been a World Biosphere Reserve since 1985, covering 84 000 ha, and there is a Special Protection Area for birds covering a similar area, in addition to the National Park designation.

Botanically, it is very rich, with about 2200 species of higher plants recorded in the whole park area, making it one of the most diverse areas in France. Within this list, there are 33 nationally protected species, 48 species endemic to the Cévennes, and about a hundred rare or threatened species. It is obviously not

Idas blues *Plebejus idas*

possible to do more than sample this vast richness of flora here. The endemics mostly occur on cliffs, screes and other open habitats, and they include the columbine *Aquilegia viscosa*, saxifrages such as *Saxifraga cebennensis*, *S. pedatifida* subspecies *prostii*, the thrift *Armeria girardii*, the germander *Teucrium rouyanum*, a butterwort *Pinguicula longifolia* subspecies *caussensis*, the bartsia *Odontites purpurea* (= *jaubertianus*) subspecies *cebennensis*, and a pink *Dianthus graniticus*, amongst others. Orchids are abundant in many parts of the park, including limestone species such as man, monkey, military, burnt, early spider, red helleborine, and the rarities *Ophrys aymoninii* and *O. avey-ronensis* (see p. 201), with a few lady's-slipper orchids here and there. In wetter areas, there are marsh helleborines, elder-flowered and marsh-orchids, lesser butterfly, summer lady's tresses, and others, with bird's-nest, Provence orchid, coral-root orchid, and violet limodore in the woods. Some other flowers of interest in the park include trumpet gentian, ciliate gentian, ferns such as forked spleenwort, and the rare *Asplenium foreziense*, large snapdragon, cobweb house-leek, the early-flowering, yellow star-of-Bethlehem *Gagea bohemica*, the striking *Carlina acanthifolia* (often collected and pinned to doors), mountain kidney vetch, broomrapes including greater, alpine

Heathland and woodland on the Corniche des Cévennes

aster, several daffodils including common wild daffodil, pheasant's-eye and the little *Narcissus assoanus* (=*N. requienii*), and the yellow-flowered pheasant's-eye *Adonis vernalis*, amongst a host of others.

There is also an enormously rich fauna which includes about half of the vertebrates known from France. In terms of bald statistics, there are 89 species of mammals, over 200 species of birds of which 135 breed, 17 species of reptiles, 18 amphibians, 24 fish, almost 1000 species of beetle, and 12 crustaceans; a remarkable diversity that translates into an abundance of interesting things to see on almost any walk or drive in the Cévennes. Some highlights among the birds include breeding Tengmalm's and eagle owls, especially in the old spruce forests, griffon vultures, black woodpeckers, golden and short-toed eagles, rock and blue rock thrushes, Montagu's and hen harriers, capercaillie, peregrine, red-billed choughs, and huge numbers of red-backed shrikes in places. Some of the special mammals include red and roe deer, red squirrels, wild boar, small numbers of genets, beech martens, polecats, and masses of bats of at least 15 species, which can be seen in some abundance on most warm evenings between about April and October.

Globeflower *Trollius europaeus*

Virtually all areas of the park are worth a visit, though a number of particular sites are described below. Many sites, such as the Gorges de La Jonte, Gorges du Tarn, and the Causse Noir, are often described as being in the Cévennes National Park, but are described separately because they lie outside the park core. **Mont Aigoual** is probably the most interesting of the higher areas in the park. It is clothed with extensive forests of beech, pine, silver fir, and spruce, partly planted, though some have the character of ancient woodland. There are some interesting plants here, such as whorled Solomon's seal, spring vetch, St. Bernard's lilies, plane-leaved buttercups, coral-root bittercress and other bittercresses such as *Cardamine pentaphylla*, Martagon lily, wood anemones, leopard's-bane, white wood-rush, herb-Paris, hepatica, *Corydalis solida*, and masses of lichens and bryophytes. Birds include black woodpecker, crested tits, Bonelli's warblers, firecrest, crossbills, and a few others. Above and below the woods there are extensive pastures that are often damp, and the richer ones have elder-flowered orchids, pasqueflower, masses of wild and poet's-eye daffodils, with occasional hybrids, early marsh-orchids, meadow saxifrages, wild tulip (in dense drifts in a few places), asphodels, globeflowers, louseworts, common butterwort, and many others. Here, and in the heathy scrub, often dominated by purging broom, there are red-backed shrikes, wheatears, and occasional Montagu's harriers and other birds, though it is not otherwise a great bird site. Butterflies can be abundant at times – though it is rather a wet and windy mountain – and species of interest include silver-studded and idas blues, purple-shot and scarce coppers, Camberwell beauties, large tortoiseshell, and many more. **Mont Lozère** is rather similar, though less well wooded. On limestone pastures lower down, there are masses of orchids and pasqueflowers. Higher up, it is more acid, and the pastures have mountain pansies, rampions, daffodils, orchids such as elder-flowered in both colour

Herb-Paris *Paris quadrifolia*

forms, lesser butterfly, and burnt, and many other flowers. In places, there are patches of sticky catchfly and long-headed clover. Birds are similar to those at Aigoual, though there are citril finches here at higher altitudes, water pipits, hen harriers, short-toed eagles, and many others. The **Corniche des Cévennes** is the D9 from Florac to St. Jean du Gard; although extending mostly outside the park, it passes through a range of habitats, with most of the Cévennes species. Most of the main limestone areas lie outside the park; the best area within the park is the eastern edge of the **Causse Méjean** between Meyruies and Florac, an almost deserted landscape in this section; and the upper part of the Gorges de la Jonte. Here, there are many of the characteristic causse plants and animals: breeding black-eared wheatears, stone curlew, Montagu's harriers, hoopoes, tawny pipits, ortolan buntings, and rock sparrows, often around old buildings. There are masses of orchids such as military, monkey, and green-winged, Mediterranean flowers such as the blue flax-like *Aphyllanthes monspeliensis* (see p. 163), waving stands of feather-grass, and masses of butterflies.

The park HQ is at Château de Florac, BP 15, 48400, Florac, and there are information centres in various villages such as Barre-des-Cévennes, Le Vigan, Meyruies, and most other larger villages. Spring and early summer are probably the best times to visit, from early April onwards up to early July, after which it becomes very busy.

Col de Montmirat

A conveniently placed pass that gives easy access to some of the best habitats of the Cévennes and causses.

The Col de Montmirat lies on the N106 south of Mende, and it is one of the easiest and best places to see Cévennes natural history. In fact, it is worth spending several days there working out in all directions, and there is a moderate hotel right on the pass. Coming up the pass from the north, the road passes through mixed habitats, with fine scarp woodland to the right, and patches of unimproved scrub and meadows here and there.

Mother Shipton moth *Callistege mi*

Ophrys *aymoninii*

Towards the pass, there are some superb pastures with masses of orchids such as bug orchids, burnt, elder-flowered orchid, frog orchids, green-winged, and early purples such as the form *Orchis mascula* subspecies *signifera*, broad-leaved marsh- orchid, and many others, together with hybrids. Other plants of interest include pheasant's-eye narcissus, pasqueflower, often in a deep purple form (sometimes called *Pulsatilla rubra*), cross gentian and yellow gentian, meadow saxifrage, the little white umbellifer honewort, mountain and sulphur clovers, mountain kidney vetch, black rampion, large speedwell, pale dog-violet, dragon's teeth, carthusian pink, meadow saffron, and much else besides. This is fine butterfly country, too, with masses of fritillaries, black-veined whites, several graylings, skippers, Cleopatras, clouded yellows, and common and scarce swallowtails, amongst others, with day-flying moths such as mother Shipton and burnet companion. Fire bugs are abundant, especially in the spring, there are glow-

worms in warm, sheltered places and stag beetles and longhorns in the woods. On the drier, more acid, outcrops there is a poorer flora with species such as perennial knawel, and an abundance of a curious little bug called *Philomorpha laciniata*, which has a fascinating indented and spiny appearance, and specializes in laying large golden-yellow eggs on the backs of other individuals of the same species to help disperse its progeny. At the top of the pass (1046 m) lies the division between the acidic and the limestone rocks; west and south of the pass lies the limestone rising up westwards to the Causse de Sauveterre and dropping southwards to the valley of the Tarn. Eastwards lies the rounded forested bulk of Mt. Lozère, on more acid rocks. At the pass itself, one can easily walk into the pine woods to the east, where there is an abundance of wintergreens such as serrated and one-flowered wintergreens, the saprophytic yellow bird's-nest, and narrow-leaved and white helleborines, together with one of the special orchids of the area, related to the fly orchids – *Ophrys aymoninii* – only found in this part of France, and the uncommon small spider orchid *O. araneola*. *Ophrys aymoninii* was only described in 1981, and seems to be largely confined to the southern part of the French *causses*. It is generally rather rare here, except for a few sites where it is abundant (see p. 201), and differs from fly orchids in having a

Firecrest *Regulus ignicapillus*

Flowery pasture on the Col de Montmirat

broader lower petal (lip) edged with yellow at the base, and light green (rather than blackish) upper petals (i.e. the 'antennae' of the fly orchid). Golden drop is common in bushy areas, and felted germander *Teucrium polium* (sometimes described here as a separate species *T. rouyanum*) grows in slightly flushed grasslands. Breeding birds here include firecrests, easily seen from the hotel windows, flocks of crossbills, nightjars, common and black redstarts, and various birds of prey such as sparrowhawks and goshawks. Short-toed eagles, and very occasionally golden eagles, pass overhead, and this is well within the feeding territory of the Jonte Valley vultures (see p. 195). Just a few hundred metres to the west, the Causse de Sauveterre begins, and there is a mass of other species to be seen.

SITE
92 Causse de Sauveterre

Wonderfully unspoilt high limestone plateau with a particularly rich flora.

The Causse de Sauveterre covers a huge expanse, commencing just west of the Col de Montmirat and extending westwards as far as Sevérac le Château and Le Massegros, lying at an average height of 900–1000 m. From early May to early July, it presents an endlessly fascinating range of possibilities for the naturalist, though it can be bleak if the wind is from the north.

The open, grazed grasslands have a steppe-like quality, reflected by the breeding birds, which include good populations of stone curlew, a few little bustard, tawny pipit, and Ortolan bunting, amongst others. Short-toed eagles are quite a frequent sight, hovering over rough grassland in search of snakes and lizards. There are rock sparrow colonies in some old buildings, such as the fortified farm at Tour du Choizal. The most heavily grazed grasslands tend to have an apparently sparse flora, with species such as alpine aster and squinancywort much in evidence. If you visit in April, there is a good chance of seeing the pretty yellow pheasant's-eye *Adonis vernalis*, or the dwarf purplish iris *Iris lutescens*,

Aristolochia pistolochia

though both have finished before most visitors arrive.

Away from the heaviest grazing, on roadsides, amongst scrub, or around patches of woodland, for instance, there is a much richer flora. Orchids are abundant, with the stately, gladiolus-like red helleborine, masses of tall lizard orchids, patches of military orchid, monkey orchid, fly orchid, and the endemic fly orchid *Ophrys aymoninii* (see p. 190). Other typical causse plants include a pink shrubby flax *Linum suffruticosum*, several rock-roses, and the rather similar *Fumana procumbens*, *Globularia cordifolia*, false sainfoin, and a vetch that looks rather like a limp bush vetch *Vicia pannonica* subspecies *striata*. It is always worth delving into patches of deeper woodland (usually of Scots pine or downy oak here) in search of wintergreens, (in a few places there are literally drifts of the pretty one-flowered wintergreen), white helleborine, bird's-nest orchid, the curious saprophytic violet limodore which tends to associate with pines, and even creeping lady's tresses in deeper shade, though these do not flower until July.

The smaller arable fields are usually a mass of colour, and are always worth a look. Common poppies and cornflowers catch the eye, but a closer look will reveal many more species such as Venus' looking-glass, an annual rock-jasmine *Androsace maxima*, corn buttercup, shep-

Adonis vernalis

herd's needle, pheasant's-eyes *Adonis* species, corn-cockle and a good range of typical cornfield poppies, goose-grasses and woodruffs such as corn cleavers and blue woodruff, and other plants now rare or extinct in Britain.

The more sheltered parts of the *causses* are good for butterflies, including small fritillaries such as spotted, heath, and marbled, larger fritillaries such as cardinal and Queen of Spain, blues, especially Adonis blue, Duke of Burgundy, skippers, marbled white, the dryad, and even montane species like Apollo. There are masses of other insects here, especially in sheltered areas and around woodlands and scrub: day-flying moths such as cistus forester, burnet companion, latticed heath and black-veined white, hawkmoths such as humming-bird, shield bugs such as the striking *Graphosoma italica*, rose chafers in bright metallic green, bee chafers, ichneumons, longhorn beetles, and many more.

Other things worth looking out for whilst on the *causses* include red squirrels in the pinewoods, green lizards in warm

Short-toed eagle *Circaetus gallicus*

scrubby places, and Montpellier snakes along the edges of woods and scrub.

Access onto the cause is easy, with numerous small roads northwards from Le Massegros, Ste. Enimie, and the Gorges du Tarn (with spectacular views on the way up), or southwards from La Canourgue, Chanac, or the Col de Montmirat. Most areas have open access unless obviously private, fenced, or cultivated. The westernmost part of Sauveterre lies in the vast Grand Causse Natural Park, with headquarters at 71, Boulevard de L'Ayrolle, BP 126, 12101, Millau. Tel: 05 65613550.

Extensive flowery *causse* grassland, dotted with scrub

SITE
93 Gorges du Tarn

Deep and dramatic limestone gorges, with marvellous birds and flowers.

Shrubby white cinquefoil *Potentilla caulescens*

The gorges of the river Tarn are a famous and popular tourist attraction. The best section lies roughly between Le Rozier (where the Tarn and Jonte meet) and Ispagnac, just north of Florac. These gorges lie almost entirely within limestone, between the Causse de Sauveterre to the north and the Causse Méjean to the south. In general, the south-facing slopes are dry and partly bare, with large areas of scrub, grassland, or bare scree, whilst the north-facing slopes tend to be more wooded, often quite humid and mossy in places.

The gorges are of particular interest for birds, especially cliff-nesting species such as rock thrush, blue rock thrush, alpine swift, crag martin, red-billed chough, subalpine warbler, and many birds of prey. The area has become famous for its reintroduced population of griffon vultures (see Gorges de la Jonte), but is also a good place for seeing kites, honey buzzard, and several eagles. In winter, wallcreepers and alpine accentors can be

spotted on and around the cliffs. Along the river, there are dippers, grey wagtails, kingfishers and common sandpipers. Beavers have been reintroduced, though you would be lucky to see one.

The Tarn is also a good river for dragonflies; apart from the assemblage of relatively widespread river-dwelling species, such as the club-tailed dragonflies *Gomphus* species and *Onychogomphus* species, there are two much less common species. The beautiful dark green and yellow *Macromia splendens* is almost confined to the Tarn and a few other rivers, while the hawker-like *Boyeria irene* is a south-western species close to its north-eastern limit here.

Apart from the more frequent lime-loving plants such as the orchids and rock-roses, the slopes of the gorges are also home to a more specialized collection of plants, including shrubby jasmine, a white potentilla *Potentilla caulescens* variety *cebennensis*, rock soapwort, the yellow toadflax *Linaria supina*, a pink bindweed *Convolvulus cantabricus*, a pretty little shrubby yellow pea with silvery leaves *Argyrolobium zanonii*, and dark-red helleborine, to name but a few. The north-facing woods share many species with the pine woods of the *causses*, though some, such as mezereon or spotted cat's ear, are more common here. Lady's-slipper orchids occur in one or two places. Fire salamanders can be found in the more humid of these woods, though you really need to go out after or during rain, or at night, to find them.

SITE 94 Gorges de la Jonte

Impressive gorges between two limestone plateaux, particularly noted for their birds of prey.

The Jonte is a tributary of the Tarn, which it joins at the pretty little village of Le Rozier. Although not quite as spectacular as the Gorges du Tarn, the gorges formed by the Jonte are nonetheless very dramatic, with some fine cliffs and pinnacles, and are much quieter and less commercialized than those of the Tarn. Le Rozier, and its twin town Peyreleau, makes an excellent base for exploring both gorges and the adjacent *causses*, with plenty of good hotels, camp-sites, and restaurants. The flora and fauna of the Jonte is broadly similar to that of the Tarn, but its best-known feature is the thriving colony of griffon vultures. These were reintroduced in 1967, and are managed by the Fonds d'Intervention pour les Rapaces, an organization concerned particularly with birds of prey, and the National Park authority, and it is now very easy to see the birds in good numbers. The colony lies just a short way up the Jonte from Le Rozier, where there is a clearly sign-posted information centre and viewpoint below the cliffs. There are live video-links to nests here. The birds themselves can now be seen in abundance throughout the area. Egyptian vultures can occasionally be spotted, too, though they are at the edge of their range, and there is rarely more than one pair. More recently, black vultures have been reintroduced, though numbers are only building up very slowly. The site is best visited in the morning or towards evening in sunny weather, though the vultures can be seen throughout the area once they have spread out to feed.

Feather grass *Stipa pennata*

Other breeding birds to be seen in the Gorges de la Jonte include blue rock thrush, crag martins, alpine swifts, red-billed choughs, rock buntings, peregrine, and short-toed and golden eagles. Eagle owls breed in the gorges, and there are Scops owls in every village. Along the river itself, there are dippers, grey wagtails, kingfishers, and common sandpipers, with serins, melodious warblers, and occasional golden orioles in waterside trees and shrubs.

Botanically, it is broadly similar to the Tarn and other limestone slopes in the area. Some obvious plants include rock soapwort, umbellifers such as *Laserpitium siler*, mountain kidney vetch, blue mountain lettuce, everlasting *Helichrysum stoechas*, Montpellier milk-vetch, horseshoe vetch, and *Coronilla minima*, pasqueflower, milkworts, *Dorycnium pentaphyllum*, and masses of orchids including military, monkey, violet limodore, and narrow-leaved helleborine. The delicate feather-grass *Stipa pennata* is abundant in places. There are also many fine trees and

Griffon vulture *Gyps fulvus*

shrubs including Montpellier maple, St. Lucie's cherry, snowy mespil, box, large-leaved lime, smoke-bush, wild service-tree, and others. In rocky places, there are other species such as *Saxifraga cevennensis*, the white-flowered cress *Kernera saxatilis*, garland flower, the endemic thrift *Armeria gerardii*, three-leaved valerian, and many more.

There is a limited range of mammals in the gorges, with red squirrels, pine marten and beech marten, roe deer, and wild boar, though there is an abundance of bats benefiting from the wealth of roosting and breeding sites and prolific insects, with lesser horseshoe, greater horseshoe, and probably Mediterranean horseshoe, Daubenton's, pipistrelles, long-eared, and others. There are green lizards in scrubby areas, with snakes such as smooth, southern smooth, and Montpellier, and fire salamanders in shadier places. The river is not as good for dragonflies as the larger Tarn and Lot, but does have populations of club-tailed, *Boyeria irene*, and *Onychogomphus*

Gorges de la Jonte

Mediterranean horseshoe bat
Rhinolophus euryale

uncatus, with damselflies such as white-legged, and banded demoiselle. Insects are abundant generally in and around the gorges, including glow-worms, day-flying moths such as black-veined, burnets, and foresters, tiger moths, hawkmoths, ascalaphids (see p. 200), stag and lesser stag beetles, longhorn and cardinal beetles, the bright blue *Hoplia caerulea* beetle along the river, and abundant butterflies.

There is a road all along the gorges from Le Rozier to Meyrueis, and side roads climbing out of them. There are masses of way-marked walks, especially close to the main villages, with leaflets available from the tourist offices.

95 Causse Noir

Unspoilt limestone plateau, edged with deep gorges.

For the naturalist, this site is rather reminiscent of paradise: unspoilt, quiet (except at peak periods), incredibly flowery with masses of butterflies and birds, and very beautiful, with generally good weather! It is made up almost entirely of limestone, with a mosaic of flowery grasslands, pine or downy oak woods, scrub, and small fields, punctuated by rocky outcrops here and there. It is bounded by the Gorges de la Jonte (p. 195) to the north and the Gorges de la Dourbie to the south, with smaller gorges and valleys within it, adding cliffs to the habitat list.

Botanically, it is enormously rich. Orchids are particularly obvious, since they often occur in great drifts. In open scrub and grassy areas, there are military, lady, monkey, green-winged, early purple, and burnt orchids, with fragrant, greater butterfly, pyramidal, man, bee, woodcock, early spider, occasional wasps, fly, and the local endemic *Ophrys aymoninii*, with stands of lizard orchids where the soil is a little deeper. In wooded areas, there are masses of narrow-leaved and white helleborines, bird's-nest orchids (often in unusual abundance, even in quite sunny places), violet limodore, the beautiful rose-pink red helleborine, lesser butterfly, and a few others. Other plants of sunny, grassy places include masses of alpine aster, much more common here than in the Alps, angular Solomon's seal, pasqueflowers, the local version of ox-eye daisy *Leucanthemum graminifolium* with its narrow leaves, rough marsh-mallow, the pretty, silvery-leaved, yellow legume

Ascalaphid *Libelloides longicornis*

Argyrolobium zanonii, winged broom, the pink flax *Linum tenuifolium*, pink bindweed, the blue composite *Carduncellus mitissimus* and its relative the coneflower *Leuzea conifera*, thyme broomrape and other broomrapes, round-headed rampion, limestone bedstraw, and others. In shadier places, there are wintergreens, including one-flowered and green-flowered, garland flower, alpine mezereon, lily-of-the-valley, and bastard balm, to name but a few. Where there are rock outcrops, there may be three-leaved valerian, southern polypody fern, the yellowish soapwort *Saponaria bellidifolia*, pinks, the pretty endemic columbine *Aquilegia*

viscosa, and many more. Any small cornfields are worth checking along the edges for cornfield weeds such as cornflower, corncockle, blue bugle, small-flowered catchfly, and pheasant's-eye, though here – as everywhere – they are declining.

Butterflies are abundant, especially in warm sheltered areas with scrub, and include woodland and tree graylings, common and scarce swallowtails, blackveined and wood whites, Moroccan orange tip, fritillaries such as knapweed, Weaver's (also known as violet), spotted, Queen of Spain, Glanville, dark green, heath, and meadow; green and ilex hairstreaks, occasional Camberwell beauties,

Intensely flowery grassland on the Causse Noir

Little bustard *Tetrax tetrax*

the beautiful Cleopatra, and many more. Other readily visible insects include broad-bordered bee hawkmoths, humming-bird hawkmoths, forester moths, black-veined moth, longhorn moths such as *Adela reamurella* and *Nemophora degeerella*, various burnets, bee chafers, ascalaphids (see below), flower-feeding beetles such as *Strangalia maculata*, and many more. In and around the woods, there are a number of longhorn beetles including, surprisingly (as it is more of a northern species), the incredible timberman, with its huge antennae. Reptiles are common here, though there is not a great diversity of species. These include green lizard, wall lizard, and southern smooth snake. There is evidence of wild boar everywhere in the form of their diggings, though you rarely see them, and there are roe deer, red squirrels, and martens.

It is also a superb area for birds. Parts of the causse have a dramatic, open steppe-like quality, stretching away into the distance, which particularly suits a number of birds that are now generally rare. The little bustard is a striking species, considerably smaller than the great bustard (which does not occur here), but still with a wingspan of over a metre. The males have a boldly marked black-and-white neck which they inflate in displays, and in flight the large patch of white on the wing is clearly visible. They are best found in the evening in early summer, when they fly and call, though they are not at all common, and most of the few

remaining birds in the area are on the military land south of the Dourbie. Stone curlews occur in similar places, and are best found in the same way. Other birds of the open steppes include black-eared wheatears, tawny pipits, short-toed eagles, both hen and Montagu's harriers in small numbers, and red-backed shrikes. There are also woodlarks, nightjars, tree pipits, cirl and ortolan buntings, hoopoe, and a few woodchat and southern great grey shrikes, with crested tits in the pines.

The Gorges de la Dourbie to the south and east of the causse are neither as impressive nor as well known as those of the Tarn and Jonte, but have a similar range of flowers, and are excellent for birds. They mainly pass through limestone, but enter an area of schist and granite towards the east, where they emerge from the Cévennes National Park, and have a more wooded character here. They have many of the birds already mentioned, with crag martins, alpine swifts, eagle owls, red-billed choughs, peregrines and kestrels, and breeding short-toed eagles.

Virtually the whole of the area is marvellous, and it is not necessary to pick out key sites. Any road across the causse passes through a range of good habitats, with different features where they drop down into gorges. On the northern edge, the corniche de causse noir is a path and track that weaves along the edge of the Gorges de la Jonte, passing through all the best habitats, with spectacular views, and vultures always overhead. Further east, around Vessac and Lanuéjols, there is more open causse with special birds. The Chaos de Montpellier-les-Vieux is an extraordinary landscape feature with an array of limestone pinnacles, arches, and 'cathedrals', which has many of the species from the causse, too. It has become rather commercialized recently

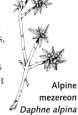

Alpine mezereon *Daphne alpina*

Ascalaphids

Ascalaphids are striking day-flying insects that are between butterflies and dragonflies in appearance, though they are actually related to the ant-lions and lacewings. They are active predators, flying strongly in sunny clearings, catching flies or similar insects on the wing, though as soon as the temperature drops, they settle on the vegetation and close their wings. The wings are semi-transparent, but partly marked with black, green, or yellow. The antennae are long and club-tipped – like knitting needles – which readily distinguishes them from dragonflies. Two species occur commonly in this area and over much of southern France: *Libelloides longicornis* and *L. coccajus*. *L. longicornis* has yellowish wing veins, quite visible on the dark areas, and limited black patches on the hind wings that do not extend as far as the tip of the abdomen; *L. coccajus* has blackish veins and a bold black hindwing patch that reaches as far as the tip of the abdomen. A third species, *L. macaronius*, is rarer and more southern, with yellowish wings and a bold black pattern that encircles an area of yellow.

and is not cheap to enter, though the area around it has some similar features if you want to avoid paying. La Roque Marguerite is an attractive spot, where a side valley joins the Dourbie, and most of the species of interest can be seen.

Southwards, the Causse du Larzac is rather similar, though bleaker and drier. It is good for steppe birds (including the military area 'Camp du Larzac' mentioned above), and has an increasing proportion of more Mediterranean species such as the blue-flowered *Aphyllanthes monspeliensis*, and sun-roses towards the south.

This area all lies within the relatively recently declared Grand Causses Regional Natural Park. The headquarters are at Millau (see p. 193 for address), which has a useful range of information. The vulture-watching centre in the Gorge de la Jonte arranges bird-watching trips to find some of the rarer species, such as stone curlew, both on Causse Noir and the Causse Méjean.

96 Causse Méjean

Marvellous, high limestone scenery, with superb flora and fauna.

The Causse Méjean lies between the Gorges du Tarn to the north and Gorges de la Jonte to the south, extending eastwards as far as Florac. The eastern part lies in the Cévennes National Park, while the remainder lies in the Grand Causses Regional Natural Park. It is broadly similar in character to the other *causses* such as Sauveterre and Noir, so it is not described in detail, but in most respects it is just as good.

There are plenty of specialist steppe birds, though little bustards appear to have disappeared from the area. Stone curlews are still reasonably common, and there are plenty of black-eared and common wheatears, hoopoes, tawny pipits, woodlarks, cirl and ortolan buntings, red-backed and woodchat shrikes, with small numbers of Montagu's harriers and short-toed eagles. In rockier areas, there are rock thrushes and blue rock thrushes, a few orphean warblers, short-toed larks, and rock sparrows, especially around old buildings.

The westernmost areas, roughly west of the D986, are more wooded and varied with more broken ground, better for flowers and butterflies though less good for steppe birds. The area around St. Pierre is particularly rich and varied, though it is hard to say exactly whether it is on the causse or part of the Gorges de la Jonte. Crested tits, red squirrels, and firecrests are abundant in the pine woods. There are green lizards, wall lizards, and southern smooth and Montpellier snakes. The orchids are superb, with the usual collection, dominated by man, monkey, burnt, military, early spider, bee, woodcock, and fly, but of special interest for the large quantities of the endemic *Ophrys aymoninii*. Other flowers of interest include masses of one-flowered wintergreen, pasqueflowers including deep purple forms, false sainfoin, mountain kidney vetch, honewort, field mouse-ear, meadow saxifrage, pink flax, swallowwort, alpine currant, long-headed clover, and the shrub *Spiraea hypericifolia* with white flowers.

There is also a superb selection of butterflies, day-flying moths (including the tiger-moth relative *Phragmatobia maculosa*), glow-worms, and much else. The stone arches at Arcs de St. Pierre are well worth walking to, with plenty to see on the way.

SITE 97 St. Rome-de-Cernon

Interesting limestone countryside with special plants.

Just west of St. Rome-de-Cernon, between the Causse de Larzac and the Plateau du Lévézou, there is fine limestone countryside, partly cultivated but with a matrix of flowery grasslands, scrub, and woodland. It has many of the flowers and animals of the *causses* to the east, or the Dordogne area to the west, and yet is slightly different. Botanically it is very rich. As usual in this area, orchids are abundant, including man, fly, pyramidal, lady, bee, woodcock, green-winged, and military, with narrow-leaved and red helleborines, and violet limodores, amongst others. The speciality of the area, however, is *Ophrys aveyronensis*, a very attractive 'spider' orchid with deep

Ophrys aveyronensis

rose-pink petals and sepals and a rich chestnut-brown furry lip marked with silvery-blue. It was only described as a species in 1983, and appears to be confined to quite a small area of central southern France around St. Rome-de-Cernon and St. Rome-de-Tarn. It is not common here, and seems to be decreasing as further sites are ploughed or sprayed for agricultural use. It is usually at its best in the last week of May or first week of June, depending on the year.

Other flowers of interest include crested cow-wheat, which is unusually common here, blue bugle, ground-pine, globularias, rock-roses, flaxes, Montpellier milk-vetch, hepatica, yellow woundwort, spotted hawkweed, Italian catchfly, and many others. Butterflies are similar to those of the more sheltered parts of the causse, and there are cream-spot tigers, bee hawkmoths, mother Shipton, burnet companions, forester moths, ascalaphids, and many other insects. Birds in the area include golden orioles, hoopoe, Bonelli's warbler, masses of nightingales, short-toed treecreepers, and tree pipits.

The nearby Tarn Valley to the north, though no longer gorge-like, is still of interest, with dippers, kingfishers, and grey wagtails along the stream, and flowers such as knotted crane's-bill, bloody crane's-bill, purple toothwort, and purple gromwell, as well as the dragonflies for which the Tarn is famous (see p. 194).

The D31 west from St. Rome-de-Cernon towards St. Rome-de-Tarn makes a good starting point for explorations.

98 Cirque de Navacelles

A spectacular area of limestone with a deep gorge, and a fine range of plants and animals.

The river Vis has cut a beautiful, deep gorge through the limestone plateaux of the Causse de Blandas and the Causse de Larzac, and in one place there is an extraordinary ox-bow etched into the high limestone, now by-passed by the main river, leaving the landscape feature known as the Cirque de Navacelles. (A cirque is a deep, bowl-shaped hollow at the head of a valley or on a mountainside, formed by high-level glaciers.) It is a picturesque and unpopulated location, with much of interest.

The cirque itself is a good starting point, with a café and fabulous views. Breeding birds here include blue rock thrush, crag martins, alpine swifts, red-billed chough, and short-toed eagles, with occasional golden eagles or griffon vultures drifting high overhead. Where there is more scrub, there are nightingales, cirl and ortolan buntings (which do particularly well here), melodious and Bonelli's warblers, and a few rock sparrows. Eagle owls breed here in the gorge, and there are Scops owls in the villages, audible every night in early summer. To hear the eagle owl's wonderful call,

Iris lutescens

you really have to be here in early spring. On the causse to the north, such as around Blandas village, there are birds more typical of open country, such as woodchat and red-backed shrikes, and occasional southern great grey shrikes, black-eared wheatear, northern wheatear, tawny pipit, woodlark, and hoopoe, amongst others. There may still be a few little bustards, though they have declined steadily in recent years. There are even a few black vultures in the area, spreading out from reintroduction sites to the north. In winter, both wallcreeper and alpine accentor feed in the gorge.

It is a good area botanically, with much in common with the *causses* to the north, though with more Mediterranean elements thanks to its southerly position. The small, spiny leguminous shrub *Genista hispanica* is common, with typical causse or gorge species such as blue lettuce, the beautiful Narbonne flax, and

the rather similar *Aphyllanthes monspeliensis* (which differs in having six-petalled flowers and almost leafless stems), hoary, common, and white rock-roses, shrubby yellow legumes such as winged broom, *Argyrolobium zanonii*, and the little *Coronilla minima*. A dwarf iris *Iris lutescens* in yellow or violet (or both) is more common here than on most similar *causses* areas, looking beautiful en masse in early May. There are orchids, though they are less abundant here than on the more northerly *causses* such as Causse Noir, where the soil is slightly less skeletal. Typical ones here include lizard, man, military, and – rarely – the pretty *Ophrys magniflora*, right at the eastern edge of its known range. Butterflies are abundant and broadly similar to those described for the Causse Noir, though Moroccan orange tips are more frequent, and map butterfly is surprisingly common. Other insects of interest include

The dramatic ox-bow that forms the Cirque de Navacelles

Moroccan orange tip *Anthocharis belia*
(Peter Wilson)

has a variety of habitats, mainly on limestone, with a wonderful mixture of flowers, butterflies, and other insects characteristic of the *causses* and the gorges. The road from Alzon towards Sauclières and La Blaquerie gives access to some fine country. The whole area is superb, and generally unspoilt.

Ophrys magniflora

praying mantises, bush-crickets, grasshoppers, and cicadas. There are green, wall, and common lizards, and a few of the large and striking ocellated lizard, together with Montpellier, aesculapian and southern smooth snakes – all food for short-toed eagles!

The gorge of the Vis is accessible at the Cirque de Navacelles, further west at Vissec, or further south near St. Maurice-Navacelles; there is no road along it, which adds to its interest, if you are prepared to walk. The roads radiating from Blandas give a good idea of the causse country.

Further north, on the edge of the Cévennes National Park, the area around Alzon, and especially just to the west of it,

SITE
99 Gorges de l'Ardèche

An impressive stretch of river with high cliffs and surrounding hills, with a particularly rich fauna.

The Ardèche is a fast-flowing river that drops sharply down from the edge of the Massif Central to the Rhône Valley north of Avignon. Along its lower course, it cuts through some high limestone hills, producing a spectacular series of steep-sided gorges with high sheer cliffs. A stretch of about 20 km covering almost 1600 ha is

designated as a National Nature Reserve, as much for its impressive geology and geomorphology as for its wildlife. Almost all the features of a karst landscape are exhibited: cliffs, caves, sinkholes, and dry valleys, as well as fine river features such as gravel banks and old flood-plain terraces. The habitats within the reserve include *garrigue*, scrub, downy oak woods, and mixed alluvial forests on the flood plain, with cliffs, screes and sand, and gravel banks.

It is an especially interesting area ornithologically. Breeding birds either here or nearby include one or two pairs of Bonelli's eagles, golden eagles, short-toed eagles, peregrine, hobby, goshawk, sparrowhawk, honey buzzard, and common buzzard, as well as alpine swifts, crag martins, subalpine warblers, blue rock thrushes, golden orioles, and red-billed choughs. Eagle owls breed in the quieter, more wooded sections of the gorges. Altogether, there are over 100 species of birds nesting in the reserve area, and it is designated as an important site for birds. In addition, bee-eaters feed over and around the reserve, and alpine accentors and wallcreepers may visit to feed in winter.

There is a wide range of flowers, mainly Mediterranean in character, though with elements from further north and higher altitudes, as the hills around rise to 500 m and beyond. The dwarf iris *Iris lutescens* is common, flowering in late April and early May, with peonies *Paeonia officinalis*, greater

periwinkle, sun-roses such as pink-flowered *Cistus albidus* and *C. crispus*, and white-flowered Montpellier sun-rose. The scrub consists of species such as strawberry-tree, Montpellier and Italian maples, snowy mespil, box, kermes oak, common, Phoenician, and prickly junipers, and Judas tree, amongst others. Other flowers of interest include the blue *Aphyllanthes monspeliensis*, lavenders such as *Lavandula latifolia*, winter savory, culinary wild thyme, goat's rue, rosemary, and three species of honeysuckles – an aromatic mixture.

Invertebrates are particularly diverse and abundant. Butterflies include the striking two-tailed pasha (whose larvae feed on strawberry-tree), cardinals, Provence short-tailed blue, and Cleopatra, amongst others. There are 5 species of scorpions, including *Euscorpius flavicauda* and *Buthius occitanus*, 30 spiders, over 150 aquatic invertebrates such as stone-flies, caddis-flies, and needle-flies, and insects such as praying mantis and the zizi bush-cricket. It is not an exceptional area for mammals, though there are genets, some reintroduced beavers, and a dozen or more species of bats, including greater horseshoe.

Besides the natural and geological interest, this is also an important area archaeologically, with cave relicts including the spectacular paintings in Chauvet Cave, only discovered in 1994.

The reserve lies just up the Ardèche from Pont St. Esprit, stretching between

Zi-zi bush-cricket *Ephippiger ephippiger*

St. Martin d'Ardèche and Vallon Pont-d'Arc. The D290 follows the gorge all the way, and there is a footpath running the whole length of the reserve. Access to the reserve is on foot only, or by organized canoe trips. There is a reserve HQ at 07700 Saint-Remèze, with information and exhibitions.

Upriver, the Ardèche rises in the Forêt de Mazon and passes through the Serre de la Croix Bauzon. This is a beautiful but entirely different area, with rounded acidic hills rising to almost 1500 m, clothed with moorland, scrub, and forests. As agricultural use has declined, huge stretches have been invaded by the broom *Cytisus purgans*, which turns whole hillsides golden-yellow in early summer. There are wild tulips, mountain pansies, pasqueflowers, wild daffodils, elder-flowered orchids, whorled caraway, and other flowers in the pastures, and tree-pipits, subalpine warblers, wheatears, and water pipits nesting. In the woods, there are goshawks, honey buzzards, and crossbills, to name but a few. It is a wild area, rarely visited except for those hurrying through on the main N102 which crosses the Col de la Chavade.

Hobby *Falco subbuteo*

Forêt de Mazon

Alps

Alps

Introduction

Although this region looks like only a tiny part of south-eastern France on the map, it seems hugely different when you are there. The land surface is much greater than a map suggests thanks to the enormous altitude range, and virtually all the roads are slow, so it takes a long time to get around the area.

The region encompasses the southern part of France's great eastern mountain wall, bordering Switzerland and Italy here. This area is much higher than the Jura or Vosges, and includes the highest mountain in Europe, Mont Blanc. It is a superb landscape for the naturalist, and much more varied than one might think. There are the mountain habitats such as screes, glaciers, and grasslands in full measure, of course, but there are also extensive woods, hay meadows, lowland bogs and lakes, major rivers such as the Rhône, and many other habitats. The total number of species cannot be counted, but it must be immense, with a very high proportion of France's species occurring somewhere within this region. The northern part, around the Chamonix Valley and along the Swiss border, contains the highest peaks, and is a superb territory, though protection is patchy and there are extensive ski-related developments. In general, the French Alps appear to suffer more from ski developments than any other mountain range, and quite large areas are disfigured. In the north-western corner of the area, north of Lyon, the Dombes is a quite different place, with hundreds of lakes spread out over a low-lying plateau, particularly good for birds.

Southwards from here, there are three major mountain National Parks, including France's oldest: Vanoise, Ecrins, and Mercantour, and three particularly important Regional Natural Parks: Vercors, Chartreuse, and Queyras, protecting an exceptional area of land between them. There are also protected locations in adjacent countries, notably Gran Paradiso National Park and Argentera Natural Park in Italy, so the total protected area is huge.

The attractions of the high alpine areas, and especially the National Parks, are obvious (and described in more detail in the following pages); less well known, though, is the vast area of pre-alpine land to the west of the Alps proper. Virtually all of this region is occupied by hills and mountains, many of which are quite spectacular and species-rich in their own right. They tend to be overlooked by people who are either heading for the spectacles of the Alps or the warmth of Provence. We have highlighted the best of these – the Vercors and the Chartreuse – but there are so many other minor ones such as the Montagne de Couspeau, Chaine de Belledonne, and Montagne d'Angèle that there is not space to mention. The vast expanse of hilly country between the Rhône and the Alps is beautiful, flowery,

Alpine marmot *Marmota marmota*

Previous page: **Pheasant's-eye narcissus (***Narcissus poeticus***) and globeflowers (***Trollius***) in the Vercors**

Alps

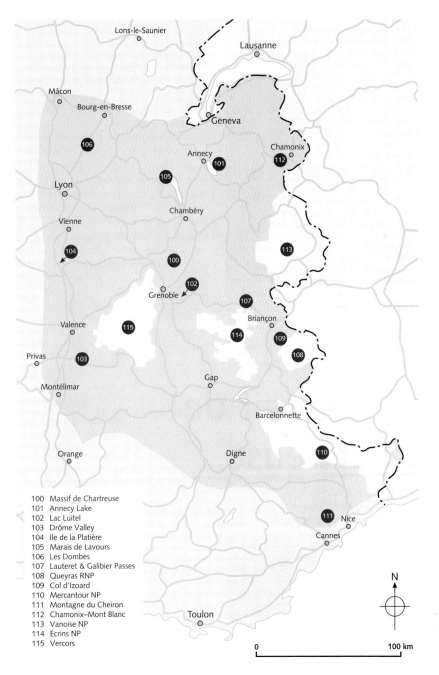

100 Massif de Chartreuse
101 Annecy Lake
102 Lac Luitel
103 Drôme Valley
104 Ile de la Platière
105 Marais de Lavours
106 Les Dombes
107 Lauteret & Galibier Passes
108 Queyras RNP
109 Col d'Izoard
110 Mercantour NP
111 Montagne du Cheiron
112 Chamonix–Mont Blanc
113 Vanoise NP
114 Ecrins NP
115 Vercors

N

0   100 km

barely populated, and always of interest, worth exploring at any opportunity.

If time permits, it is fascinating to follow the Alps southwards, perhaps along the 'route des grandes alpes', observing the steady change in species as you go. Some plants and animals occur throughout the Alps, while others are confined to more

Lady's-slipper orchid *Cypripedium calceolus*

northern or southern parts, and a few places have their own endemics. In general, the southern Alps are the richest, and the Maritime Alps are exceptional with their combination of high alpine species and warmth-demanding species on the hot southern slopes running down to the Mediterranean.

This is a marvellous region, impossible to do justice to in a lifetime let alone in a single visit. The southernmost areas, especially the southern slopes of the Maritime Alps, are of interest from March onwards, while higher and more northern areas are best visited as late as June to August. Many of the higher minor roads are closed by snow through the winter and on into early summer, even as late as June in places, which needs to be taken into account.

SITE 100 Massif de Chartreuse

Dramatic, wooded hills, with a fine mixture of plants and animals that are partly alpine and partly lowland.

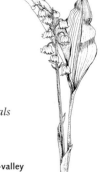

Lily-of-the-valley
Convallaria majalis

Alpine squill *Scilla bifolia*

The Massif de Chartreuse is a strikingly beautiful range of mountains, with peaks reaching to just over 2000 m. It is often described in local tourist information as a land of charm and mystery, which is apt enough. There are dramatic cliffs, peaks and gorges, vast forests, old villages, high grasslands, and a general air of undiscovered tranquillity. Anywhere else, it would probably be a major tourist site, but here,

Guiers Mort

squeezed between the Vercors and the Alps, it is largely overlooked except by locals, though skiing – and some consequent habitat destruction – has increased in recent years. Since 1995, 63 000 ha of the range have been designated as a Natural Park, and since 1997 a core high area of 4500 ha has been declared as a

Trumpet gentian *Gentiana kochiana*

National Nature Reserve, though active protection and management are not yet fully organized.

There are extensive forests of beech and Norway spruce, with smaller amounts of oak and larch, and scattered trees of wild cherry, wild service-tree, whitebeam, yew, and juniper. These forests have a rich flora, especially where they have not been re-planted or heavily managed. Flowers include wintergreens such as common and green, whorled and angular Solomon's seals, yellow bird's-nest, large-flowered calamint, hepatica, herb-Paris, lily-of-the-valley, snowdrops, spring snowflake, dog's tooth violet, lungwort, and many more. Orchids include narrow-leaved, broad-leaved, and white hellcborines, bird's-nest, creeping lady's-tresses, lady, coralroot, and the prize of them all, the lady's-slipper. Although not as frequent as in the Vercors (see p. 247), the beautiful lady's-slipper orchid occurs here and there, in woods or more open locations, never failing to impress with its beauty. Along roadsides and tracks, there are white butterburs, large-flowered foxgloves, *Adenostyles*, and several montane ragworts.

There are some fine, flowery pastures both within the forests and above the tree-line. These can be a mass of wild daffodils or poet's-eye narcissus, elder-flowered orchids (in both colour forms), early purple orchids, pasqueflowers, and alpine pasqueflowers in spring (usually May), followed by milk-worts, several forget-me-nots including alpine forget-me-not, alpine squill, martagon lily, gentians such as the tall spikes of yellow gentian, the intense blue cushions of spring gentian, or the striking trumpet gentian, perennial cornflower, masterwort, the bluish-purple spikes of aconite, and pinks such as fringed pink. The more sheltered places are perfect for butterflies and other insects, especially where there is old woodland nearby. These range from more widespread species such as orange tip, wood white, fritillaries including Queen of Spain, Glanville, spotted, heath, and knapweed, marbled whites, black-veined whites, ringlets, and skippers such as grizzled, large grizzled, chequered, and marbled, to more specialized mountain species such as Apollo and clouded Apollo.

It is a fine area for montane and alpine birds (though interestingly it is not identified as one of France's 277 important bird areas, nor does it appear in any bird-watching guide). In the higher areas, alpine choughs are common (and often quite tame), with alpine accentors, citril finches, snowfinches, and occasional golden eagles. Lower down, in and around the forests, there are abundant crossbills and nutcrackers, a reasonable number of the increasingly scarce black grouse, honey buzzards and sparrowhawks, and a few short-toed eagles. Woodpeckers include black, which one tends to associate with these montane forests, though nowadays they are more widespread, and there are several owls in the forests such as tawny, the majestic eagle, and Tengmalm's. Wallcreepers appear in the gorges from time to time in winter, and may nest on some of the higher cliffs.

Lynx *Lynx*

It is superb walking country, with many minor roads, tracks, and marked paths, and there are a number of caves. On the west side, the gorges of Guiers Mort and Guiers Vif are both impressive, and there are spectacular waterfalls in the latter. There is also the monastery of Grande Chartreuse, where the liqueur is made; one can enjoy the drink and take pleasure in looking for the 130-or-so flowers that are said to be used in its production!

It is also a good place for mammals, though as usual you have to work for them. The list for the National Nature Reserve (only a small part of the area) gives 43 mammal species as having been recorded. Some of the key ones include chamois in good numbers, and now partially protected from shooting – try scanning the high grasslands, especially on and around cliffs, to find them; mouflon, originally from introduced animals, marmots which normally advertise their presence with high-pitched calls of contact or alarm, and red and roe deer. To most peoples' surprise, lynx have recently reappeared (and are generally welcome), and other species include wild boar, badger, fox, beech marten, polecat, weasel, and a variety of others.

Owls

The easiest way to detect the presence of forest owls, and to identify them, is to go out at night and listen. Apart from tawny owls, with which most people are familiar, the two most likely species here are eagle owl and Tengmalm's. Both call mainly in late winter and early spring at night. Eagle owl most commonly produces a single deep call that slides from one note to another and lasts for about a second; Tengmalm's owl has a lighter, more ringing call consisting of 8–10 notes, rising then falling. It is an eerie and exciting experience listening to either in an area of wild mountain forest.

101 Annecy Lake

A large pre-alpine lake, with two nature reserves which between them protect a marvellous range of wildlife.

Annecy is a large natural lake lying in the hilly areas to the west of the high Alps, in the pre-alpine zone. The lake itself lies at about 450 m, and the hills around rise to almost 2000 m, making a very attractive

Narrow-leaved marsh-orchid *Dactylorhiza traunsteineri*

Orange-spotted emerald *Oxygastra curtisii*

setting. There are two key National Nature Reserves here, described below, on the east side and at the southern end, but many of the forests and rocky slopes around the lake are also worth exploring. The woods above Talloires, towards Col de Nantets, are especially good for flowers.

The Roc de Chère Reserve lies midway along the east side, just north of Talloires and close to Echarvines. It is essentially a small limestone headland, projecting into the lake, with scrub and woodland, open grassy areas, cliffs, and small areas of marsh. It is particularly rich in flowers (over 500 species) thanks to a variety of

habitats and a warm climate. Orchids are common, including military, monkey, lady, narrow-leaved helleborine, and pyramidal, and the woods have a mixture of lily-of-the-valley, several wintergreens, yellow bird's-nest, bird's-nest orchid, and many more. In more open areas, you can find wood crane's-bill, globeflowers, snowy mespil, *Cotoneaster nebrodensis*, alpine mezereon, and European Michaelmas daisy. There are also boggy places in the higher parts, where sundews, sedges such as *Carex limosa*, and clubmosses grow. It is also a superb place for insects, with about 80 species of butterflies revelling in the warm sheltered conditions, and a surprising range of dragonflies and damselflies, including orange-spotted emerald.

It is also a good place for animals of all sorts. Forty species of bird breed here, including red kite, goosander, and Bonelli's warblers, together with abundant nightingales, and peregrines often breed nearby. There are sand-lizards and green lizards in and around sunny clearings, and the aesculapian snake is frequent (a non-venomous relative of the

Roc de Chere

grass snake, which can grow to 2 m under favourable conditions). Perhaps surprisingly for an essentially warm, dry site, there are also six species of amphibians here, including the little yellow-bellied toad, which is often active in the day and has a musical 'boop…boop…boop' call, and alpine newts which are distinctively dark above and orange or red below.

There is a footpath into the reserve leading southwards off the golf course access road at Echarvines, but there is no public road access.

At the south-eastern corner of the lake, two small rivers – the Ire and the Eau Morte – have formed a marshy delta, 84 ha of which is a protected reserve. The habitats include reedbeds, fen, carr and drier woodland, and the lake margin. There is a particularly rich flora here, especially in the calcareous fens, with almost 500 species of higher plants, including 17 orchids and 27 species of sedge. Some species of special interest include narrow-leaved marsh-orchid, fen orchid, marsh helleborine, the form of loose-flowered orchid known as *Orchis palustris*, great sundew (a rare species in

France), marsh gentian, and fen ragwort in the fens, with sowbread in the damp woodland. There are similar amphibians (five species) to Roc de Chère, with the addition of the delightful little fire salamander, plus 11 species of reptile.

In recent years, beavers have been reintroduced on the Eau Morte Valley and are doing reasonably well. It is also a good location for birds, with about 60 species breeding, including kingfishers, goosander, great-crested grebe, water rail, great reed warbler, reed, grasshopper and marsh warblers, and many others.

Two good roads – the N508 on the west, and the D909 on the east – run alongside the terrestrial parts of the site, and there is a good path to the lakeside from a signposted parking area.

The Dranse Delta, which lies on Lac Léman (Lake Geneva) just east of Thonon les Bains, is rather similar. A reserve of 52 ha protects the woodlands, reedbeds, and marshes where the Dranse reaches the lake. There is a fine range of birds, flowers, fungi (over 700 species!) and much else, with access from a parking area on the west side, near the lake.

SITE 102 Lac Luitel

A small lake and marsh at high altitude, surrounded by forest.

Although the Lac Luitel Reserve covers only 17 ha it is an interesting site, and lies on the edge of a vast area of unspoilt and little-known mountain country, making a visit here more rewarding.

The lake lies at about 1230 m in a hollow surrounded by forest and moorland. It is a good example of a *Schwingmoor* – where living bog is gradually encroaching onto a circular lake, leaving a central area of open water surrounded by floating bog surface. Pines, and occasionally other

trees, attempt to colonize the drier parts of the bog, but as they grow larger their weight pushes the roots through into the acid water below, and they die, so the bog remains naturally open (until the whole system eventually becomes peat-filled and dries out). These are relicts of the last ice age, changing slowly towards becoming forest.

It is of interest botanically, particularly for the specialized bog plants, including 12 species of bog-moss *Sphagnum* such as *S.*

magellanicum, a similar number of sedges including *Carex limosa*, Rannoch-rush, sundews, round-leaved wintergreen, cotton-grass, and a good number of lichens, especially *Cladonia* species. Other groups are of interest, too; for example, although only 15 species of dragonflies and damselflies are recorded, these include the Arctic emerald, northern damselfly, and black darter. There are aesculapian snakes, common frogs, and resident crossbills and nutcrackers. It is an unusual location, with an Arctic rather than alpine feel to it. Access

is easy via minor roads, either up from Séchilienne on the N91 east of Grenoble, or from Uriage les bains, which lies about 8 km to the north.

Lac Luitel lies at the south-western end of the Chaine de Belledonne, a largely forested range of mountains running north-east towards the Vanoise (see p. 237). The peaks rise to around 3000 m towards the north, and there are high-altitude lakes and other glacial features, yet it is quieter than the main area of French Alps.

Floating bog and pool in the Lac Luitel reserve

1̤0̤3̤ Drôme Valley

An interesting stretch of the Drôme Valley, where multiple channels have produced a mosaic of unspoilt habitats.

The Ramières du Val de Drôme Reserve covers 350 ha of the Drôme Valley between Livron and Crest, close to where it joins the Rhône. The Drôme is a typical

alpine river, forming braided channels between gravel banks where it slows down in the lowlands, and this protected area includes a variety of stable and

The braided channels of the Drôme river

unstable habitats such as willow scrub, poplar woodland, mobile gravel banks, backwaters and main river channels, and flowery grassland.

It is notably rich in species. Over 600 species of higher plants have been recorded, including almost 100 trees and shrubs (some of which are introduced). Many are plants of disturbed habitats (sometimes known as weeds!), such as redshank or the naturalized *Ambrosia abrotanifolia*, but others are more specialized, such as the love-in-a-mist *Nigella gallica* (confined to disturbed areas in south France and adjacent Spain), bur-marigolds, 12 species of orchids, and 15 aquatic plants such as pondweeds and water-crowfoots.

The Drôme is generally quite rich in dragonflies, and sites such as this, where there is a variety of water levels and flow-rates, are best. Over 30 species have been recorded, including southern damselfly, scarce chaser, and the club-tailed dragonfly relative *Onychogomphus forcipatus*. There is a strong population of beavers

here, doing well, and 16 other species of mammal. It is also an important bird site, with about 70 breeding species. These include a large colony of little egrets, abundant black kites (about 200 birds), a thriving colony of bee-eaters, common sandpipers, little ringed plovers, hobby, kingfishers, and abundant warblers.

Several minor roads cross the site, and there is parking on the north bank, south of Eurre, with tracks through much of the reserve. There is a no-hunting reserve a few kilometres to the west, where the Drôme joins the Rhône.

About 15 km to the south east, Saou Forest is a superb hilly woodland with cliffs, home to a fine mixture of breeding birds, including short-toed and golden eagles, eagle and Tengmalm's owls, honey buzzard, alpine swifts, black woodpecker, alpine chough, and many others. It is also a good area for flowers and butterflies, and generally quiet and unspoilt. From Crest, take the D538 south, turn east towards Bourdeau, then left at Saou to head into the Vèbre Valley via Le Pertuis.

^{SITE} 104 Ile de la Platière

A remarkable reserve, consisting of an 8-km stretch of the Rhône with associated islands, and a rich flora and fauna.

The Rhône Valley is an important ecological corridor, though it is largely unprotected from a nature conservation point of view. This reserve of about 500 ha, the Ile de la Platière, protects and allows for the management of an important stretch of the main river about 50 km south of Lyon, and contains an intimate mosaic of river channels, gravel banks, grasslands, carr woodland, scrub, and mature forest.

It is an important bird site, at most times of year: 190 species of birds have been recorded, of which about 60 breed. There is a fine mixed heronry, one of the largest in the area, with large numbers of

Inula britannica

grey and night herons, and smaller numbers of little egrets. The activity can be viewed from the riverbank hide. Other breeding birds include kingfisher, a colony of bee-eaters, hobby, good numbers of black kites, purple heron, little ringed plover, Cetti's and other warblers, and many more. Eagle owls nest nearby and hunt over the reserve. At passage periods, large numbers of birds pass through, including hundreds of duck of various species, grebes, cormorants, and a few ospreys which linger for a while both on spring and autumn passage. There are usually large numbers of waterfowl in winter, too.

Otters used to occur but are probably no longer present, though beavers still are (5–6 family groups), and can often be seen along the edges of the water in the evening. Within the reserve 26 species of freshwater fish have been recorded (the Rhône has a particularly diverse fish population), and natterjacks and midwife toads can be both seen and heard. It is also very rich entomologically, and some groups have been well studied. For example, about 670 species of beetle have been recorded, of all groups – perhaps not to everyone's interest, but a good indication of the diversity and condition of the site. There are at least 20 species of dragonflies and damselflies, including scarce chaser, club-tailed dragonfly, and the protected southern damselfly. In addition, there are 32 butterflies, and over 60 species of molluscs known from here.

Botanically, it is also very diverse, with 550 species of higher plants, including flowering rush, two naiads: *Najas marina* and *N. minor* (rare relatives of pondweeds, which need particularly clean water to thrive), frogbit, fen bedstraw, bladderworts, *Inula britannica*, *Sisymbrella aspera*, and many more.

Access is from the D4 running west from Rousillon (on the N7), across the canal to a parking area. From here there are paths, including one to the riverside hide.

Just to the west of here lies the Pilat Regional Natural Park (actually in the Auvergne region, but conveniently mentioned here). This is a pleasantly unspoilt area of hills and low mountains, rising to 1434 m at the Crêt de la Perdix, covering 70 000 ha in all, between St. Etienne and the Rhône Valley. This is a very pleasant area to visit, with a high percentage of for-

est, and some fine bogs, lakes, and grasslands. The underlying rock is mainly granite, and there are distinctive granite outcrops on some of the hills. Breeding birds include Bonelli's eagle, hobby, black woodpecker, crag martins, citril finches, firecrests, whinchat, and ortolan buntings, among others. There are wild boar, red and roe deer, red squirrels, and martins in the woods, and some of the higher pastures are a mass of wild daffodils, poet's-eye narcissus, early purple and elder-flowered orchids, and other flowers in spring and early summer. It is an easy place to visit, with a good road network, endless marked paths, and information centres in most villages, as well as a park HQ at Pélussin.

105 Marais de Lavours

A combination of a large wetland reserve, the Rhône, and a large natural lake.

The Marais de Lavours Reserve covers almost 500 ha of fen, bog, carr woodland, open water, and mature woodland just west of the Rhône, at the northern tip of

the Lac du Bourget. It lies on a deep lens of peat up to 9 m deep in places, with surrounding deposits of clay and sand. Just within the reserve alone, there is a superb array of species, and most of the area around it has some fine habitats with additional species.

It is an important site for birds. Over 200 species have been recorded, of which at least 75 breed. Nesting birds include bluethroat, curlew, snipe, Savi's, marsh, and grasshopper warblers, and kingfisher, while many others which breed nearby feed in the reserve, such as short-toed eagle, honey buzzard, black woodpecker, and peregrine. It is also an excellent place for amphibians, with natterjacks, yellow-bellied toads, agile frog, pool frog, and tree frog amongst others, as well as the attractively named parsley frog, and reptiles such as aesculapian and grass snakes. The parsley frog is a curious little creature,

Large heath *Coenonympha tullia* (Peter Wilson)

rarely more than 5 cm long, and more toad than frog. It is pale greyish or greenish, rather warty, with numerous bright green spots (a bit like chopped parsley!); to continue the culinary association, it often smells of garlic! It can quickly be distinguished from young frogs of other species by its vertical pupils.

Lavours is a particularly good place for insects and other invertebrates, which benefit from the association of a variety of habitat types. Although by no means fully recorded, there are known to be almost 200 species of spider (including one new to science), 120 beetle species, about 260 flies (including two new to science), and hundreds of moths. Amongst the butterflies, perhaps the most interesting are the dusky large blue, scarce large blue, false ringlet, large heath, and large copper. The false ringlet is considered to be one of Europe's most endangered butterflies, declining throughout its range; it is actually more closely related to the heaths, but looks a bit like a ringlet. The two large blues are both uncommon species, towards the western edge of their ranges here. There are also 35 species of dragonflies and damselflies on the site, including bog specialists such as the white-faced dragonfly and small red damselfly.

Not surprisingly, the reserve is also a good botanical site. Almost 400 fungi and 350 flowering plants have been recorded. The latter total includes fen orchid, summer lady's-tresses, marsh spurge, grass-of-Parnassus, marsh pea, bladderworts including the inconspicuous lesser bladderwort,

Marshland and open water in the Marais de Lavours

two species of sundew, marsh fern, gratiole, loose-flowered orchid in its *Orchis palustris* form, fen ragwort, the uncommon willowherb relative Hampshire-purslane, and a variety of sedges and white-beaked sedge (probably the main food-plant of large heath here). It is a fascinating area, though not particularly easy to study, apart from along the paths.

The only realistic access to the reserve is southward from the main D904 Lyon to Aix-les-Bains road onto the D37 to Ceyzérieu, then left to Aignoz where there is parking and information.

To the south-east of the reserve lies Lac du Bourget, which is surrounded by wooded hills and generally quiet towards the northern end, with some fringing aquatic vegetation such as reedbeds. It is not a protected site, and does suffer both from disturbance and steady loss of habitat. However, there are still breeding grebes, various marshland warblers, little bitterns, and herons, and it is an important wintering place for large numbers of ducks, including up to 5000 pochard at times. The D914 along the west shore at the northern end gives good access and views.

SITE 106 Les Dombes

A vast area of land studded with lakes and marshes, with an exceptional range of birds.

Les Dombes covers about 1000 square kilometres between Lyons and Bourg-en-Bresse, centred roughly on Villar-les-Dombes, at an altitude of approximately 300 m. Although almost 80 000 ha have been designated as an Important Area for Birds (a non-statutory designation), there are no significant reserves or officially protected sites within the area.

The lakes are the key feature of Les Dombes, and there are at least a thousand of them. Some are of ancient, natural post-glacial origin, while many others are artificial. Although this is a superb place for birds, it is not the same as going to a good reserve – the lakes are hunted, fished, drained, and flooded at will, and often disturbed, and local tourist information gives much more information on what is there to be eaten rather than what you can see. Given this caveat, it is still worth visiting as there is so much to see. Breeding birds include great-crested and black-necked grebes (up to

Water-chestnut *Trapa natans*

200 pairs), small numbers of little bitterns, colonies of night heron, a few squacco heron, lots of purple and grey herons, little egrets, and small numbers of white storks, often to be seen nesting on pylons and artificial platforms. Marsh harriers are present, though not as common as one might expect, perhaps because the habitat is so discontinuous, and there are good numbers of breeding gadwall, pochard, red-crested pochard, black-winged stilts, and large numbers of

Grey Heron *Ardea cinerea* **(Mike Lane)**

wing, goldeneye, cormorant, mallard, and other wildfowl in winter; at passage periods, there are interesting species such as black stork, white-tailed eagle, osprey, common cranes, black terns, and many smaller birds. Probably the best time for a visit is late spring or early summer, though almost any time can be good, avoiding July–August, and the autumn hunting period can be depressing.

As you might expect, it is also a good area for amphibians, including edible frog, tree frog, and natterjacks. Fish are abundant, though they are mainly carp thanks to artificial rearing, and this does not really help the diversity and abundance of other wetland life. Coypus are quite conspicuous in places, and the muskrat is equally common, but harder to find. It is a good area for dragonflies and damselflies, though not as good as the rather similar Brenne (see p. 76). There is an abundance of wetland and aquatic flowers, including conspicuous ones such as yellow iris, purple loosestrife, arrowhead, yellow and white water-lilies, frogbit, var-

whiskered terns. Amongst smaller birds, there are great reed, reed, Savi's, and melodious warblers, woodchat and red-backed shrikes, bee-eaters, hoopoes, and many more. There is an interesting combination of southern and northern species, perhaps because the Rhône Valley corridor allows such easy access from the south.

In winter, and at passage periods, there can be very large numbers of birds, with over 20 000 regularly counted. There are particularly good numbers of coot, lap-

Les Dombes – Lake

ious water-crowfoots, water chestnut, bladderworts, duckweeds, pondweeds, loose-flowered orchids, and many others.

The area can be easily surveyed from the network of roads, many of which pass by lakes and associated habitats. It is hard to predict where will be best in view of the problems mentioned above. However, a good starting point is the Parc Ornithologique (bird park) just south of Villars-les-Dombes. Many of the birds here are local species, and the habitats within it are the nearest thing to a protected area in Les Dombes. It is a good place for photography, and there is a certain amount of information on the rest of the area, including leaflets on suggested lake trails to follow. There are good lakes around Birieux and Lapeyrouse in the south, Dompierre sur Veyle in the north, and Bouligneux west of Villars, but it is best to explore the area thoroughly.

~~SITE~~ 107 Lautaret and Galibier Passes

Marvellous alpine flowers and high-altitude birds and butterflies, together with a fascinating alpine botanic garden.

The main road from Grenoble to Briançon, the N91, crosses the Alps at the Col du Lautaret (2058 m), and a minor road northwards crosses the even higher Col du Galibier (2545 m). These areas lies just outside and to the north of the Ecrins National Park (see p. 242), and are unprotected. The roads, and paths leading from them, give easy access to some fine high-mountain country, with a rich flora and fauna. The geology in the area between the two passes is complex; it is mainly acid, but includes some limestone and calcareous schist, producing conditions for a wonderful range of flowers. In grassy areas, there are elder-flowered and burnt orchids, Pyrenean buttercups, a pretty pink-flowered daphne *Daphne striatum* (like garland flower but hairless), alpine plantain, Snowdon lily, alpine skull-cap, rock-roses including the large-flowered alpine form, pansies such as *Viola calcarata*, alpine garlic, *Gentiana alpina*, often in abundance, alpine ox-eye daisies, yellow star-of-Bethlehem, several *Primula* species, and many others. In stonier places, the flowers include alpine cabbage, rock-jasmines such as *Androsace carnea* and *A. obtusifolia*, the pretty white-flowered *Callianthemum coriandrifolium*, and various cinquefoils such as *Potentilla frigida*, *P. brauneana*, and *P. nivalis*, amongst many others. In July, the flowers here are superb.

The garden on the Col du Lautaret is particularly famous, and well worth a visit. Most of the plants are well labelled, and many are growing in virtually natural conditions, often in masses such as Jacob's ladder. There are over 3000 species here, many from the Alps, though it includes mountain plants from around the world. The garden is open every day from the last Sunday in June to the first Sunday in September.

The mountains around the Col du Galibier

The area is good for high-altitude birds, too. Golden eagles breed within the area and can be seen overhead, with both red-billed and yellow-billed choughs, alpine accentor, ptarmigan, ring ouzel, redpoll, marsh warbler, and a few black grouse, though you would need to work hard to see all these.

The scenery throughout is spectacular, and there are good paths in most directions.

108 Queyras Regional Natural Park

A quite exceptionally beautiful high mountain area on the Italian border, with a wonderful array of flowers, birds, insects, and mammals.

Queyras Regional Natural Park covers 65 000 ha of high mountain country from Guillestre eastwards to the Italian border. It is one of the most remote parts of the French Alps, not only far from urban centres, but in something of a backwater, with only one minor road leading out over the mountains. The Regional Natural Park designation gives little protection, and both tourism and ski-related developments are increasing, as well as agricultural changes, though to date these have not been too damaging. It is a spectacular landscape, with peaks rising

mixture of alpine, southern, and central European. Over 2000 species of flowers occur here, including some special ones.

The lower areas are largely of limestone, and here there are many orchids such as military, globe-flowered, burnt, early purple in the form *Orchis mascula* subspecies *signifera*, elder-flowered, frog, and others, with cross gentian, pinks, globeflowers, wild tulips, pheasant's-eye narcissus, martagon lily, flaxes, and many more. The rare (and locally much-celebrated) milk vetch *Astragalus centralpinus* is fairly common in lower grassy places – it is a striking plant, with clusters of yellow flowers, though by no means confined to Queyras. In higher pastures, there are gentians such as a form of spring gentian *Gentiana rostanii*, yellow gentian, short-leaved gentian, and a sub-species of the yellowish-brown *G. burseri* subspecies *villarsii*; a pretty fritillary *Fritillaria involucrata*, alpine bartsia, louseworts such as leafy and whorled, the striking white-flowered *Anemone narcissi-*

above 3000 m all around, and up to almost 4000 m at Mont Viso on the Italian border. The habitats in the park include extensive alpine pastures, spruce and larch woodland, meadows, rivers, cliffs, screes, and small-scale snowfields. Despite the altitude, it is actually quite a sunny area (though very cold in winter), and the flora and fauna are a fascinating

Lichens

flora, grass-of-Parnassus, rampions such as *Phyteuma globularifolium* subspecies *pedemontanum*, bellflowers such as the impressive spiked bellflower and large-flowered bellflower, and many more. In wet flushed areas, there are willowherbs, the pretty *Swertia perennis*, Tofield's asphodel, more orchids, and a fine mixture of sedges and mosses.

In the cliffs and screes of the highest areas, there are many more flowers: saxifrages including purple saxifrage, *Saxifraga biflora, S. adscendens, S. diapensioides*, and *S. retusa*, primulas such as *Primula pedemontana, P. latifolia*, and *P. marginata*, and their close relative vitaliana, pansies, pinks, the pretty cress *Petrocallis pyrenaica*, valerians, and many others.

The woodlands have a different range of species, more typical of coniferous woods elsewhere, such as wintergreens, yellow bird's-nest, round-leaved bedstraw, yellow foxgloves, with alpine clematis common in open areas. The higher-altitude trees are particularly good for lichens, and some are covered with the striking yellow wolf's moss in

Black grouse *Tetrao tetrix* (Mike Lane)

combination with beard lichens and *Pseudevernia furfuracea* doing particularly well.

Queyras is excellent for bird-watching, with many alpine and forest specialities to be found here. In the extensive forests, there are abundant nutcrackers, crossbills, firecrests, crested tits, black (and other) woodpeckers, and several species of owl. Tengmalm's and pygmy owls breed in the forests, and eagle owls can be found in the lower gorges. The tiny pygmy owl has quite a high-pitched call, just a single note, almost like that of a bullfinch, or several notes uttered quickly, and a variety of less describable squeaks. It can be active in the day, particularly at dawn and dusk, and may sit in the tops of trees calling; if seen, it can be identified by its small size (smaller than any other European owl) and the calls. (See also p. 213). Black grouse are protected here, and are tolerably common around the edges of woods and in clearings, usually at higher altitudes. Rock partridges can be found on warm, rocky south-facing slopes, common and alpine choughs wheel and call overhead, and red-backed shrikes do well in open bushy country. There are citril finches in the higher areas, and occasional golden eagles, probably breeding elsewhere. On the rivers, there are dippers and grey wagtails, and ring ouzel breed in rocky places. Wallcreepers breed here and there on suitable cliffs.

Astragalus centralpinus

Nutcracker *Nucifraga caryocatactes*

It is also quite a good place to see mammals. Red squirrels are abundant in the coniferous forests, together with the less conspicuous pine martens and polecats. Marmots are common in the higher grassland areas and can quickly be located by their piercing calls. Nearby, there may often be chamois, especially around Mont Viso, and there are a few ibex. Wildcat are not infrequent in rockier woods – I followed the tracks of one for some distance after fresh snow on the slopes of Sommet Bucher.

The whole area is marvellous for butterflies, particularly in late June and July. Apollos and clouded apollos are quite frequent, and there are mountain clouded yellows (as well as the more common

ones), chequered, alpine, and large grizzled skippers, fritillaries including Niobe, Queen of Spain, shepherd, and dark green, rock grayling, dryad, and various ringlets such as sooty, water, and the rare Larche ringlet (confined to here and an area to the south, and named after the Col de Larche – see p. 233), and numerous blues such as baton and iolas. Other insects abound, especially grasshoppers such as *Gomphocerus sibiricus* (distinctive because the males have strongly swollen front legs) and *Podisma pedestris*, beetles, and moths including the striking Spanish moon moth with pale green wings and long 'tails', confined to a few upland coniferous woods.

There is little need to recommend specific places, as the whole area is good. Some locales of special interest include the Sommet Bucher, just south of Château-Queyras, where there is a driveable track up through marvellous woods; the high valleys above Ristolas, the high slopes of Mont Viso, or the unspoilt Val d'Escreins Reserve south-east of Guillestre, where a large area is protected by local community effort. There are various 'discovery paths' here and elsewhere in the park, including an Astragalus trail! The park HQ and information centre is in Guillestre.

109 Col d'Izoard

SITE

A spectacular and dramatic high pass in the southern Alps, with a rich flora.

The Col d'Izoard, on the road from Briançon into the Queyras Regional National Park, is a marvellous place, reaching 2300 m at its highest point. The col marks the boundary of the Queyras park, but this is treated as a separate site which many people visit while following

the 'route des grandes alpes' without intending to visit Queyras.

The north side is relatively gentle, with extensive open woods and scrub of arolla pine and juniper, with masses of montane or alpine flowers such as spiked bellflower, the burnt orchid *Nigritella cor-*

Alps

matic steep screes, punctuated by rock pinnacles and overtopped by cliffs – an area known as the casse deserte. Although at first sight it appears lifeless, apart from dwarfed larches and arolla pines, there are many flowers of interest, including alpine cabbage, the valerian *Valeriana saliunca*, the stemless composite *Berardia acaulis*, alpine toadflax, and creeping avens.

In the higher parts of the coniferous woods (mainly larch, arolla pine, and Norway spruce) there are nutcrackers, jays, crested tits, and crossbills, with citril finches at higher levels. Both red-billed and yellow-billed choughs fly around the high cliffs and feed in the flowery pastures, and alpine swifts 'chitter' overhead. Wallcreepers can sometimes be seen on the cliffs. There are rock buntings here and there, and rock sparrows lower down on the north side.

Not far away to the west (though longer by road) is the Bois des Ayes – Ayes Wood – one of the designated important bird areas. It

neliana (not to be confused with *Orchis ustulata*), a rather distinctive form with pale pink flowers that darken towards their tops, snowbells, the white-flowered Mt. Baldo anemone, garland flower, shrubby milkwort, the delightful one-flowered wintergreen, Mt. Cenis lousewort, spring gentian, pansies such as *Viola cenisia*, and many others on a rather calcareous substrate. The south side, however, is quite different, with dra-

The Casse Déserte in winter

consists of extensive coniferous woodland with moorland and bogs, home to black grouse (an estimated 100 birds), pygmy owls, black woodpecker, and ring ouzel, in addition to the more widespread coniferous woodland birds. It is reached from Briançon southwards to Villard St. Pancrace then on the D236/GR5 to Les Ayes and on upwards.

SITE
110 Mercantour National Park

Fascinating high mountains and associated habitats, with an exceptionally rich flora and fauna.

The Mercantour National Park covers most of the high sections of the Maritime Alps, the southernmost of France's alpine areas. It has a curious convoluted boundary, which is more a reflection of political issues and objections than an indication of the highest quality area, so we have not

Saxifraga florulenta

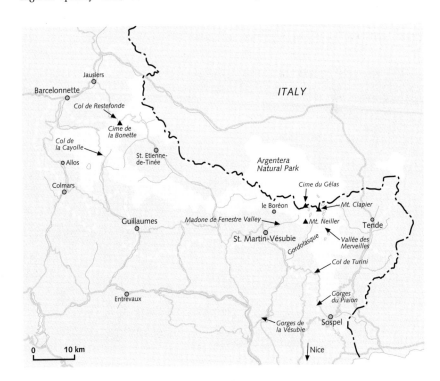

followed the boundary precisely in defining sites. The park covers almost 70 000 ha in two departments, and partly adjoins the Argentera Natural Park in Italy to the east. There is, as usual in French National Parks, a core zone sited in the higher areas and a peripheral zone around it. The area consists essentially of chains of high mountains rising to over 3000 m, dropping steeply towards the coast where it is heavily eroded into a series of gorges. Its position near the Mediterranean provides generally warm sunny conditions on the southern slopes, with the high places and north-facing areas being cooler and wetter. The geology of the terrain is complex, with large stretches of limestone in the lower and southern parts, and granite and other acid rocks towards the northern or higher areas, as a broad generalization. The flora is exceptionally rich, with over 2000 species, including 40 that are endemic to the area. There is also a vast insect flora, including about 100 species endemic to the Maritime Alps as a whole. The whole area is superb, and there is little need to pick out highlights – aim for the cols and experience everything along the way – but we have tried to

select a few sites of particular interest for certain specific things. There are a few nature reserves within the National Park, but they do not seem to offer anything extra. The National Park service runs various guided walks and other activities in the park through the summer, advertised in a free newspaper leaflet, or at the various information offices.

The Le Boréon area at about 1500m, north of St. Martin-Vésubie (an excellent centre) is an unspoilt mixture of grasslands, mixed coniferous woods, and high cliffs stretching northwards and eastwards to the Italian border. It is a fine area for the larger mammals of the park, especially chamois, mouflon, ibex, and marmots, all best seen towards the edges of the day. There are endless good walks in this area, such as north to the Col de Cerise, or north-east to the refuge at Cougourde. Birds to be seen along these routes include nutcrackers, black woodpeckers, crossbills, crested tits, firecrests, and possibly pygmy owls in the wooded areas, with citril finch, both choughs, alpine accentor, ptarmigan, ravens, and occasional golden eagles higher up. Flowers of interest around here on

The Col d'Allos with large yellow restharrow *Crocus versicolor*

the mainly acidic rocks include *Crocus versicolor* (endemic to the area) in spring, *Viola valderia* and *V. argenteria*, lesser twayblade and burnt orchid, alpine bellflower, *Cardamine asarifolia*, the endemic ragwort *Senecio balbisianus*, alpenrose, trumpet gentian, and many common and widespread mountain species. There is a famous cascade at Le Boréon, and the whole area is good for butterflies.

Madone de Fenestre Valley is lovely; the road passes through coniferous forests before reaching the meadows and ending at the Madone. From here, paths radiate out

Mercantour in autumn

Crocus versicolor

into marvellous mountain country such as the Cime du Gélas (3143 m) on the Italian border or Mt. Neillier (2786 m) to the southeast. The birds are broadly the same as for Le Boréon, and it is another good terrain for ibex, mouflon, chamois, and marmots. In the woods there are one-flowered and other wintergreens, and in the meadows and nearby rock areas there are orchids such as globe orchid, burnt orchid as *Nigritella corneliana* and the form of early purple *Orchis mascula* subspecies *signifera*, two attractive primulas: *Primula marginata* and *P. latifolia*, white false helleborine, houseleeks, gentians, pansies, and many more. Further up the valley, into the high granite peaks, there are masses of rosettes of the park's emblem, *Saxifraga florulenta* – a rare endemic saxifrage that sends up striking spikes of pale pinkish flowers from beautiful spiral rosettes, but which flowers only rarely. Here, you can also find the bright blue King-of-the-Alps, rock-jasmines such as *Androsace vandellii*, globularias, the endemic violet *Viola argenteria*, and many more. Butterflies here are abundant in summer and include Apollo, small Apollo, swallowtails, wood white, scarce copper, long-tailed blue, shepherd's fritillary, and many others. Dragonflies of note include the relative of golden-ringed *Cordulegaster bidentata*, and alpine emerald at the southern edge of its range.

The Gordolasque valley running northeastwards from the village of Belvedère is another fine area, with good flowers such as the bluish-violet *Hyacinthoides italica*, fritillaries such as the yellowish *Fritillaria tubiformis* subspecies *moggridgei*, wild tulip in its reddish-yellow southern form,

the composite *Adenostyles leucophylla*, and many more. There are superb walks onwards into high country around the Refuge de Nice and Mt. Clapier – spectacular country with high lakes – where ibex and chamois are common and sometimes quite tame, and alpine grasshoppers live in their thousands. The Vallée des Merveilles is a quite extraordinary place by virtue of its thousands of prehistoric rock-paintings, mostly in the open air, dating from the Bronze Age and mostly at an altitude of over 2000 m. Access is now controlled, due to vandalism and theft, and can be arranged through National Park centres.

The road between Jausiers (east of Barcelonnette – a good centre) and St. Etienne-de-Tinée (the D64) passes through some fine high country at Cime de la Bonette and Col de Restefonde, providing easy access to high peaks and valleys; this is one of the highest through-roads in Europe. Not surprisingly, it is normally closed between November and June, though one can use it to reach high areas for part of this time. These are good places to see birds of prey such as golden and short-toed eagles, and possibly lammergeiers (which have been reintroduced into the area), both choughs, ptarmigans, snowfinches, ravens, alpine accentors, and rock thrushes amongst others, with the more widespread forest and hill birds, such as crossbills and ring ouzel, lower down. Marmots are pleasantly common here, and are often close to the road early in the morning. Flowers are abundant, with drifts of narcissus-flowered anemones, elderflowered orchids, the pretty blue-mauve

King-of-the-Alps *Eritrichium nanum*

Peak white *Pontia callidice*

Primula marginata on rocks, purple sax-ifrage, alpine mezereon, and garland flower, cushions of yellow vitaliana, Mt. Baldo anemone, several mountain butter-cups such as *Ranunculus seguieri, R. glacialis* and *R. keupferi*, gentians such as the local version of trumpet gentian *Gentiana ligustica* with long pointed petals, and masses of the distinctive rosettes of *Berardia subacaulis*, a sessile composite with yellowish flowers. It is not the best spot for butterflies – perhaps too exposed and treeless – but there are high-altitude specialists such as peak white and Apollo, and you may see the endemic Larche ringlet (amongst other ringlets) which is named after the Col de Larche just to the north. Lower down on the north side, there are fine walks through forest and pas-tures, such as up the Valle de Terres Pleines to the lake of the same name, with an endemic sainfoin *Hedysarum briganti-acum*, the clover *Trifolium thalii*, saxifrages

such as *Saxifraga exarata* and *S. caesia*, alpine bartsia, and many others.

West of Cime de la Bonette, there are two other superb passes, the Col de la Cayolle (2327 m) and the Col d'Allos (2247 m). Both give access to some good high-altitude woods (mainly larch and spruce), high pas-tures, and mountain areas, with a fine mix-ture of wildlife. The birds and mammals are broadly similar to those of Cime de la Bonette. There is a small botanic garden on the south side of Cayolle, at Estenc, which is worth a visit. The south side of Allos is badly affected by ski developments, but there is a rich flora away from these, including the pretty Cottian bellflower, large-flowered bellflower, alpine mezereon, saxifrages such as purple and *Saxifraga lingulata*, the pretty reddish-flowered *Ononis rotundifolia*, and martagon and orange lilies.

On the east side of the park, there are some fine areas around Tende, including the upper Levense and Minière valleys near St. Dalmas-de-Tende. This is a classic area for some of the special flowers of the Maritime Alps, such as the beautiful dwarf rose-pink *Primula allionii*, which flowers in April on cliffs and ledges here.

There are many other places of interest in the park and surrounding area, includ-ing the Col de Turini and the valley leading south to Sospel, the gorges such as Gorges de la Vésubie and Gorges du Piaion – and almost everywhere else!

Alps

Montagne du Cheiron

Low mountains north-west of Nice rising to 1800 m, with a rich flora and fauna.

Northwards from Vence, the limestone hills climb steeply and become steadily more wild as the busy coast roads are left behind. On the southern slopes, there is a broadly Mediterranean flora with the pret-ty blue *Aphyllanthes monspeliensis*, lavenders, sun-roses such as the pink *Cistus incanus*, and the spring-flowering rarity *Leucojum nicaense*, a tiny white snowflake, and the dwarf iris *Iris lutescens* with purplish or yellow and purple flowers. In higher areas, such as on the Col de Vence, there are orchids including toothed, giant, lady, lesser butterfly, broad-leaved marsh, narrow-leaved helleborine, and various tongue orchids, with the fritillary *Fritillaria involucrata*, dog's tooth violets (which are actually pink-flowered members of the lily family, flowering very early), the striking lemon-yellow composite *Urospermum dalechampii*, and occasional poet's-eye narcissus. There are scattered bushes of a wild pear *Pyrus spinosa*, kermes oak, Christ's thorn, smoke bush, and others, with occasional wild peonies amongst them. The attractive everlasting flower *Catanche caerulea*, known to florists as cupidone, is common in open scrub and on roadsides in summer.

In the highest places, there are breeding blue rock thrushes, red-billed choughs,

short-toed eagles, subalpine and Sardinian warblers, and a few little bustards in open areas, at the eastern edge of their breeding range in France.

The Gorges du Loup is a superb limestone gorge north-east of Grasse, with good flowers including orchids such as pink butterfly, lady, military, and early spider, and breeding crag martins and blue rock thrushes. Peregrines can often be seen overhead.

The whole area is rich in butterflies, bush-crickets such as the distinctive zi-zi, beetles such as stag beetles and the enormous *Cerambyx cerdo* (one of Europe's largest insects, associated with oak trees), and there are fireflies in abundance in rough, flowery places. Fireflies are actually beetles; the males fly at night emitting a flashing greenish-yellow light to which the flightless females respond. The sight of a whole field full of flashing lights on a warm summer's night is magical. They are an eastern species, not found much further west than here.

SITE 112 Chamonix–Mont Blanc

Marvellous mountain country around the highest mountain in Europe, with a wealth of interesting natural history.

Around the town of Chamonix, running up to the borders with Switzerland and Italy, there is some superb high-mountain scenery. Although there is no National Park here, and there has been a fair amount of ski-related and other development, there is a series of large nature reserves which protect most of the habitats. North of Chamonix, there are five contiguous reserves: Sixt-Fer-à-Cheval,

Cetraria islandica

Carlaveyron, Passy, Aiguilles Rouges, and Vallon de Bérard, which collectively cover over 15 000 ha of fabulous mountain country, reaching to over 3000 m and including extensive forests, scrub, high-level pastures, cliffs, glaciers, snow fields, lakes, bogs, river valleys, and more – a complete cross-section of alpine nature.

Botanically it is very rich, though this is not a special region for endemic plants or many rarities. There is a very diverse flora of most of the more common alpine and montane plants, with just a few rarities. About 900 species of flowers occur in the whole reserve, obviously too numerous to mention in detail; a few highlights include: about 30 orchids such as globe, lady's-slipper (rare here, mainly found in the Sixt Reserve), fragrant, military, and the arctic–alpine dwarf mountain orchid; a dozen species of gentian including spring, cross, spotted, and trumpet; 16 species of saxifrages, 30 or so sedges *Carex* species, and others such as alpine

A mountain stream in the Aiguilles Rouges, passing through a larch forest

columbine, primulas such as *Primula auricula, P. farinosa,* and *P. hirsuta,* rock-jasmines such as *Androsace vandellii,* martagon and St. Bruno's lilies, alpine garlic, mountain bladder-fern and the rare alpine woodsia, alpine clubmoss, giant knapweed, and many more. It is also a good area for lower plants, especially lichens, particularly the map lichens *Rhizocarpon* species, *Umbilicaria* species, numerous *Cladonia* species, *Cetraria islandica, Stereocaulon* species, beard lichens, the bright orange *Xanthoria elegans,* and many more, which do especially well on the hard granite of the Aiguilles Rouge area.

There are most of the mammals of the northern Alps that one might expect: marmots, chamois, ibex (reintroduced here, but doing well in places), mountain hare, stoats, weasels and martens, red squirrels, red and roe deer, and the rather endearing snow vole. There are also interesting amphibians, including the alpine salamander (a true mountain species, easily distinguished from the fire salamander – which also occurs, mainly lower down – by being all black, rather than bold black and yellow) in the higher woods and some alpine pastures, and alpine newt (which is not really an alpine specialist).

The birds of the area are marvellous, including most central European high-

Wallcreeper *Tichodroma muraria*

altitude species. Wallcreepers are not uncommon on higher, more mossy cliffs, where they breed, golden eagles and occasional lammergeiers (from a nearby reintroduced population) soar overhead, and both species of choughs wheel around the cliffs. There are ptarmigan, ring ouzels, alpine accentors, snowfinches, rock thrushes, and rock partridges in open rocky areas, and crag and house martins and alpine swifts around the cliffs. In the more wooded valleys, eagle owls and Tengmalm's owls both breed (see p. 213), with nutcrackers, crossbills, crested tits, and firecrests among others. Hazelhen and black grouse can both be found here, though neither is easy to see.

It is also – not surprisingly – a good location for butterflies and other insects. Amongst the long list of butterflies, some highlights include Apollo and small Apollo, moorland clouded yellow, large blue, peak white, and dozens of other coppers, blues, ringlets, and fritillaries.

Entry to these reserves is free and open, though mainly it is necessary to walk. The Chamonix to Martigny road passes by the Aiguilles Rouge Reserve, and there are good marked paths from it. A minor road westwards from Taninges reaches into the reserve at the spectacular Cirque de Fer-à-Cheval; on the way, it passes close to the Plateau de Loex, just east of Les Gets, which is a good area for black grouse and other forest birds.

South of Chamonix, the Contamines-Montjoie Reserve protects an area on the

Ibex *Capra ibex*

Purple saxifrage *Saxifraga oppositifolia*

western flank of Mont Blanc, reaching up to just over 4000 m at the Aiguille de Bionnassay. The reserve covers 5500 ha of superb high-mountain scenery, including spruce forest, alpine grassland, cliffs, scrub with alpenrose, green alder woods, and glaciers. A large glacier, the glacier de Tré la Tête, occupies much of the higher part of the reserve.

The bird life is broadly similar to the group of reserves described above, with virtually all of the same breeding species (about 60 species of birds breed in the reserve). It is botanically rich, with about 650 species recorded, including many high-altitude and snowfield species, with 56 specifically alpine species. Alpine columbine, rock-jasmines such as *Androsace alpina*, *A. vandellii*, *A. pubescens*, and *A. helvetica*, primulas such as *Primula hirsuta* and *P. farinosa* (as well as oxlips and cowslips), alpine garlic, saxifrages such as purple saxifrage, the dull yellow *Saxifraga seguieri*, and the striking spikes of pyramidal saxifrage, Queen-of-the-Alps with its lovely electric blue flowers that are especially good for insects, alpine yarrows such as *Achillea erba-rotta*, alpine saussurea, *Arenaria biflora*, and the pretty little blue arabis, to name but a few. The rather rare and mainly eastern marshorchid *Dactylorchis sudetica* occurs here.

Mammals are similar to the northern reserves. The snow vole is notable here, because it has been recorded as occurring at altitudes of up to 4000 m on Mont Blanc – a remarkably inhospitable environment for a non-migratory mammal. They live in grassy areas above the tree-line, where their network of tunnels often betrays their presence, emerging as the snow melts to bask in the sun, feed on grasses and seeds, and mate.

1̇1̇3 Vanoise National Park
SITE

A spectacular mountain National Park in the central French Alps, with a very rich flora and fauna.

The Vanoise National Park was the first to be declared, and is still one of the best known and most scenic. Its core zone covers 529 square kilometres, where there are no permanent human residents, surrounded by an inhabited peripheral zone

Northern beaked milk-vetch
Oxytropis lapponica

of 1450 square kilometres. It occupies the eastern half of the great Massif de la

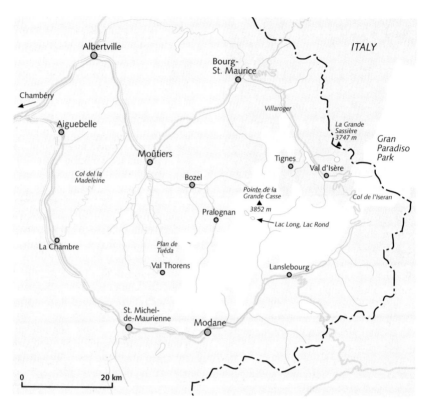

Vanoise, extending as far as the Italian border (where it abuts the Gran Paradiso National Park), and the highest point is the Pointe de la Grande Casse, at 3852 m. Within the park, there is a full range of mountain habitats – deciduous and coniferous woods, meadows, alpine pastures, lakes, cliffs, rivers, glaciers, screes, snowfields, and others. There are five major reserves in the park: Tigne-

Champagny (in two parts), La Grande Sassière, L'Iseran, Plan de Tuéda, and Les Hauts de Villaroger – all worth visiting, though it should be added that all parts of the park, and many of the surrounding parts, are also worth visiting!

Overall, it is botanically very rich, with about 1200 species of higher plants, of which 107 are legally protected at some level in France; there are also about 300 species of mosses and liverworts, and many lichens and fungi. Mammals within the park as a whole include large numbers of ibex (almost 2000) and chamois (about 5000), marmots, mountain hares, stoats, martens, snow voles, and 10 species of bats. The ibex move between the high pastures and cliffs in summer, where they breed, and the lower wooded areas and adjacent grasslands in winter (which is a long season here). Some 125 bird species have been recorded, of which 72 breed; there are currently 20 pairs of

Apollo butterfly *Parnassius apollo*

golden eagles in the park, as well as lammergeier, eagle owl, and many others.

L'Iseran is a large, high-level reserve on the east side of the park, covering 1500 ha on either side of the Col de l'Iseran (2770 m) on the road between Bourg-St. Maurice and Modane, which gives easy access to the high areas. The reserve is entirely at high altitude, between 2200 and 3428 m, so it lacks forest but has extensive expanses of high-altitude scrub, pastures, rocks and screes, and glaciers. It is particularly rich botanically, with 75 notable species (in addition to many more common ones); of these 18 are rare, with 11 protected nationally, and 7 regionally. Some special plants here include the rock-jasmines *Androsace*

Plan de Tuéda

Alps

Astragalus sempervirens

flower and more striking large-flowered bellflower *Campanula alpestris*, saxifrages such as the pale lemon-yellow *Saxifraga muscoides* as well as more common ones such as purple saxifrage, gentians such as bladder, spring, and trumpet, the beautiful *Primula pedemontana* on high rocks, mountain avens, dwarf mountain orchid, frog orchid, snowbell, several mountain willows, and many others. In wet places, there are dozens of sedges such as *Carex microglochin*, *C. atrofusca*, and *C. bicolor*, Scottish asphodel, louseworts, and many others. It is a good area to see ibex, chamois, and marmot, and birds of special interest include breeding wallcreeper, alpine accentor, rock thrush, and ptarmigan, in addition to the more widespread species of the park.

Not far away across the Isère Valley lie the two parts of the Tignes-Champagny Reserve, effectively two reserves; the southern part covers the spectacular Grande Motte Glacier, which extends from 3500 m down to 2500 m, while the less

helvetica, *A. alpina*, and *A. pubescens*, the beautiful, pinkish-red flowered *Primula pedemontana*, the very rare hawksbeard *Crepis rhaetica*, several saxifrages such as *Saxifraga valdensis*, *S. diapensioides*, and purple saxifrage, dwarf mountain orchid, bladder and spring gentians, and a grass that occurs nowhere else in France – *Sesleria ovata*, amongst many more common species such as moss campion, one-flowered fleabane, and edelweiss. In summer and early autumn, there are vast numbers of alpine grasshoppers, especially *Gomphocerus sibiricus* and *Podisma pedestris*, huddling together in warm hollows out of the wind, and high-altitude butterflies such as Apollo and peak whites are frequent.

La Grande Sassière is another superb high-level reserve, slightly more varied in character, extending from the Val d'Isère at 1798 m up to the high peaks on the Italian border. It has a complex geological structure, composed partly of the exposed ancient core of the Alps, giving rise to varied conditions and a rich flora. Species of note to be found here, mainly in the high pastures, include two uncommon milk-vetches Tyrolean milkvetch and mountain tragacanth, the closely related northern beaked milk-vetch, several rock-jasmines including *Androsace helvetica*, *A. villosa* subspecies *villosa*, and *A. pubescens*, the pretty alpine bell-

Masses of Arnica in the Vanoise National Park

Podisma pedestris

spectacular, but much more diverse, high valley of the Sache forms the northern section. The glacier is protected more for scenic and geomorphological reasons, and there is little in the way of resident species here (though the area round about is of interest, anyway). The Sache Valley part consists mainly of high grasslands, screes, cliffs and river, and lakes, mostly beautiful and wild, but rather spoilt by some ski developments (in a nature reserve within a National Park!). It is botanically rich, broadly similar to Sassière, with several species of rock-jasmine, fine grasslands with vanilla, frog, and dwarf mountain orchids, spring gentians, yellow bellflower, and others. Butterflies are not abundant, but they are of interest with Apollo, small Apollo, peak white, and scarce copper, amongst others.

The Plan de Tuéda Reserve lies at the western end of the park, and is very different in character. The Plan de Tuéda itself is a small lake at the base of the valley which extends upwards from 1700 to 3150 m to cover over 1100 ha of fine mountain country, with some particularly fine forests of arolla pine and Norway spruce on the slopes of the valley of the river Fruit. The lower forests have a similar general flora and fauna to those elsewhere in the area – crossbills, nutcrackers, crested tits, and fire salamanders, with the pretty little twinflower and one-flowered wintergreen amongst the flowers of interest. Higher up the valley, there are breeding golden eagles, rock thrushes, ring ouzels, and wallcreepers, amongst others. The artificial Tuéda Lake is not of exceptional inter-

est, though alpine newts and frogs breed here, and there are a few dragonflies.

Finally, amongst the special reserves there is Les Hauts de Villaroger Reserve (Villaroger Heights), which lies in the north-east corner of the park, covering 115 ha of mountain scenery up to 3650 m at Mont Turia. Although it is barely forested, it is managed by the Office National des Forêts (the forestry authority), though relatively little management is needed here. It is of particular value for its populations of black grouse, which are strictly protected here (though it is a pity that other hunting is not more strictly controlled) and breed around the forest margins in good numbers. Other features of special interest in the reserve include southern smooth snake, black woodpeckers, mountain hares, 400 or so flowers, and a good range of alpine lichens and mosses.

Access to all the mountain reserves is generally open and easy, and some, such as Tuéda, have information boards and trails.

Apart from the reserves, almost all parts of the park are worth investigating. Roads east from Bozel lead up valleys from where there is access into the high parts of the reserve on foot or by lifts, or there are particularly fine walks into the highest parts northwards from La Chavière chalets (north-west of Lanslebourg), reaching as far as Lac Long and Lac Rond, if you are fit and well prepared. The National Park HQ is, rather unexpectedly, in Chambéry, over 100 km away, at: BP 705, 135 Rue du Docteur-Julliand, Chambéry. Tel: 479 623054. They have a helpful range of information and organize guided walks in summer. There are information offices in all the villages around the park which can help with their own locales.

The mountains to the west of the park are also of interest, and less well visited. For example, the Col de la Madeleine on the D94 northwards from La Chambre is a good area, and gives easy access to high mountains such as Le Cheval Noir (2382 m) and Grand Pic de la Lauzière (2829 m).

SITE 114 Ecrins National Park

A large and spectacular mountain National Park, with a rich and varied flora and fauna.

Saxifraga pedemontana

The Ecrins National Park covers 918 square kilometres in its central zone, and a further 1789 square kilometres in its surrounding peripheral zone – a huge territory. Unlike the Vanoise National Park (p. 237), which is confined almost entirely to the higher areas, Ecrins includes a substantial amount of lower forested or open ground, and thus has a wider range of habitats, over a total altitude range of 800–4102 m. Within its borders, there are 17 000 ha of glaciers, 36 750 ha of high summer-grazing pastures, and 3000 ha of forests, together with cliffs, screes, lakes, rivers, snowfields, scrub, and other habitats. In 1999, there were an estimated 380 000 visitors to the park, though it can feel like more at peak periods in July and August.

Ecologically and climatically, it lies both between the northern Alps and the southern Alps, and between the western pre-Alps and the Alps proper. So its species have a complex mixture of affinities. The climate is complex – like most mountains – affected by warmth from the south, rain from the west, and other factors, together with its own complexities. For example, the south-western parts of the park are warm but damp, with well-forested hills; in contrast, the south-eastern part of the park is unusually dry for a mountain area. Briançon, for example (the highest sizeable town in Europe, at 1350 m) has a rainfall of only 55 cm per year, which is less than Marseilles. Broadly speaking, the west is wetter than the east, and the south is warmer and sunnier than the north, with many local variations.

Altogether, there are over 1800 species of higher plants in the park, with many additional lower plants, especially lichens and bryophytes. Of these, 40 are rare or endangered, and 35 are endemic. In recent years, the National Park staff have been compiling maps of all the rarest plants in the park. European larch is the commonest tree, with Norway spruce, especially in the damper west, arolla pine at higher altitudes, and beech and oak here and there. Within the park boundaries, 64 species of mammal have been recorded, including a number of particular note. Chamois numbers have increased in recent years (thanks to protection from uncontrolled hunting) and there are now about 12 000 animals in the park. Ibex were reintroduced in the early 1990s, and have increased steadily to the present total of about 200, mainly in the Valbonnais and Champsaur parts of the park. There are probably still small numbers of lynx, and wolves are occasionally recorded, while marmots are common almost throughout the region. There are mountain hares, red squirrels, martens, snow voles, and a dozen or so bat species, including the parti-coloured bat. This was only discovered in the park in 1995; it is very rare in France, and at the western edge of its range here.

About 210 species of birds have been recorded within the park, of which 110 breed regularly. The list includes most of the species you might expect in an extensive mountain and forest area. There are currently 37 pairs of golden eagles – a high

Waterfall in the Beranger valley

Alps

Alps

proportion of the French population, with peregrines, eagle and Tengmalm's owls, wallcreepers, a substantial population of the rare and declining black grouse (recently estimated at about 600 birds within the park area), and lammergeiers visit frequently. There are plans to reintroduce both griffon vultures and lammergeiers as breeding species here. An atlas of vertebrates has recently been produced by the National Park, giving localities for a wide range of species. Not surprisingly, it is also a good area for invertebrates, with a wealth of insects including about 140 butterfly species, the rare and very striking longhorn beetle *Rosalia alpina* in at least three localities, and much else. Altogether, the park contains 200 protected species under French legislation, and 80 protected in the whole of Europe.

Within the park, there are a number of specially protected reserves, described below, but anywhere in the park is of interest to naturalists and walkers. The largest park reserve is the Pics de Combeynot which covers almost 700 ha in the north-east, extending from 1800 to 3155 m. It includes a wide range of mountain habitats such as bogs, high-altitude scrub, alpine pastures, green alder and willow woods, cliffs, and screes. It lies immediately south of the Col du Lautaret (see p. 242), from which there is access, and partly outside the park boundary. There are 27 species of breeding birds here, including black grouse, ptarmigan, alpine accentor, rock thrush, and red-billed chough, and good populations of chamois, mountain hare, and marmot. The flora is broadly similar to that described for the pass in general, and includes 17 nationally pro-

Rock thrush *Monticola saxatilis* (Mike Lane)

tected species such as alpine columbine, alpine garlic, alpine clematis, several species of rock-jasmine, King-of-the-Alps, which is a very striking blue but only 10–15 cm high, and a number of species of primula such as bird's-eye primrose, and viscid primrose. The Séveraisse Valley Reserve covers 155 ha in the Valgaudemar area, southwest of the centre of the park. Although a relatively small area, it is something of a microcosm of the park, with woodland, pastures, the river itself, and cliffs, and breeding wallcreepers, rock partridges, nutcrackers, chamois, marmots, and wall lizards all occur. It is moderately rich botanically, and the flora includes five protected species: alpine clematis, *Primula pedemontana*, bird's-eye primrose, the willow *Salix daphnoides*, and the yellow star-of-Bethlehem *Gagea fistulosa* (= *G. liotardii*). In fact this whole valley is of interest, including the side valleys running north and south of La Chapelle-en-Valgaudemar, particularly for birds such as golden eagles, black grouse, ptarmigan, alpine accentor, crossbills, and many others.

The Cirque du Grand Lac des Estaris Reserve comprises an impressive high-altitude cirque and lake, covering 145 ha, at an altitude of between 2540 and 3086 m. The main habitats within the reserve are alpine pastures, grazed by sheep, and the lake with its surrounding wetlands. The nearby cliffs and screes, though outside the reserve, add to the visual and natural interest of the site. There is a rich flora which includes large-flowered leopard's-bane with its large solitary orange flowers, King-of-the-Alps, the pansy *Viola cenisia*, two

Golden eagle *Aquila chrysaetos*

Androsace alpina

uncommon rock-jasmines *Androsace alpina* and *A. pubescens*, two uncommon primulas *Primula pedemontana* and *P. latifolia*, the distinctive flat rosettes of the yellow-flowered composite *Berardia subacaulis*, and a rare grass Gerard's foxtail. Breeding birds here include snowfinch, ptarmigan and alpine accentor, and mountain hares produce their young in 'forms' next to rocks or amongst the bushes.

The Hautes Vallées du Béranger and du Vénéon Reserves are two separate valleys in the north-western quadrant of the park, rather similar to each other in character. Béranger, sometimes described as a gorge (but much more open than the average gorge) has a fine mixture of larch and spruce woods on steep stony slopes, with enclosed pastures on the valley floor lower down, and alpine pastures higher up. Tengmalm's owls breed here in addition to the usual range of mid-altitude forest birds; there are green lizards and southern smooth snakes in the scrub and grassy areas, while higher up there are chamois, ibex, marmots, and mountain hares. Amongst the flowers, the purple and yel-low spikes of a cow-wheat *Melampyrum nemorosum* stand out, and other interesting plants include the striking giant knapweed, and a dragonhead *Dracocephalum austriacum*. Vénéon is a splendid high valley, around the hamlet of La Bérarde up the valley from St. Christophe-en-Oisans, and on upwards to 1850 m. It is a particularly rocky area, with granite mountains all around, and moraines on the valley floor. Breeding birds here include black grouse, rock thrush, and alpine swifts, towards the northern edge of their range. Flowers include bird's-eye primrose, alpine clematis, alpine columbine, *Salix daphnoides* and the pretty purplish umbels of viscid primrose. There are also two other reserves: the integral Reserve of Lauvitel, beautiful but with restricted access, and the very small Reserve of Saint Pierre. This is too small to be of great significance, but it lies in a lovely valley that is well worth exploring; the D994 follows the St. Pierre valley up from Vallouise (on the east side of the park), passing through interesting montane habitats, rich in flowers and butterflies. There is a large car park at the end, from where paths radiate to many of the best high spots in the park, including the highest point, the Barre des Ecrins and some fine glaciers.

The park HQ is at Domaine de Charance, 05000 Gap. Tel: 0492 402010. There are park information centres dotted around the park at La Chapelle-en-Valgaudemar, Châteauroux, Vallouise, Entraigues, and Le Bourg d'Oisans. There is a good programme of walks and other activities.

115 **Vercors**

An impressive mountain area with an exceptionally rich flora and fauna.

There are many beautiful, spectacular, and species-rich places in France, but Vercors is undoubtedly one of my per-

Haller's pasqueflower
Pulsatilla halleri

sonal favourites for its landscape, marvellous diversity of plants and animals, easy accessibility, and remarkably unspoilt character. The Vercors mountains are a dramatic limestone range running roughly north–south, to the south of Grenoble, but the rock is clearly tilted downwards to the west, so the range ends abruptly on the east side in a line of high cliffs. Within the 1300 or so square kilometres that make up the range there is a marvellous variety of habitats and scenery – flowery high pastures, old hay meadows, pine, beech, oak, and other forests, gorges, rivers, screes, and cliffs, reaching to 2341 m at the highest point,

Grand Veymont. The Vercors are part of the western pre-Alps, that wonderfully hilly region to the west of the main French Alps, and as such seem to be slightly overlooked – they are almost completely uncommercialized and very quiet except at peak periods. About 135 000 ha of the Vercors, covering most of the best bits, are within the Vercors Natural Park, and within this there is a Nature Reserve – Les Hauts Plateaux du Vercors – which covers 16 662 ha, the largest reserve in France. The whole area is of interest, and we have strayed outside these boundaries where appropriate.

The main part of Vercors is considered to be ornithologically important, and a Special Protection Area under European legislation. At least 80 species of bird breed here, including good numbers of golden eagle, short-toed eagle, peregrine (about six pairs), honey buzzard, eagle owl, Tengmalm's owl (up to 20 pairs), rock partridge, black woodpecker, wallcreeper, alpine swift, ptarmigan, and about 200 black grouse, amongst many others. There are also 33 mammals, including ibex (reintroduced in 1989–90), chamois, marmot (also reintroduced), mountain hare, and a high diversity of bat species. Green lizards are common, and there are several snakes including southern smooth snakes, and various amphibians such as alpine newt and fire salamander.

Botanically it is extremely rich, with a good mixture of alpine, montane, lowland, southern, and northern species, though somewhat limited by the lack of acid soils or extensive wetlands. There are a number of protected species, such as alpine columbine, alpine bellflower, rock-jasmines such as *Androsace villosa* and *A. pubescens*, wild tulip, bear's ear primrose, the stemless yellow composite *Berardia subacaulis*, edelweiss, Haller's pasqueflower (very rare in France) – a noticeably alpine list. Lower down, there are some beautiful and distinctive flowers such as the pretty *Eryngium spinalbum*, a redflowered shrubby restharrow *Ononis rotundifolia*, and abundant orchids

Chamois *Rupicapra rupicapra*

including the little-known small spider orchid *Ophrys araneola* and the elusive lady's-slipper orchid. It would be fair to say that lady's-slipper orchids are more common in the Vercors than anywhere else I know, and are relatively easy to find once you tune into their most frequent habitat requirement of semi-shaded, moderately stable limestone clitter or morainic material.

The area is too large to describe in detail, but it may be helpful to recount one walk which encompasses most of what is best about Vercors, with some other sites suggested in outline later. The N75 (E712) runs along the eastern edge of Vercors; south of Monestier, there is a turning to St. Michel-les-Portes, the D8a, which climbs on through the village towards the Col de L'Allimas; about 5 km after St. Michel, on a sharp bend where the road leaves a valley, a track heads left up the valley, signposted to Mt. Aiguille, Col de l'Aupel, etc. (no vehicles). An ideal walk follows this valley up to the col on the west side of Mt. Aiguille, then down through the woods to Richardière or

even Chichilianne. Depending on your transport arrangements, you can then walk back via forest tracks on the east side of Mt. Aiguille if required.

The lower parts of the valley consist of a patchwork of hay meadows, scrub, rough grassland, and beech and spruce woods. The meadows are full of greater hay rattle, at least three species of rampions, pheasant's-eye narcissus, pasqueflowers, orchids such as common-spotted and burnt, while drier, grassier patches have military, lady, and fragrant. There are globe orchids in a few fields. Butterflies such as Queen of Spain and Glanville fritillaries, chequered skipper, clouded and pale clouded yellows, Duke of Burgundy, and many others are abundant, with day-flying moths such as broad-bordered bee hawk, humming-bird hawk, and other insects such as bee chafer and rose chafer. In and around the woods, there are Jupiter's staff, lily-of-the-valley, may lily, orchids such as bird's-nest, coral-root, and a few lady's-slippers, mezereon, lungworts, whorled Solomon's seal, and the beautiful yellow and blue cow-wheat

Pheasant's-eye narcissus *Narcissus poeticus*

Melampyrum nemorosum. Black wood-peckers can be heard calling in the woods, and on one occasion a golden eagle flew over carrying a young marmot! Eventually, the path starts to climb more steeply towards the col, giving access to a different range of species on scree and upland pastures. There are crested tits and crossbills in the upper woods, alpine and red-billed choughs can be heard calling from the cliffs, and eagles and buzzards are liable to pass overhead. In the higher grasslands, there are snowbells, stemless carline thistles, globularias, broomrapes such as the distinctive *Orobanche gracilis*, the pretty *Eryngium spinalbum*, gentians such as spring and narrow-leaved trumpet gentian, pyramidal bugle, additional orchids such as the rare *Orchis spitzellii*, creamy-yellow *O. pallens*, fly and late spider orchids, and more lady's-slippers; crocuses, daffodils, Seguier's buttercup, alpine honeysuckle, alpine pasqueflower … and more. There are wood white butterflies, masses of skippers and blues, a few apollos, and the occasional Camberwell beauty. The views at the top of the pass are spectacular: Mt. Aiguille (2086 m) is probably the most distinctive and impressive feature in the area, an isolated needle or buttress (depending where you look from) with high cliffs and a skirt of screes. The choughs, eagles, and buzzards are all much closer to you here, and marmots can be heard calling from the grassy

Mountain hare *Lepus timidus*

slopes. There are snow voles in the high grasslands, and roe deer and wild boar in the woods. The walk down is a steady descent through grassy screes, scrub, and eventually extensive woods with many of the species mentioned for the ascent, often in abundance. Around Richardière, there are flowery hay meadows, and an attractive limestone river with masses of stoneflies, frogs, and a few wetland plants. Glow-worms and bats are common at night, and Scops owls call in some of the villages. Altogether, it is a superbly varied and interesting area, within a small compass.

Other fine sites within the Vercors area include the Cirque d'Archiane and the Gorges des Gas on the south side of the hills. Superb minor roads run along the eastern flanks of the range around Gresse-en-Vercors and Château-Bernard, crossing passes such as Col de L'Allimas and Col de Deux. These roads and passes give access to some splendid high hay meadows full of flowers, and some fine areas of woodland, always with marvellous views. On the north side, the Gorge d'Engins has good flowers and butterflies, and lots of green lizards. On the west side, the Combe Laval and Col de la Machine are both beautiful, with extensive forest, but Vercors is one of those areas where almost anywhere is worth investigating. There are also numerous caves in the region, many of them well known.

The park HQ is at Chemin des Fusilles, Lans-en-Vercors, though there are additional information centres at many other villages such as Chamaloc, St. Jean-en-Royans, and Autrans.

Globe orchid *Traunsteinera globosa*

Pyrenees

Pyrenees

Pyrenees

Introduction

The Pyrenees are one of the most striking and important mountain ranges in Europe. They stretch for 450 km like a huge wall across the 'neck' of the Iberian Peninsula, not only separating France from Spain, but also creating a major climatic, ecological, and social barrier. Although they do not contain the highest peaks in either France or Spain, the Pyrenees are nevertheless formidable, with many peaks over 3000 m, and few low passes in the central area. Structurally, there is quite a noticeable difference between the French side and the Spanish side; in France, the Pyrenees rise sharply from relatively low-lying plains and foothills, and are a major geographical feature, whereas on the Spanish side, there is a vast and complicated area of lower mountains stretching away southwards and westwards.

As with most significant mountain regions, they create their own climate, and are considerably wetter and cooler than the surrounding areas of land. Their climate is complicated by the fact that they stretch roughly west–east, from the Atlantic Ocean to the Mediterranean Sea; since most of the wet weather sweeps in from the north-west, off the Atlantic, this creates two distinct trends within the range. The northern side, almost entirely in France, receives much more rain than the southern side, which lies partly in a rain shadow, and there is also a distinct lessening of rainfall eastwards along the range, particularly on the French side. The western parts of the Pyrenees are amongst the wettest places in France, whereas the area around Perpignan, close to the eastern end of the Pyrenees, is the

driest. Broadly speaking, the border between France and Spain follows the crest of the range, but there are anomalies, especially as the crest is by no means clear-cut. The Val d'Aran, for example, is in Spain but has more of the character of France, whereas the area around Bourg-Madame in France is decidedly trans-Pyrenean, with a much drier climate. The state of Andorra lies between France and Spain in the east-central Pyrenees, which complicates the border further, and there is also a curious enclave of Spain within France at Llivia.

The Pyrenees are superb for the naturalist, with an abundance of things to see throughout the spring, summer, and autumn. They are noticeably less developed and spoilt than the French Alps, and have been described as the last great wilderness in western Europe (though perhaps some areas in Scandinavia would qualify better for this designation). They are high enough and large enough to have a full development of species, yet are quite isolated from other high mountains, especially on the French side, which has allowed a number of endemics to evolve, though because of the structure of the mountains on the Spanish side, many of these endemics are shared with the mountains to the south or the Cordillera Cantabrica stretching away westwards. The flora is particularly rich: in the Pyrenees as a whole, there are over 3000 species of flowers recorded, and in the relatively small area of the French National Park alone (see p. 264), there are 120 endemic species or varieties. In general, the flora is a splendid mixture of northern, southern, Atlantic, alpine, and Arctic, with the added bonus of many special Pyrenean species, which means that you

Pyrenees

are always seeing something new. Other groups are not quite so rich in endemics, partly because they are more mobile, though amongst the vertebrates there is the delightful Pyrenean desman (a sort of aquatic mole – see p. 252), the local version of chamois, known as the isard, and the Pyrenean brook salamander, amongst

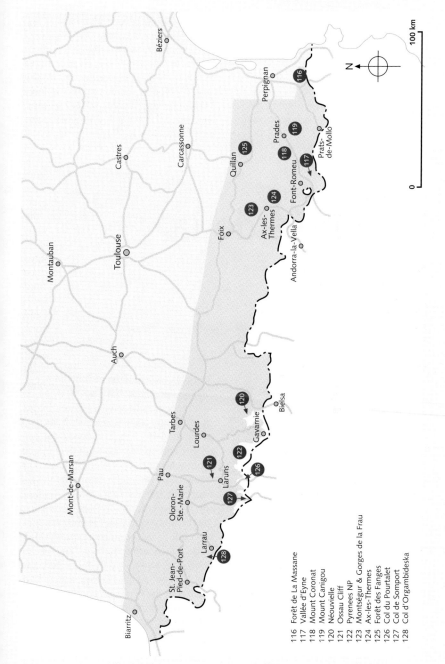

100 km

N

116 Forêt de La Massane
117 Vallée d'Eyne
118 Mount Coronat
119 Mount Canigou
120 Néouvielle
121 Ossau Cliff
122 Pyrenees NP
123 Montségur & Gorges de la Frau
124 Ax-les-Thermes
125 Forêt des Fanges
126 Col du Pourtalet
127 Col de Somport
128 Col d'Orgambideska

Pyrenees

Pyrenean desman *Galemys pyrenaicus*

others. There are a few endemic species or varieties of butterflies, such as the Gavarnie blue (which is not quite as

restricted as its name suggests), the Gavarnie ringlet, and Lefèbvre's ringlet.

The Pyrenees are worth visiting at any time of the year, though the winters are cold and snowy, and access is likely to be very restricted between November and May. Any time between April and early November will be of interest, with peak flowers in May and June at lower levels, or in July higher up; butterflies are at their best in June and July, while for birds May–June and again in September– October (for spectacular migration) are the optimum times.

SITE 116 Forêt de la Massane

Ancient woodland in the eastern foothills of the Pyrenees, especially rich in invertebrate life.

The Forêt de la Massane National Nature Reserve covers 336 ha of fine old woodland on the slopes of the eastern Pyrenees, in a range of hills known as the Albères, running up to the Spanish border. It is dominated by beech and oak (mainly downy and holm oaks), with field maple, Montpellier maple, sweet chestnut, and other trees in smaller amounts. Some, especially the beeches, are very old, and this is one of the reasons that the site is so good entomologically. It is one of the few remaining fragments of mid-altitude ancient Mediterranean forest, and has not been exploited for over a hundred years. The Albères hills are slightly separate from the rest of the Pyrenees, and they have as many links, ecologically, with the Spanish hills to the south as with the Pyrenees.

Thus they are the northernmost outpost of some Spanish species, and some of the Pyrenean species occur in slightly different races here.

The forest is an outstanding place entomologically, partly because it has been well studied, but also because of its habitat structure, long continuity, and geographical position. Well over 3000 species of invertebrates have been recorded, including 1415 beetle species, 7 of which are endemic only to the reserve, 58 species of ants, 317 moths and butterflies, 358 spiders, 390 species of flies, 39 species of annelid worms, 23 crustaceans, and many others. A number of records new to France have been made here, and there are many endemic French, Pyrenean, or regional species.

Some highlights include the striking bright blue beetle *Hoplia caerulea*, the pretty metallic *Anthaxia midas* subspecies *oberthuri* (known only from three or four other places in France), and the impressive coppery-green ground beetle *Chrysocarabus rutilans*, amongst the usual mixture of stag beetles, longhorn beetles, and rove beetles; and 106 species of hoverflies have been recorded including the rare *Syrphus lapponicus*, and *Scaeva dignota*, amongst others.

It is also rich in other forms of animal life. Well over 50 species of birds breed here, including red-backed shrikes, woodlarks, Thekla larks, Dartford and subalpine warblers, and green woodpeckers as the Iberian race. There are over 30 species of mammals, including a dozen or so bat species such as Savi's pipistrelle (mainly Mediterranean) and Leisler's bat, as well as edible dormouse at the southern edge of

Hoplia caerulea

its range, garden dormouse with its distinctive black face mask, and water shrew. Painted frogs are common in and around the streams, midwife toads breed in suitable places amongst rocks or under logs, and there are several snake species, including southern smooth, aesculapian, and ladder snakes, amongst others.

It is not quite so special botanically, though there is plenty of interest. Lichens are particularly rich here in the unpolluted mountain air, with almost 300 species recorded, together with 63 bryophytes, 17 ferns, and about 200 species of fungi. Most flowers that you might expect here in a woodland on acid soil occur, such as cowwheats, bastard balm, orpine, wood-sorrel, and fly honeysuckle, and there are rare species such as the pink *Dianthus subacaulis* and the purplish-red lousewort *Pedicularis asparagoides*, confined to this end of the Pyrenees.

You must walk to visit the wood. The GR10 long-distance footpath passes through the upper parts. Alternatively, there is access up a track from south-east of Aregelès-sur-Mer past Mas Christine, and finally via a footpath towards the Col de la Place d'Armes (below Tour de la Massane); or you can travel by road southwards from St. André to Lavall, then on up the valley on foot – a lovely walk.

The whole of the Chaîne des Albères westwards from here to the motorway (and southwards into Spain) is of interest, with many fine wooded mid-altitude hills, or eastwards towards the coast.

Dianthus subacaulis

<small>SITE</small> 117 Vallée d'Eyne

A high flowery valley in the western Pyrenees, reaching up to the Spanish border.

The Vallée d'Eyne National Nature Reserve covers almost 1200 ha of a pretty valley reaching high into the Pyrenees, with an altitude range of 1700–2850 m. It is made up mainly of open grassland and scrub, with small patches of mountain pine and dwarf mountain pine *P. mugo* at the highest altitudes. There are great patches of alpenrose and purging broom revelling in the acid soils here, with screes, cliffs, and moraines at the highest altitudes.

It is an excellent all-round site for the naturalist, with good flowers, mammals, birds, and butterflies and other insects. For the botanist, there is a fine mixture of both widespread mountain plants and Pyrenean specialities, often in abundance, including the yellow flowers of Pyrenean pheasant's-eye (a Pyrenean endemic), the pretty umbels of viscid primrose, shrubby cinquefoil (which has a curiously interrupted distribution – rare, but with sites in western Ireland and north England), an unusual yellowish umbellifer *Xatardia scabra* confined to high-altitude screes in the Pyrenees,

and saxifrages such as the endemic water saxifrage, and reddish saxifrage *Saxifraga intermedia*. There are gentians including *Gentiana burseri*, and the violet Pyrenean gentian, the pretty red endemic Pyrenean hemp-nettle, Pyrenean lily, Pyrenean thistle, and the lovely alpine rose (a true rose, deep pink in colour, not to be confused with *alpenrose* which is a rhododendron), and many others. Higher up, on the scree slopes, there are three mountain buttercups, *Ranunculus parnassifolius*, *R. glacialis*, and *R. pyrenaeus*, with alpine poppies and pretty clumps of the candytuft *Iberis spathulata*.

It is a superb site for birds. Apart from the breeding red-billed chough, capercaillie, citril finch, black woodpecker, and others, it is also on a major migration route, and designated as a Special Protection Area for birds for this reason. In spring and autumn, vast numbers of birds of prey such as honey buzzards, black kites, harriers, and eagles, with bee-eaters, pigeons, and other passerines are forced to cross the Col d'Eyne at a relatively narrow bottleneck, and at times this can be spectacular, though hard to predict precisely.

There are also abundant butterflies, plenty of amphibians and reptiles, and some of the more conspicuous mountain mammals including chamois (known locally as isard – see p. 265), marmot, mountain hare, and wildcat.

Access is up the valley from Eyne village, where there is an information centre at Cal Martinet, 66800 Eyne, open all year but with more varied displays in summer.

Shrubby cinquefoil *Potentilla fruticosa*

SITE
118 Mt. Coronat

A mid-altitude forested mountain range with a notably rich flora and fauna.

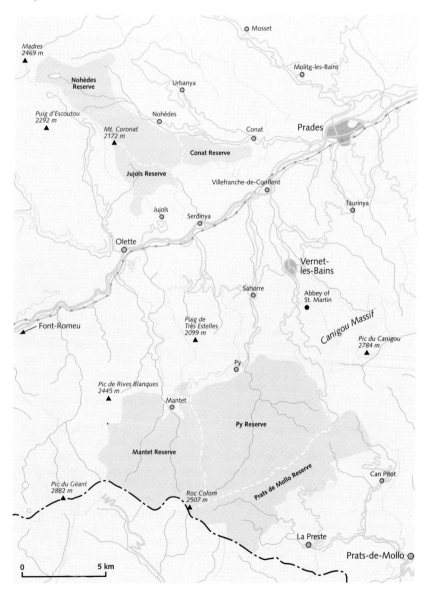

Ononis aragonensis

Strictly speaking, this is a group of three separately named National Nature Reserves known as Conat-Bettlans, Nohèdes, and Jujols, but since they are entirely contiguous it is easier to refer to them collectively. Between them, they cover over 30 square kilometres of the Massif des Madres and Mt. Coronat, a range of mid-altitude wooded mountains north of the Têt Valley. They are dominated by Scots pine forest, some mountain pine, patches of beech forest, and extensive areas of grassland and scrub, lying mainly over limestone and dolomite. The altitude range of the protected zone is from 760 to 2549 m, encompassing a marvellous variety of vegetation types and life forms. As with most large mountain reserves, they are protected primarily as areas of unspoilt habitat, rather than for a specific group of species, and are naturally rich in most life forms. They are recognized as one of France's Important Bird Areas, but have no international designations of significance.

Botanically, this is a very rich area, with a huge collection of species, many of them rare or endemic, or both. In the lower areas, there are warmth-demanding species such as box, lavenders, culinary thyme, Etruscan honeysuckle, Montpellier milk-vetch, and the pretty yellow *Fumana procumbens*. Higher up are more typical mountain plants, including many Pyrenean or specifically eastern-Pyrenean endemics, such as the alyssums *Alyssum pyrenaicum* and *A. macrocarpum* (both endemic, and formerly

in the genus *Ptilotrichum*), the lavender-leaved sage, alpenrose, caraway, great pignut, wild tulip, the endemic pink *Dianthus pyrenaicus* subspecies *catalaunicus*, and yellow stars-of-Bethlehem including *Gagea pratensis*. On rocks and cliffs, there are clumps of the endemic Pyrenean ramonda (related to African violets), and saxifrages such as *Saxifraga paniculata* and *S. pentadactyla*, amongst others. On the moraines, screes, and high grasslands above the tree-line, there are other flowers including trailing azalea, mountain avens, alpine toadflax, *Potentilla caulescens*, burnt candytuft, a restharrow *Ononis aragonensis*, the dragonhead *Dracocephalum austriacum*, Pyrenean columbine, Pyrenean figwort, rock-jasmines, and the pretty rock stork's-bill, among others.

At least 85 species of bird nest in the area, and many more are recorded on passage or just visiting. Amongst birds of prey, there are several pairs of peregrines, golden eagles, short-toed eagles, and honey buzzards, as well as a couple of pairs of eagle owls. Red-billed choughs are common, and there are crag martins, ptarmigan, grey partridges, and ring ouzels around the cliffs and rock outcrops, and dippers along the streams. In wooded areas, capercaillies are still tolerably common, and there are black woodpeckers and Tengmalm's owls, amongst other species. At passage periods, there can be good numbers of birds of prey such as honey buzzards, with common cranes, bee-eaters, and much else, but there is no clear-cut funnel where they can be seen in abundance.

Most of the mountain mammals of the Pyrenees occur here, with some of them in abundance: chamois, marmots, lynx, genet, wildcat, red squirrel, and the little aquatic Pyrenean

Salvia lavandulifolia

desman (see p. 252), as well as a fine range of bats such as Natterer's, Daubenton's, Leisler's, common, Savi's, and Kuhl's pipistrelles, and various others. Brown bears have been recorded, but they are so rare in the Pyrenees now that any sighting here is unlikely. There are midwife toads, natterjacks, stripeless tree frogs, smooth snakes and southern smooth snakes, Montpellier snakes, aesculapian snakes, ocellated lizards, and many other reptiles and amphibians.

As you might expect from such a varied and unspoilt landscape, it is also very rich in invertebrates. Almost a thousand moths and butterflies have been recorded, including marbled skipper, mountain small white, Apollo, and several burnet moths such as *Zygaena carniolica*, *Z. romeo*, and *Z. viciae*. There is a rare scorpion, numerous spiders including rarities, crayfishes in the streams, and much else.

Peregrine *Falco peregrinus*

Access is open on foot, with the easiest routes leading into the site from the D26 that runs through Conat and Nohèdes. This eventually degenerates into a track that crosses the range at the Col de Portus. There are information centres in the main villages, and refuges in the high peaks north-west of Mt. Coronat, suitable for overnight stays.

SITE 119 Mt. Canigou

A vast area of mountain habitats, rich in all forms of life.

Mt. Canigou, or the more appropriate Massif du Canigou (since it covers a huge area), dominates the eastern end of the Pyrenees. It rises to 2784 m at Pic du Canigou, but there are other high peaks

Gavarnie ringlet *Erebia gorgone*

around here, and it is sufficiently separate from the main range to stand out as a major geographical feature. Its huge area of convoluted slopes encompass an enormous range of habitats, from hot Mediterranean *garrigue* and *maquis* in the lower eastern parts, through holm oak and downy oak, to beech woods, coniferous woods, acid and calcareous grassland, boggy areas, snowfields, screes, cliffs, and other habitats, often covering considerable areas. On the south-western slopes, there are three large nature reserves covering over 9000 ha between them, and the whole site covers several hundred square kilometres.

Pyrenees

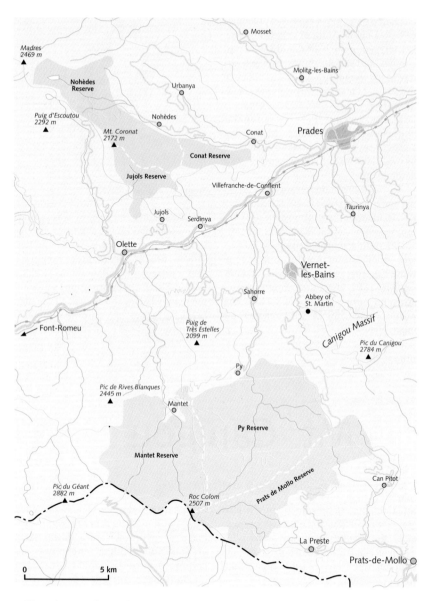

There is something of interest here for any naturalist, though it is particularly good for birds. Part of the area (contiguous with the three nature reserves) is a Special Protection Area for birds, and the whole mountain is of interest. About 90 species breed here, and many more pass through. In the higher regions, there are golden and Bonelli's eagles (which are rare), short-toed eagles (rather more common), a few lammergeiers, peregrines, red-billed and alpine choughs, alpine accentors, water pipits, ptarmigans and grey partridges, rock thrush,

Saxifraga geranioides

ring ouzels, citril finches, and rock buntings. In the higher forests and the adjacent scrub, there are red-backed shrikes, goshawks, Tengmalm's and eagle owls, black and other woodpeckers, capercaillie, crested tit, crossbills, nightjars, and Bonelli's warblers, amongst others. On the warm lower slopes, there are Dartford, Orphean, subalpine, and Sardinian warblers, with cirl buntings, woodchat shrikes, and a few blue rock thrushes. It is also an important migratory bottleneck in parts, and hundreds or thousands of honey buzzards, kites, bee-eaters, and even cranes, amongst others, pass through.

There are at least 35 species of mammal here, including most of the forest and mountain species that one might expect. There are isard (chamois) herds on the higher slopes in summer (or the upper parts of the woods in winter), genets, wild boar, pine martens, red squirrels, a few wildcats, and even occasional lynxes. The curious and little-known Pyrenean desman also occurs in some of the streams on the northern slopes. An aquatic relative of the moles, it is only 10–15 cm long, and was widespread in Europe before the ice age but is now confined to the Pyrenees and north Iberian mountains. They are very

hard to see, being mainly aquatic and mainly nocturnal, as well as being rare and shy. Their presence is best detected by the droppings, which are small, black, and twisted, deposited on any suitable perch protruding above the water. Midwife toads and ocellated lizards are quite common in lower areas, fire salamanders are frequent in the woods, and there are sand lizards, green lizards, wall lizards, western whip snakes, and various other reptiles.

It is also a marvellous place for invertebrates, including two endemic beetles: the ground beetle *Chrysocarabus punctatoaureus* subspecies *canigouensis* and *Cechenus pyrenaeus* subspecies *costulus*, together with many other beetles including the green and black longhorn *Chlorophorus varius*. Butterflies are abundant, including Apollo, clouded Apollo, ringlets such as Lefèbvre's, Gavarnie, almond-eyed, sooty, and dewy, and many more widespread grassland and woodland species. The strikingly beautiful Spanish moon moth occurs in the pine woods, and bush-crickets such as the upland green bush-cricket and the squat *Isophya pyrenea* are abundant.

It is rich botanically, too, though most species are widespread Pyrenean or southern flowers. The woods, and especially the beech woods, have species such

Chlorophorus varius

as green-flowered and common wintergreens, bird's-nest and coralroot orchids, yellow bird's-nest, whorled Solomon's seal, large-flowered calamint, purple lettuce, and many others. In open areas, there are Pyrenean lilies, Pyrenean eryngo, Andorran milfoil *Achillea chamaemelifolia*, and Pyrenean sneezewort, along with more common flowers. Higher up, amongst screes and cliffs, there are more special plants such as viscid primrose, the pretty red entire-leaved primrose, gentians such as spotted gentian and Pyrenean gentian,

the rock-jasmine *Androsace vandelii*, the uncommon umbellifer known locally as chamois parsley *Xatardia scabra*, saxifrages such as *Saxifraga geranioides*, *S. nervosa*, and *S. bryoides*, the small-flowered Pyrenean pink, alpine garlic, and many more. In wet places, there are butterworts including large-flowered, aquatic saxifrage, and an abundance of sedges. In addition, the lichens are outstanding, both in the open alpine areas and in the woods, especially those with old beeches. The ragwort *Senecio leucophyllus* with grey

Mt. Canigou Beech woods

leaves and heads of deep orange flowers is frequent on Canigou. There is a botanical nature trail sign-posted from near Prats-de-Mollo.

Access is open over more or less the whole of Canigou, and large sections of it are grazed by wandering flocks. The reserve areas of Py, Mantet, and Prats-de-Mollo–La Preste form a continuous large area in the headwaters of the Tech, lying roughly between La Preste (above Prats-de-Mollo) and Mantet. Access is open on foot to any of the reserves. Various minor

roads wriggle their way around the slopes of Mt. Canigou, such as from Arles, Vernet-les-Bains and Prats-de-Mollo, or jeep rides almost to the top can be arranged in Vernet or Prades. The GR10 footpath passes across the top of the peak.

If you are on the northern slopes of the mountain, the abbey of **St. Martin du Canigou** is well worth a visit for its architecture and position, and there is a fine range of lower-altitude nature in the vicinity.

SITE 120 Néouvielle

A large high-altitude reserve, with a spectacularly rich flora and fauna.

Although this showpiece reserve lies within the Pyrenees National Park (see p. 263), we have treated it separately as it is right on the edge of the park, and access is from a quite different direction from the rest of the park. This is one of the

oldest reserves in France, dating from 1936, though not officially designated by law until much later. The National Nature Reserve now covers 2313 ha of high-altitude wild country, between 1800 and 3091 m, reaching to the summit of the Pic du Néouvielle. The underlying rock is almost exclusively granite, and the habitats include permanent snowfields, screes, cliffs, lakes, pine forests (Scots pine lower down and mountain pine higher up, reaching to 2500 m), mixed forests, grassland, moorland, and bog. The natural life is extremely rich in all respects here.

Botanically it is outstanding, despite the lack of limestone. Over a thousand species of higher plants have been recorded, together with hundreds of mosses, liverworts, lichens, algae, and fungi. The flora is a fascinating mixture of different biogeographical types – such as the Atlantic cross-leaved heath, the Mediterranean umbellifer *Molopospermum peloponnesiacum* (which, curiously enough, does not occur in the Peloponnese) and the north

European marsh cinquefoil, together with alpine and endemic Pyrenean specialities. In grasslands and other open patches, there are plants such as alpenrose, bearberry and bilberry, garland flower, clubmosses including alpine and interrupted, oxlips, yellow star-of-Bethlehem, orchids such as the burnt or vanilla orchid, dwarf juniper, sedges such as *Carex depressa*, pansies, alpine pasqueflower, rampions (including a long-bracted species sometimes called *Phyteuma gaussenii* and considered to be endemic), wild daffodils, and gentians such as *Gentiana alpina*, amongst many others. On shady rock faces, the endemic *Ramonda myconi* is frequent, often with *Primula integrifolia*, and large-flowered butterworts in wetter spots. Higher up, there are rock-jasmines including *Androsace vandellii*, *A. villosa*, and the cushion-forming *A. pyrenaica*, alpine onion, primroses such as bird's-eye, viscid, *P. hirsuta*, and the closely related yellow-flowered vitaliana, the pretty *Chaenorhinum origanifolium* (related to snapdragons), perennial snapdragon, the so-called English iris, the striking Pyrenean saxifrage, and many others. There are also bog plants such as sundews and 22 species of bog-moss *Sphagnum*, an endemic bur-reed *Sparganium angustifolium* subspecies *borderi*, and many more. Because of the great altitude range, there is something different to see at any time right through the spring and summer.

The bird life is broadly similar to Mt. Canigou and other higher mountains, though this is probably not the easiest area in which to see the full range of species. There are red-billed choughs, citril finches in pleasant abundance, snowfinches, alpine accentors, and ring ouzels, amongst others in the higher open areas; lower down, there are capercaillie, black and other woodpeckers, crested tits, firecrests, crossbills, and other typical montane woodland birds. Birds of prey are surprisingly thin on the ground, though lammergeiers and golden eagles pass overhead occasionally. There are herds of chamois on the high slopes,

marmots are common, and red squirrels, pine martens, and roe deer live in the woods. The Pyrenean desman (see p. 252) occurs in the streams and other wet areas, along with the similarly restricted Pyrenean brook salamander – an inconspicuous, newt-like amphibian.

Not surprisingly, Néouvielle is also excellent for insects and other invertebrates. Almost 400 species of beetle have been recorded, with 124 flies and 150 spiders, to name but a few. Amongst the butterflies, the Apollo, clouded Apollo, several ringlets, the Glandon blue and the Gavarnie blue, and numerous fritillaries stand out as highlights. In high summer, from early July onwards, large numbers of butterflies (mainly blues and skippers but with others, too) often gather on wet patches where there are concentrations of mineral salts.

The only realistic road access to the reserve is via the minor road which turns off the D929 at Fabian above St. Lary-Soulan, signposted to the reserve and the lakes. The last 6 km of the road (which is closed by snow for much of the year) is open to vehicles only before 9.30 am (you can return at any time) to restrict numbers in the highest parts; after this, parking and a bus shuttle are available. The long-distance GR10 passes through the reserve, and there are many other marked paths. Access on foot is open.

Pyrenean saxifrage *Saxifraga longifolia*

SITE
121 Ossau Cliff

Striking limestone cliffs, best known for their vulture colonies but with many other features of interest.

This National Nature Reserve covers 83 ha on the map (though much more in effect as a good deal of it is vertical), and was established specifically to protect a breeding colony of griffon vultures. The main habitats are limestone cliffs, with downy oak, beech, and hazel woodland on the less steep slopes. When the reserve was established, in 1974, there were 10 breeding pairs of griffon vultures; now there are over 100 pairs, with five pairs of the rare Egyptian vultures, short-toed eagles, and several peregrines breeding here or nearby. In fact, there are about 50 breeding bird species within the reserve, including ravens, eagle owls, black and red kites, cirl buntings, blue rock thrushes, and kestrels, and dippers and grey wagtails breed on the river nearby. The griffon vultures are essentially resident and begin to breed in January, when there is often snow on the ledges. At this time of year, there are also red kites, ravens, peregrines, and a few other resident birds, and often there are wallcreepers feeding on these lower cliffs

before returning to the high Pyrenees in summer. The Egyptian vultures arrive in March, at about the same time as the black kites. The vultures are fed nearby, which not only keeps them around the cliff during the day, but has probably also encouraged the development of the breeding colony to its present level.

Although the reserve is primarily for breeding birds, and especially the vultures, there is also a certain amount of botanical interest – similar to most limestone cliffs in the area – and there are six reptiles and four amphibians recorded. However, since access is largely restricted between mid-January and mid-August (the vulture breeding season), there is little scope for studying these other aspects, and they are not described in detail.

The reserve is well signposted from the main D934, and there is an information centre and shop at La Falaise aux Vautours, 64260, Aste-Béon, just below the reserve, where you can watch live video links to vulture nests. It is open from April to September.

SITE
122 Pyrenees National Park

One of the most beautiful mountain areas in Europe, with a wonderful diversity of plant and animal life.

The Pyrenees National Park lies in the central part of the French Pyrenees, where many of the highest peaks are sit-

uated. It is a linear area along the Spanish border, over a distance of about 100 km, with six main valleys running

Pyrenees

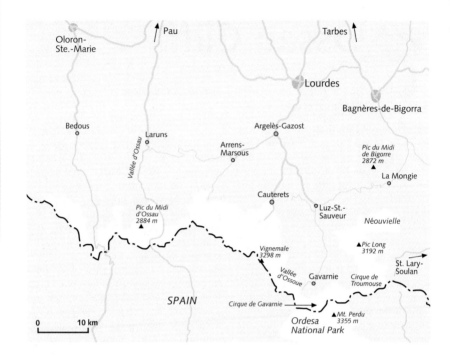

roughly northwards from the high peaks. The core zone of the park covers 45 700 ha – a relatively small area, tightly drawn around the higher peaks – with a peripheral zone of 206 000 ha, and it adjoins the Ordesa National Park on the Spanish side of the Pyrenees. It is an area of quite spectacular scenery, encompassing huge glacial cirques with high waterfalls, screes, snowfields, huge forests, alpine pastures, hay meadows, scrub, open water, and other montane habitats, over an altitude range of 1067–3298 m (the highest point in the French Pyrenees). Not surprisingly, it is also a superb area for its natural history, with an immense diversity of flowers, butterflies, and other insects, and a marvellous range of birds and mammals.

The National Park is very rich botanically, with a mixture of species. Some are ancient endemics that have clearly persisted and adapted from a period when the Pyrenees were warmer, others are more recent endemics that have

evolved here in isolation since the last ice age. In addition, there are essentially northern species, alpine species, and lowland species, making a total of about 1200 higher plants in the core zone, or about 1650 if the peripheral area is included. It is obviously not possible to cover all of these in detail, but a good selection is included in the locations described below. It is unlikely that anyone would be disappointed by the plants of this park unless you are specifically searching for orchids, which are not particularly varied here.

At least 40 species of mammals occur regularly. The most obvious are the marmots, which are now found in broken grassy slopes in virtually all of the valleys, though they are a relatively recent reintroduction (1950). They constantly advertise their presence by piercing alarm and contact calls and are easily seen, though they are not generally as tame as some of those in the Alps. Chamois (or isard) numbers have

Lammergeier *Gypaetus barbatus*

steadily risen, and now stand at around 5000 in the park; some consider the Pyrenean animals to be a separate sub-species of the chamois – the isard – but not everyone agrees that it is sufficiently distinct. The rarest and most locally endangered animal in the park is the brown bear, with numbers down to an estimated 5–7 adults. A recent re-introduction attempt nearby has been abandoned, due largely to local opposition, so their future here looks very bleak. There are Pyrenean desmans in the streams (see p. 252) up to over 2000 m, red and roe deer, wild boar, red squirrels, six species of shrew, and 19 species of bats altogether. Amongst the birds, the lammergeiers are perhaps the most exciting, with 11 pairs in the park, and more chance of seeing them here than almost anywhere in Europe. There are also abundant griffon vultures, 9 pairs of Egyptian vultures, 25 pairs of peregrines, and 17 pairs of golden eagles; the latter have increased steadily in recent years thanks to the increase in the marmot population. There are also strong populations of capercaillie, currently estimated at 170 adult males, ptarmigans, several pairs of wallcreepers, red-billed and alpine choughs, alpine accentors, snowfinches, citril finches, alpine swifts, and many other birds.

There is also a marvellous abundance and diversity of insects. For example, over a thousand species of beetles have been recorded, and over 200 species of spiders, and insects are in evidence everywhere. In a recent stay of 5 days in the park in late June, we recorded over 80 butterfly species (without especially concentrating on them), often in startling abundance.

Gavarnie makes a perfect starting point for seeing the best of the park – its only drawback is that it becomes extremely busy in summer and other holiday periods. However, anywhere that has Apollo butterflies in the main street, orchids by the car park, and lammergeiers and golden eagles overhead, with one of the most spectacular views anywhere, has to be worth a visit! The walk from Gavarnie towards the cirque is superb. Birds here include dippers and grey wagtails along the river, crossbills and crested tits in the pine woods, and citril finches and red-backed shrikes here and there. Golden eagles, lammergeiers, and griffon vultures are always likely to be seen overhead, red-billed and alpine choughs can be heard or seen, and there may be snowfinches, black redstarts, and alpine accentors near the cliffs. The damper cliffs are breeding sites for wall-creepers, though they are surprisingly hard to see.

Flowers are abundant all along here, in woods, grasslands, scrub, bogs, streams, and other habitats. Amongst the many species to be found are horned pansy, Pyrenean vetch, narrow-leaved helleborine, burnt orchid, wintergreens, mezereon, welsh poppy, the pretty pale blue *Hyacinthus amethystinus*, St. Bernard's lily, martagon lily, both alpenrose and alpine rose, and hepatica in woods and clearings. In wet places, there are water saxifrages, large-flowered butterwort, orchids such as *Dactylorhiza majalis*, the pretty little *Sesamoides pygmaea*, Pyrenean scurvygrass, the asphodel *Tofieldia calyculata*, the speedwell *Veronica ponae*, and several sedges. The ancient endemic *Ramonda myconi* (one of the few European relatives of the African violets) produces its purplish-blue flowers on shady rocks, sometimes with holly ferns and other accompaniments, and the striking spikes of Pyrenean saxifrage droop from rosettes on some of the bigger cliffs. There are also cowslips, oxlips, butterfly orchids, irises, Pyrenean fritillaries, rampions, cinquefoils such as *Potentilla montana*, *P. rupestris*, and *P. crantzii*, and a wealth of other attractive flowers. Insects are abundant here, too, with butterflies such as Camberwell beauty, Apollo and clouded Apollo, fritillaries such as Glanville and heath, Duke of Burgundy, chequered skipper, and sooty and Gavarnie ringlets; also on display are day-flying moths such as latticed heath, chimney sweep, black-veined and burnet companion, and other insects such as ascalaphids, stoneflies, longhorn beetles, field crickets, and many more.

There is a hotel/refuge at the end of the track, from where paths lead into the cirque or up the sides, with a whole variety of possibilities depending upon how strong you feel. Higher up, there are abundant saxifrages, rock-jasmines including the endemic *Androsace ciliata*, dwarf soapworts such as *Saponaria caespitosa*, alpine forget-me-nots, several species of *Primula*, speedwells, dwarf willows, vitaliana, several mountain buttercups, bellflowers, mountain avens, and the curious little endemic member of the yam family *Dioscorea* (*Borderea*) *pyrenaica* amongst many others. The possibilities are endless. There is a small botanic garden at Gavarnie which may be worth a visit, though its state of upkeep seems to vary.

Other worthwhile visits within the area include the valley of the river Héas leading from Gèdre up to the **Cirque de Troumouse** and a reservoir, for marvellous flowers and a wealth of butterflies; and the road from Gavarnie up to the **Port de Gavarnie (or Puerto de Bujaruelo)** at 2270 m, for superb access to the high peaks and screes (with several refuges), with excellent flowers, masses of mar-

mots, and all the high-altitude birds including some tame alpine choughs (though it is unlikely to be open before June). The **Vallée d'Ossoue**, running westwards from Gavarnie, is a noted botanical site, but also good for birds, marmots, Pyrenean desmans, and brook salamanders amongst other things; and the area south of **Gabas**, especially up towards the striking **Pic du midi d'Ossau** (2884 m) is lovely from every point of view.

Access is generally open within the park, except for obviously private areas, and there are many good waymarked paths. The park headquarters is at: 59, Route de Pau, F65000, Tarbes. Tel: 05 62443660. There is an excellent park information centre and shop at Luz-St.-Sauveur, and similar ones in Gavarnie, Gabas, Arrens-Marsous, Cauterets, and St. Lary-Soulan. The whole area becomes extremely busy in July and August, though this is the only time that some of the highest parts become accessible.

Alpenrose *Rhododendron ferrugineum*, Troumouse

SITE 123 Montségur and Gorges de la Frau

Beautiful, well-wooded limestone hills, with a fine range of birds and flowers and a spectacular historic castle.

Montségur is famous as one of the series of Cathar castles strung across this part of France, all in spectacular sites thanks to the Cathars' need to protect themselves from attack. It is well worth a visit for historic, cultural, and visual reasons, but it also lies in an area of unspoilt limestone hills with extensive woodlands and some fine gorges.

The Gorges de la Frau, which runs southwards from Fougax-et-Barrineuf up into the forests of Comus and Prades, is particularly good, with fine cliffs and screes, and extensive woodland, scrub, and grassland. It is botanically rich, with orchids such as military, monkey, green-winged, burnt, woodcock, bee, early spider, greater and lesser butterfly, and several helleborines. Angular and whorled Solomon's seal are both common, with globularias, kidney vetch and mountain kidney vetch, Butcher's- broom, cowslips,

The Gorges de la Frau in spring

autumn crocuses, Pyrenean bellflower, trumpet gentians *Gentiana occidentalis*, fairy foxgloves, hairy saxifrage, and many more. On cliffs and rock outcrops, there are species of *Ptilotrichum* (now *Alyssum*) such as *A. laeprousianum*, and Pyrenean valerian. Perennial honesty and large-flowered meadow-rue make fine displays in bushy places. It is also a great place for butterflies, with Camberwell beauties, orange tips, and large tortoiseshells in spring, building up through early June to masses of fritillaries, blues, skippers, hair-streaks, and many others.

Black woodpecker *Dryocopus martius*

Black woodpeckers are quite common in the woods (as they are through much of the Pyrenees), with great and lesser spotted woodpeckers, short-toed treecreepers, goshawk, sparrowhawk, honey buzzard, and masses of nightingales in the scrub. Both eagle owls and Tengmalm's owls nest in the more remote parts of the gorge, and there are red-billed and alpine choughs (at one of their lowest-altitude breeding sites), peregrines, ravens, and short-toed eagles higher up. Wallcreepers regularly winter here, down from their high Pyrenean breeding sites, especially in the cliffs of the upper part of the gorge. There are wild boar and red squirrels in the woods, and the rare Pyrenean desman (see p. 252) has been recorded in the unpolluted stream here (which is also excellent for invertebrates such as stone-flies, caddis-flies, and mayflies).

A minor road runs much of the way up the gorge from Fougax, with easy access to some lovely places, and a footpath carries on up into the higher and more remote parts, all well worth visiting. Around Montségur itself, there is a small flowery gorge to the east of the village, with Pyrenean fritillaries, trumpet gentians, and mountain kidney vetch, and some fine woods and pastures, all rich in flowers, birds, and butterflies.

Not far to the west, **Mont d'Olmes** offers an excellent opportunity to reach some high-altitude areas out of the main Pyrenean chain. There is a good road to a small ski station, and the nearby peaks reach 2348 m. There are extensive beech, silver fir, and Norway spruce woods, with the usual assemblage of wintergreens, large-flowered calamint, purple lettuce, bird's-nest orchid, hepatica, Irish spurge, bittercresses such as *Cardamine hepta-phylla*, and many other flowers on a pre-dominantly acid soil. In the high grassy pastures and scrub, there are yellow stars-of-Bethlehem, gentians including trumpet and yellow gentians, orchids such as early purples, alpine rock-cress, mountain lungwort, autumn crocuses, alpenrose, the bluebell relative *Scilla liliohyacinthus*, often in abundance, and green and stinking hellebores. In wet places, there are masses of the deep pink bittercress *Cardamine raphanifolia*, with starry and yellow saxifrages, marsh-marigolds, and many more. Water pipits breed here, and there are snowfinches, alpine accentors, and alpine choughs at the highest levels, with crossbills, crested tits, and Bonelli's warblers in the woods.

The small, but good road climbs up from Montségur to a considerable altitude, and is liable to be snowy well into the spring. There are ski-lifts, though they are closed whenever there is no skiing, which limits their value to the naturalist.

SITE 124 Ax-les-Thermes

Marvellous mountains close to the Andorra border, particularly good for birds and mammals.

Ax-les-Thermes is a pleasant, small town in a valley on one of the main roads from France to Andorra. It acts as a useful centre for various interesting sites in this part of the Pyrenees, which is a beautiful region of heavily wooded valleys and high peaks with glacial lakes. The underlying geology is complex and varied, though much of the terrain is underlain by granite which gives rise to acid soils.

To the south-east of the town, the **Orlu National Reserve** is a large no-hunting

Orlu Reserve

reserve, run by Office Nationale de la Chasse, consisting of a vast area of woodland, pasture, lakes, and high peaks to the south-east of Orlu village. Although primarily established to protect some of the larger mammals, it is a superbly pristine and varied area, with a fine range of marked trails, and a wealth of general natural history (though the difference between hunting reserves and National Nature Reserves is quite marked in that there is no information about the flora and fauna here at all). The main purpose of these no-hunting reserves is to allow the populations of quarry species, such as chamois or red deer, to thrive and repopulate the neighbouring hunting areas. Chamois, for example, have increased here since the reserve was established, and there are now several thousand individuals. There are also red and roe deer, abundant marmots, red squirrels, pine and beech martens, wild boar, and a fine diversity of bats including European free-tailed (the largest European bat, and distinctive by virtue of its size, narrow wings, and protruding tail). A few young bears have been seen here, from the reintroduced population not far to the west, but the sudden recent end to this project has ended the possibility of bears coming back to this part of the Pyrenees permanently. There are extensive old forests of beech, pine, and fir, which are good for black woodpeckers, crossbills, firecrests, crested tits, and marsh tits, and Tengmalm's owls breed here. Higher up, there are ring ouzels, water pipits, citril finches, black redstarts, and alpine accentors, with the possibility of seeing golden eagles, lammergeiers, and other large birds of prey.

Although Orlu is not a noted botanical site, it is still a superb place for flowers, with all the characteristic species of acid or neutral soils, such as alpenrose, arnica, vanilla and small white orchids, moonwort, bilberry and cowberry, trumpet gentians, yellow gentian, and many more.

In autumn, there are masses of both meadow saffron and the true autumn crocus *Crocus nudiflorus*, and a fine range of fungi in the woods. To reach Orlu Reserve, take the D22 minor road running east off the N20 just south of Ax, signposted to Orlu, and turn left at the end of the road onto a minor road signposted to the reserve. There is a huge car park at the end, from where paths radiate out into the reserve.

West of Ax, there is an area of forest and upland pasture and scrub, known as **Gudanes wood and the Beille Plateau.** There are huge tracts of beech, pine, and other trees here, particularly good for forest birds such as black woodpecker, capercaillie, crossbills, and Tengmalm's owl, while higher up there are the usual upland species such as ring ouzel, water pipit, and choughs. There is easy road access from Les Cabanes on the N20, signposted to the plateau because this is a cross-country skiing area.

Further west again, the D8 runs southwards from the N20 to Vicdessos; just beyond Vicdessos, at Auzat, there is a minor road running south into the high peaks around Pic de Tristagne and Pic de Montcalm, giving easy access to some marvellous high country that harbours marmots, chamois, golden eagles, alpine choughs, alpine accentor, rock thrush, and good flowers and butterflies, all in a relatively unvisited and unspoilt environment.

Finally, although it is a separate country, it is worth mentioning **Andorra,** which is so close to Ax-les-Thermes. It is a small and very mountainous state covering less than 500 square kilometres, squeezed between France and Spain. The first impression may be of busy roads and developments, but away from the main town and any ski stations, there is some marvellous species-rich mountain country, such as at Coll d'Ordino, between Ordino and Canillo, the Val d'Incles north of Soldeu, and the high area north of El Serrat amongst others.

SITE 125 Forêt des Fanges

A beautiful hilly forest on limestone in the Pyrenean foothills, with marvellous flowers and butterflies.

Forêt des Fanges is a large woodland south-east of Quillan, covering the slopes of hills reaching to over 1000 m. The woodland is mixed, with beech, oak, pine, and fir, and, although managed, is largely natural in character. Around the edges, there are extensive patches of flowery *garrigue* or scrub, open grasslands, and enclosed meadows, and within the forest there are cliffs and rock outcrops. Collectively, it makes up an impressive matrix of unspoilt habitats, rich in flowers, invertebrates, and birds.

The open areas are probably the richest part botanically, with orchids such as lady, military, monkey, burnt, early purple, greater and lesser butterfly, bee, woodcock, fly, early spider, and many

Garrigue and mixed forest in the Forêt des Fanges

others. There are broomrapes including clove-scented, tall, ivy, purple, and thyme, together with horseshoe vetch, cowslips, *Coronilla minima*, Pyrenean honeysuckle, sun-roses, rock-roses, and many other flowers. In the wooded areas, there are hepaticas, helleborines such as red, narrow-leaved, white, and broad-leaved, plus lily-of-the-valley, whorled Solomon's seal, Mediterranean coriaria, swallow-wort, and a wealth of other species. The whole site is good for insects, including butterflies, particularly swallowtails, Adonis blue, long-tailed blue, large blue, brown argus, Provence chalkhill blue, various fritillaries, Camberwell beauties, and many more, as well as ascalaphids (see p. 200), longhorn beetles, praying mantids, and cicadas. The birds are those characteristic of mid-altitude forests, including honey and common buzzards, red and black kites, crossbills, Bonelli's warbler, nightingales, short-toed treecreepers, red-backed shrike, and many more.

The D9 running from Caudiès (on the main D117) up to the Col de St. Louis and beyond passes through some of the more interesting sites, and there are roads and tracks throughout the forest.

Fontanille Forest and **Pic d'Estable** lie just to the south, across the D117, and this is another lovely area, with rocky peaks and cliffs rising to almost 1500 m, with the attractive Gorges de St. Georges at the western end. About 15 km to the east, the **Gorges de Galamus** is a striking limestone gorge with an ancient hermitage, just north of St. Paul-de-Fenouillet, with excellent flowers, birds such as crag martins, and impressive scenery.

SITE 126 Col du Pourtalet

Marvellous, easily accessible high-altitude flowery habitats, with special birds and butterflies.

Although the Col du Pourtalet lies within the Pyrenees National Park (see p. 263), we have given it separate site status here as it is a long journey by road from the heart of the park, and it provides very easy access to some high areas with their special species. The steady climb up to the pass from Gabas (where there is a park information centre) goes through some fine woodlands before opening out to high scrub, grasslands, screes, and cliffs, often with snow nearby until well into summer. Flowers of interest here in the pastures and scrub include bird's-eye primrose, cowslips, Pyrenean fritillary, elder-flowered and vanilla orchids, snowbells, wild daffodils, white crocuses

Merendera montana

Crocus albiflorus (which, confusingly, can often be purplish), Pyrenean aster, houseleeks, gentians such as spring, snow and Pyrenean, white false helleborine, horned pansies and many more. By late summer, there are masses of the beautiful pink or purple *Merendera pyrenaica* (= *M. montana*), related to *Colchicum* but with petals that separate right to ground level, as well as blue-purple leafless crocuses, autumn felwort, goldenrod, and the pretty fringed gentians. Lower down, in and around the woods, there are masses of Pyrenean squill (rather like bluebells), bitter-cresses, oxlips, spotted and bird's-nest orchids, orpine, Irish spurge, and a host of others.

Butterflies are common here, peaking in diversity in about late June or early July. There are too many species to mention individually, but some frequent ones include Camberwell beauty, scarce and common swallowtails, Apollo and clouded Apollo, Piedmont and other ringlets, and masses of fritillaries, skippers, coppers, and blues. Marmots are common, and there are herds of chamois nearby. The birds are good here, too, and often easily seen; there are red-billed and alpine choughs (the latter often very tame), golden eagles, lammergeier, alpine accentors, water pipits, rock sparrows, ortolan bunting, whinchats, and rock thrush, amongst others.

Apart from the shops (mainly on the Spanish side), this is a beautiful place, and it also gives access to some higher country nearby such as the Pic d'Anéou and the fabulous Pic du Midi d'Ossau.

---

127 Col de Somport

A mid-altitude pass surrounded by beautiful woods and flowery pastures.

The Col de Somport lies at 1632 m on the N134 from Oleron Ste. Mairie to Jaca in Spain. The road up to the col on the French side passes through some splendid woodland, such as the Bois de Lazarque, before emerging into the higher scrub and mountain pastures. The woods have a similar range of species to those mentioned for the Col du Pourtalet. Higher up, the grassy pastures are rich in flowers following the melting snow – white crocuses, spring gentians, wild daffodils, Pyrenean fritillary, elder-flowered orchids, the form of cowslip known as *Primula veris* subspecies *columnae*, mountain kidney vetch, speedwells such as large speedwell, Pyrenean vetch, globularias, and the endemic globularia-leaved

valerian, amongst others. On rocks and scree, you can find the pretty St. John's-wort *Hypericum nummularium*, the white or pink *Petrocoptis pyrenaica*, fairy foxgloves, the little toadflax *Chaenorhinum*

White-backed woodpecker
Dendrocopos leucotos

Crocus nudiflorus

origanifolium, the gorgeous endemic saxifrage *Saxifraga longifolia*, and several little rock-jasmines. Small shrubs of Pyrenean honeysuckle flower prolifically around rocky outcrops, and there are junipers and snowy mespils amongst more common shrubs.

The birds are typical of most places in the Pyrenees at this altitude, with citril finches, water pipits, ring ouzels, and black redstarts around the pass, and alpine choughs, snowfinches, and alpine accentors higher up. Golden eagles breed in the area, and can be seen overhead at times, and it is within the feeding range of the lammergeiers from further east along the chain. Butterflies are abundant though not exceptional here.

The Col du Somport lies within the Pyrenees National Park. The Forêt d'Issaux,

however, lies outside the park to the north, to the west of the Aspe Valley. It is a craggy area of old forest on limestone and other rocks, and is noted as a particularly good site for the rare white-backed woodpecker, particularly where there are quantities of dead or dying wood. There are other woodpeckers, too, including black, as well as crossbills, honey buzzards, and other more widespread woodland species. In autumn, the pretty blue-purple *Crocus nudiflorus* is abundant around the upper edges of the forest, and there are good flowers throughout the year. The forest can be reached via the D241 to Lourdios-Ichère off the N134, turning off soon after the village, following signs to the forest. The gorge at the lower end of the forest is noted as a wintering site for wallcreepers.

SITE 128 Col d'Orgambideska

One of the best of the Pyrenean passes for watching bird migration, especially in autumn.

The Col d'Orgambideska (or Orgambidexka) has long been known as one of the very best of the western Pyrenean passes for watching migration. Unfortunately its value – and its attraction to visiting naturalists – is sometimes greatly marred by the presence of large numbers of hunters, shooting mainly at woodpigeon, but also killing and maiming other birds, including many birds of prey. A small area is now leased by the Orgambidexka Col Libre and managed as a reserve, though unfortunately this scandalous and wholly unnecessary hunting goes on both nearby and on other key passes, which have no protection at all. The Orgambidexka Col Libre was created specifically to try to protect the migrating birds, and subsequently to study them in more detail.

The numbers of birds passing through is impressive and can be spectacular, though, as with most migration points, numbers vary widely according to season, weather, and other factors. In recent years, up to 18 000 honey buzzards, 13 000 black kites, and almost 5000 red kites have been recorded as maximum numbers, together with all three west European harriers, osprey, black stork, hobbies, and vast numbers of swallows and martins, amongst other birds. Most pass through in the first half of September, though red kites peak in October, and up to 15 000 common cranes pass through in November. The site is manned by volunteers between mid-July and November, and there is something happening for most of this time. Bird-watchers (and especially volunteers) are welcomed as it helps to combat the infringements by hunters. Orgambidexka Col Libre can be contacted at: 11 Rue Bourgneuf, F-64100, Bayonne.

The hills here overlie acid rocks, and the flora is not rich, though there are interesting species such as St. Dabeoc's heath, Cornish heath, Kerry lily, alpenrose, marsh gentian, and other species of damp acid sites. The col can be reached via the D19 running westwards from Larrau, about 30 km south-east of St. Jean Pied-de-Port.

The Forêt d'Iraty to the west, spreading across the Spanish border, is a huge expanse of beech, spruce, and other woodland, noted for forest birds and, probably, a few remaining brown bears. The Forêt des Arbailles, some 8–10 km north of the col, is scenic woodland on limestone, noted especially for its birds of prey such as red kite, honey buzzard, booted eagle, and a few griffon vultures, as well as black woodpeckers, other forest birds, and much else besides.

Mediterranean

Introduction

This region includes the whole Mediterranean coast of mainland France, stretching from the Spanish border beyond Perpignan in the west to the Italian border beyond Nice in the east. This is the warmest part of France, with the archetypal Mediterranean climate of mild, wet winters (though with many sunny days) and very hot dry summers. Not surprisingly, this is the goal of millions of tourists from all over Europe and beyond, coming for the sun, sea, good food and wine, and the scenery, and this puts tremendous pressure on the infrastructure and natural habitats of the region. However, this is a complex area scenically and geologically, with a vast range of habitat types, and a quite remarkable amount remains to interest the naturalist.

The coast is mainly flat, of alluvial origin, with lines of dunes in a few places (notably in the Camargue), and studded with dozens of coastal lagoons. These vary in size, from tiny or largely filled-in to huge, and support a surprising range of wildlife from flamingos and egrets to horned pondweeds and masses of invertebrates. Some of them are reserves, though most are unprotected and may be heavily fished, shot over, polluted, and built around. The most celebrated of France's coastal reserves is undoubtedly the Camargue – a vast expanse of wetlands and coastal habitats around the mouth of the Rhône – one of the deltas for which the Mediterranean is noted.

Away from the coastal plains, the inland countryside is hilly, with enormous tracts of quite wild countryside. Most of it is underlain by limestone which supports a

Horned pondweed
Zannichellia palustris

dry, often overgrazed vegetation of shrubs and bare ground – *garrigue*, normally rich in herbaceous plants such as orchids. In places, such as at Mont Ventoux, Montagne Sainte-Victoire, and around the Gorges du Verdon, the mountains rise to considerable heights, bringing a touch of northern or alpine climates and species to the area. Where the soil is more impermeable and acid, there tend to be more extensive forests, of which the Massif des Maures and the Massif de l'Esterel are the best mainland examples, though both have suffered from that bane of the Mediterranean region – fires – and Esterel is a devastated remnant of its former self. Offshore, the island of Port-Cros (a National Park) holds some fine native Mediterranean forest on the same underlying rock, and there are similar areas on the St. Tropez Peninsula.

It is hardly surprising that this coastline has a huge number of species not found elsewhere in France. Few of them are

Two-tailed pasha Charaxes jasius

Opposite page: **Cerbère–Banyuls**

Mediterranean

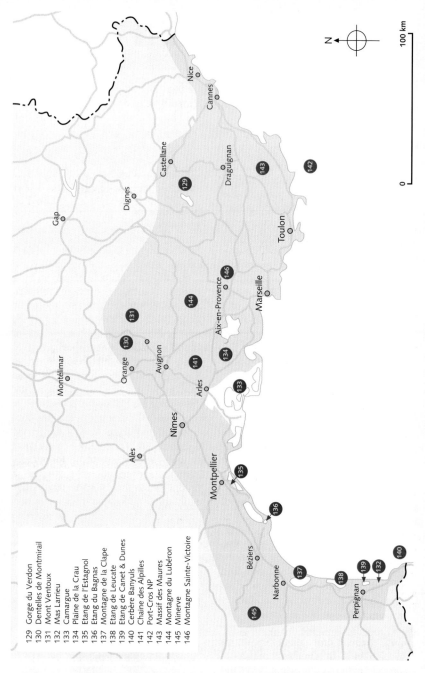

129 Gorge du Verdon
130 Dentelles de Montmirail
131 Mont Ventoux
132 Mas Larrieu
133 Camargue
134 Plaine de la Crau
135 Etang de l'Estagnol
136 Etang du Bagnas
137 Montagne de la Clape
138 Etang de Leucate
139 Etang de Canet & Dunes
140 Cerbère Banyuls
141 Chaîne des Alpilles
142 Port-Cros NP
143 Massif des Maures
144 Montagne du Lubéron
145 Minerve
146 Montagne Sainte-Victoire

endemic, since there is little in the way of restriction to colonization into and from adjacent countries, but they are unable to colonize far into mainland France since the winters become rapidly colder as you go north. A typical indicator of the Mediterranean climate is the olive tree, but there are huge numbers of wild

Grey-leaved cistus *Cistus albidus*
Aphyllanthes monspeliensis

of other flowering plants, the two-tailed pasha butterfly, and many more.

The climate is broadly similar throughout the zone, though it cools off rapidly inland and usually becomes wetter wherever there are hills; and there is a cline of increasing rainfall from west to east. Unusually, the western end, around Perpignan, is the driest because it lies in the rain shadow of the Pyrenees, while further east the rainfall is higher.

The Mediterranean is best visited in spring for most reasons, between March and early June. This avoids the worst of the crowds and the heat, yet catches the best of the flowers and birds and most of the butterflies. Autumn can be good, too, for birds, insects, and some flowers.

species that are confined to here within France – for example pallid swift, great spotted cuckoo, several species of gecko, sea daffodils, Neptune-grass, and dozens

SITE 129 Gorge du Verdon

One of the longest and most spectacular gorges in Europe, with a rich flora and fauna to match.

The Gorge du Verdon, or even Grand Canyon du Verdon, is an impressive and deservedly popular geographical feature where the Verdon River cuts through the mountains of Haut Provence to the north-east of Marseille. Apart from being both beautiful and scenic, it is also a remarkably varied place; the river wriggles its way through the mountains, giving a great variety of aspects, but there are also variations in width, slope, and rock character, and the result is a combination of woodland, cliffs, scrub, grassland, and slow-flowing and fast-flowing water, with gravel banks. It is an excellent place for wildlife, especially out of the busy high-summer period. In 1997, 1770 square kilometres of varied hill country around the gorge were declared as the Verdon Regional Natural Park; the park extends to the borders of the

Maritime Alps, with the gorge as its centrepiece.

The predominant rock is limestone, with high peaks on the north side of the gorge rising almost to 2000 m, rather lower to the south. Most of the park has a very low population density, and there are vast swathes of deserted countryside here.

Botanically, it is very rich. There is a large variety of trees and shrubs (which turn to some splendid colours in autumn), including Montpellier, field and Italian maples, smoke bush, Scots pine, downy and holm oak, terebinth trees, wild service-tree, true service-tree, whitebeam, and wild cherry, with black poplar, alders, and false acacia along the river valley. Shrubs include junipers, spindle, Mediterranean buckthorn, snowy mespil, St. Lucie's cherry, dogwood, cornelian

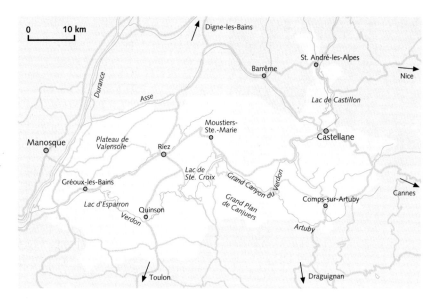

cherry, and many others. There are a number of special plants to be found in and around the gorge: spiny spurge, an endemic rampion *Phyteuma villarsii*, the sandwort *Arenaria cinerea*, a spleenwort *Asplenium jahandiezii*, with rather distinctive, coarsely pinnate leaves, found only in the main gorge area downstream from Castellane, and a pale yellow golden drop *Onosma fastigiata*, in addition to more widespread species such as the pretty pink rock soapwort, culinary thyme, narrow-leaved lavender, winter savory, scorpion vetch, and numerous others, making a colourful and aromatic mixture. Orchids are not especially common, but in places, espe-

cially where there are grassy areas or *garrigue* on less steep soil, one can find lady, military, toothed, woodcock, early spider, red helleborine, and occasionally the uncommon *Orchis spitzellii*, looking rather like an early purple orchid, but with green sepals. In a few places there are springs whose water drips down the cliffs, and steep slopes forming tufa and colonized by fen vegetation, including black bog-rush, marsh helleborine, broad-leaved marsh-orchid, and other flowers. On cliffs, there are clumps of the whitish-flowered cinquefoil *Potentilla caulescens*, with a harebell *Campanula macrorhiza* and the St. John's-wort *Hypericum coris*. In a few places, you can find martagon lily (and possibly the striking *Lilium pomponum*, which is at the western edge of its range here), a fritillary *Fritillaria involucrata*, wild peony, and the shrubby yellow rest-harrow *Ononis minutissima*. An uncommon plant found mainly in the higher hills to the north of the gorge is the pretty pink-flowered rock-jasmine *Androsace chaixii*.

The whole area, including the high plateau of Valensole to the north and the Grande Plan de Canjuers to the south, is

Montpellier maple *Acer monspessulanum*

Verdon Gorge

very rich in birds. The gorge itself has choughs, crag martins, alpine swifts, blue rock thrush, and many scrub birds such as subalpine warblers, with visiting alpine accentors and wallcreepers out of the breeding season. On the plateaux, there are breeding Montagu's harriers (with up to 50 pairs recorded on the Valensole), a few little bustards, stone curlew in reasonable numbers, Calandra larks, short-toed larks, hoopoes, cirl buntings, and many others. Short-toed eagles are scattered throughout the area.

The lower part of the gorge, below the Lac de Ste. Croix reservoir, is also worth a visit, though not as spectacular as the main canyon. Many of the plants and animals are similar, though some additional plants include the milk vetch *Astragalus vesicarius*, the umbellifer *Opopanax chironium*, and a spleenwort *Asplenium petrarchae*.

There are good roads along most of the length of the gorge on both sides which vary in their height above the river, giving a nice variety of views and habitats.

SITE 130 Dentelles de Montmirail

Limestone hills with jagged peaks and cliffs, particularly good for birds.

The Dentelles de Montmirail is a low range of limestone hills lying to the west of Malaucene, north of Carpentras. The rockier parts rise from a sea of vineyards (mainly grown for Muscat de Beaumes-de-Venise, which lies just to the south), with higher cliffs and pinnacles pushing up from a skirt of pine and oak forests. It is a compact and well-defined area, which makes visiting and bird-watching relatively easy, though the tracks into the central area are really only suitable for dry weather driving if you are coming by car.

Short-toed eagles breed in the area, and hunt over and around the peaks looking for snakes and lizards, and ravens and occasional red-billed choughs fly around the cliffs. There used to be breeding Egyptian vultures, but they seem to have gone, in keeping with a general decline and increasing disturbance here. Other birds to be seen on and around the

Limestone pinnacles in the Dentelles de Montmirail

cliffs include alpine swifts, crag martins, common kestrels, and a few pairs of blue rock thrushes. In scrub and open woodland, there are woodchat shrikes and the Mediterranean race of great grey shrike, with hoopoes, Bonelli's and Orphean warblers, and colonies of bee-eaters where there are suitable breeding sites. Orphean warblers are larger than the much more common Sardinian warblers (which are abundant here in scrub), with a yellow (not red) eye and a rather less scratchy, gentler song. In scrub, especially on the southern slopes, there are Dartford and subalpine warblers, too. Eagle owls breed in the area, and Scops owls are common in and around the villages. In winter, alpine accentors, wallcreepers, and even occasional snowfinches visit.

It is not exceptional botanically, though there is a reasonable range of orchids including bee, early spider, woodcock, and lady. In the woods, there are Aleppo pines, holm and downy oak, wild cherry and whitebeam, with the curious shrubby *Osyris alba*, butcher's-broom, lily-of-the valley, a hare's ear *Bupleurum rigidum*, and wild hepatica flowering very early in the year.

Access is easy by minor roads westwards from Malaucene, and numerous tracks and paths within the area.

SITE 131 Mont Ventoux

A large mountain ridge, one of the most famous landmarks in Provence, with a varied mixture of flowers and birds.

Mont Ventoux is a long ridge running eastwards from Malaucene, distinctive from some angles but rather obscure from others. Its highest point is 1912 m, high enough to have bare limestone scree and clitter around the top, and to be snow-covered for much of the winter and spring. The ill-defined lower slopes, which extend south into the Plateau de Vaucluse, east towards the Montagne de Lure, and north into the Montagne de Bluye, are well wooded. The forests are varied, with large tracts of beech, much planted Austrian black pine and spruce, some planted Atlas cedar, with smaller amounts of downy oak, and scattered rowan, Montpellier and Italian maples, whitebeam, and wild cherry, amongst others. Red squirrels, wild boar, roe deer, and pine and beech martens are all frequent, and quite often seen, except perhaps during the hunting season, as there is no protection here and it may become very disturbed.

It is a fine place for birds, with a good mixture of alpine, montane, and Mediterranean species in an accessible site. Breeding birds include alpine accentor (only close to the top), citril finch,

Alpine columbine *Aquilegia alpina*

Mediterranean

Mont Ventoux

red-backed and woodchat shrikes, black kite, buzzard, blue rock thrush, crossbills, black woodpecker, subalpine and Bonelli's warblers, crested tit, woodlark, rock bunting, and firecrests. In winter, snowfinches are frequent and quite tame.

Botanically, it is surprisingly good, though it looks unpromising. In the woods, one can find stinking hellebore, hepatica, box, white, and narrow-leaved helleborines, wintergreens, yellow bird's-nest, and occasional martagon lilies. Higher up, the flora is more unusual and

Eryngium spinalbum

alpine: spikes of blue-flowered monks-hood, the silvery eryngo *Eryngium spinalbum*, the golden-yellow Rhaetian poppy, low cushions of yellow vitaliana, purple saxifrage, yellow whitlow-grass, creeping globularia covered with blue pom-pom flowerheads, the common rock-jasmine *Androsace villosa*, purple flowers of Mt. Cenis pansy, and an endemic candytuft *Iberis candolleana*, amongst others. In shadier places, especially on the north side, there are dark-red helleborines, the pretty yellow *Orchis pallens*, alpine columbine, and many other flowers. It is not a great site for butterflies, perhaps because the top is very windy, though there is a reasonable range of limestone species plus Apollo.

There are roads around the mountain, and virtually across the top, making bird-watching and general exploration very easy.

The Plateau de Vaucluse to the south, and especially the Gorges de la Nesque, are worth a visit, with crag martins, alpine swift, blue rock thrush, and short-toed eagle, amongst other birds.

<small>SITE</small> 132 Mas Larrieu

A small but interesting nature reserve made up of coastal habitats around the estuary of the Tech River.

The Reserve of Mas Larrieu (Mas is an old name for farm or estate) protects about 150 ha of mixed coastal habitats where the Tech meets the Mediterranean. Unfortunately, the reserve is very busy in summer as it lies between busy resorts, and protection and management are quite lax. However, it is hard to find areas of Mediterranean beach that are at all unspoilt, and this is worth a visit if you are in the vicinity.

The dunes have a good mixture of flowers, including sea-holly, sea bindweed, sea spurge, sea rocket, joint-pine, a pink endemic to the Catalan area *Dianthus pyrenaicus* subspecies *catalaunicus*, blue globe thistle, and sea medick, amongst others. In slightly damper areas, there are tongue orchids, giant orchids, and a form of loose-flowered orchid *Orchis palustris*. The pretty chaste tree occurs along the flood plain, producing long spikes of

Sand dunes in the Mas Lameu reserve

blue-purple flowers in summer that are very attractive to butterflies. Altogether, about 350 species of flowers have been recorded from the reserve.

At least 10 reptile species have been recorded, including green lizard, Spanish psammodromus (a little-known, slender, brownish-grey lizard), wall lizard, and Europe's largest lizard, the ocellated. These can grow to 80 cm (though I've not seen them as large as this here) and are green spotted with blue along the flanks. There are also Montpellier snakes and ladder snakes (so-called because the young are boldly black-striped in a ladder pattern, which fades to two longitudinal stripes in the adults). Painted frogs, western spadefoot toads (see p. 39), and tree frogs add to the interest. It is also an inter-esting location for insects, with almost 100 beetles recorded, ant-lions, a good range of grasshoppers and crickets, and many butterflies and moths.

It is not an exceptional place for birds, though there are over 40 breeding species, particularly along the river course. Penduline tits and golden orioles nest amongst the poplars, melodious warblers sing from the scrub, and king-fishers and bee-eaters breed along the banks. Woodchat shrikes and Cetti's warblers are frequent, and Kentish plovers and fan-tailed warblers breed in more open coastal parts.

There is access via rough tracks towards the beach off the D81, alongside the river, to a large car park. Entry to the reserve is unrestricted.

(see p. 39)

SITE
133 Camargue

Probably the most famous of the natural history sites in France, rich in birds and other forms of wildlife.

The Camargue is a vast stretch of flat, low-lying land on the south coast to the west of Marseille. It is essentially the delta of the great Rhône, formed from the huge quantities of silt brought down and steadily remodelled by the sea and by floods to form an enormous mosaic of lagoons, marshes, and other habitats. Along the outer edge of the delta, a line of sand dunes (the best in Mediterranean France) has been formed by the action of the sea. Since 1860, when embankments were completed along the two arms of the Rhône and a sea defence wall was built, the water levels in the Camargue have been largely artificial. Nowadays, very large sections of the delta are used agriculturally for rice-growing, wheat, vines, grazing, and other uses, though large areas of semi-natural habitat, especially saltmarshes, lagoons, freshwater, grazing marshes, reedbeds, and dunes still survive. Some 850 square kilometres are designated as a Regional Natural Park, and 13 000 ha within this are designated as a National Nature Reserve, with other smaller reserves. The Regional

Red-crested pochard *Netta rufina*

Natural Park designation provides relatively little protection for the wildlife – one of its aims is to 'allow the inhabitants of the Camargue to lead a life which they themselves have chosen', which inevitably includes a certain amount of intensive agriculture, tourism-related development, and industry. Considerable areas of prime habitat have been lost over the last 30 years and the value of the Camargue has diminished, though it is so large that anyone coming fresh to it will still be impressed, and it undoubtedly remains an important and fascinating place for its wildlife.

The core National Nature Reserve protects the central part of the site around the famous Etang de Vaccares lagoon. It is a marvellous location but unfortunately – from the point of view of the visiting naturalist – access is all but forbidden, except where the D36b road skirts it, or in the southernmost coastal sections of dunes and along the sea wall. There is a private reserve to the east and a communal local reserve to the west, near Stes. Maries-de-la-Mer, making a total of 18 000 ha, all with limited or forbidden access. It is worth describing this area in detail, however, as a microcosm of the Camargue, and because most of the wildlife can be seen in surrounding parts.

It is particularly good for birds, reflected in the international designations of Ramsar Site (76 500 ha) and

Flamingos *Phoenicopterus ruber*

Special Protection Area for birds (16 000 ha). At least 345 species occur, of which about 70 breed, and in winter there are large concentrations of waterfowl, waders, and other birds. At passage periods, very large numbers of migrants pass through, often staying for a few days to re-fuel. Breeding birds include at least 10 000 greater flamingos (still the largest colony in the Mediterranean, though they have been steadily increasing in other areas), which can be seen almost throughout, avocets, little and cattle egrets, bittern, collared pratincole (now quite rare), red-crested pochard, marsh harrier (perhaps 40 pairs), black-winged stilts, Kentish plover, fan-tailed warbler, Mediterranean and slender-billed gulls, whiskered tern, oystercatcher, purple heron, kingfisher, and many others in the saltmarshes and wetland areas. Where there is scrub or woodland, there are moustached, spectacled, reed, Cetti's, and great reed warblers, bearded and penduline tits, golden orioles, woodchat shrikes, and cirl buntings. Colonies of bee-eaters live in sandy banks, and little, Sandwich, and common terns breed on the sand and around the lagoons. Small numbers of rollers still breed here, but they are increasingly rare. At passage periods, almost anything can turn up, including thousands of each of Kentish plovers, curlew sandpipers, black-tailed godwits, spotted redshank, black and whiskered terns, and smaller numbers of glossy ibis, great white egret, white-winged black terns, great spotted cuckoo,

Asparagus acutifolius

Part of the vast line of dunes fringing the Camargue

and hundreds of others. In winter, very large numbers of wildfowl and waders pass the time here; for example, up to 15 000 wigeon, 14 000 gadwall, 25 000 teal, 30 000 mallard, 14 000 shoveler, 30 000 coot, and over 2000 red-crested pochard. There are smaller numbers of waders, grebes, sawbills such as red-breasted merganser, swans including Bewick's, and visiting birds of prey, including spotted eagle, harriers, and merlins. It is a good site for birds!

The Camargue is also of great interest to the naturalist for other reasons. There are eight species of amphibians, including substantial numbers of the stripeless tree frog (see p. 160), which can occasionally be almost blue here and is frequent enough even to appear in houses at times; western spadefoot toad, midwife toad, marsh frog, and others; and 14 species of reptiles, including pond terrapins, Spanish psammodromus, Montpellier snake, and southern smooth snake. There are 32 species of mammals, though generally these are much less in evidence than the birds, except perhaps for the coypu (introduced) which can be seen along the ditches, and often as corpses on the roads.

Other noteworthy mammals include the tiny pygmy white-toothed shrew (Europe's smallest mammal, and one of the smallest terrestrial mammals in the world), and a number of bats including Kuhl's pipistrelle (a mainly southern species, though currently spreading northwards). It is also good for invertebrates; for example, there are over 50 molluscs and a fine range of dragonflies. I once visited in August, when it is very busy, too hot, and windy, but it does have the advantage of flowering sea daffodils (see below) and peak dragonfly numbers. Behind one set of dunes, sheltering from the wind, there were literally hundreds of lesser emperors, together with three or four species of darter.

Finally, it is also a good site botanically, though admittedly many of the 500+ species are not the most popular of plants – glassworts, saltworts, goosefoots, grasses, and other difficult groups often associated with saltmarshes. On the dunes, there are masses of beautiful sea daffodils, whose fragrant white flowers are produced in July and August, with sea dock, sea flax, sea bindweed, cottonweed, sea stock, and sand crocuses (which flower early in spring). Where the dunes are more stable or shaded, there are pretty flowers such as the intense blue dyer's alkanet, the yellow-flowered poppy relative *Hypecoum procumbens*, yellow-flowered shrubby restharrow *Ononis natrix*, and the curious little bluish-flowered *Coris monspeliensis*, related to primroses but looking quite unlike them. There are a few orchids here and in other grassy places, such as giant orchid, bug orchid, woodcock orchid, early spider, and bee orchid, including an unusual form with bicoloured lips known as *Ophrys apifera* variety *bicolor* (or *O.*

Cattle egret *Bubulcus ibis*

mangini). Summer snowflakes grow in some of the damp semi-shaded spots, sometimes with loose-flowered orchids and *Narcissus tazetta*, and there are a few patches of the pretty iris *Iris spuria* subspecies *maritima* in damp pastures.

Some of the best ways to get to grips with the Camargue wildlife include: walking or cycling along the Digues (sea wall) footpath eastwards from Stes. Maries-de-la-Mer, with excursions into the dunes or saltmarsh edge; visiting the ornithological park (*parc ornithologique*) north of Stes. Maries, which has rescued birds and many visiting wild birds; following the D37 (with a southward diversion to Méjanes) along the north side of the Etang de Vaccarès, stopping as necessary, visiting the information centre with hides and walks at La Capelière, then going down the east side of the reserve. Access into another reserve, the Salin de Badon, can be booked at this centre. It is also worth visiting the Regional Natural Park information centre on the main D570, though it is mainly concerned with matters other than wildlife.

1^{SITE}34 Plaine de la Crau

A sprawling stony desert at the mouth of the river Durance, unique in France for its flora and fauna.

The Plaine de la Crau is large, flat, and featureless, formed from the vast quantities of stony material brought down from the mountains by the Durance, before it changed course during the last ice age. Once, it covered about 60 000 ha, a vast reserve of wildlife, but it has steadily been encroached on by industry, housing, and intensive agriculture, with a large area of military training, and only about 11 500 ha remain as reasonable habitat. It is also heavily shot over. A Special Protection

Stone curlew *Burhinus oedicnemus* (Peter Wilson)

Area covers the remaining habitat, with small reserves within this, but in general protection and management are still poor. Most of the plain is grazed by large flocks of sheep and goats, which contribute to its character and are an essential part of its survival.

It is best known as a bird site. This type of habitat is very rare in France, more like parts of Spain or North Africa, and there is no comparable extent elsewhere in the country, so it is hardly surprising that there are species here that are found nowhere else. The most characteristic species, typical of dry, open steppe country, are little bustard (about 300 males in the breeding season, some 30% of the French population), small numbers of pin-tailed sand-grouse (perhaps 70 pairs), stone curlew (150 pairs), large numbers of short-toed larks, and a few Calandra larks, mainly in the military training area. Rollers are more common here than anywhere else in France (about 50 breeding pairs), together with woodchat and lesser grey shrikes, black-eared

Pin-tailed sandgrouse *Pterocles alchata*

wheatear, tawny pipits, corn buntings, and black-eared wheatears. There are also a few of the strikingly distinctive great spotted cuckoo, which parasitises the abundant magpies. A few Montagu's harriers breed, and can occasionally be seen quartering the plain, and there is a good population of lesser kestrels, which are generally rare in France. Apart from in old buildings, they also nest here (as do hoopoes) in the old stone piles assembled in the last war by the Nazis to prevent landings by allied planes. One or two

Plaine de La Crau

Egyptian vultures still occur around the area, but they are very rare now. In more wooded areas, there are golden orioles, black kites, turtle doves, and melodious warblers, to name but a few.

At passage periods, there are red-footed falcons and other birds of interest. Little bustard gather in flocks of up to 1000 birds, with a total of about 1600.

The Plaine de la Crau is also noted for its unusual invertebrate life, though many of the species are both obscure and hard to find. There are three species of praying mantis, including the large green or brown *Mantis religiosa*, and the endemic grasshopper *Prionotropis rhodanica*; this is a rather squat greyish insect, which only occurs in the Plaine de la Crau, where it is reasonably common but threatened by habitat loss. There are tarantulas and scorpions (nei-ther dangerous), a few butterflies, dragonflies in the damper areas, and the striking ocellated lizard (see p. 286) lives around stone piles.

It is not a great site botanically, though there can be some quite impressive displays at times. In late spring one may see masses of slender asphodel, followed by the thistle *Galactites tomentosus*, field eryngo, and sweet alison, which smells beautiful.

The best area lies south of St. Martin-de-Crau, and there are reserves at Vergière (Peau de Meau Reserve) and the damper Vigneirat Reserve close to the Grand Rhône. There is an Ecomusée in St. Martin-de-Crau, where information and visiting permits can be obtained: Ecomusée de la Crau, Avenue de Provence, 13310, St. Martin-de-Crau. Tel: 90 470201.

SITE 135 Etang de l'Estagnol

A freshwater lake close to the Languedoc coast, with extensive reedbeds and a rich bird fauna.

Westwards from the Camargue, there is a long line of lagoons and associated coastal habitats stretching as far as Perpignan. Here and there within the coastal plain, there are freshwater habitats such as the Etang de l'Estagnol Nature Reserve, which occupies an ancient solution hollow in the underlying limestone bedrock. The reserve covers about 80 ha, mainly made up of reedbeds and open water, with patches of carr. It is an important area for breeding reedbed birds such as bearded tit, moustached, great reed, reed, and Cetti's warblers, purple heron, marsh harrier, water rail and reed bunting, with fantailed warbler in more open areas. The noise of all the songs and calls can be deafening on a fine morning in spring! In winter, large numbers of ducks gather here, including teal, shoveler, mallard, and coot. Fish are abundant

Reed bunting *Emberiza schoeniclus* (Mike Lane)

and, unusually, fishing is banned, though numbers drop dramatically in dry years when the whole lake dries up. It is not an exceptional botanical site, though there is a good variety of fen and aquatic plants, including seven species of stonewort (charophytes).

The adjacent coastal lagoons of Etang du Vic, Etang du Prévost, and Etang du Grec, through which the Rhône–Sète canal flows, are all good bird-watching sites, with coastal fringes of sand dunes and associated habitats that are rich in flowers. Breeding birds on and around the lagoons include greater flamingos, avocets, black-winged stilts, little egrets,

purple and grey herons, common and little terns, and fan-tailed warblers. There are good numbers of ducks, waders, grebes such as great-crested and black-necked, red-breasted mergansers, and others in winter, with visiting birds of prey. At passage periods, there can be a marvellous variety of terns, harriers, waders, gulls, chats, shrikes, warblers, and birds of prey, including osprey.

Estagnol lies about 8 km south-west of Montpellier, between the D186, N112, and railway, with limited access and a hide at the south end. There is easy access to the coastal lakes from the roads around Palavas-les-Flots, on the coast.

136 Etang du Bagnas
SITE

A wetland reserve close to the coast, with a marvellous diversity of birds and much else besides.

The Etang du Bagnas Reserve lies at the southern end of the Bassin de Thau lagoon (but quite separate from it), on the edge of the Herault river delta. Its 560 ha include a mixture of freshwater lakes, reedbeds, scrub, woodland, grassland, dunes, and saltmarshes. It is a particularly important bird site covered by a Special Protection Area exactly contiguous with the reserve. The 100-ha reedbed holds large numbers of nesting birds, particularly sedge, reed, great reed, and moustached warblers, reed buntings, penduline and bearded tits, and bittern, and there were up to 50 pairs of purple herons, though numbers have declined since the mid-1980s. In more open areas, such as the saltmarsh, there are avocets, black-winged stilts, fan-tailed warblers, kingfishers, and Calandra larks, amongst others. Greater flamingos are frequently seen nearby. At passage periods, there can be good numbers of gulls, terns

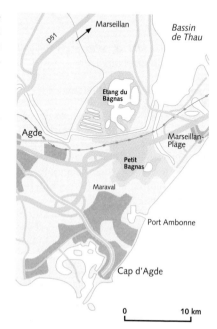

(including Caspian), waders, ospreys, marsh harriers, egrets, both black and white storks, and many other species. One census showed that over a million swallows and sand martins roosted in the reedbeds in autumn, prior to migration. In winter, there are large numbers of waterfowl such as shoveler, pintail, wigeon, teal, and garganey, with black-necked and great-crested grebes, marsh harriers, cormorants, little egrets, and a variety of smaller birds.

There are also large numbers of stripe-less tree frogs, including the unusual blue variety, green lizards, and Montpellier snake. It is moderately rich botanically, though not exceptional, and access restrictions prevent one from looking at much of the vegetation anyway.

The reserve lies just east of Agde. The N112 towards Sète passes through the reserve, and there is limited access south-wards. The D51e which runs northwards towards Marseillan skirts the reserve at a point where there is parking and a good

Purple heron *Ardea pupurea*

view, or check the saltpans to the south. Visits to the reserve can be organized through Société de Protection de la Nature du Languedoc-Roussillon, which manages it, at: Institute de Botanique, 163 Rue Auguste Broussonet, 34090 Montpellier. Tel: 0467 022707.

The Bassin de Thau lake to the north-east, which is much larger but harder to study, has good numbers of flamingos. There is some sand dune and saltmarsh vegetation along the N112 between the lake and the sea, though it is well used.

SITE 137 Montagne de la Clape

A fascinating area consisting of limestone hills combined with a series of coastal lagoons and associated habitats.

Neither Narbonne nor Narbonne-Plage are especially prepossessing places, but they are surrounded by a variety of inter-esting – and relatively unspoilt – habitats.

The Montagne de la Clape is a rugged range of limestone hills, clothed with *gar-rigue*, which used to be an island in prehistoric times. It is crossed by the D168 and a number of minor roads that give good access. The *garrigue* has a fine

range of flowers, including white aspho-del, stemless stork's-bill, pinks including *Kohlrauschia* species, small-flowered catchfly, sun-roses such as *Cistus albidus*, rock-roses including *Fumana* species, rosemary, culinary thyme, and the shrubby *Bupleurum fruticosum*, together with a number of orchids such as man, early spider, bee, woodcock, and dense-flowered *Neotinea maculata*. In the

Aleppo pine woods, there are violet limodores and other attractive flowers.

It is surprisingly good for birds, with a resident pair of the uncommon Bonelli's eagles, short-toed eagles, a couple of pairs of eagle owls, nightjars, warblers such as orphean and spectacled, ortolan bunting, black-eared wheatears, and blue rock thrush, as well as more common species such as Sardinian warblers. It is also quite rich for butterflies revelling in the warm, open, flowery conditions, including the striking two-tailed pasha – a large unmistakeable butterfly whose larvae feed on strawberry-trees – nettle tree butterfly, scarce and common swallowtails, Spanish festoon, Moroccan orange tip, clouded yellows, Cleopatra, hermit, grayling, and many blues and skippers.

Between La Clape and the mouth of the river Aude to the north lies the Etang de Pissevaches, a brackish coastal lagoon with saltmarshes. It is a good area for birds such

as breeding black-winged stilts, avocets, Kentish plovers, little terns, and fan-tailed warblers, with Scops owls and golden orioles in the poplars. At passage periods, there can be large numbers of waders, terns, gulls, wagtails, and many more.

Just south of La Clape, there are further good lagoons around the small town of Gruissan, with associated scrub, salt-marsh, woodland, and reedbeds. In winter, there are flamingos, ducks such as wigeon, pintail, teal, and shoveler, marsh harriers, and the resident penduline and bearded tits. There are breeding black-winged stilts, avocets, and a similar range to those of Pissevaches, plus a few great spotted cuckoos in the surrounding scrub. Passage visitors include both black and white storks, osprey, Eleonora's falcon, and much else of interest. The road from Narbonne to Gruissan, or southwards from Gruissan across the Isle St. Martin to the coast, give easy access into the area.

138 Etang de Leucate

An interesting combination of a coastal limestone headland and a large coastal lagoon, collectively good for birds and flowers.

Etang de Leucate

The Etang de Leucate is one of the series of large brackish lagoons located all along this stretch of the coast. At the northern end, there is a limestone headland – Cap Leucate – with a lighthouse, long known as a good spot for watching migrant birds, but also with a good flora.

The cape is particularly good between March and May, when large numbers of birds may pass over or stop for a while, in addition to the resident species and summer visitors. In good conditions, thousands of raptors such as honey buzzard, black kite, marsh harrier, short-toed eagle, and a few ospreys stop here or fly over, plus hundreds of thousands of passerines in total, which makes for exciting bird-watching. Typical species include finches, bee-eaters, red-rumped swallows, pipits including red-throated, warblers, shrikes, and many others. Breeding birds in the scrub and rocky areas include blue rock thrush, spectacled and orphean warblers, short-toed lark, black-eared wheatear, hoopoe and occasional great spotted cuckoos.

In early spring there is quite a colourful flora, including the shrubby violet *Viola arborescens*, orchids such as yellow bee, sombre, and naked man, pink bindweed and the woolly *Convolvulus lanuginosus*, spurges such as *Euphorbia segetalis*, broomrapes such as the striking *Orobanche gracilis*, the yellow-flowered *Pallenis spinosa*, two species of *Dorycnium*, the pretty rock-rose *Fumana thymifolia*, bluish-flowered *Coris monspeliensis*, labiates such as *Sideritis* and *Phlomis lychnitis* (related to Jerusalem sage), a shrubby gromwell *Lithodora fruticosa*, henbane, annual yellow flaxes such as *Linum trigynum*, the distinctive *Cneorum tricoccon*, and many others. It is too windy for butterflies to be abundant, except in sheltered hollows.

Etang de Leucate, and the smaller Etang de Lapalme to the north, are both worth looking at for the greater flamingos, breeding black-winged stilts, avocets, Kentish plovers, fan-tailed warblers, and various other birds, though they are not the best lagoons on the coast.

To reach the lighthouse, head for Leucate village then on towards Leucate Plage; turn left (north) following signs for *phare* (lighthouse). There is parking here and open access, though it can be busy, and watch out for car thieves. Roads more or less encircle the lagoon, with many viewpoints.

Mediterranean

139 Etang de Canet and dunes

A mixture of coastal habitats, including a large shallow lagoon and some species-rich dunes.

Bearded tit (reedling)
Panurus biarmicus

The Etang de Canet (also known as the Etang de St. Nazaire), the associated dunes to seaward, and some marshland to the west, are all protected as Local Nature Reserves. This is a very popular stretch of coast for holidaymakers in summer, and the reserve inevitably becomes busy, though it seems well protected and people rarely penetrate far.

The lagoon is about 5 km long by 3 km wide, shallow and variably brackish, with a surrounding fringe of reeds and other aquatic emergent vegetation. Despite the disturbance, it is an excellent site for birds, at almost any time of year. Breeding birds here include warblers such as great reed, reed, Savi's, moustached, and fan-tailed, bearded and penduline tits (see below), purple herons, reed buntings, and others. Little terns fly back and forth, and there are large numbers of greater flamingos, some of which breed here. Normally hidden from view, though occasionally showing themselves, there are several pairs of breeding little bitterns, and a good number of short-toed larks. Canet is not far from the Spanish border, so it is hardly surprising that one or two essentially Spanish birds are beginning to breed here; the striking purple swamp-hen (like a large iridescent purple moorhen) has been breeding in small numbers since 1996, probably from the reintroduced population at Aiguamolls d'Emporda not far over the border. Spotless starlings are also now breeding in small numbers, giving the opportunity to compare them with common starlings; they are very similar but lack the spots, not surprisingly (except in winter), and have a much simpler song than common starling, with less mimicry.

The lake shore has typical lagoon flowers such as yellow iris, sea club-rush,

Swamp-hen *Porphyrio porphyrio* (Mike Lane)

flowering rush, pondweeds, reed-mace, and reeds. The low dunes are more interesting, with masses of beautiful bright blue dyer's alkanet *Alkanna lehmanii*, the curious joint-pine, related more closely to conifers than flowering plants, with red berries following its greenish-yellow flowers, stocks such as *Matthiola sinuata*, sea bindweed, silvery *Paronychia* species, sea medick, an umbellifer *Thapsia villosa*, and large quantities of *Senecio inaequidens*, an introduced shrubby ragwort from South Africa. There are masses of blue-flashing and red-flashing grasshoppers (*Oedipoda* and *Sphingonotus* species) with other grasshoppers and bush-crickets. Stripeless tree frogs call from the reeds and other tall vegetation.

Flamingos on the Étang de Canet

On the west side of the lake there is a separate reserve, the Delta du Réart, where a river enters the lake. There are scrub, woodland, grassland, and other rough habitats, alive with grasshoppers and bush-crickets such as *Ruspolia nitidula* (which can be bright green or brown), Roesel's and coneheads, and good for bee-eaters, and occasional rollers amongst other things.

Not far away to the west, the partly artificial lake of Villeneuve-de-la-Raho is of some note. It is heavily disturbed by water sports, but part is a reserve, and there can be good birds, especially when water-skiing is out of season.

Bearded and penduline tits

These two similar birds both breed in large reedbeds or associated habitats, and may occasionally be seen together. Neither is a true tit, though they bear some resemblance, perhaps, to a large, long-tailed tit. Of the two, bearded tits are distinctly larger and more boldly coloured, with a rich orange-brown above and clear black and white margins to the wings. The male has a very distinctive long, drooping black moustache (hardly a beard), and both sexes have inordinately long tails. Penduline tits are rather paler, without the long tail, and the male has a shrike-like mask in place of the moustache. The bearded tit has a distinctive, easily heard pinging call (amongst others), whilst that of the penduline tit is thinner, more like a coal tit's. Bearded tits nest close to the ground, often amongst reeds, whilst penduline tits usually hang their distinctive nests on a branch of poplar or willow overhanging water. Both species are resident here.

---

140 Cerbère–Banyuls

The only exclusively marine reserve in France, protecting an enormous diversity of sea life.

Where the Pyrenees become the Chaine des Albères and reach the Mediterranean, the coastline is rocky and undeveloped. Along a short section of this, south of Banyuls-sur-Mer almost to the Spanish border, an area of sea is designated as a Marine Nature Reserve. The outer reserve is huge, but since most activities are allowed within it, this carries little weight. Within it, there is a stricter reserve of 650 ha, and a smaller 'integral reserve' within that. This is a rocky coast with clear water and very little sand, and a rich diversity of marine life has developed. Over 500 species of invertebrates have been recorded here, including a number of corals such as the beautiful red or 'precious' coral *Corallium rubrum*. The delicate and intriguing seahorses (such as *Hippocampus hippocampus*) are doing

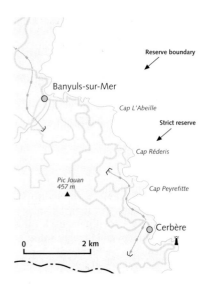

Reserve boundary

Banyuls-sur-Mer

Cap L'Abeille

Strict reserve

Cap Réderis

Pic Jouan
457 m

Cap Peyrefitte

Cerbère

0   2 km

Pinna nobilis, which had been virtually wiped out by collecting before the establishment of the reserve. There are beds of Neptune-grass – a protected species in France – which are always a good sign of clean water and a rich invertebrate life. There are also several endangered marine algae here, including *Cystoseira spinosa* and *C. stricta*.

There is open access to the area, except in the strict integral reserve. An information centre is located at: 18 Avenue de Fontaulé, 66650, Banyuls-sur-Mer.

The coastal vegetation here is disappointing, often either cultivated or burnt. The best sectioin of remaining semi-natural vegetation, with a good mixture of species, is actually over the border in Spain at the Cap Creus Natural Park. Inland from Banyuls, the Albères hills are quite interesting, with cork oak woods and scrub, and a good range of birds such as short-toed eagle, both rock and blue rock thrush, alpine swift, woodchat shrike, subalpine warbler, and rock bunting, to name but a few.

well here, despite their declines elsewhere, and there are lobsters such as *Scyllarides latus*, and spiny and common lobsters, fish such as groupers, and a few individuals of the impressive vertical shells of the 'grand nacre' or fan mussel

SITE 141 Chaine des Alpilles

A striking range of partly wooded limestone hills, with a remarkably rich flora and fauna.

The Chaine des Alpilles rises sharply from the low-lying land north of the Camargue and the Crau (see p. 289), forming a striking landscape feature with their glistening white cliffs. The lower slopes are mainly cultivated for vines and peaches, but there are large tracts of Aleppo pine and holm oak woodland, and the higher parts are largely bare or scrub-covered.

It is a remarkably good place for birds, within a relatively small area. Two places are especially noteworthy: the beautiful

and spectacularly sited old village of Les Baux, and the woods around the peak of La Caume (387 m). Les Baux is a fascinating place, anyway (though almost always busy with tourists), and there are blue rock thrushes, black redstarts, alpine swifts, and Dartford and subalpine warblers all breeding, with peregrines in the area. Wallcreepers may visit the cliffs in winter. Eagle owls breed in the vicinity, and you can sometimes see them hunting at dusk, and there are Scops owls around the village.

Les Baux

The radio mast of La Caume has a dirt track leading to it off the D5 north of Les Baux, usually closed to traffic. In the woods there are crested tits and firecrests, with scrub birds such as Dartford warblers in open areas. Closer to the top, there are breeding Bonelli's and short-toed eagles, alpine swifts, crag martins, blue rock thrushes, and occasional Egyptian vultures (with possibly two breeding pairs hanging on here). Nightjars churr at dusk, and eagle owls can sometimes be heard. La Ligue pour la Protection des Oiseaux has an information centre open through the summer from April, concentrating particularly on birds of prey.

It is a good area botanically, too. In scrub and light woodland, there is a fine selection of orchids including giant, sombre, bee, early and late spider, yellow bee, *Ophrys bertolonii*, *O. arachnitiformis*, and occasional violet limodores, amongst others. There are masses of the pretty blue *Aphyllanthes monspeliensis*, with pink cistuses, lavender, *Helichrysum stoechas*, swallow-wort, and many more. There is a good range of typical Mediterranean butterflies here, and the rare orthopteran *Saga pedo* has been recorded – a fearsome creature, up to 12 cm long, that is known only as females, which feeds almost entirely on other grasshoppers and bush-crickets.

The D5 runs through the area southwards from St. Rémy to Les Baux, with good access into the hills all along this stretch.

142 Port-Cros National Park

SITE

A fascinating group of offshore islands together with an area of sea, protecting an unexploited fragment of Mediterranean ecosystem.

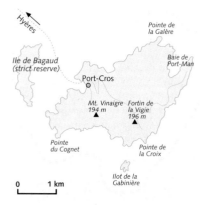

Ile de Port-Cros is one of the Iles d'Hyères, which are offshore fragments of the Massif des Maures along the coast south of Le Lavandou. The National Park, created in 1963, is tiny, covering only 675 ha of land (plus 1800 ha of surrounding sea), and has to be viewed more as a nature reserve than a normal National Park. It comprises the main island, the adjacent small Ile de Bagaud, the management of 1000 ha of neighbouring Ile de Porquerolles, and 300 ha of Cap Lardier on the mainland, east of Cavalaire.

The islands are composed of acidic rock, similar to that of the Massif des Maures, and are covered mainly with semi-natural evergreen Mediterranean forest, dominated by Aleppo pines, holm oak, strawberry-tree, wild olive, mastic, myrtle, juniper, and other trees and shrubs. There is a rich flora, made up of just over 600 species, though most of them are widespread and common, and

easily seen elsewhere on acidic rocks in the region. Some of the more interesting or distinctive plants include wild gladiolus, the shrubby yellow-flowered cineraria *Senecio bicolor*, Jove's beard (related to kidney vetch, but up to several metres high), masses of tree spurge and other spurges, lavender, both pink and white *Cistus* species, an endemic thyme, and many more. It is well worth a visit, but the dense evergreen vegetation does not support the same sort of colourful masses of spring flowers found elsewhere in the Mediterranean area. There are good numbers of fungi to be seen here, including the distinctive red *Clathrus ruber*, which usually appears in spring.

It is a good place to see some of the Mediterranean coastal birds. Out of the 114 species of bird recorded for the island, about 25 breed; a relatively low number,

Yellow-legged gull *Larus cachinnans*

Cory's shearwater *Calonectris diomedea*

There are kestrels and sparrowhawks, Eleonora's falcons (seen occasionally and which may sometimes attempt to breed), and nightingales, Scops owls, and nightjars, amongst others.

One of the key features of Port-Cros is its populations of reptiles, and in particular geckos. All three French species are found here – the more widespread Turkish and Moorish geckoes are quite common, and often seen in buildings, while the rare leaf-toed gecko (only found in this area) is mainly found in more natural situations amongst trees and rocks, and particularly on old junipers. There is also a population of the rare Tyrrhenian painted frog, which only occurs in Corsica, Sardinia, and a few adjacent areas. They are not quite as distinctive as their name suggests, looking rather like a

but it does include some unusual ones. For example, there are breeding colonies of both Cory's and Yelkouan shearwaters, both alpine and pallid swifts, blue rock thrush, and the usual abundance of Sardinian warblers and yellow-legged gulls (the southern form of herring gulls).

Port-Cros

Swift *Apus apus*

brownish edible frog, but with a round (not horizontally elongated) pupil. There are also ladder snakes and Montpellier snakes here, the latter reaching up to 1.6 m long and best avoided if possible, though they are unlikely to bite and it is not normally serious if they do. There are also black rats, and seven species of bats. It is not a great site for butterflies, though there are two-tailed pashas feeding on the strawberry-trees, and a wealth of other insects.

The surrounding marine area is protected from hunting and fishing, and has a wealth of life to be seen. There are said to be almost 500 species of marine algae – an extraordinary total – and 180 species of fish, of which 18 are endemic to the area. There are extensive beds of Neptune-grass, covering up to half of the seabed here, and areas of coral. One part is described as being 'one of the last *Posidonia*-barrier reefs of the Mediterranean'. Fish are abundant, including sea bream, rainbow wrasse, painted comber, and the huge grouper, which can be well over a metre long. There are masses of sea fans including yellow gorgonia and *Paramuricea clavata*, with red branches, on rock faces, and a good colony of the endangered fan mussel *Pinna nobilis*.

Access to the National Park is easy, by boat from Port d'Hyères or other ports in summer, with the journey taking about an hour. It is busy in high summer and on warm holidays and is best avoided then

Swifts

Both pallid and common swifts occur around Port-Cros, though they can be hard to separate at first. Most people are familiar with common swifts; pallid swifts (which may often be the more common species along the coast, but are often overlooked) are a paler brownish colour rather than black, with a more marked white throat patch, and more distinctly two-tone wings as the pale coverts contrast with the dark leading edge. The size, calls, and flight are too similar to distinguish without long experience, but one other helpful distinction is the fact that the pallid arrives up to a month or so earlier than the common. Alpine swifts are quite different, much larger, and white below with a dark 'collar'.

(there are about a quarter of a million visitors to Port-Cros per year). A glass-bottomed boat, the aquascope, gives good views of the submarine life, and possibly birds and cetaceans. There is an underwater trail, many opportunities for snorkelling, and nature trails on the island. There is an information centre, café, and hotel on the island.

On nearby Porquerolles to the west, the National Park manages 1000 ha in conjunction with the botanical conservatory as part of the National Botanical Reserve. Apart from research, and a collection of hundreds of cultivated fruit varieties, there is also a selection of local wild plants. It is open to visitors from the beginning of May to the end of September. The rest of Porquerolles, though much more cultivated than Port-Cros, has sizeable areas of wild habitats.

SITE
143 Massif des Maures

Beautiful and unspoilt wooded hills on acid soil, with a marvellously varied flora and fauna.

The Massif des Maures is a large area of hills running north-eastwards from Toulon, not far from the coast. They are heavily wooded, rising to only 779 m at the highest point, yet they seem to present a considerable barrier, and are wide enough to make up an important area of habitat. They overlie acidic schistose rocks which gives them a quite different character to the many limestone hills in the south, with more surface water and woodland, but fewer orchids and some other flowers. To the north lies an area known as the Plaine des Maures, relatively level and low-lying, and stretching away northwards. The combination of these two fine habitats provides a wonderful range of species.

In the hills, there are extensive woods of sweet chestnut, pine, and scattered oaks, with strawberry-trees and other shrubs below. On the lower slopes and on the plain, there are considerable areas of cork oaks, often with heathland below them. Within the forests, there are patches of grassland, cultivated clearings, and open scrub and streams, in a mosaic of habitats.

One of the special features of the Massif des Maures is the presence of a good population of Hermann's tortoise, the only species of tortoise in France in its only significant mainland locality (though it can also be found in small numbers in southwest France along the Spanish border, and in Corsica). It is quite common in the Maures, though numbers vary considerably, and are badly hit by extensive fires. They occur mainly in scrub and light woodland, and can often be located by listening for a rustling in the undergrowth, especially in the morning. There is a tortoise rehabilitation centre – the Village des Tortues – just east of Gonfaron, which is the easiest place to see tortoises at all stages, and some other local reptiles. There are also Montpellier snakes, ladder snakes, and ocellated lizards, amongst other reptiles in the Maures, and moorish geckos in the villages.

It is a fine place for birds, and the Plaine des Maures is considered to be one of the Important Bird Areas of France. Here, you can still see rollers (up to 50 pairs), related to crows and fond of perching on wires, colonies of bee-eaters, hoopoes, golden orioles, woodchat and red-backed shrikes, and others – some of the most brightly coloured of all French birds. There are also nightjars, cirl and ortolan buntings, serins, Dartford and melodious warblers, woodlarks, and many more. Scops owls breed in and around a number of villages.

Golden oriole *Oriolus oriolus*

It is a marvellous location for flowers in spring, though quite different from the limestone hills. The richest areas are the open *garrigue*, where there is French and narrow-leaved lavender, the impressive ragwort *Senecio bicolor* with its silvery-grey foliage, large Mediterranean spurge, several cistus species such as *Cistus monspeliensis*, often with their little root parasites *Cytinus* species, anemones such as *Anemone hortensis*, spotted rock-rose and its rarer yellow-flowered relative *Tuberaria lignosa*, wild rue, rosemary, everlasting *Helichrysum stoechas*, mallow-leaved bindweed, and many more – a colourful and aromatic mixture. Tree heather is abundant in places. It is not the richest part of France for orchids, but there is a good range of species including at least three tongue orchids *Serapias lingua*, *S. vomeracea*, and *S. cordigera* with a broad, heart-shaped lip, pretty pale yellow Provence orchid in shady places, narrow-leaved helleborine,

lesser butterfly orchid, dense-flowered orchid, and a form of green-winged orchid known as *Orchis champagneuxii*, which has an unspotted lip that is pale in the centre and darker at the sides.

The Massif des Maures is also an excellent place for insects. There are over 60 species of butterflies, including the dramatic two-tailed pasha, which feeds on strawberry-trees in its larval stages and may visit gardens and orchards for fruit in late summer. Ascalaphids are abundant in flowery clearings, and cicadas are omnipresent and very noisy, with several species, including the largest European species, *Tibicen plebejus*, most often found on pines.

Any of the minor roads through or across the hills are worth following, and there is a good network of paths. La Garde-Freinet makes a good base. The plain lies to the north of the massif, partly across the motorway and N97, towards Besse sur Issole.

Massif des Maures

SITE
144 Montagne du Lubéron

An attractive range of limestone mountains with cliffs, gorges, and forests, and a fine mixture of birds and flowers.

The Montagne du Lubéron is a rounded limestone mountain range stretching for about 60 km between Cavaillon and Manosque, rising to 1125 m at the highest point. The mountains are often divided into the Petit Lubéron to the west of the D943 and Aigue Brun River, and the larger Grand Lubéron to the east. The eastern section has a fine mixture of downy oak woodland, some beech, Montpellier maple, and other woodland, with areas of grassland, rock, scrub, and agricultural land, including many vineyards. The western section is lower, but has more cliffs and gorges, and there is a large tract of planted old cedar forest. An area of 165 000 ha is designated as the Lubéron Natural Park, including both Grand and Petit Lubéron.

The flora is rich, especially in the east. There are good quantities of orchids such as narrow-leaved, bird's-nest, lady, and early spider including the form now known as *Ophrys araneola*. Other flowers include narrow-leaved red valerian, Montpellier milk-vetch, pale St. John's-wort, rock soapwort, hepatica, burning bush, martagon lily, meadow saffron, and daffodils such as pheasant's-eye, in addi-

tion to more widespread species such as rosemary and wild thyme. In dry scrub areas, there is shrubby jasmine, with pretty yellow flowers, sun-roses, especially the pink *Cistus albidus*, the gromwell *Lithodora fruticosa* with intense blue flowers, and the shrubby yellow flax *Linum campanulatum*.

The Petit Lubéron is the better site for the bird-watcher, and most of it (over 16 000 ha) is designated as a Special Protection Area under European legislation. There is a fine range of breeding raptors, including one or two pairs of Egyptian vultures, a pair of Bonelli's eagles, short-toed eagles, and a few eagle owls. There are also blue rock thrushes, alpine swift, red-billed chough, Dartford warbler, and other species of cliffs and scrub. The narrow Gorge de Regalon, leading northwards from the D973 (and marked on most maps), is an excellent site, as is nearby Font D'Orme. The Combe de Loumarin, which splits the Lubéron into its two parts, is also worth a look.

The HQ for the park is at: Maison du Parc, 60, Place Jean-Jaurès, BP122, 84404 Apt. Tel: 04 90044200, and there are other information centres in the villages.

ABOVE LEFT: La Garde - Freinet is
where Janet's
friend "Leedy" lives!

SITE
145 Minerve

A marvellously unspoilt area of rocky garrigue with forests and gorges around the old town of Minerve.

Minerve comes as something of a surprise; for such a well-known town it is very small, and its setting is quite spectacular, surrounded by cliffs, caves, gorges (and some extraordinary natural rock bridges) and *garrigue* in the barren limestone country known locally as Minervois. The wines from the area are also well known, but the vineyards occupy only a small proportion of the countryside, and there are large expanses of wild, open countryside

running northwards from here, becoming more forested as you go towards the Montagne Noire. Most of the area around here – totalling 19 000 ha – is classified as an Important Area for Birds, yet there are no statutory designations or nature reserves, so it is wholly unprotected. The optimist might be pleased that there is still so much superb habitat left in France that it does not need to be officially protected, while the pessimist might fear that it will

A vast natural rock arch at Minerve

go the way of many other good sites! Fortunately, it is a harsh terrain, rather like the *causses* of further north (see pp 197–201), with little surface water and extremely rocky conditions, so any change can only be slow.

It is indeed a superb area for birds. Around the town itself, there are rock sparrows (listen for their distinctive, single-note, wheezy call), ravens, alpine swifts, and crag martins, in addition to more typical village birds such as black redstart, serin, and Scops owl. Westwards from the town, there is a good small gorge, the Gorge de la Cesse, which extends the area of interest. Wallcreepers may visit in winter to feed on the cliffs. The rocky *garrigue* around the town has an abundance of open country birds such as black-eared wheatear, red-backed, woodchat, and southern grey shrikes, Dartford, Orphean, and subalpine warblers, cirl and Ortolan buntings, and other more common species. There are good numbers of tawny pipits breeding, and Montagu's harriers are as common here as almost anywhere in France, with up to 100 birds recorded. Woodlarks sing mournfully from any areas with scattered trees, nightingales sing from impenetrable scrub, and there are stonechats everywhere. Occasionally, short-toed eagles float over (though they probably do not breed nearby), and there are several pairs of peregrines, while eagle owls call at night from the gorge areas.

It is also a marvellous place botanically, with an intriguing mixture of southern and central European species, or lowland and montane. The orchids are superb on the hilly and grassy areas northwards from the town, and the list includes man, green-winged, pyramidal, early purple, lizard, bee, yellow bee, woodcock, early spider, and the distinctive *Ophrys magniflora* (see p. 163), amongst others, often in considerable abundance. Other interesting flowers here include drifts of the

Black-eared wheatear *Oenanthe hispanica* (Mike Lane)

pretty china-blue *Hyacinthus* (*Brimeura*) *amethystinus*, an essentially Pyrenean plant (and a little further north, the Pyrenean squill is common), brown bluebell, an essentially southern plant, wild jasmine, poet's-eye narcissus, vetchlings such as *Lathyrus sphaericus*, and all the typical limestone *garrigue* flora such as blue *Aphyllanthes monspeliensis*, sunroses, and lavender.

Green lizards and Montpellier snakes can be seen in scrub areas, and even occasional larger ocellated lizards. Bats of half a dozen species are common around the town, no doubt roosting and breeding in the extensive caves in the vicinity. Butterflies are common in places, including common and scarce swallowtails, Bath white, Moroccan orange tip, Cleopatra, hairstreaks such as ilex and brown, Provençal short-tailed blue, baton blue, idas blue, marbled whites, woodland and tree graylings, and Camberwell beauties for sure, and no doubt many others.

It is an easy area to work; apart from the town itself, any road or track northwards or north-westwards will provide plenty to see.

Not far away to the south, just southwest of Olonzac, is Jouarres Lake, partly kept as a no-hunting area. There is a good range of breeding wetland and reedbed birds, and it can hold large numbers of waterfowl in winter. It is signposted from Homps village.

SITE 146 Montagne Sainte-Victoire

Two adjacent limestone mountain ranges with a remarkably rich flora and fauna, despite their location in such a busy part of Provence.

Montagne Ste.-Victoire is a striking landmark to the east of Aix-en-Provence, rising to over 1000 m and famous for its artistic associations. It is also an important bird site, and of great value geologically. Both of these mountains have a roughly east–west alignment that means there is a great difference between the north and south slopes, with dry *garrigue* and cliffs to the south and well-established woodland to the north. On Ste.-Victoire, the south side is particularly important for its breeding birds of prey, which include short-toed eagle, Bonelli's eagle, and eagle owl, together with smaller birds such as blue rock thrush, crag martins, Dartford and subalpine warblers, nightjars, and woodlark. There is also a geological reserve of 139 ha on the western end of the mountain. It contains some striking red soils adjacent to the limestone in which, amongst other things, there are fossilized dinosaur eggs.

Massif de la Ste.-Baume has similar birds, but is more important botanically, with extensive, surprisingly humid deciduous forest on the north slopes below the cliffs. Plants of interest here, in addition to the usual widespread limestone *garrigue* plants, include the dwarf yellow or purple iris *Iris lutescens*, which flowers abundantly in spring, orchids such as giant, woodcock, narrow-leaved helleborine, and even elder-flowered orchid, meadow saxifrage, tuberous comfrey, and the southern form of wild tulip. In more shady areas, there is yellow bird's-nest, wintergreens, bird's-nest orchid, martagon lily, herb-Paris, spurge laurel, and poet's-eye narcissus, amongst other things. There is a private nature reserve on the north side of the main peak, St. Pilon (994 m), above the *hostellerie*.

The D95 provides good access all along the north side of the Massif de la Ste.-Baume, from Mazauges through to Plan d'Aups, and paths depart from this in various places, including by the *hostellerie*. Montagne Ste.-Victoire is ringed with roads, and the GR9 footpath crosses it.

Corsica

Corsica

Introduction

Corsica is an extraordinary island. Although part of France, it lies 160 km from the nearest point of mainland France, yet within 12 km of Sardinia, which is part of Italy, and only 80 km from mainland Italy. Historically and ecologically, it shares a great deal with Italy, and particularly with Sardinia. It is a remarkably rugged, almost entirely mountainous island, with peaks rising to a dramatic 2706 m at Monte Cinto, and it is the least populated and developed of the larger Mediterranean islands. The amount and diversity of habitats, and the beauty of the landscape, is quite breathtaking. Much of the island is made up of granites, dominating the main mountain areas, with hard schists in the north-east corner (including the finger – Cap Corse), and limestone here and there, most notably outcropping on the coast at Bonifacio (see p. 319) to produce quite spectacular white eroded cliffs.

The relative isolation of Corsica has allowed a number of endemic species and varieties to develop, quite distinct from their mainland equivalents, and sometimes without close parallel nearby. Thanks to the unspoilt nature of the island, most such endemics have survived. In practice, many of them are shared with Sardinia – and known as Tyrrhenian endemics, after the Tyrrhenian Sea – and sometimes other nearby islands. It follows that most such endemics do not occur on mainland France, and Corsica is the only place in France that they can be seen. There are most endemics amongst the plants; if you include endemic varieties and subspecies, there are almost 300 endemic taxa in Corsica, of which 131 are confined to

Corsica alone; this is out of a total native flora of about 2500 plants, so more than 10% are endemic at some level. For the visiting naturalist, this immediately provides a huge number of species which cannot be seen in the wild elsewhere. There are also endemic birds such as the Corsican nuthatch, and varieties of other birds such as citril finch and spotted flycatcher which are slightly different, as well as a few endemic butterflies, the Tyrrhenian painted frog, and an endemic race of mouflon, amongst other things.

A large part of Corsica is designated as a Regional Natural Park, covering 3750 square kilometres – well over a third of the island. We have not treated this as a site, partly because it covers so much of the island, but also for the reasons given about Regional Natural Parks on p. 19. However, the park authorities can be contacted for information at: 2 Rue Major Lambroschini, BP 417, 20184 Ajaccio Cedex. Tel: 04 95517910. The park encompasses many of the finest landscapes and sites in the mountainous centre of the island.

Climatically, Corsica is typically Mediterranean, with mild winters and long hot summers, though it is slightly wetter than, say, Perpignan, with more of a tendency to receive rain in late spring and early summer. Unless you are planning to spend much time in the mountains, it is definitely an early island, with a good range of flowers from mid-March onwards and plenty of bird activity at this time. The orchids and other choice flowers around Bonifacio, for example, are at their best in late March. If you are going into the mountains, the best times are from mid-May onwards, depending on how high you intend to go. The island does become busy

Opposite page: **The dramatic chalk cliffs at Bonifacio**

Corsica

147 Etang de Biguglia
148 Cap Corse
149 Iles Lavezzi and Iles Cerbicale
150 Scandola
151 Asco Valley & Monte Cinto
152 Spelunca Gorge
153 Bonifacio
154 Vizzavona Forest
155 South-eastern Mountains
156 Propriano Bay
157 Désert des Agriates & Regino Valley

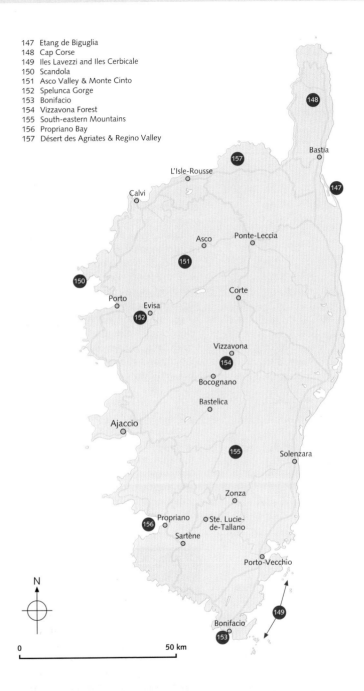

in high summer, and it is increasingly being discovered, which naturally means increasing developments. It is a superb place for the naturalist – one of the gems of the Mediterranean, yet still surprisingly little known.

SITE 147 Etang de Biguglia

A large coastal lagoon with a particularly rich bird fauna and many other features of interest.

ter and rain, but also connects with the sea via a channel (*grau*) at the northern end, so there is a gradation from saline, through brackish, to fresh, which varies according to the state of the tide and the groundwater levels. The whole reserve is both a Ramsar Site and a Special Protection Area for birds, an indication of its international importance.

It is particularly good for birds, though they are not very easy to see here. Breeding birds include red-crested pochard, purple herons, marsh harriers, kingfishers, hundreds of coot, and a fine selection of wetland warblers including Cetti's, reed, great reed, fan-tailed, moustached, and melodious. White-headed duck were regular here until 1966, when the last ones were seen, and they are now being reintroduced from Spanish populations. The hunting pressure used to be intense and few species did well, though the declaration as a reserve in 1994 has improved matters. The lake becomes more important at passage periods and right through the winter, and regularly holds well over 20 000 birds. Visiting or wintering birds of prey include ospreys

Etang de Biguglia National Nature Reserve covers about 1800 ha, of which about 1450 ha is the lagoon – easily the largest lake in Corsica – with marginal reedbeds, saltmarsh, scrub, and other habitats. The lake measures 11 km from north to south, and up to 2.5 km across, so it is a substantial body of water, separated from the sea by a sandy bar about 1 km wide (mainly outside the reserve and unprotected). The lake is fed by freshwa-

White stork *Ciconia ciconia*

Fringing reeds on the Étang de Biguglia

(which breed on Corsica – see p. 316) and red-footed falcons, and one may see night herons, purple herons, white storks, glossy ibises, greater flamingos, black-winged stilts, avocets, Terek sandpiper, wood sandpiper, ruff, and many other waders. Little egrets and a few great white egrets occur, with gulls such as Audouin's and slender-billed, and most of the terns. In winter, there are thousands of pochard, tufted duck, and coot, with smaller numbers of red-crested pochard and ferruginous duck. In surrounding scrub and other open habitats, there are red-backed and woodchat shrikes, Sardinian warblers, hoopoes, bee-eaters, and a few short-toed larks.

Other vertebrates of interest here include the Tyrrhenian painted frog (see p. 301), marsh frog, green toad (an eastern species virtually absent from mainland France), and the Corsican–Sardinian variant of common tree frog. This differs from the usual tree frogs in being smaller, with a less well-developed stripe, and the hind legs may often have dark cross-bars. They are often classified as *Hyla arborea* subspecies *sarda*. There are pond terrapins here, with several snakes and lizards, and

the most obvious mammals are the bats which hunt over the lake at dusk and through the night. The lake is full of fish, including mullet, eels, and *Aphanius fasciatus* (a characteristic Mediterranean lagoon fish). Dragonflies such as emperor, darters, and the striking *Crocothemis erythraea* are abundant.

It is not an exceptional place botanically. African tamarisk (with darker bark and whiter flowers than other tamarisks) is considered to be native here, and other interesting species include the dwarf eel-

Woodchat shrike *Lanius senator*

grass, pondweeds such as *Potamogeton pectinatus*, and *Ruppia cirrhosa* and *R. maritima.*

There are roads around the lake, especially on the east side, and a footpath/cycle track runs along the edge of the lake. There is a hide and part-time reception on the east side, a few kilometres south of the exit

channel. There may eventually be better access and visibility, though at the moment it is difficult.

Down the east coast south of Biguglia, there are some similar lagoons – Etang de Diane and Etang d'Urbino – with similar species, though neither is protected, and both are badly disturbed at times.

148 Cap Corse

SITE

The mountainous north-east tip of Corsica, with good flowers and special seabird colonies.

Borago pygmaea

Cap Corse is the finger that projects northwards from the main bulk of Corsica, with offshore islands around its tip. It is actually very mountainous throughout, rising to over 1300 m at Monte Stello, with many peaks over 1000 m, and is composed mainly of acidic schists. There are steep and impressive cliffs on the west side, sloping more gently on the east. The hills are primarily covered with *maquis* (dense and 2 m or more high) or *garrigue* (shorter and more open), with very little established woodland.

It is quite rich botanically, with a few Corsican specialities and many of the more widespread species. At the southwest corner, the soil is more calcareous and there are orchids such as man, pink butterfly, heart-shaped tongue orchid, bumble bee, and early spider. In the more acidic areas, the endemic yellow-flowered shrub *Genista corsica* is common (as on many other parts of the island), with strawberry-tree, myrtle, tree heather, pink and white-flowered cistuses (sometimes parasitized by the little flowering plant *Cytinus* species on the roots), French lavender, and other shrubs. The endemic white-flowered *Pancratium illyricum* (a relative of sea daffodil, but flowering in May, usually

away from the coast) is quite frequent in grassy places and on roadsides, and the endemic figwort *Scrophularia trifoliata* (with distinctly trifoliate leaves) grows in shadier, damper places. Other interesting species include ferns such as the huge *Woodwardia radicans* and the spleenwort *Asplenium onopteris*. There is another special plant here – a pretty little yellow-flowered crucifer, *Morisia monanthos*, with rosettes of leaves and a pile of flowers in the middle, that just grows in two areas in Corsica, on Monte Stello, and near Bonifacio. It is an ancient endemic, worth seeing, though it is rather easier to see at the Bonifacio site (see p. 320).

The northern tip of the Cape, at Barcaggio, is a well-known spot for watching migration, and about 170 species have been recorded here, including black and white storks, and the Audouin's gulls from the islands can sometimes be seen.

The Finnocchiarola Isles lie off the north-eastern tip of Cap Corse. They are only tiny, but are protected as a reserve for the strong breeding colonies of Audouin's gulls. There are also two species of gecko (Moorish and leaf-toed) and Tyrrhenian wall lizards. Landing is restricted in the breeding season, though it is possible to take boat trips and see the birds from Macinaggio.

SITE
149 Iles Lavezzi and Iles Cerbicale

Offshore islands with superb birds and other wildlife, including a sizeable marine reserve.

There are two important groups of islands off the southern coast of Corsica, protected as reserves. The Iles Lavezzi lie off the southernmost tip, in the straits between Corsica and Sardinia, and the reserve here protects both the islands (totalling 80 ha) and an area of sea totalling 50 square kilometres. The islands are particularly important for breeding Cory's shearwaters, shags (rare in the Mediterranean) and storm petrels, and there are also blue rock thrushes and pallid swifts amongst other species. It is a haven for the rarer reptiles and amphibians including leaf-toed gecko, Tyrrhenian lizard (both of which are slowly evolving different forms on different islands), and the Tyrrhenian painted frog. There is also quite a rich flora, although restrictions on where you can go prevent the visitor from seeing much. The marine reserve is very important in an area where over-exploitation was common, and it has a superb flora and fauna including at least 166 species of fish, including some enormous examples of the grouper.

Boat trips can be arranged from Bonifacio, and some landing is permitted on beaches and marked paths.

The Iles Cerbicale lie further northeast, not far from Porto-Vecchio. Only the islands are protected here, without any marine reserve. They are another important breeding colony for Cory's shearwater, storm petrel, shag, and a few Audouin's gulls, and there are also special reptiles, and an interesting flora which includes the tall pink catchfly *Silene velutina*, confined to just a few islands and coasts here and off neighbouring Sardinia. Boat trips can be arranged from Porto-Vecchio, but landing is prohibited in summer. Good views of the islands and some of the birds may be obtained from the adjacent Punta Cerbicale.

Most of the coast in this south-east corner is unspoilt, with some lovely bays and headlands; for example, the Baie de Rondinara has lovely flowers and a wealth of seashore life. Since 1999, a further 800 square kilometres of sea has been designated as a marine reserve, though little has changed, practically, at the time of writing.

Corsica

<small>SITE</small> 150 Scandola

One of the most impressive and unspoilt stretches of French coast, almost untouched by human influence.

The Scandola Peninsula juts out westwards at the northern tip of the Gulf of Porto, and almost 1000 ha of the tip of the peninsula are protected as a reserve, together with an offshore island and a further 1000 ha of sea. There are no roads anywhere near the reserve, nor even any proper footpaths, and the nearest village, Girolata, is only accessible on foot or by sea, which is about as remote as it is possible to be in France. It is a Special Protection Area, and there is an additional large no-hunting zone. The list of species from the reserve is almost dauntingly impressive, though somewhat academic for everything but the birds and marine mammals, as walking in the reserve is virtually impossible. There are over 600 species of flowering plants, including 34 endemic species or subspecies, and about 20 nationally protected species, in addition to huge numbers of marine algae. The rare and impressive fan mussel *Pinna*

nobilis grows to a huge size here in the clear water. There are three amphibians (all Corsican specialities) and seven reptiles, including geckos, Tyrrhenian lizard, and the tiny and inconspicuous pygmy algyroides. There are also six species of bats – including the largest European species, the free-tailed bat – and the last French monk seals were seen here, in 1968.

However, it is the birds that command attention, because they can be most easily seen. Perhaps the most significant feature is the loose colony of ospreys, currently doing well with perhaps 25 pairs; this was the only breeding colony in France, though now they also breed in small numbers in central France. Other breeding birds here include peregrine, shag, alpine and pallid swifts, crag martins, rock doves, blue rock thrushes, and Cory's shearwaters, with Dartford and Marmora's warblers in the scrub. There is also always the possibility of seeing cetaceans around here, one of the best places in Corsica.

Access is effectively by boat only, usually from Porto. This allows time ashore at Girolata, and then gives good views of Scandola from the sea. The Col de La Croix, on the D81 north-west of Porto, passes through fine *maquis* and gives good views towards Scandola.

Osprey *Pandion haliaetus* (Mike Lane)

SITE
151 Asco Valley and Monte Cinto

A superbly varied high-altitude area around Corsica's highest mountain.

The Asco Valley runs westwards from the N197 near Ponte-Leccia, followed by a minor road, the D147, which reaches Haut Asco, close to Monte Cinto (or Monte Cintu). The road passes through scrub and stony plains, a beautiful gorge, and extensive Corsican pine forests before finally reaching the damp grassy pastures and scrub around Haut Asco, at the upper edge of the forest. From here, the huge bulk of Monte Cinto (at 2706 m the highest mountain in Corsica) dominates the view. There are trails, including long-distance footpaths, radiating out from the end of the road and allowing exploration of the high country.

The wildlife is marvellously varied. Botanically it is very rich, with many of Corsica's special flowers found here. Lower down, there are sand crocuses *Romulea* species, the little *Crocus minimus* (which flowers very early, from January onwards), *Crocus corsicus*, often in abundance, cyclamens, Corsican hellebores, red and narrow-leaved helleborines, and many others. Higher up, there are flowers such as the endemic pearlwort *Sagina pilifera*, the pretty little

Monte Cinto, with Corsican pines, in spring

daisy *Bellis bernardii*, alpine meadow saffron in its endemic form *Colchicum alpinum* subspecies *parvulum*, alpine pasqueflower in its Corsican form *Pulsatilla alpina* subspecies *cyrnea*, the tiny little endemic basil thyme *Acinos corsicus*, a yellow whitlow-grass *Draba loiseleurii*, yellow stars-of-Bethlehem, and many others. The Corsican pines themselves are of interest, strikingly large and often clad with lichens.

It is a good area for high-altitude birds, such as golden eagles, lammergeiers (this is probably the best place in Corsica to see them), masses of Corsican nuthatch in the pine forests, crossbills, citril finches, cirl buntings, and Corsican or Tyrrhenian forms of goshawk, buzzard, wren, and spotted flycatchers. Hermann's tortoises occur here in *maquis* (and elsewhere on Corsica), and the regional park runs a tortoise village rescue/visitor centre. There are also Bedriaga's rock lizards higher up and Tyrrhenian rock lizards lower down, plus a wealth of butterflies and other insects. Paradise!

SITE 152 Spelunca Gorge

A wild and dramatic area running down to the west coast with superb birds and special flowers.

East of Porto, the D84 passes through a striking gorge – the Spelunca Gorge – before climbing through Evisa and then the old Forêt d'Aitone, and eventually on up to the Col de Vergio in amongst the high peaks, traversing a marvellous cross-section of Corsica's habitats. There is *maquis* and *garrigue* lower down, with cliffs and rocky outcrops, mixed forest, mainly holm oak, sweet chestnut, and

Leucojum longifolium

Corsican pine, and finally scrub and open grasslands at the highest levels.

It is a good bird-watching area. Ravens are abundant, especially around rubbish tips, citril finches can be found at almost any altitude here, and there are crossbills, red kites, buzzards, treecreepers, firecrests, and Corsican nuthatches in the forests. In more open places there are Marmora's and subalpine warblers, red-backed shrikes, and the local version of spotted flycatchers, with more citril

Raven *Corvus corax*

Spelunca Gorge

It is a good area botanically, too. Lower down, there are patches of the dainty endemic snowflake *Leucojum longifolium*, the more widespread *Cyclamen repandum*, both endemic crocuses, and pretty shrubs such as the legume *Anthyllis hermanniae*. Higher up, there is a collection of more specialized mountain plants, including the yellow star-of-Bethlehem *Gagea nevadensis*, endemics such as the plantain *Plantago sarda* variety *sarda*, and the thyme *Thyma herba-barona* – a pretty dwarf thyme smelling of lemon and pepper by turns and often used in cooking locally. Other plants of interest up here include the milk vetch *Astragalus genargenteus*, common juniper in its alpine form, and the dwarf barberry *Berberis aetnensis*, which occurs on several of the central Mediterranean islands.

There are endless possibilities for exploration around here. The Col de Vergio is a good starting point for walks into the higher mountains, and eastwards there is the lovely Valdu Niellu forest. The road running southwards from Evisa crosses the Col de Sevi, with fine mountain country all around.

finches. Higher still, there is a good chance of seeing golden eagle and lammergeier floating overhead, and crag martins and peregrines.

1̠5̠3̠ Bonifacio

An impressive piece of coast with marvellous flowers and other features of interest.

Coming southwards through the southern part of Corsica, you cross the low range of granite hills known as the Trinité range, and enter another world; the rock changes from the acidic volcanic or plutonic rocks, which make up most of Corsica, to a soft white Miocene limestone, which spreads in a wide band across the southern tip of the island. Around the spectacular town of Bonifacio, it reaches the coast in a line of

breathtakingly beautiful overhanging cliffs, with offshore islands including a distinctive one known as the 'grain of sand' (see photo on p. 309).

Botanically this is an outstanding location, with many different species not found elsewhere on the islands. Orchids are abundant, with their preference for calcareous soils, including beautiful forms of the long-spurred orchid, many forms of sawfly orchid, pink butterfly, bumble bee, mirror, yellow bee, sombre bee, early spider, including the endemic form now known as *Ophrys praecox*, late spider, *Ophrys bertolonii*, the uncommon but undistinguished *Gennaria diphylla*, and tongue orchids such as the small-flowered, amongst others. In scrub areas, there are the usual cistuses, rosemary, mastic, immortelle, Phoenician juniper, and other shrubs, with more maritime species such as the pretty *Asteriscus maritimus* in low mats covered with large golden-yellow flowers, tree mallow, one of the rues *Ruta chalepensis*, the undistinguished shrub *Thymelaea hirsuta*, a milk vetch *Astragalus massiliensis*, and the yellow-flowered, curiously named white henbane. Above the town there is a colony of the striking *Ornithogalum arabicum*, possibly an old introduction, together with many widespread Mediterranean wasteland flowers such as squirting cucumber, starry clover, several species of stock, and crown daisy. In the hilly area towards Capo Pertusato, some of the Corsican endemics occur: the pretty yellow crucifer *Morisia monanthos* (see p. 314), much easier to see here than on Cap Corse, Corsican stork's-bill, which is probably the most beautiful of the *Erodium* species, the little silvery rosettes of *Evax rotundata*, sand crocuses such as *Romulea requienii* and *R. revelieri*, an endemic orchid *Ophrys morisii*, and a distinctive dwarf sea-lavender *Limonium obtusifolium* on the limestone cliffs.

Surprisingly, the endemic sea-lavender *Limonium bonifaciense* does not grow here, but on the granite headland at the western end of the Trinité range. There are also typical coast flowers such as rock samphire, sea holly and sea alison. Later in the year, the blue spikes of the Corsican autumn squill and the rather similar but more robust *Scilla obtusifolia* subspecies *intermedia* flower, with the two smaller species of sea squills *Urginea undulata* and *U. fugax*; neither is endemic, though both are very limited in their European distribution. *U. fugax* is smaller (to 35 cm) and has very narrow, thread-like leaves.

Bonifacio is also a good place to watch birds. In the *garrigue* and *maquis*, there are Marmora's warblers, with the more common Dartford and Sardinians, red-backed shrikes, black redstarts, and cirl buntings. There are Spanish sparrows here, in their only Corsican site, in addition to the more widespread Italian ones, and a few rock sparrows. The Corsican variant of citril finch occurs here and there, such as around ruined buildings – it is normally a mountain species in mainland Europe, but occupies a much wider range of niches here. On the cliffs and offshore islets, there are breeding Cory's and Yelkouan shearwaters, rock doves, blue rock thrush, alpine and pallid swifts, and more common birds. The shearwaters can often be seen over the sea towards dusk.

Inland from Bonifacio, on the more acid soils, there are marshy fields with *Narcissus tazetta* in late winter and *N. serotinus* in autumn, and also the rare, winter-flowering arum relative *Ambosinia bassii*. North of Bonifacio, along the N196, the Plage de Tonnara (Tonnara beach) offers a good selection of coastal flowers, including sea heaths, spotted rock-rose, yellow centaury, the endemic *Stachys glutinosa*, the endemic catchfly *Silene succulenta* subspecies *corsica*, and many others. It is signposted from the main road and beach developments are just beginning.

Marmora's warbler *Sylvia sarda*

^{SITE}154 Vizzavona Forest

Beech forest and high mountains, with good birds and flowers.

The main central road of Corsica – the N193 – passes through a mountain woodland landscape around the Col de Vizzavona at 1163 m. Around the col, and particularly to the north as far as Vivario, there is a superb forested region, dominated by beech in the forest of Vizzavona, but with pines and oaks, too. It grades eastwards into other forests, and westwards towards the peak of Monte d'Oro (2254 m) where there is high-altitude scrub, grassland, and cliffs. The beech forests at this height have the feel (and many of the species) of more northerly woods such as those in the Auvergne, but there are also special Corsican species.

It is a particularly good locale for birds. Corsican nuthatch (recognizable by its white eye-stripe) is tolerably common here, mainly in the Corsican pine forests at higher altitudes, with red kites, citril finches, goshawks, common redstarts, crossbills, firecrests, and great spotted woodpeckers; along the larger streams there are dippers and grey wagtails. In the highest areas, such as on the slopes of Monte d'Oro, you can reasonably hope to see lammergeier (a few breed here) and golden eagles, which are quite common in these central mountains (with perhaps 20 pairs in the central forested mountain area). There are also Corsican brook salamanders in the area.

Botanically, the forests are interesting but not outstanding. There are more typically northern plants such as sanicle, wood-sorrel, wintergreens, and others, with red, white, and narrow-leaved helleborines, bird's-nest orchids, the pretty hepatica and stinking hellebore, and a few more distinctive Corsican species such as Corsican hellebore, *Crocus corsicus*, and the dead-nettle *Lamium corsicum*. In the highest parts, there are some of Corsica's special plants such as *Cymbalaria hepaticifolia*, the plantain *Plantago sarda* variety *sarda*, the dwarf eyebright *Euphrasia nana*, the speedwell *Veronica repens* variety *repens*, and many others.

There is easy access into the area from forest tracks and paths directly off the main road.

To the north lies the wild and high mountain region of Monte Rotondo (or Ritondo). This is a remote and rugged area, with masses of lakes, the wet grassy areas (known locally as *pozzines*), and cliffs. It has a fine flora and all the Corsican mountain birds, though it involves long walks to reach it, so it is not treated in detail here. Part of this area lies in the Biosphere Reserve of Fango, which has a core zone of 4400 ha.

Beech woodland in the Vizzavona Forest

^{SITE} 155 South-eastern mountains

Wild forested mountains with many of the Corsican special plants, birds, and other wildlife.

The mountains of the south-eastern part of Corsica, running roughly southwards from Monte Renoso (2352 m) to Col de Bavella, and including the high area of Monte Incudine (2136 m), form a marvellous montane habitat with few roads. The area as a whole supports many of Corsica's rare plants, most of the special upland birds, plus a few mammals and butterflies of interest, amongst other things. For the keen walker there are endless possibilities, with *grands randonées* and other paths reaching to most parts. For those with less time or energy, we

have selected two main sites where a good selection of the species can be seen more easily.

In the north, on the southern slopes of Monte Renoso, the Plateau d'Ese can be reached by a pleasant quiet road from the attractive hill town of Bastelica on the D27. The woods above the town have some superb old chestnut trees and here and in open areas there are plants such as the endemic columbine *Aquilegia dumeticola*, a local variant of round-leaved saxifrage *Saxifraga rotundifolia* variety *insularis*, and the endemic *S. cor-*

Ancient Corsican pines on the Col de Bavella

Corsican nuthatch *Sitta whiteheadi*

sica, mats of *Arenaria balearica*, two endemic greenweeds, *Genista salzmannii* (which is prostrate) and *G. corsica* (which is taller), the endemic *Barbarea rupicola*, and more widespread species such as tongue orchids. Red kites float over the village, and there are nettle tree butterflies and Corsican wall browns here and there.

At its highest point, the road ends on the plateau where there is a *pozzine* (wet grassy area) with streams, scrub, and woodland. Some of the special plants one might find, often in abundance, include yellow wood violet, pyramidal bugle, *Crocus corsicus*, Mt. Etna barberry, the endemic variety of rock cinquefoil *Potentilla rupestris* variety *pygmaea*, rock soapwort as the endemic variety *alsinoides*, snowy mespil as the endemic variety *rhamnoides*, an endemic buttercup *Ranunculus cordiger* subspecies *cordiger*, the little white Corsican butterwort, related to alpine butterwort, two pretty mountain daisies *Bellis bernardii* and *Bellium nivale*, the mouse-ear chickweed *Cerastium soleirolii*, and many others including endemic alders along the stream – *Alnus alnobetula* subspecies *suaveolens*. There are remnants of beech woods higher up,

but it is a mainly open landscape with a few birds such as citril finches and ravens. There are Corsican swallowtails here, with Corsican wall browns and Corsican fritillaries lower down.

Further south, the D268 running from Ste. Lucie de Tallano across to Solenzara on the east coast passes over the Col de Bavella (1218 m) and the lower Col de Larone, which lie on the south-eastern slopes of Monte Incudine. Some fine Corsican pines grow here, towards the upper limits of their altitudinal range, and a range of woodland flowers including *Anemone apennina* and other anemones, cyclamens, narrow-leaved helleborines, Roman marsh-orchids in the form now known as *Dactylorhiza insularis*, and others. From the Col de Bavella up to the heights of Monte Incudine, there are masses of special plants, including, amongst many others, the following endemic species or subspecies: the little mint *Mentha requienii*, two columbines *Aquilegia bernardii* and *A. littardierei*, the pretty little *Cymbalaria hepaticifolia*, related to the more familiar ivy-leaved toadflax, two species of sea-pinks *Armeria leucocephala* and *A. multiceps*, the pretty little violet *Viola argentaria* with almost round leaves, some endemic forget-me-nots, *Crocus corsicus*, and two whitlow-grasses. There are other non-endemic plants here such as yellow wood violet, willow gentian, starry saxifrage, and alpine rock-cress. It is an excellent place in which to see both Corsica's higher-altitude native plants and interesting birds such as Corsican nuthatch, citril finch, alpine chough, red kites, and even a few lammergeiers and golden eagles, with luck. This is also the most likely area in which to glimpse the Corsican/Sardinian variant of mouflon.

The Tova Forest, lower down on the east side of the Col de Bavella, also has much of interest.

<small>SITE</small> 156 Propriano Bay

A good example of Corsica's sandy beaches and associated coastal habitats.

Although Corsica is much less developed than most parts of coastal France, or indeed most parts of the Mediterranean, it is nevertheless steadily losing its sandy beaches and the flora and fauna that go with them. Propriano Bay still has some good locations with a rich beach flora, such as along the north coast, and south of the airstrip on the south side (the 'Plage des Vaches'). Typical species to be found here include the endemic blue-flowered alkanet *Anchusa crispa*, with bristly leaves, the little pink campion *Silene colorata*, a yellow toadflax *Linaria flava* subspecies *sarda*, and more widespread coastal species such as sea stock, three-horned stock, yellow horned-poppy, pink and white *Bellardia trixago*, milk thistle, blue hound's tongue, *Lotus cytisoides*, vetches, and numerous others, in a lovely mixture of colours.

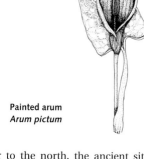

Painted arum
Arum pictum

Not far to the north, the ancient site of Filitosa (well worth visiting for its own sake) has a fine mixture of flowers such as the striking flowering ash, masses of the endemic relative of sea daffodil *Pancratium illyricum*, which is much more a plant of inland grassy places than the true sea daffodil (which grows on dunes), loose-flowered orchids, and the distinctive painted arum with dark red-purple spathes and a bluish-purple spadix, followed by bright red berries; it is endemic to the Balearics

Pancratium illyricum at Filitosa

and Corsica–Sardinia. Other plants here include bear's breeches, Narbonne vetch, and several tongue orchids. It is a pleasant place to watch the lowland birds of Corsica, including spotted flycatchers, black redstarts, Italian sparrows, cirl buntings, woodchat shrikes, spotless starlings, nightingales, and bee-eaters, amongst others. There are banded demoiselles along the stream, and good butterflies including Mediterranean skipper (not found elsewhere in France), two-tailed pasha, Corsican dappled white, and the local version of wall brown.

The site is well signposted from the coast road along the north of the bay, or from the main N196. It is busy in high summer, but good at other times.

SITE 157 Désert des Agriates and Regino Valley

An interesting combination of a varied lowland river valley and a large deserted peninsula.

The Désert des Agriates is a rounded peninsula projecting northwards, just to the west of the finger of Cap Corse. As the name suggests, it is indeed virtually deserted (though not a desert in the sense that nothing grows there), and dominated by rocky, hilly *garrigue* and *maquis*. Along the coast, where small rivers meet the sea, there are lagoons, often with associated marshland, and a series of sandy beaches. It is not particularly a place for rare species, but anything that likes these conditions does well here. There are endemic plants such as *Stachys glutinosa* and *Genista corsica* – both widespread in Corsica – with asphodels, sun-roses, sea squills, autumn squills, mastic, juniper, strawberry-tree, and other plants that survive grazing by one means or another, as the area is well grazed by wandering flocks. Around the lakes, there may be loose-flowered orchids, yellow iris, and other wetland or brackish water species. The striking blue-flowered stonecrop *Sedum caeruleum* occurs along the coast. In a few places, there are orchids such as green-winged,

pink butterfly, tongue, small-flowered tongue, and sometimes *Dactylorhiza insularis*. Typical scrub birds such as Sardinian, Dartford, and Marmora's warblers occur in some abundance, with tawny pipits, woodchat and red-backed shrikes, blue rock thrushes, woodlarks, nightingales, and many others.

Access is difficult but the D81 crosses the south of the site, and there are roads in northwards from there.

The Regino Valley, just to the west, runs for a short distance from the hills to the sea east of L'Ile-Rousse. It is an important area for birds and a good place to see some interesting species. Red kites are especially common, with 10–15 pairs breeding in the valley, as well as Scops owls, nightjars, bee-eaters, rock sparrows, tawny pipits, cirl buntings, and many of the species mentioned above for Agriates. Golden eagles from the mountains may pass over at times. The D113 runs right through the area, passing the reservoir, which is worth investigating.

Corsican *garrigue* in May, in full flower

Further reading

Abbs, B. (1994). *Gardens of France.* Quiller Press, London.

Bernard, C. (1997). *Fleurs des Causses.* Editions du Rouergue.

Boucher, C. (1998). *La flore des Alpes de Haute-Provence.* Edisud/Adri, Aix-en-Provence.

Crozier, J. (2000). *A birdwatching guide to France south of the Loire.* Arlequin Press, Chelmsford.

Delforce, P. (1995). *The nature parks of France.* Windrush Press, Gloucestershire.

Dupias, G. (1990). *Fleurs du Parc National des Pyrenees* (2 vols). Parc National des Pyrenees, Tarbes, France.

Gamisans, J. (1996). *La flore endémique de la Corse (Corsica).* Edisud, Aix-en-Provence.

Gibson, R., Hextall, B., and Rogers, A. (2001). *Photographic guide to sea and shore life of Britain and North-west Europe.* Oxford University Press.

Heath, M. and Evans, M. (ed.) (2000). *Important bird areas in Europe.* Vol. 2: *Southern Europe.* Birdlife International, Cambridge.

Jestin, P. (1998). *Flore du parc national des Cévennes.* Editions du Rouergue.

Molina, J. (1996). *Flore de Camargue.* PNR de Camargue, Arles.

Mosse, F. (1996). *À la découverte des réserves naturelles de France.* Nathan/RNF, Paris.

North, C. (1997). *A botanical tour round the Mediterranean.* New Millennium, London.

Snow, D. W. and Perrins, C. M. (ed.) (1998). *The Birds of the Western Palearctic* (concise edn). Oxford University Press.

Tolman, T. (2001). *Photographic guide to the butterflies of Britain and Europe.* Oxford University Press.

Yeatman-Berthelot and Jarry (ed.) (1995). *Atlas des Oiseaux nicheurs (nesting birds) de France.* Soc. Ornithologique français.

Geographical Index

KEY TO SITE MAP SYMBOLS

— - — -	National border		National park
	River, stream or canal		Reserve or area of interest
	Road		Marine reserve
	Dual carriageway		Marsh
	Path or track		Reedbed
— • — •	Railway		Sand or mudflats
	Ferry		Dunes
✈	Airport, airfield		Rock
ⓘ	Lighthouse		Woodland
⌶	Castle or tower		
i	Information point		
P	Parking		
☗	Hide or observation point		
1155 m ▲	Peak, height in metres